Scenes From a Misbegotten Life

My Struggle with Mental Illness

Victoria Maiden

Tampa, Florida

Scenes From a Misbegotten Life

Published by Gatekeeper Press
7853 Gunn Hwy, Suite 209
Tampa, FL 33626
www.GatekeeperPress.com

The cover design, interior formatting, typesetting, and editorial work for this book are entirely the product of the author. Gatekeeper Press did not participate in and is not responsible for any aspect of these elements.

Library of Congress Control Number: 2023944896

ISBN HC: 9781662943478
ISBN PB: 9781662943485
eISBN: 9781662943492

I dedicate this book to my brother Jimmy, whose strange, sad life was like a series of starbursts -- sudden eruptions of brilliant light, dark energy, random impulses and unbridled thoughts that came out of nowhere and sometimes made him think he was at the gates of heaven, when he was really on the high road to hell.

And to all those whose lives have been disfigured by mental illness. For we, too, are God's children, His windswept wildflowers scattered far and wide, fated to be ever out in the elements, never a part of any floral arrangement. We are the bruised, misshapen fruit that won't get put on display in the produce aisle but are none the less sweet for that.

Table of Contents

1. Why I Bothered Writing This 7
2. A Solemn Decision 9
3. True Confessions 20
4. Not Hiring 27
5. Two Doctors, No Cures 35
6. Kneesocks 41
7. Hot Tantrum in a Firehouse 45
8. Poetry and Raw Milk 55
9. A Motley Crew 66
10. How I Spent My Summer Vacation 72
11. A Scarlet Letter 80
12. West Side Story 89
13. The Beat Goes On 97
14. From Church Basement to Sugar Hill 102
15. Belly Dancing in Bloomingdale's 112
16. Anger Management 101 130
17. King Tut's Tomb and a Belated Christmas Gift 138
18. Crime and Punishment 145
19. Sweet Georgia Brown 158
20. Trip the Light Fantastic 180
21. The Sun God's Revenge 188
22. Water Sports 195
23. Swinging on a Star 210
24. Ruffles, Feathers, and Lace 217
25. Saints and Sinners 226
26. Makes Me Wanna Holler 247

27. Born to Lose 258
28. Lost in the City of Fallen Angels 266
29. Midnight Desperado 276
30. Death Begins at Forty 282
31. Tall, Dark, and Stark Raving Mad 292
32. The Magic Fades 305
33. Carolina Blues 315
34. Mania Meets Music 326
35. The Day the Towers Fell 347
36. Moonlight in Vermont 354
37. Goodbye, Mom 360
38. You Can't Go Home Again (Until You Have To) 368
39. Blood and Treasure 378
40. 'Tis the Season...Sigh… 388
41. It's a Family Affair 393
42. Minus Two 398
43. Totally Unedited 410
44. The Unraveling 430
45. Soul Searching Across the Pond 432
46. Rocky Mountain High 447
47. Epilogue 458

1
Why I Bothered Writing This

YOU KNOW WHAT it looks like. Have you ever wondered what it *feels* like? Everybody recognizes it in its most extreme and disturbing form. The oddly dressed man badly in need of a haircut who is muttering to himself on the subway platform, then suddenly lunges at a perfect stranger and throws her onto the tracks. The woman sitting cross-legged on the sidewalk next to a shopping cart piled high with bags of junk, who is wearing a tattered fur coat on a 90-degree day. The shy, quiet student who one day shows up at his school all dressed in black and starts shooting. The sounds of a teenager furiously vomiting in the bathroom after having stuffed herself with burgers, pizza, and ice cream, on the downside of a bulimic binge-purge cycle. The old lady at the bottom of the dead-end street whose house emits earsplitting noise and a foul stench she seems not to notice, because she is housing nineteen stray dogs.

Mental illness is not an easy subject to talk about. Besides the unfair stigma that often attaches to it, there is the bewildering array of symptoms and conditions it encompasses. Many of us who suffer from one form or another of it have been labeled, or have even seen ourselves as, freaks, weirdos, oddballs, eccentrics and outcastes. With the possible exception of lepers, victims of physical ailments and disabilities are rarely looked upon that way. So it is no surprise that many of us attempt to keep our illness hidden from view, to the extent we can do so.

The truth is, "mental illness" is an amorphous concept, hard to pin down. Is it a disease of the mind? Of the brain? Of the soul? We know it has existed in all times and in all cultures. It can be so severe and so obvious that a person has to be institutionalized or put behind bars. It can be perfectly harmless, if disruptive, as with the person who has to wipe the kitchen counter exactly thirteen times, repeatedly check her door locks, or make sure all the socks in his drawer are facing east. Often it is accompanied by a special kind of genius and the world is graced with a great artist, writer, inventor, or musician.

But for most of its everyday sufferers, mental illness is much more subtle than that, afflicting people who appear “normal” on the surface, and who go about their lives much as anyone else does, keeping their demons and their crazy thoughts and strange compulsions carefully camouflaged. I am talking about people who experience periodic, debilitating bouts of crippling anxiety or deep depression, who can’t stop thinking certain troublesome thoughts, who undergo roller-coaster mood swings, or nervous breakdowns, or intense and inexplicable shyness in social settings, or irrational fears and phobias, or mild OCD or bipolar tendencies. Look around you. Those people are your friends, your neighbors, your relatives, your coworkers. This is the garden-variety, unremarkable kind of mental illness that plagues millions of us, though we tend not to like to talk about it. For us it is just something we learn to live with -- like having freckles, or being short. While medication and therapy as well as supportive, caring friends and family can go a long way toward keeping the illness in check, they can never eradicate it. It is our cross to bear.

If you’ve ever wondered what life must be like for someone who suffers from this type of mental illness, you will certainly get a close-up view in the pages that follow. Maybe too close for comfort. Today there are so many voices out there clamoring for attention, demanding recognition, rights, a place at the table. Consider mine another voice from the garret, willing to share “a day in the life,” a small sampling of my existence with anyone who cares to listen.

2
A Solemn Decision

I SUPPOSE YOU could call me a terminal misfit. The Encarta online dictionary defines the word "misfit" as *somebody who does not belong, somebody who does not fit comfortably into a situation or environment.* The Oxford English Dictionary defines it as *a person whose behaviour or attitude sets them apart from others in an uncomfortably conspicuous way.* Well I'm afraid that's me. I feel that I do not really belong in modern-day society. Perhaps I could have "fit comfortably" in an earlier time or place, say, among the ancient Celts, or in the lost civilization of Atlantis. Maybe I would have fared better as a member of a primitive hunter-gatherer tribe in the Amazon Rain Forest. Sometimes I am not sure if I'm even supposed to be on this planet. At any rate, as I begin writing this, I am a single woman now in my fifties, who lives on the outskirts of New York City with her eighty-seven-year-old father and drug-addicted younger brother. I have not worked full-time since the age of 40, and my only source of income is a Social Security disability check.

Whenever you hear a politician or a journalist or a sociologist refer to those unfortunate denizens of our society who have "fallen through the cracks," they are talking about me. If you saw me walking down the street you probably would not guess that I am "disabled." You would not know that my eyes are permanently damaged because I once had an irresistible compulsion to "stare down" the sun. Nor would you guess that when I am feeling a bit anxious I often comfort myself by rocking back and forth, whether sitting or standing -- kind of like religious Jews do when *sitting Shiva*. I try, not always successfully, to suppress the urge when in public. You would never suspect that I have stayed in the shower for as long as three hours because the water pressure on my skin and scalp relieved unbearable tension and helped me concentrate. Or that I cannot turn lights on in my home until the sun has gone down completely and dusk has settled over the land. And of course, you couldn't know that I have been hospitalized at least seven times on account of "major depression" or that I've been subjected to dozens of electric shock treatments over the course of my adult life. And, unless you were walking right past me, you probably wouldn't notice the little nervous tremors and tics I have developed as a result both of the medications I must take and what has been done to my brain.

I am a self-proclaimed social outcaste. I avoid people as much as possible, and if someone approaches me in a friendly manner I usually shy away because I always assume that when they come to know the whole, unappetizing "truth" about me they will certainly not want to be my friend. I have never married and have no children. I have been expelled from school, evicted from apartments, thrown out of college dorms, fired numerous times, arrested, handcuffed, and even straitjacketed, during various episodes of my life.

I currently live with my father and brother because I cannot afford to live independently on what Social Security Disability provides. I have never owned a car, and have to depend on buses, trains, and my elderly dad to take me wherever I need to go. I hate to wallow in self-pity, but sometimes I think that this life of mine must be a punishment for something very bad that I did in a former life.

My mother thought I exhibited some strange tendencies as a child, but somehow I managed to eke out a happy childhood in spite of my oddness. I liked to show off in class a lot and make the other kids laugh. I invented games, told wild stories, and got a kick out of doing really neat things like climbing up onto the billboards overlooking the highway and rummaging through vacant lots and junkyards. The other kids always invited me to their birthday parties. The trouble seems to have started shortly after puberty, when I was about 12. In that year our family moved from the Bronx to a new suburban development just outside of Fort Lauderdale, Florida. That move marked the official end of my "childhood." I was never the same again. At the time, it seemed, several elements of fate converged in a particularly unfortunate and sinister way. The end result was to turn my life into a bad dream I have yet to wake up from.

First there was the terrible culture shock of the move -- me, a native New York City child suddenly plunged into a foreign way of life, into the sterility and boredom of suburbia. No familiar friends on the block to run around with, no more playing stickball or hopscotch in the streets. No gathering with the neighbor kids on the curb to flip baseball cards. No snowball fights or sledding down hills, no white Christmases. No candy stores or corner newsstands or Italian bakeries. Only cookie-cutter houses and strip shopping malls, paved parking lots, and manicured lawns soaked in pesticides that seemed as artificial as potted plastic plants. No neighborhood "bodegas" with Spanish music playing on a cheap portable radio and a stray cat napping in the back, no place to get a good slice of pizza, no next-door neighbors sitting out on the stoops shooting the breeze.

I had to transfer from P.S. 71 in the Bronx to *Driftwood Elementary School* -- from a solid, five-story red brick building to a ranch style school that resembled a cheap motel. The teachers were not the dowdy middle-aged women with bifocals I remembered from home, but were men in their thirties, wearing knit sweaters and slacks. Guys being teachers? That was a novelty for me. No wonder then, that on my first day at the new school I was greeted with howls of laughter and incredulous stares. I had shown up clutching my little briefcase, dressed in a formal navy blue jacket and skirt, with white blouse, plaid knee socks and polished penny loafers. That was not the way they did it down south. After that first humiliating day at school, it seemed as though a part of me had slipped away, never to return.

Second, the onset of puberty itself had been traumatic and confusing. The morphing into adolescence was twice the wrenching ordeal for me that it was, and is, for normal kids. All throughout elementary school I must have been, to use the Freudian term, "polymorphous perverse." That is to say, I felt physically and emotionally attracted to both boys and girls. I had friends of both sexes. When I was nine my best friend was Michael down the block; two years later it was Claudia around the corner. I liked boy things and girl things and wanted both. It seemed only natural. I resisted getting trapped in some "girly-girl" identity. Climbing trees, digging for buried treasure, and playing cops and robbers were as much fun for me as dressing up my Barbie Doll. I enjoyed baking cookies with my grandmother as much as I enjoyed washing the car or playing catch with my dad.

I got crushes on cute boys and pretty girls. I had romantic fantasies about certain boys in my class -- and certain girls. I just assumed everyone felt the same way -- how could they not? But of course, I wasn't really paying attention. When it came time to start thinking about things like lipstick, nylon stockings, and nail polish, about dances and dates, I was totally lost. I resented having to change into another person, having to suddenly shift into a "feminine" as opposed to "masculine" persona. I just wanted to be myself -- my original, androgynous self, that is. And I didn't see why I had to stop fantasizing about girls and focus exclusively on boys.

But this was hardly the worst of it. At about age 13, I began withdrawing into myself, preferring solitary reading in my room or listening to music rather than playing out in the backyard or with my two siblings. I had made a couple of friends at school, but they lived too far away to be able to just walk over and see. Mom worked and didn't get home till suppertime, so she couldn't take me anywhere. Eventually, I came to feel unaccountably sad, even distraught, most of the time. I could feel something dark and heavy, but invisible, pressing down on me. Gradually I came to look at life as if through a grimy, streaked windowpane. I saw the world in varying shades of gray; everything seemed dust-covered, mute, and leaden.

It was as if a scent of death and devastation, a foretaste of the ruins into which all that lives and breathes will one day crumble, had wafted over to where I was sitting, lingered a while, and finally decided to take up permanent residence in my mind. I had no way of knowing that I had been stricken with an illness now recognized as clinical depression. I could only assume that this was the gloomy, sullen, unpleasant person I was turning into. And so did my mother, who became increasingly irritated about what she called my "antisocial attitude." Before long, the two of us were at loggerheads all the time and I began to think of her as my sworn enemy.

Eventually our family tired of Florida and returned to New York, but I took no joy in being back home. If anything, my condition worsened, and junior high school was a miserable nightmare. I made no friends, avoided the popular cliques like the plague and, rather than face the raucous scene in the cafeteria every day, I chose to eat my brown-bagged lunch standing up in a toilet stall in the girl's restroom. I couldn't bear gym class -- *Dodge Ball* became a frightening metaphor for how I would be targeted if I became too conspicuous, let my weirdness show too much. High School was hardly any better. I began regular sessions with the school's in-house psychologist, but all of the "talk therapy" failed to make a dent in my depression. At lunch time I carried my tray to the farthest away corner of the dining hall, where no one else was sitting. Although I generally got good grades, I managed to score an "F" in Phys Ed. I had to take and pass a summer school course in swimming or else I would not have been allowed to graduate.

Not all was hopeless -- I did get asked out on dates by a couple of nice guys, attended a few basketball games (my high school team were regional champions), and did exceptionally well in my English and History classes. But by now I had become convinced that the pathetic individual who showed up weekly, sat in a chair and stared at the stuffed animals in Dr. Biaggi's office was simply who I was. This was the way God made me and I could not be altered. After spending much of my junior and senior year indulging in racy fantasies about the cool girls at school, I decided I was probably gay. Boys had become boring, and my longings for girls -- especially since I never would have dared act on them -- became all the more compelling, more "forbidden," and hence even harder to resist or suppress.

I knew I was some kind of freak who didn't belong, but as much as I resented and even feared those from whose inner circle I was excluded, I also began to nurture a growing disdain, even hatred, for these *normal* people -- these stubbornly "ordinary" folks living their vapid Good Housekeeping Seal of Approval lives in their bland *Pleasant Valley Sunday* communities. These were people with limited imaginations, people who didn't know what it was to live on the fringes or walk on the wild side, people who feared and rejected that which they could not understand. They were intellectual featherweights, with a stunted view of this beautifully complex world and without an ounce of poetry in their hearts. A creeping sense of superiority gave me a needed defense against those to whom I was, for all intents and purposes, invisible.

Although you wouldn't notice my "disability" at first glance, I often do look the part of a socially challenged eccentric. I can often be found sitting alone on a park bench basking in the sun -- even if it's 22 degrees outside. My face is somewhat odd. I am of Italian, Scotch/English, and Panamanian extraction, which makes for a strange mixture. I have an olive-ish complexion, with dark, wavy hair, a "Roman" nose, and a long, oval face. Over the years, people have asked me if I am Greek, Turkish, Brazilian, Middle Eastern, a Sephardic Jew, and other exotic ethnicities.

Some find my looks attractive, some not so much. I have been called by men both "beautiful" and "an ugly Italian girl" and everything in-between. During my "rebellious" college days I stalked around campus in my favorite costume: a heavy double-breasted fatigue-green man's trench coat that I bought secondhand at an Army/Navy Supply store. Nowadays I don't dress quite as drably, or walk around with my eyes looking down. Though I seldom wear dresses, I do use makeup and regularly visit a hair salon. That might give you some kind of picture of me, if you happen to be interested. There are no photographs of me in either my high school or college yearbooks (I refused to sit for them) and there will be no current ones in or on this book.

But if you were to look at me right now through a camera lens as I am writing this and snap a photo, the picture would be an unsettling one, not suitable for the dust jacket of any book. My brows would be knitted with anguish, my mouth would be twisted into a sullen pout and my fingers would be banging the keyboard like a drum. Because now I've come to a strange kind of crossroads, and I have to take a step back and carefully consider my next move. I have a pivotal decision to make. You see, I am now at a point where I must, in dreary middle age, deal with the stark consequences of a life that began to spin out of control when I was 13. All I can do now, it seems, is sift through the wreckage, hoping to find something worth salvaging.

Before I went on disability I worked as both a paralegal and a copy editor. I was accepted into law school a couple of years after graduating college, but decided not to attend because it would have meant giving up my job and my apartment and moving back in with my parents. Ironically enough, today I could never work in a law office, or any other office. I could never sit at a desk or in a cubicle under fluorescent light tubes for seven hours a day. That would give me a panic attack -- especially on a clear day when the streets below are bathed in natural sunlight.

I have a thing about the sun, see. When it shines down on me directly it never fails to quell my anxiety and smooth out frayed nerves (which likely has something to do with the brain chemical serotonin and the way it responds to light). Indeed, if it weren't for my darker complexion, the abundance of sun rays I have absorbed since I stopped working would be enough to cause skin cancer ten times over. Although the current crop of anti-anxiety and antidepressant medications have done much to ease my depression and control my obsessive-compulsive tendencies, they are by no means a perfect solution. The pills have damaging, unavoidable side effects, and they tend to lose their effectiveness after a while. Often a hospitalization came about because a medication I had used successfully for five to seven years suddenly stopped working.

Today I somehow cope and go through the motions, but there's no dancing around the fact that my life is pretty much a wretched mess. I have absolutely nothing to show for over fifty years of living on this earth -- no accomplishments, no career, no home of my own, no children, no husband or partner, no valuable possessions, no money in the bank, not even a damn car. The only thing that has changed, and keeps changing, is my age. I am getting older and now that I am almost officially a "senior citizen," all I have to look forward to, it appears, is a slow steady decline in my abilities, my prospects, and my health.

The future appears darker to me than it ever has before. I am almost unemployable now; the more years I spend out of the workplace, the harder it will be to find a job that pays a living wage. And I worry about whether I can even hold down a steady job were I lucky enough to find one. Dear old Dad won't be around forever. The idea of one day having to choose between paying the electric bill or refilling my antidepressant medication is truly frightening. The thought of turning 65 fills me with inexplicable horror. What will I have to "retire" from, or to "save up" for? With no children or grandchildren, who will come to visit me on Thanksgiving and Christmas? In a world that worships youth, I will feel even more invisible than I do now.

If I try really hard, I can imagine myself walking on the moon in a spacesuit, slaving away in a coal mine, crossing the Sahara Desert on a camel, or taking the stage at Carnegie Hall. I cannot imagine ***turning 75***. I try to picture myself at the Senior Center playing a tenth round of bingo or in the OR having a hip replaced, or thanking a handsome young kid who just stood up to offer me his seat on the bus. It just feels too weird. And what happens if I should make it to ***80?*** My small handful of friends, if they're still alive, will likely be out of reach or dealing with their own problems. Day to day life will demand dealing not only with my recurrent depression, but with bodily aches and pains and other physical ailments. I envision canes, walkers, hearing aids, a dozen plastic bottles of pills on the dresser. Looking ahead there is nothing to see but encroaching decrepitude.

Finally -- fast forward to me all alone and barely conscious, lying on a bed in the ICU hooked up to a ventilator, various tubes, IV bags. Just beyond me a symphony of frenetic but coordinated activity proceeds at a stirring tempo. Visitors pour out of elevators, but none of them are visiting me, doctors bustle about with their patient charts, technicians wheel gurneys down gleaming corridors, nurses change catheters and bedpans, other staff dispense painkilling drugs and answer anxious phone calls -- all to the tune of whirring high tech machines, whistles, bells, electronic beeps, and the occasional emotionally wrenching human wail. And then, in the midst of this random cacophonous blur -- my final breath on this earth will be marked only by some squiggly line on a monitor going flat and some anonymous voice intoning: "Time of death, 3:16 pm."

Do I need this? I think not. And, as we all know, there is one surefire way to prevent this whole nightmare scenario from ever becoming reality. The French philosopher Albert Camus famously said that the only serious question in life is whether or not to kill yourself. I am now on the brink of posing that question to myself. I have become weary of the struggle, exhausted from dragging around the ball and chain of my existence. When I look toward my future I do not see a life worth living. Frankly, I am scared. Fear has become my constant companion. It starts first thing in the morning, the instant I wake up and realize that I am still me. I 'm just plain tired of myself, tired of my own company from which I cannot escape. Tired of the nagging "existential" questions that won't go away: What if all of us have been lied to? What if there really is NOTHING out there -- no "Maker" to meet, no heaven, no afterlife. What if all the meaning and sanctity and specialness we have tried to attach to our lives is for naught? What if "God" turns out to be, like Santa Claus and the tooth fairy, just another form of make-believe?

I ask myself how it will feel to have the sneaking suspicion, as I am lying on my death bed, that there will be no day of judgment, no final reckoning, no rewards or punishments. To suddenly realize in one naked glimpse of cold hard truth that you've come all the way to the end of this arduous journey only to find there is nothing waiting for you but the abyss. I don't know about you, but I would prefer to find this out sooner rather than later.

Once, at age 15 and in the midst of a severe depression, I made a feeble attempt to dispatch myself by trying to swallow poison. Though I have contemplated it many times, I have not made any actual suicide attempts since then, restrained by mostly moral and philosophical considerations. You know, the shock and hurt to my family, the fear of committing "mortal sin" (I was raised Catholic), the shame of being an abject coward who "took the easy way out," and even the superstitious notion that if I left this life with "unfinished business" I would be condemned to return until I'd worked out all my "karma" -- or, worse still, would become a ghost, forever haunting my old stomping grounds, unable to find peace even in death.

But now all of those considerations have fallen by the wayside. It has become simply a matter of applying a practical solution to an intractable problem. To go on living, knowing I can never be happy, that I don't seem to belong anywhere, that I am making no real contribution to society, that I am helping no one -- this seems almost a crime in itself. Why should I take up space, use precious resources like food, water, and energy, be supported by the U.S. taxpayer, be a burden on others? Why should I when it would be so easy to just end it?

Looked at that way, the idea of ending my life begins to seem like a prudent and moral decision. A simple act that would save me countless hours of misery and tears. It would be a way to undo the aberration that my whole unruly existence appears to be. Yes, it would mean "giving up," but isn't that exactly what one must do at long last, when they realize they have embarked on a futile enterprise? Everyone knows you can't get blood out of a stone -- no matter how many times you stubbornly refuse to give up trying. Mine seems to be a life that is damaged beyond repair, that has outlived its usefulness, that is without meaning or purpose. I am a broken person who, like Humpty Dumpty, simply cannot be put back together again. I am, in other words, *terminal*, as I said in my opening line.

Moreover, it is a rare privilege indeed, to be able to choose the exact time, place, and manner of one's own death. When we take our death into our own hands, we are in control. We alone determine when, where, and how. I find the idea of having this choice, which the vast majority of people on earth will never exercise, appealing and significant. I have not yet chosen a method, but have narrowed it down somewhat.

But method is not important to me now. Because I must first make the determination whether to take this drastic and irrevocable step or not. Snuff out my existence now or continue the endless struggle. Deliver myself while I have the chance, or keep on falling into a bottomless pit of misery. Just do it and get it over with, or keep contemplating it over and over for the next twenty or so years -- like some recurrent dream that won't let go. This is a decision I would like to make carefully and thoughtfully, and to make once and for all. If I am to live, I must never think about suicide again, at least not in a serious way. If I am to die it had best be soon. At this point neither you nor I know how it will all turn out.

They say that when a person is on an airplane that's about to crash, scenes and images of her entire life flash before her rapidly as if on a video screen. If it were me on that plane, I wonder what that screen would show. And I wonder what comfort, if any, such a life review would bring. Perhaps for folks who had enjoyed a happy and fulfilled life it would make it easier -- knowing one had truly lived -- to confront sudden unexpected death. On the other hand, for those who, like me, have lived lives full of pain, rejection, anger and confusion, such a life replay might bring only relief that the awful movie is finally over.

In an attempt to answer these questions, I have decided to revisit some of the scenes of my own past, to review key episodes and experiences over the last fifty-plus years that have shaped and colored my life. I will scour my memory and dredge up pieces of old grainy footage showing me trudging through the various stages of my life journey. I will consult my collection of diaries and journals, in which I have recorded many of the disturbing and traumatic, bizarre and unbelievable occurrences which have marked my life. I will resurrect and distinctly portray some of the strange and unforgettable characters I have encountered along the way. No matter how uncomfortable, raw, or hurtful the memories, I am prepared to look them in the eye with brutal, unsparing honesty, and write them down on paper in as vivid detail as I can recall.

Yes, write them all down. It will not be sufficient to simply replay these incidents and experiences in my mind in rapid sequence, as with the doomed airline passengers. Rather I must take the time to spell them out, one word at a time, to ensure that I truly and accurately recreate them just as they happened, using the words to paint a picture that I will recognize. A painting with no unnecessary brushstrokes, no omissions, no embellishments -- just plain unvarnished truth, however much it makes me cringe. I want to know if, like Ebeneezer Scrooge in Dickens's classic, *A Christmas Carol*, I will be enlightened by taking a hard look at my past, be transformed and made a better person. Is this possible? I tend to doubt it, but I owe it to myself to find out.

If completing this exercise forces me to take a second look at my experiences and find in them a significance or value that seemed to be missing before, if after this project is over I can look in the mirror without guilt or shame and see, not one of God's worst mistakes, but maybe just a child with a rare birthmark -- off-putting at first but on closer inspection intriguing, like some elaborately colored tattoo, pregnant with hidden meaning and purpose and well worth pondering -- THEN I suppose I can go on living.

But if, on the other hand, all of this anguished writing and torturous remembering results in nothing more than deepening my depression and reinforcing all of my prior notions about the uselessness of my life, then, my friend, I am checking out. This fateful adventure will be either my very last, or the prelude to a new beginning. And if you happen to be a curious tourist willing to explore a dark, rocky landscape, you are welcome to join me. So climb aboard.

3
True Confessions

I'M IN A small dark room and the door is shut. I am lying on my back on a narrow table. My hands are tied down. Approximately every fifteen minutes a nurse pushes the door ajar and peeks in on me. They think I'm insane, or maybe tripping out on drugs. Hah -- I should be so lucky. Why do they think this? Because it looks like I tried to set the dorm on fire. What I had actually done was to set aflame the contents of a small metal wastebasket. It was a silly mini-conflagration, totally contained and under control. I never would have wanted to hurt anyone or destroy property. It was just that damn conference at the U of Rochester, a few miles west of the state college I was then attending in upstate New York. It was what happened at that wild off campus party I'd been invited to by Wendy and Joyce. The politics and the movement stuff got tossed into the mix with my own identity crisis to create a recipe for disaster.

You see, I had just started college, was away from home for the first time, and this was the era of "radical feminism" and "gay liberation." For the past five years I had been struggling with issues pertaining to my own sexuality and womanhood. In truth I was probably bisexual, but had never explored the "gay" side of that, and all through high school I felt self-conscious, confused, and afraid. Now, freshly arrived on a college campus among a world of strangers, I was feeling lonely and full of escalating anxiety about the secrets I felt forced to keep yet desperately needed to share. Instead, out of fear, I had taken great pains to hide them from everyone I knew. It was all making me crazy and I felt a growing sense of urgency that the issue needed to be resolved once and for all.

So one day I see a flyer pinned to the bulletin board in the student lounge. A major Feminist Conference was to be held at the University of Rochester, expected to draw attendees from all over the East Coast. Issues to be discussed included women's issues like equal pay and reproductive rights, sex and sexuality, and the burgeoning "Gay Pride" movement. I thought I ought to go -- perhaps I would learn something or meet others "like myself." So I made a note of the dates and as the event approached I told my two roommates (yes, two -- on-campus living space was scarce) that I would be out of town for a day or so.

The following Friday -- it may have been the first or second day of the conference -- I walked out to the main drag in the tiny town of Brockport and boarded a bus to Rochester. I quickly located the campus. Evidence of the big confab was everywhere -- signs, banners, balloons, and, I had to admit, a whole lot of weird looking people. The sound of blaring dance music attracted me to a large hall where a "gay disco party" was taking place. As the thundering bass lines of Isaac Hayes's *Shaft* reverberated painfully in my ears, all I could do was stand and stare. The odd sight of boys dancing with boys and girls dancing with girls made me wince just a bit. It seemed like a world turned upside down. I noticed there were far more men than women, and the women seemed particularly unattractive, most of them overweight and wearing ill-fitting clothes. Were they gay because no man would have them? I myself had been asked out by guys numerous times, both in and out of school. I had lost my virginity on a remote stretch of beach with an older third cousin who looked like Paul McCartney. And so, looking at these heavyset gals with their close-cropped haircuts, mannish clothing, and no makeup or jewelry (not even earrings) I thought to myself: "How can I possibly be one of *those people*?" But then, what about all of those Sapphic, girl-on-girl fantasies..

I wandered around curiously, at one point stumbling into what looked like an office; the door was wide open and a pile of papers on a desk indicated it was the headquarters of the Gay Student Union on campus. A man was talking on the phone and I overheard some of the conversation: "She's waiting where? At what diner? Right, well see, I never met her, don't know what she looks like. . . yeah, uh huh, really tall, you say?"

Taped to one wall was an official poster announcing the conference, larger and more detailed than the flyer I had seen in my student lounge. Among other things it listed the speakers and activists scheduled to appear. A few were quite well-known in lesbian-feminist circles, including a popular writer and former arts critic who had a regular column in the

Village Voice, by the name of Jill Johnston. Noting her name on the poster while hearing the guy on the phone I suddenly realized that she was the person waiting at the diner to be picked up. I had seen her around town and she was, indeed, quite tall. So I politely interrupted, saying "Oh -- are you talking about Jill, I know what she looks like." He smiled, asked me to come along for the ride, and we jumped into his car and drove out to get her. On the way back I observed her carefully and considered her own strange coming out of the closet story. For years she had been a professional dance critic, penning her weekly column in the arts section of the paper. Then, one day she just "came out" as a lesbian in a dramatic announcement to her readers. From that point on, all of her columns dealt exclusively with "the movement."

Back on campus, I listened to Ms. Johnston's talk and attended a few of the workshops. There were other rousing speeches by other activists, but aside from the dance parties there wasn't much in the way of social events or opportunities to get to know people. It was all very political, with the usual attitudes, slogans, and militant rhetoric I had heard a thousand times. I found it difficult and awkward to strike up a conversation with anyone while listening to yet another heated discussion about whether heterosexual marriage was in and of itself an oppressive patriarchal institution that kept women in bondage and needed to be scrapped for good, or whether all sex between men and women was essentially rape. It was all just too angry and discordant.

After the day's activities wound down, Jill invited a small group of us to join her at a campus cafe for dinner, then offered her hotel suite to anyone who wanted to crash for the night and get up early for the next day of the conference. At the cafe I got a sandwich and coffee and looked around the table to see if there was anyone I might want to know better. Maybe one or two, but I didn't have the nerve to initiate eye contact, so I just ate and listened. And when it came time to head for Jill's suite I politely declined, feeling I had seen and heard enough of the conference.

I left the University of Rochester campus armed with a couple of pounds of literature -- booklets, magazines, poetry journals and other material that had been handed out or picked off tables. When I got back to my dorm I hid the stuff in a drawer. I tried to assess what, if anything, I had accomplished. An introduction to the "community" perhaps? But nothing that suggested a convenient way for me to reach out and make friends, find women to talk to or date, or make my own "coming out" any easier. Clearly it would be up to me to figure out the next step if I wanted to move from the safety of romantic daydreams and sexy fantasies to the unpredictable untidy world of real live people. At the moment I didn't have a clue.

It so happened that about a week after the conference, my friends Wendy and Joyce announced that a good buddy of theirs who lived off campus was throwing a party at his house. Both Wendy and Joyce were bona fide "hippies" who had gone to Woodstock, attended Grateful Dead concerts, and experimented with acid. I met Wendy while wandering through the corridors of the dorm one afternoon. When I first arrived on campus I had been somewhat shocked at how suburban and scrubbed-behind-the-ears the student body, particularly the girls, appeared. It seemed nearly everyone was blonde, majoring in Phys Ed, and always had the latest Carpenters album spinning on their turntables. So imagine my surprise when I turned a corner and heard the sublime sounds of John Coltrane's soprano sax solo from *My Favorite Things*. I walked right through the open door and encountered a generously proportioned gal in a granny dress and wire-rimmed glasses, sporting a wild mane of frizzy dark hair. We instantly bonded and later on she introduced me to her friend Joyce. The three of us soon became inseparable on campus, laying claim to our own little corner of the dining hall.

But the party turned out to be a train wreck -- for me, that is. That Saturday, after we all downed a few beers in Wendy's room, she, Joyce and I got into Joyce's car and drove the few blocks to a mock Tudor house on a quiet residential street. Their friend David and his roommate had managed to find a cheap rental on the first floor that featured spacious living quarters and even a fireplace. There were maybe eight people already there when we arrived. The stereo was on playing some kind of jazz fusion and everyone was sitting on comfortable couches around a large coffee table.

David and his roommate greeted us, introductions were made, and the three of us found seats and plopped down. Before I knew it, a stick of hashish (more potent than ordinary weed and something I was not used to) was being passed around in a water pipe. The person next to me cheerfully offered the pipe for me to take a hit. Then it came around again. Having never before indulged, I quickly got into a disoriented trance-state that turned the sofa I was sitting on into a flying carpet, the music into liquid colors, and laughter into whooping jungle cries.

A few more guests showed up. Somebody turned up the music. There were copious amounts of white wine and I distinctly recall someone, perhaps enjoying the sight of me seriously strung out, who -- like a dutiful servant -- was always right there to refill my glass before I could ask. We were all sitting more or less in a circle, munching on cheese and crackers, talking about movies, classes, items in the news. Soon the animated voices, high-pitched giggles, and ambient music all blurred into a silky fabric that wrapped itself luxuriously around my body.

Before long all became dreamy and surreal and suddenly Joyce, sitting next to me on the couch, became one of the girls in my fantasy world. My attention became fixated on her flowing chestnut locks and smooth cheeks. Feeling sensual and warm I suddenly reached out and made a very conspicuous and aggressive pass at her, and when she rebuffed me in no uncertain terms it torpedoed me back to reality with a massive thud. Ugh!! Mortified, and realizing I had just made a pathetic fool of myself in front of a dozen people, most of them strangers, I broke down crying. As all eyes turned toward me and someone came over to help, I felt compelled by a need to "come clean." So, in front of all who had witnessed the sorry spectacle I "confessed" that I was indeed one of *those people.*

Jeremy, David's roommate and a gay man himself, assured me that there was nothing wrong and nothing to apologize for. Others looked on with a strange mixture of pity and bemusement. Somebody walked up to me and gently patted my forehead. But all of the kindness could not prevent me from having the worst headache I ever had in my life and feeling as flush with shame as if I had just lost control of my bladder in first grade and left a telltale yellow puddle on the floor for all to see. David and Jeremy insisted I sleep over that night so I could get my head back together.

The next afternoon when I got back to my dorm room I found it empty. Both of my roommates had gone home for the weekend. I locked myself in and wanted to tear my hair out. Hating myself for last night's embarrassing incident I felt I had to do something, anything, to redeem myself and wipe away the humiliation. For hours I just sat on my bed and agonized. I wondered if Joyce would ever speak to me again, or would look upon me in a different way from now on. But even if she was perfectly cool with what had happened, I knew that I wasn't. I tried to sit at my desk and read over some class assignments but I couldn't concentrate. As it began to get dark I thought I ought to head for the dining hall to get some dinner, not having consumed any solid food since the day before. But I made sure to leave an hour earlier than usual, dreading the possibility of encountering Wendy and Joyce there. Later on I tried to sleep but could only toss and turn restlessly. The night wore on. Midnight came and went and I was still wide awake, sitting up, anxious and upset.

Then I suddenly recalled all of that "queer" literature from the Rochester conference tucked away in my dresser. A feeling of rage swept over me as I pulled open the drawer and wrenched out all those papers, throwing them in a heap on the bed. I looked over the loosely scattered array of . . . what? The literature of liberation long overdue? Or the propaganda of perverts? Without a second thought I gathered up everything and dumped it into the metal wastebasket. Then I found a match, lit it, and tossed it into the basket. Slowly the flame caught and spread, and I watched the papers burn with a sigh of relief. It was as if all the emotional anguish I had been feeling since arriving on campus thoroughly confused about my sexuality could somehow be off-loaded and dispersed in an instant, transformed into a fine ash that would vanish into the air without leaving a trace.

Lost in my reverie I scarcely noticed when the smoke alarm out in the hall started ringing and the frightened students began spilling out of their rooms to find out where the fire was. As soon as the truth was known, shocked pajama-clad young women could be seen whispering among themselves and pointing fingers towards my room. Somebody called the campus infirmary as well as the police. Within a few minutes I saw several people approaching me with baffled or concerned expressions on their faces. Someone who looked like a campus security guard attempted to grab hold of me and slip on what appeared to be handcuffs. When I jerked away suddenly and tried to bolt, two men tackled me and put a straitjacket on me, obviously thinking I was a would-be terrorist or a dangerous mental case. I was strapped to a gurney and ushered away to some "quiet room."

All this because of a little bonfire in a trash can? I thought the overreaction ridiculous, uncalled for, and fully expected it would all blow over as soon as I had a chance to explain myself. That was until I overheard campus officials talking about "immediate expulsion" and "sick leave." Next thing I knew someone was on the phone with my parents, hundreds of miles away, at three o'clock in the morning. They needed to come right away -- it was an "emergency." I shuddered to think what Mom and Dad must be imagining and whether they would ever forgive me. My college career, which my father had dreamt about, looked forward to with pride, and prepared for financially since the day I was born, had been stopped in its tracks less than three months after it had taken off.

4
Not Hiring

WHAT I REMEMBER most is the green cookies. It was during that giddy euphoric week between Christmas Eve and New Year's Eve, and I was about to be discharged. For the past six weeks my home had been the North Wing, Ward Three at St. Vincent's Hospital, a psychiatric institution tucked away in a leafy suburb of Westchester County, New York. I was admitted there shortly after getting expelled from college two and a half months into my freshman year. That expulsion had shocked and angered my parents and led to my having a nervous breakdown. They decided to put me in the hospital for a thorough evaluation and subsequent treatment. During my stay I was scrutinized by headshrinkers, showered with condescending compassion, pumped up with happy pills, zapped with electric bolts to my brain, taught how to make log cabins out of popsicle sticks, how to turn wet clay into a glossy, woefully misshapen coffee mug, and befriended by my fellow lost, disjointed souls.

Now I was feeling pretty good, my spirits elevated, my mental and emotional state considerably improved. I was greatly looking forward to being with my family and enjoying home-cooked meals again, not to mention no longer having to listen to crazy Betty play the Beatles song *O-Blah-Dee-O-Blah-Da* over and over and over a dozen times in a row. (Oh! -- how often had I been tempted to stomp on that portable pink record player they kept in the rec room!) All of the hall monitors had donned red Santa Claus caps and were giving away candy canes. The kitchen staff on the ward had baked several batches of delicious butter cookies, shaped like Christmas trees, dyed green with Easter egg food coloring, and covered in red and gold sprinkles. They were walking down the hallway with platters, grinning widely, freely handing them out. The cookies, still warm, literally melted in your mouth and both the patients and their visiting relatives, all awash in Yuletide glee, were indulging with gusto. I left St. Vincent's with a small boxful of the holiday treats

-- a souvenir of my stay, if a perishable one -- and could barely wait to sleep in my own bed again.

But alas, the festive spirit was soon to evaporate. A brand new year was about to unfold, and it found me back at home instead of away at school, with no opportunity to enroll again until the fall. What would I do all winter, spring, and summer? My mother had a ready answer. I would, of course, go out and find a job. Just about any job would do so long as it got me up early every morning and out of the house. My psycho-emotional health was hanging by the thinnest of threads -- to keep the thread from snapping I had to be occupied, productive, and firmly planted in the real world. Okay -- well, a cursory check of the neighborhood revealed that they didn't need any checkout girls at the *Pioneer* supermarket or salesclerks down at *Genung's* department store. I had no experience as a babysitter or waitress. And in an era before the *McDonald's* golden arches were as ubiquitous as pickpockets in Rome, there were simply no places around where I could get a gig flipping burgers.

So I went to an employment agency and told them I'd take anything they had, any job I was qualified for. But all they had to offer was a job working at a radio factory in an industrial part of Mount Vernon, NY, the town we were living in. My task would be to fold large heavy sheets of corrugated cardboard into boxes. As the fully assembled radios came down the conveyor belt another worker would lift and place them into the finished cartons. Feeling lucky to have found a job I could actually perform, I gladly accepted the assignment.

For the first few weeks all went smoothly. The pay was decent and the factory was clean and well-lit. The work itself was not too taxing, although my hand and arm muscles became fatigued from the constant repetitive motion. I dealt with the monotony by getting into a certain rhythm as I worked, playing favorite songs in my head and using them as soundtracks for my escapist fantasies. And the best part of all was that when I got home at the end of the day I felt genuinely beat, tired in a visceral, physical way -- like someone who had *really* put in a hard day's work. The result was that I slept like a baby and woke up refreshed and invigorated.

Then everything changed. One day, after I'd been on the job almost two months, a new supervisor took over and he was none too pleased at the sight of me dutifully assembling my cardboard cartons. Maybe he feared a lawsuit or a visit from an OSHA inspector -- who knows -- but on his second day there he announced that the job they had assigned me was "too strenuous to be performed by a female." Instead, he wanted to put me on a workstation right on the assembly line, where, working with tweezers and other precision tools, I would be attaching different colored wires to various connector ports inside the rear panel of what would shortly become a new radio.

I took the tweezers into my hand and, squinting, struggled to grab hold of the tiny protruding wires and attach the right color to the right port. Sometimes they were slippery and I had to make several attempts. Turning the very small screw I had to use to fasten the wire required a certain finesse and patience. Before I was done with one, the next radio would be right in front of me. Apparently my fingers were not as nimble as those of the other women on the line. After about ten minutes I thought my eyes would glaze over and my hands cramp up. Another ten minutes and I started to feel like one of those ancient Chinese embroidery workers who went blind sewing intricate imagery into the fine silk robes worn by the aristocracy. Fifteen more minutes and I felt like I was going insane.

I protested vigorously, insisting that I much preferred folding boxes to jabbing little wires into tiny holes and was perfectly capable of executing the task without keeling over. But my complaints failed to move the supervisor. I tried to reason with him, begged and pleaded, but to no avail. For whatever reason, he had made up his mind and was impervious to all counterarguments. Back on the assembly line I fumed silently, refusing to work any faster than was comfortable for me, even if it meant letting an occasional radio go by without its wires properly connected. As I watched myself being transformed unwillingly from a diligent dedicated worker into an insubordinate troublemaker, I felt helpless and ill-used. At one point, just after pricking my finger with the tip of a wire, I was suddenly struck by the sheer absurdity and stupidity of it all. Without another sigh or murmur I just threw down my tools and stormed out the door, vowing never to return -- not even to collect my last paycheck.

My mother had little sympathy for my plight, saying I should have never taken such a job in the first place. So it was back to *The New*

York Times Help Wanted section and the employment agencies. I began regularly going into Manhattan and registering with every agency I could find. I showed up unannounced at the HR departments of dozens of companies scattered among a cluster of midtown skyscrapers. But I was a recent high school grad with zero job experience. Unlike my two siblings, I had been too lazy and too uninterested in money to knock myself out trying to line up summer jobs for when school let out every June. So I had nothing to even put on a resume.

In most cases, before I could even ask to fill out a job application, the receptionist or administrative assistant would quip, without even making eye contact, "We're not hiring now, sorry" or, "What experience do you have?" The identical scenario kept repeating itself, as if someone were hitting the REWIND button on a tape recorder. Before long I began to feel like Charlie Chaplin or Buster Keaton in an old silent film going through the motions of a silly ritual: there I was entering the glass revolving door of an office building, stepping onto an elevator and going up, only to reappear mere moments later exiting the elevator car and shuffling along the corridor in the opposite direction, eyes downcast, heading for those same glass doors. Like some hapless mime whose signature skit is riding elevators up and down all day long.

But if there was any humor to be found in my predicament, it quickly wore off as soon as I got home. My mother scolded me, saying I wasn't trying hard enough or pointing out that if only I had taken my typing class more seriously in high school, I surely could have landed some kind of office clerk position. "Mark my words" she barked, peeling potatoes over the kitchen sink, "if you think you're just gonna lay around here and do nothing for the whole summer you've got another thing coming, no matter *what* your father says!" My dad, who was never home during the day, didn't care what I did around the house or what "chores" I managed to avoid as long as I did well in school.

But Mom had a point. Almost six weeks had passed since I'd left the radio factory. Spring was turning into summer and I was no closer to landing a real job than I had been the first day of winter. Frustration mounted, and a dreary sense of hopelessness began to creep up on me like a drop of black ink spilled onto a napkin, slowly spreading out in all directions. Somewhere in the back of my head I could hear a dark discordant sound that became increasingly irritating. Something getting scraped, friction, screeching, comb-dragged-across-a-blackboard sounds. Ouch! I could sense my pre-hospital, broken self returning with a vengeance, and I started to panic.

I redoubled my efforts to find employment, even tried to brush up on my typing skills. Out the door I rushed each morning armed with sheets of job postings and classified ads clipped from several newspapers, marked here and there with hopeful red circles. One advertisement read: "Waitress Wanted -- No Experience Necessary." When I arrived at the "cabaret" I soon learned that the word *Topless* had been intentionally omitted from the ad. I seemed to be having a streak of bad luck or maybe it was the economy or maybe it was just *me*. I must have given off those misfit vibes, a kind of freaky radar that could be detected a hundred yards away. I began to dread going home and having to face my mother after yet another futile day of job-hunting.

But never could I have imagined the way it would all end. My suspicions about what might be happening to my mental state, my fears that a crisis was brewing, were about to be horribly confirmed. It happened one raw rainy day. I had taken the commuter train to Grand Central Station and then hopped a subway for the umpteenth time. Somehow, I had managed to score an interview after calling the number on a small help-wanted ad that sounded promising. The job site was located in a townhouse in Greenwich Village and appeared to be a small antiques business dealing in vintage postcards, Tiffany lamps, French posters, and similar collector's items. The position involved mostly filing and answering phones. I had an afternoon appointment so there was plenty of time to eat a good breakfast and get all dressed up.

When I arrived I immediately saw that there were only a handful of employees, and the place had a warm cozy feel to it. A well-dressed white-haired matron who looked to be in her sixties -- probably the owner -- asked me to take a seat. I dared get my hopes up as she explained how I would be sorting postcards by country and date, cataloging posters, creating labels and inventory lists, and answering customer inquiries. If accepted for the position, she continued, I would be given a two-week orientation that would include extensive training about the type of merchandise the store specialized in. The salary she quoted was well above average for a file clerk. Then she said something about a "brief audition."

"Our clientele is quite refined," she began, "and very knowledgeable about the kinds of collectibles we deal in. This job entails long phone conversations with customers seeking very particular kinds of rare items. They will expect to talk to someone not only well-informed about our catalog, but exhibiting a certain level of. . . well, elocution, a certain manner of speaking, you know?"

"So you want me to give a demonstration of how I would speak to a customer?" I offered.

"Well, we have a little script prepared that we ask all prospective hires to read for us," she said, pointing towards an assistant. "Gretchen will play the role of a client calling you -- you answer by reading the script."

She then handed me a sheet of paper containing about half a page of text, which included terms like "figural powder jars," "depression glass," "millefiori paperweights" and "rose tapestry vases." As Gretchen posed each question I read aloud from the appropriate place on the sheet. I read smoothly and clearly, without stumbling over anything, and thought I had performed well enough. I began trying to imagine the look on Mom's face when I told her I had finally landed a really nice job. It seemed like it would be a pleasure to have to report to such a place each morning, instead of to a sterile bank of cubicles in some midtown office tower. After I finished reading they asked me to please sit and wait while the two of them consulted in the next room.

As soon as they closed the door I sat nervously, playing with my fingers, wondering if I needed to upgrade my wardrobe to work in this classy place. Somewhat impatient as the moments passed, I silently crept over to the door, crouched down and placed my ear against the crack, hoping to catch bits and pieces of their conversation. Within a few seconds I caught wind of the words, "thick Bronx accent" and "maybe a bit too ethnic." Instantly I knew I wouldn't get the job. At length the two of them came out, thanked me very much for coming, assured me they thought highly of my qualifications, shook my hand and said, smiling, "We'll let you know."

As I left the handsome townhouse my eyes welled up with tears, try as I might to hold back the flood. I ran all the way to the West 4th Street subway station in the pouring rain, relieved I needn't bother trying to hide my own gushing waterworks. I caught my train at Grand Central and by the time I got back to Mount Vernon the tears had subsided. But the weather had taken a turn for the worse. The rain was coming down in sheets. Terrible wind gusts were whipping tree branches and knocking over trash bins, sending them rolling down the street. Those ominous howls signaled a *Nor'easter* barreling in from offshore, unusual for late spring.

I still had eight long blocks to walk from the station and despite my umbrella, I was getting soaked. And then, just as I was walking past the library, my cheap fold-up umbrella blew inside out. In an instant it had turned into a useless piece of junk. I folded it back up and ran into the library for cover, not sure what to do. Should I try to wait out the storm, or call my mom to pick me up?

As I stood by the window watching frenzied raindrops pelt the pavement without mercy, I became aware suddenly of a desperate, teeth-clenching, stiffening feeling sweeping over me. My whole body felt like a huge screw being slowly tightened. I realized I was no longer sad, but furious. How had it come to this? Had I become the bull's-eye in some sinister game of darts being played by the Arbiters of Fate? I happened to be standing in the exhibition room, which fronts the main library. A small dimly lit hall that most folks just walked through without stopping, it featured items of local historical interest. Rare old photographs, hundred-year-old maps, an early handwritten draft of the first state constitution -- stuff like that. The artifacts were all secured in glass cases, safe from human fingers. I glanced at the exhibits, then continued to pace around the room, looking out the door helplessly, watching the angry storm lash out at everything in its path. Leaves, twigs, and pieces of trash were swirling about wildly in the wind. I felt lost as the screw tightened further.

And then, without warning, I saw my arm rise up, hand clutching the stub of my broken umbrella, and come down crashing into one of the glass cases with a resounding clatter. And then into the one next to it, and then the next, and the next, and the next -- until the sound of shattering glass became deafening and every single case in the room had been smashed. I barely noticed when library attendants came running, and shortly after that, the police. I stood looking at my thumb covered in blood and hanging oddly -- it had almost been torn off. I was rushed by ambulance to the nearest hospital. The next thing I knew I was lying in a bed with my hand all stitched up and wrapped in bandages. A nurse mentioned that my mother was on the way.

About fifteen minutes later she appeared at the door looking flabbergasted. Before I knew what I was saying I began shouting, "No! Don't let her in. I don't want her here! Make her go away!" Then I broke down sobbing, feeling as if my insides were spilling out, and could not be calmed until she left, saying she would return later.

After that shocking incident my mom stopped pestering me to find a job and began worrying about whether I needed to be hospitalized again. A close relative suggested she consider taking me to a family practitioner. After all, he advised, the problem could be rooted in something physical or glandular. And he knew a good doctor -- a family friend -- who specialized in a condition called "low blood sugar," a kind of reverse diabetes in which there is too little glucose in the blood instead of too much. It was known to greatly affect mood, he explained, and could be a key factor in depression and other emotional disorders. Mom took down the doctor's name and phone number and after a day or two we decided to call. An appointment was scheduled for the following week.

5
Two Doctors, No Cures

DR. V. LOOKED to be in his early sixties, had lots of wavy black hair and wore thick-rimmed glasses. He seemed experienced and knowledgeable and had a pleasant bedside manner. After a battery of tests, it turned out that I did indeed suffer from low blood sugar, or -- to use the proper medical term -- hypoglycemia. It was a case of insulin overkill. As a person eats throughout the day, insulin, secreted by the pancreas, is supposed to continually collect glucose from the bloodstream and ferry it to the liver where it can be made available for fuel. But my body was producing too much of the hormone in response to carbohydrate intake, removing the sugars so aggressively and so fast that my blood glucose level plummeted even lower than it had been before I ate. The condition caused mood swings, blues, lethargy, and constant hankerings for sweets and starches. But the remedy was quite simple: avoid carbs as much as possible so as not to trigger this overreaction.

For someone who loved nothing better than a heaping bowl of macaroni (what non-Italian Americans call "pasta") smothered in tomato sauce and grated cheese, and who could devour an entire column of Ritz crackers at a single sitting, this was no easy task. But with a bit of willpower and my mom's cooperation I managed to conquer my cravings and stick to the recommended diet. Surprisingly, after six weeks on the hypoglycemic diet I actually did feel considerably better. I also shed some of those excess pounds I had put on and never dropped since leaving St. Vincent's Hospital with my stash of green butter cookies.

It was now mid-May and everything outside looked soft and fuzzy like an Impressionist painting and all kinds of surprising scents and bits of pollen and warm ripply breezes wafted through the air. In other words, that lighthearted sensual feeling of springtime was back. I faced an entire late spring and summer with nothing to do. Wendy and Joyce from college wrote me letters for a while after I'd been expelled, but I had no real friends in my neighborhood. And, except for that one amorous adventure at the beach with my cousin I had had little or no sexual experience. There had been a few make-out sessions with a couple of the boys I'd gone out with in high school ("dated" hardly seems the right word), but that was about the extent of it.

As for girls, there were nothing but fantasies. I wondered, could a person really be gay without having had a single same-sex experience? And what if I were to deliberately seek out sex with men and found that I enjoyed it -- would the feelings for girls fade away? I thought it was high time I resolved this nagging question once and for all. With so much time on my hands and the whole summer ahead -- well, why not go out and experiment? Men were always approaching me -- the fate of every reasonably attractive teenage girl, I suppose -- so there was no shortage of opportunity.

And so, without becoming an all-out slut, I allowed a few guys to pick me up. For birth control I used a spermicidal sponge that I could buy at the drug store. Then I would just go into the city and walk around at random, noticing attractive guys and not averting my glance when they looked back. There was the cute Puerto Rican dude I met in Washington Square, a Polish construction worker with great biceps, and a gorgeous, fashionably dressed black dancer who I just knew had to be gay when I spotted him leaning against a pole in a subway car. He wasn't. I found that while I could enjoy the sexual gymnastics as well as any "normal" woman, a key part of me seemed not to be there, seemed withheld somehow. It was as if the essential kernel of myself was up on the ceiling, looking down at this confused young woman in bed with a stranger.

I couldn't know it at the time, but despite the new diet regimen my depression was beginning to return in full force. I became aware of a peculiar feeling as I walked about town or had dealings with others. I noticed it at the supermarket, the train station, the post office -- anywhere I went where there were other people. It was a feeling of *receding*, of slowly disappearing to the point of being barely visible, of shrinking into the black hole of my being. I became convinced that the person interacting with me -- the clerk at the post office, the conductor on the train, the teller at the bank -- was not talking to the "real" me but only to an actor playing the part of me. Whatever they saw was not really me, because the real me was hidden, invisible, at least to them.

Lodged somewhere deep in the back of my consciousness, squeezed and compressed like a crumpled-up lunch bag, sat the true ME, armed with a pair of binoculars, surveying the scene out there. Part of that scene was the actor playing me and her every move was being watched, her every word monitored, her performance evaluated and critiqued. Her function was to say and do whatever was necessary to make her way in the world and to keep transactions with others to a bare minimum. She was the faithful house servant opening doors and answering phones to shield her master from having to deal directly with the public. Safely ensconced in my dark upper chambers behind velvet curtains, the real me was free to study, reflect on, and record life as it transpired out there. The true me had no real responsibilities other than to observe. Nothing that happened to my decoy moving about in the real world, be it hurtful or pleasant, nothing that she did with or to others, or even to her own body, could affect the real *me*, securely hidden in the dark.

As the essential inauthenticity of my behavior became increasingly obvious to me, I began to withdraw, to shrink into myself, more and more. I gave up my sexual escapades, put myself in solitary confinement, and tried to have as little to do with the world outside my mind as possible. My mother decided it might be time to take me to a genuine head doctor, a psychiatrist who would be better equipped to handle my severe "emotional problems." I had already applied to and been accepted by another college closer to home and would be relaunching my freshman year come September. My parents agreed it was critical that I get some kind of treatment before going away to school again. So I began regular sessions with a shrink.

Dr. Q., tall, slender, and mysterious looking, began by administering some diagnostic tests. I was asked to count to 100 by sevens, to name the current vice president, to spell "earth" backwards, and to draw a picture of a clock reading 11:40. Then there was a four-page questionnaire to answer, containing at least one hundred items. One of the questions read: "Have you ever been attracted to a member of your own sex in a romantic or sexual way?" Those one-night stands with men had done nothing to "cure" my attractions to women. The issue had become something of an obsession that often kept me awake at night. Perhaps if I were totally honest, Dr. Q. could help me to finally resolve it. So I checked the little box in front of "Very frequently," completed the rest of the questionnaire and handed it back to him.

But at our next session there was no mention of the subject. Instead, the good doctor wrote out a prescription for some mood-elevating drug in vogue at the time, telling me it would "lift and lighten" my spirits. After two more sessions with no mention of the gay issue, I decided I would have to bring it up myself. It took me a while to get the nerve to broach the subject, but finally I just let it out. Dr. Q. didn't seem to find my revelation all that earth-shattering. In fact, he rather dismissed it as probably a "phase" I was going through and no big deal. "But" I said, "Does this mean I'm a homosexual even though I've never done anything?" His reply: "Probably not -- you won't really know until you get out into the world and meet more people, have more real-life experiences. At any rate it's nothing to be concerned about."

So I left his office feeling no more enlightened on the subject than I was the first time I walked in. I wished there was someone, anyone, that I could confide in. But there wasn't. I had no real friends, no trusted older sister, and I certainly couldn't tell my mother. (And in those hush-hush days before Ellen, Martina, Rosie O'Donnell, etc. there were no "role models" to look to.) All I had to consult were library books. But then, I thought of Dr. V. He had helped me so much with the low blood sugar problem and he was a family friend besides. And, as an experienced and fully trained physician, such matters surely wouldn't shock him. So, I called him and asked for an appointment.

I went to see Dr. V. and explained that I was totally confused about my sexuality, that although I had experienced several intimate encounters with men, the fantasies about women continued, had, in fact, become even more consuming. I told him I felt "abnormal," as if something was not quite right with me. He said that we should first find out if there was anything physical or medical that could account for my "confusion." Once we ruled that out, he explained, we could then consider psycho-emotional factors.

He asked me to undress and to put on a gown, with the opening in the back. He then stood behind me and began by putting his hands under my arms and massaging the lymph nodes, saying this could indicate if there was a "glandular imbalance." I stood quietly as he slid his hands down to my breasts, which he began to squeeze. He reminded me that all young women should examine their breasts regularly in order to detect any lumps that could signal breast cancer.

I wondered what this examination could possibly reveal that would shed light on my problem. I started to feel somewhat uncomfortable as he moved his hands down toward my hips. I had become aware of his hot breath on my neck and his breathing seemed to be getting heavier. He said he would briefly check my genital area for any "abnormalities." I squirmed a bit as I felt his fingers brushing against my pubic hair, moving toward the spot where my clitoris was. All of a sudden I felt something firm and fleshy from behind pushing in between my legs, then pulling back. What!! *What the fuck!* I could not believe what was happening. Was this guy actually trying to jerk off against my naked butt, or maybe even trying to *rape* me!!!

Horrified, I pulled away quickly, turned around and there he was with his zipper down, holding his stiff pink dick, looking almost as shocked as I was. Had all of my talk about sex turned the old man on? I began dressing immediately, too dumbfounded to hear his mumbling attempt at an explanation. I chastised myself severely. How could I have allowed this to happen, not seen it coming? How naive and stupid could I be! I grabbed my things and flew out the door, practically running all the way home.

I could not bring myself to tell my parents what had happened. I simply never mentioned Dr. V. again. It was not until almost six months later that my father found a copy of a letter I had written to a trusted cousin describing the incident. I had intentionally left it in a conspicuous place in the hope that one of my parents *would* find it and learn the truth. I wanted the whole family to know and to sever all ties with the lecherous bastard.

After that awful episode I felt more alone than ever. I decided to just keep to myself and forget about sex altogether. Fantasies would have to do -- and with luck, maybe they too would fade away. It was now mid-July and it felt like a steam bath outside. I was still taking the medicine Dr. Q. had prescribed for me. It did lift my mood somewhat but always made me feel like I'd just gulped down nine cups of coffee. Still, I couldn't afford to stop taking it. I was so afraid of falling again into the sinkhole, down into that place where I can hear my own echo but no one hears me. It was too hot to stay home and too hot to go outside. I sought out air-conditioned places -- stores, movie theaters, the train.

I couldn't wait for the fall when I would start college again. This time it would be a small private college in a sleepy little town along the Hudson River, not a large state-run institution like the last school. On several occasions I had taken the train north to Tarrytown and visited the campus. I walked all around admiring the bucolic scenery and wondering which dormitory I'd be living in. But college was still two months away and I had all this time to kill. Since I'd already spent all the money I had earned in that factory job, I was reduced to depending on my parents for my "allowance."

How humiliating! Maybe I could find some kind of job before school starts, I thought as I wiped my sweating brow with a rag and reached into the fridge to steal another one of my dad's *Budweisers*. Then I shook my head and laughed. Just the thought of putting on makeup and stockings and dressing up for yet another *job interview* in this kind of weather. . .hell no! There was just no way. I was going to have to get through this sweltering summer with pocket change, cold showers, and dangling, unresolved issues that I pretended not to notice.

6
Kneesocks

A SULTRY SUMMER afternoon and I'm trudging home in the sticky heat. I've just left the cool environs of *Baron's* Stationery store, where I had browsed through the display of notebooks, three-ring binders, pens and markers, all in anticipation of starting college in the fall. I also picked up that week's *Village Voice*. The *Voice* was the standard counterculture, anti-establishment newspaper of New York and I read it avidly. As I approached the library I noticed a group of teenagers loitering on the street. I immediately recognized some of them as delinquent girls from high school who had taunted me about my clothes in the ninth and tenth grades. Ever since that humiliating first day of class in Florida when a roomful of kids laughed at my appearance, I never knew quite how to dress in school (jeans and t-shirts not allowed in those days!) And all through my freshman year in high school, all I would have to do is walk into the girl's restroom and there they would be, leaning against the sinks, smoking cigarettes, applying eyeliner, trash talking, and giving me the once-over.

There was always something about my dress -- maybe my skirt was too long or my shoes too flat or my sweater too "square" or my belt not cool enough. They would glare at me and make sarcastic comments: "Hey, are those orthopedic shoes?" or "Yo, what style is that blouse you got on, early Salvation Army?" These were tough Italian girls from the wrong side of the tracks. They were Sicilian, in fact; their people had come over from Sicily, the same place where the Mafia crime families hailed from originally. They had often been suspended for truancy and gross misbehavior -- one girl had even smacked a teacher.

As I continued walking up Prospect Avenue I could see there was no avoiding them. They had spotted me before I had time to cross over to the other side of the street. Just as I was passing the library I heard one of them shout: "Hey look, there goes *Kneesocks* -- I remember you!" referring back to an incident that took place one chilly November morning when I was in the tenth grade. I was running late for school and the only clean pair of nylons left in my drawer had a jagged run from thigh to ankle. I hurriedly pulled on a pair of navy blue woolen knee socks, like the kids in Catholic school wore, and ran out to catch the school bus. It was just my lousy luck to encounter them by the school entrance, smoking their *Marlboros.* I could hear their hoots and howls of laughter all the way till I got to my locker.

At the moment Josephine, the heavyset one, was coming towards me. "Hey, can I look at your newspaper a second?" she said with mock politeness, starting to reach for the paper under my arm. I quickly snatched it away, said "Go fuck yourself" and kept on walking.

"Ex-CUSE me -- did you just swear at me? Hey Angela, did you hear her swear at me? Now where the fuck do you get off swearing at me like that, you sicko bitch! I'll come over there and teach you some respect."

Next thing I know she's shoving me while Angela grabs my *Village Voice* and throws it in the air, scattering pages all over the sidewalk. I pushed Josephine back and then felt Angela pulling my hair really hard. There was no way I could take both of them on myself. Worse, they had the rest of their posse still waiting on the corner, which included two boys. Luckily the custodian at the library, hearing the ruckus, came out to break it up. The girls finally left, giving me the "evil eye" and vowing revenge.

Shaken, I sought shelter in the library -- the very same library I had vandalized in broad daylight just a few months earlier. I had intended to stop in there anyway to do some reading but now I couldn't concentrate. I imagined the whole mob of them huddling behind a tree somewhere waiting for me to come out (the library would be closing in just 20 minutes) and then ambushing me on my way home, determined to mete out the "punishment" I truly deserved for my offense.

I started to panic -- what would I do -- would they leave me in a bloody heap on the sidewalk, triumphantly shouting *"That oughta teach her a lesson!"* I tried to figure a way out. I didn't want to call my mom like some frightened little kid. Besides, she probably wouldn't be home. Should I ask someone to accompany me out of the library and walk with me until I was within running distance of my house? No, that would be too embarrassing.

I paced around trying to think. Then I noticed the large open window in the Science section, which was located towards the back of the building. I walked over to the window and looked out at the parking lot below. If I exited the library from the back, Josephine and company would never see me coming and I could take a detour and get home in one piece. I stared at the ground below. It did not look like a very steep jump. I was on the upper level of the library, only two stories above the ground. Surely if I braced myself and jumped cautiously, I could land on my feet like a cat. This was my only escape. Two people were in the immediate area, looking through the bookshelves. I waited patiently until both of them moved out of view, then walked over to the open window. Carefully hoisting myself onto the ledge, I took a good look below and then "took the plunge" -- literally.

Well, I did land on my feet alright -- the only problem was I could not move. The drop onto the concrete blacktop was so hard that I had actually splintered the small bones in my heels, creating hairline fractures which radiated outward all through the soles of my feet. I fell back to the ground. When I tried to get up the pain was excruciating. I could not stand on my feet, much less walk. There was no one around and I just lay there in the parking lot pondering the irony of it all. Angela and Josephine might have smacked me around, but they could never have crushed my very bones, not unless they were planning to use a sledgehammer!

I waited desperately for someone, anyone, to come by. I didn't feel like screaming. Finally, some man came into the parking lot and walked over to his car. I yelled out to get his attention, told him I had fallen and couldn't get up, and asked him to please call an ambulance. He went inside the library to make the call. Before I knew it I was surrounded by library personnel who had witnessed my earlier misadventure. They looked at me pitifully and I soon realized that they assumed I had tried to commit suicide. One just shook his head, muttering "Tch tch. . .ah, that poor girl."

My feet had to be set in casts, which extended all the way up to my knees. I left the hospital in a wheelchair. My mother was stunned as were all of my family. I tried to assure them that I had *not* tried to kill myself. But I never told them the true story of what had happened -- I was too ashamed. At last, the sight of me in a wheelchair elicited some real sympathy from my mother. There would be no more scolding or rebuking, at least not for a while.

7
Hot Tantrum in a Firehouse

MOM WAS NOT a mean or a cold person, far from it. I'll never forget the day -- I must have been about eight or nine years old -- when we found a wounded parakeet in our driveway. The bird was probably a pet that had escaped out of a neighbor's window. Mom felt so bad that she picked it up gently and brought it into the house. She laid it on a towel; it appeared to have a broken leg and an injured wing. My mother got some bandages, gauze pads and cotton and proceeded to bandage the animal's leg and tenderly wrap the wing. She went to the local pet store and bought bird feed and a small cage. Within a couple of weeks the bright green and yellow parakeet came back to life and chirped loudly in our kitchen every morning. He was our first and only family pet until he died the following year.

But she simply didn't know how to handle me. My mom grew up in a heavily Italian neighborhood in the Bronx, her family having originated from a part of Italy called Calabria. After graduating from high school she took a job as a switchboard operator and worked until she got married. Today she would be called a "stay at home mom," as were most married women in the 1950s and early '60s. I was her firstborn child. Signs that I might be "different" appeared almost immediately.

My mother told me she could never understand why, when she picked me up out of my playpen and let me crawl around on the living room carpet, I would whimper and cry until she put me back behind bars in my pen with my toys and stuffed dolls. At about age 2, I began sitting up in bed and rocking myself to sleep, a habit that continues *to this day*. At the same age I would constantly pester her, insisting that she take a crayon and show me how to write my name. Whenever she put a frilly dress on me or a bow in my hair, I would pull up the skirts and try to rip it off or would yank the bow out and throw it on the floor.

As I grew a bit older I tried to entertain my mother by dancing around and inventing clever tales and funny stories to tell her, because she always looked so serious. She was forever cleaning -- dusting, vacuuming, wiping, sweeping, scrubbing down the bathroom. I rarely saw her without a dishrag or towel in her hand. After a while I just couldn't understand what made her tick, no more than she could me. She was always on the move. My mom was as efficient and businesslike as an office manager. Unlike my dad, she showed little interest in my schoolwork or report cards, believing that academic pursuits took second place to practical living skills and social etiquette -- especially for girls.

She would routinely lecture me, solemnly reciting a laundry list of my shortcomings: First, I tried to avoid household chores and would rather "bury my head in a book." Second, I was "antisocial" and never reached out to other girls to make friends. Third, I showed no interest in "feminine" things like learning how to cook and iron clothes. Fourth, my manners were crude and "uncouth" -- why couldn't I be more "dainty?" Fifth, I was eccentric and standoffish. Mom often told me I had a weird personality and that all of the criticism she leveled at me was of the "constructive" kind, meant only to help me improve my character. Of course, neither my mother nor I knew anything about clinical depression at that time. It was assumed that all of my moods, attitudes and behaviors arose naturally from my personality.

Now that the accident in the library parking lot had rendered me "crippled," just like that unfortunate bird, I basked in the extra attention I was getting, as my mother saw it as her first duty to attend to the needs of her injured child. And so I luxuriated in the tender loving care that Mom exuded in her new role as nurse. I breathed a deep sigh of relief knowing there was no longer any pressure on me to do anything. Mom was always there to help me do whatever I had difficulty with, whether bathing myself, dressing, or even going to the bathroom.

After about two weeks in a wheelchair I graduated to crutches. I spent most of my days reading and when it was not too hot outside, hopping about in the yard. I could feel my feet getting stronger. When my arms got tired from swinging the crutches I would lie down on the bed with a book or the latest copy of the *Village Voice*. One day I happened to be scanning the Bulletin on the back page, where announcements about various goings-on in the city could be found. I noticed one posting in particular. It read: "**GAY HOTLINE -- Call us anytime for info or friendly conversation**." Underneath was the phone number. I clipped it and decided to call. I waited for a day when my mom wasn't around and, after a few nervous false starts, I managed to dial the number.

At first I spoke with a gay man named Presley. In the safety of anonymity, I told Presley everything I had once attempted to tell Doctor Q. and Doctor V. and the high school psychologist but that none of them seemed to hear. He told me about his own coming out struggles and how he'd thought he was the only gay person in Junction City, Kansas. He knew all about being taunted and teased and beat-up on a regular basis. At last, I thought, what a rare comfort to be able to talk to someone who could and would truly listen, understand, and share.

The next time I called I got a woman. Her name was Morgan and she was about my age, or just a few years older. Morgan was very friendly, vibrant, loved to talk. Over the next several days I called the Hotline every other night and it was almost always Morgan who picked up. Soon we were having hour-long conversations about politics, movies, music, sexuality, religion. She had a keen sense of humor and often cracked me up with some comment or bit of sarcasm. I found I could talk to her about anything under the sun without feeling awkward, shy, or uncomfortable. Morgan worked the Hotline three nights a week and before long I was calling regularly, asking for her by name. I finally had a friend. And for once I could belong, could feel part of a community that was warm, accepting, and made up of people who knew the same kinds of feelings and attractions I did. I told Morgan that as soon as I got back on my feet – literally -- I would go down to 'the Village' and we could meet in person.

In my idle mind I began to conjure up an image of the woman whose voice was the only thing about her I could describe. She would be slender with shoulder-length hair and dark glistening eyes, maybe wearing a black leather jacket and cowboy boots. She'd be a woman who could be sexy without eye makeup, padded bra or stiletto heels. A woman that a man could lust after but wouldn't want to mess with. I could see the two of us walking proudly down the street, my arm draped over her shoulder, hers around my waist…

But first I had to have these annoying plaster casts removed. And in two weeks I was scheduled to attend the *Wine and Cheese Orientation* at Marymount College, a reception intended to welcome new freshmen and their parents to the campus. I could scarcely believe the long hot summer was over at last. My dad was so relieved I was finally going back to school and so was I. After the casts were taken off, I would take the train to Tarrytown on clear crisp days and visit the college, spending an hour or so strolling the picturesque grounds. I admired the surrounding Hudson River Valley landscape, the big old trees, the fine-looking academic buildings. It seemed a much more welcoming place than my former state university. This was a small Catholic women's college and there was a lovely chapel in an impressive golden-domed edifice called Butler Hall. I could see nuns walking around with their black and white habits, long strings of rosary beads hanging from their hips. As September got underway all my thoughts turned to school.

I moved into my dormitory on the Marymount campus on a Saturday, one week before the start of classes. My room was large, bright, and comfortably furnished with nice wooden desks and reading lamps. I wondered who my roommate would be and the next day I found out. She was a charmingly shy, pleasantly plump, very sweet looking gal whose name, appropriately enough, was Candy. She had big pale blue eyes, long eyelashes, and naturally rosy cheeks. At times she looked more like 13 than 18. Indeed, she had this air of dewy innocence about her that seemed almost comical or put-on, if not downright scary. Candy made me think of marshmallows and teddy bears and all things pink. For a moment I found myself considering whether I should warn her to keep her distance, lest contact with someone like me mess up her Peter Pan world. As it turned out, she would have been grateful, I'm sure, had she received such a warning.

So my new college career began on what seemed a hopeful note. But less than three weeks into the Fall semester, I felt a familiar deep purple gloom beginning to descend. I felt isolated among my fellow students, uncertain how to reach out and make friends. Trying to make small talk or carry on a conversation with Candy seemed to require a concerted effort that I just wasn't up to. I was getting anxious to actually go and meet Morgan, feeling certain it would usher in a whole new life for me, a life that would be free at last from the kind of murky headache-inducing confusion I was so used to being steeped in.

And so finally came the night when I went into the city to meet Morgan and her friends for the first time. We all gathered at *Bonnie & Clyde's*, a popular lesbian bar in the West Village. Morgan was a doll -- a curly-haired blonde, she looked exactly like the silent film star Mary Pickford. As we walked in the door my eyes beheld a typical Saturday night hot-to-trot crowd -- typical but for the fact that they were all women. The place had a small dance floor and a DJ spinning records. A James Brown jam with a phenomenal baseline was booming out of the speakers. We danced and drank and danced some more. There was sparkling conversation at the bar, lively female bartenders refreshing our drinks, lots of laughter. Morgan's friends were cool, curious, interesting characters to say the least. Everyone appeared happy, mellow, relaxed. It seemed wonderful just to be there. I felt like I had been initiated into some secret society that had its own rituals and was privy to knowledge unattainable by outsiders. When it was all over at nearly 4:00 am I kissed Morgan goodnight and rode the train back up to Tarrytown feeling wildly intoxicated -- in more ways than one.

But alas, something dreadful happened the next time I went to see Morgan. Our second meeting, which I had daydreamed about and anticipated even more eagerly than our first, took place on a Friday night. Compared to that joyful "intro" I'd been given at *B&C's*, which had lingered with me for two weeks, this second rendezvous could not have been more different. Morgan had invited me to check out the weekly "Jam Session for Women," a musical event held at a venue I had never heard of in the neighborhood that people were starting to call "Soho." Apparently a group of activists had taken over an abandoned firehouse on Wooster Street and turned it into a gay community center. Friday nights were reserved for the ladies. It was an ideal place to meet women and make friends, Morgan assured me. People brought their own instruments, their own creative ideas. There would be guitars, harmonicas, flutes, singing -- maybe even some poetry reading. It all sounded enchanting.

But when I got there I saw no guitars, heard no poetry. What I did see was an odd assortment of about forty women sitting on the floor, women of all shapes, sizes, colors and ages. Some were shaking tambourines, one was playing a fife, another was banging on a pair of conga drums. Some of the women seemed to be chanting. But it was all a random disconnected cacophony -- everyone was doing their own thing. I asked Morgan what was going on and she said that this was "a chance for women to empower themselves through spontaneous self-expression, unencumbered by patriarchal rules." Oh really? Evidently, obnoxious "rules" like harmony, counterpoint, or keeping time, threatened to cramp a woman's style. This was militant feminism in full flower, coupled with Gay Liberation, movements that were just coming into their own in the early seventies. "But that's not why I came here," I thought but didn't say.

Morgan then recognized a couple of her friends on the other side of the room and, without giving me another look, rushed over to where they were. I just sat down cross-legged and tried to take it all in. To me, everybody looked spaced-out, stoned. I saw joints being passed around. There was too much noise for any attempt at conversation. I didn't know what I was supposed to do. I sat there confused and dismayed. Should I have brought along a pair of castanets or maracas? My mom's uncle had recently returned from a trip to Spain bearing those souvenirs among others. But it all seemed so silly, so. . .so. . *kindergarten*. I looked around helplessly at the strangely animated faces. They were really getting into it now – the gal with the conga drums was on a tear. Soon the whole room was shaking with what sounded like an Indian war dance on steroids.

And then I started to disappear. There it was -- that receding feeling again; I was shrinking into myself. Suddenly I could see my form, my body, sitting among a bunch of crazy people. I saw the actor -- my double -- looking perfectly ridiculous in some theater of the absurd. The feeling startled me. I stood up and walked toward the back of the room. Or more accurately, the actor playing me walked over there. I was invisible again.

Along the back wall a dozen or so metal folding chairs were neatly stacked. Obviously, the room was used for civilized events as well. A physical sensation had come over me that I can only describe as what happens when you bite into something that is very bitter. Except that the instant revulsion was not confined to the mouth but radiated throughout my entire body. I paced back and forth uncomfortably. The drumbeats were getting louder. I looked on hopelessly, feeling left out, erased. But what they were doing seemed too stupid to even want to be a part of. And yet that was all I wanted, wasn't it?

I wanted to say something, shout something, but it seemed no use. Suddenly I grabbed one of the chairs and threw it to the floor. The thud could barely be heard above the unceasing din. I threw down another chair, then another. Next, I began hurling chairs against chairs to make a louder, clanking metal sound. Soon there were more chairs on the floor than against the wall.

People were beginning to turn around; the drumming and chanting subsided. Now everyone was staring in my direction. I knew that what I was doing was spiteful, childish, even bizarre, and certainly wouldn't win me any friends. I won't say: *"but I couldn't stop myself."* That would be slightly disingenuous. I could have forced myself to stop doing it, only it wasn't really *me* that was doing it. I, invisible, was watching the entire scene from the hidden dark corner in my head. And it was an unbelievable show.

Some dyke with a crew cut got up and walked over to me. She gently put her hands on my arms and said, "Are you okay? Why are you doing that?" I heard another one say, "Hey -- we worked really hard to even *get* this space. Somebody paid for those chairs, why are you trying to fuck everything up!" I also heard, "Just get her the hell out of here," and, "Should we call the cops?" I backed off, looked at the gal with the crew cut and said, "Oh, I was just making some noise -- same as you guys were. Not a big deal, right?" I didn't wait to hear her answer but flew down the firehouse steps and out onto Wooster Street. A bit shaken and very angry, I hopped on the subway and rode up to Grand Central Station. It was well past midnight by the time I got back to the dorm and I slipped into my room as quietly as I could so as not to wake up Candy. I must have looked like hell.

I had happily assumed I would be spending that weekend with my new friends in the Village. All summer long, all through my recovery from the accident I had been waiting anxiously for my chance to join the "community" as a full-fledged member. Instead, Saturday saw me sitting in front of my typewriter all day and into the night working on a paper. It was about Samuel Beckett's play *Waiting for Godot*. How appropriate, I thought. After completing the paper I put it into a binder to bring back to class on Monday. Then I felt restless and decided to take a walk into downtown Tarrytown. "Downtown" was nothing more than a quaint village square with a post office, bank, police station, and a few retail shops.

One of them was a liquor store. I thought back to that first night I'd gone out with Morgan's crowd and partied at the wildly popular *Bonnie & Clyde's*. I recalled with a smile how strong the drinks were at that bar. I had consumed at least three tequila & sodas. Someone had once told me that tequila, unlike other whiskeys, produced a very subtle "psychedelic" effect because of some mild hallucinogen found in the blue agave cactus plant from which it was fermented. I didn't know if that was true, but it sure seemed so that night. I had felt almost stoned and it was a sublime feeling.

So I decided to throw my own party, a party-for-one, in my room. I walked into the liquor store and purchased a bottle of *Cuervo Gold*, then hiked back up the hill to the dormitory. Candy had gone home for the weekend just as she did every weekend. I poured some of the tequila into a plastic-coated paper cup. Then I went out to the vending machine and bought three cans of soda. I poured some cola into the cup and took a sip. The next time I used ginger ale. As I imbibed, I tried to focus on and replay the entire scene from Friday night in my mind. I racked my memory to recall every last detail from the moment I met Morgan on West 4th Street to the minute I bolted down the stairs at the firehouse-turned-lesbian-lounge.

Onto my mental movie screen I projected the faces of the women who had sat across from me and those I sat next to at that raucous "Jam Session." Would I have really wanted to date any of them, even if I had not been so turned off by their antics? With the exception of Morgan, probably not. Besides, they were too political. I didn't want to hang out with women who refused to shave under their arms or who viewed men as "the enemy." I pictured myself standing up and addressing them as a group. I poured myself some more tequila, then stood up, red paper cup in hand, and began speaking out loud as I paced across the room.

For six hours I fed myself the cocktail, taking another gulp maybe once every fifteen minutes. I wanted to get wasted, to be able to blot out all that was lonely and hurtful. I wanted to drift into the land of nod, where the anguish and the pain would just melt away. I wanted to leap into a dreamscape where the laws of physics were turned upside down, where a cat could morph into a horse and then into your Uncle Joey, where time was bent, future was past, and actions had no consequences. I continued pacing back and forth across the floor like someone engaged in an anxious phone conversation, my hands making emphatic gestures, still speaking aloud to the assembly of women from last night. I was giving a lecture, telling them what was wrong with the women's movement, pausing every now and then to refill the red cup.

By the time I had consumed almost two thirds of the bottle I was slurring my words and could barely walk. My ranting had gotten louder and more incoherent. Someone must have heard my gibberish because now I could hear loud knocking at the door. I thought I recognized the voices of Donna and Francine who lived two doors down from me. I opened the door. As soon as they saw my condition and the half-empty whiskey bottle on the night table they pushed me over to the bed. Someone ran to get a pot, thinking I might be sick. Amazingly I did not vomit, even though I was high as a kite.

When a few of my dorm mates reported to Candy, in graphic detail no doubt, what had happened, she went immediately to Sister Mary Ellen, who managed student housing and demanded to be given another room and/or another roommate. Who could blame her? The next day Candy brought her mother over to help her gather up all her stuff and move out of the room. I didn't really mind, as I relished the prospect of having my own private abode. Ultimately it was decided that Candy would move to another dormitory, I would take a slightly smaller unused room located at the end of the hallway, while the room I had shared with Candy would be given to a couple of transfer students. I looked forward to decorating my new sanctuary and secretly thanked heaven for the odd bit of luck that allowed me the luxury of a private room on campus.

However, I was more than a little taken aback when, wide awake and stone cold sober, I reviewed the events of the past forty-eight hours. Immediately I made a vow to myself to stay out of trouble from now on -- lest there be a repeat of what happened at my last school. I was no longer seeing Dr. Q. and had stopped taking his pep pills. I had to find some other way to keep depression at bay. At length I decided to go on an ultra-strict diet and begin daily exercise routines to keep myself grounded and free of hypoglycemic symptoms. I was able to get up to one-hundred sit-ups and forty push-ups a day. I gave up alcohol and cigarettes. All attention and focus now shifted to my studies and my health. I tried to pretend that Morgan and her crew, *B&C's*, the firehouse, the chanting and the drums, were all parts of a demented nightmare I was lucky to have awakened from. I would pretend, that is, as long as I could get away with it.

8
Poetry and Raw Milk

I WAS TAKING courses in English literature, European History and Philosophy. I especially liked Philosophy. Knowledge and ideas for their own sake -- yeah. Cutting right to the chase, to the *sine qua non* of BEING itself -- this struck me as an awesome way to spend one's time. I seemed to be headed toward a perfect 4.0 GPA for that semester -- not a bad start for my freshman year. But by the end of October, I was starting to feel like an outcaste among my classmates. I was starting to miss the company of fellow gay people. I had finally come to accept that I must be queer -- whether I did anything about it or not. Despite the fiasco with Morgan's friends at the firehouse, I still looked back with longing to that wonderful night dancing and feeling so free at *Bonnie & Clyde's*. Sometimes I would go to the college mixers or the local Rathskeller with a group of other freshmen just so I could listen to music, have a drink (just one or two), and dance. But watching the girls dancing and making out with their boyfriends only made me feel lonely. So when I happened to see an inch-high announcement in the *Village Voice* about some lesbian dance to be held on the campus of Columbia University, I made up my mind to go.

Thanks to my new diet and exercise regimen I had lost quite a bit of weight and looked pretty good, I thought. I bought myself some flashy earrings and a colorful silk scarf for my head -- I was aiming for a kind of exotic gypsy look. I had a nice pair of leather boots too. On the night of the dance I left my dorm, walked down the hill to the train station and boarded the next train to Grand Central Terminal. Then I took the subway uptown to 116th Street and walked to the Columbia campus. The hall where the dance was being held was as large as a discotheque and had a superb sound system. I looked around to see if by chance Morgan might be there, but there was no sign of her. The dance floor was crowded with women. Those not dancing were either standing around with cigarettes or drinks in their hands, or else lounging on cushions that had been placed against the walls. It was too dark to really see anyone clearly. I headed for the bar to get a beer. There were three women standing at the bar as I approached. I could hear snatches of laughter and happy talk.

As I listened, I thought I recognized one of the voices. It had a kind of twang to it that was not quite southern and not quite Midwestern. Yes, I had definitely heard that voice before. Then it hit me. I had spoken to this woman on the telephone. She volunteered at the Gay Hotline and often when Morgan didn't show up, she was the one who answered the phones. We had a few conversations and I thought she sounded like an interesting character. She had told me she was from Springfield, Missouri, had been "raised by the Jesuits" and had dropped out of college to come to New York and write poetry.

I thought I should walk over and introduce myself, so I did. When she heard my voice she remembered me. Her name was Sadie. She looked quite different from what I had pictured while talking to her on the phone. For some reason I had envisioned a mature woman in her late fifties, perhaps a schoolteacher, slightly overweight with a sweet grandmother countenance. Instead, Sadie was a good deal younger, trim and slender with an athletic build. Her eyes were crystal blue, intense and intelligent, and set in a handsome face shaped by high cheekbones. Her hair was just beyond shoulder-length and hung so dead-straight that she reminded me of one of the Seminole Indian girls I had gone to school with in Florida. Except that her hair was dirty blonde rather than jet black. I thought she made a striking appearance.

We moved onto the dance floor and reveled in the music for a while, then spent the rest of the night talking. She told me she had turned 33 only a few days before, and her friends had thrown her a big party at the community center on Wooster Street. (Hmm...what if I had shown up for that event instead of the Jam Session?) I was impressed by her wit, sardonic tone, and articulate manner of speaking. It was obvious that, college dropout or no, she was highly educated and gifted with words. She told me she was a published poet, and had once been very active in "the movement." I was immediately attracted and hoped that she wouldn't consider me, at 19, too young to hang out with. Evidently she didn't, because after the dance was over we made a date to go out the following Saturday night. I walked off the Columbia University grounds in a state of unabashed glee. For once there was something I could honestly smile about, and the smile held all the way back to my dorm room.

Two weeks later we were lovers. It was my first sexual experience with a woman and I found it somewhat surprising and quite gratifying. In truth it had never really been sex that I was after. If I had mainly wanted sex, I'd just as soon have done it with a man. My attraction to women did not seem to be primarily physical. I did not get turned on looking at half-nude sirens in the pages of *Playboy* or *Penthouse* magazine. What I craved was the softness, the tenderness, the intimacy that only another woman could offer. Just touching, holding, kissing -- what some would call "foreplay" -- was often just as satisfying to me as raw sex, sometimes even more.

Sadie was a sensitive and gentle lover and she told the most captivating stories in bed. I heard about her job grooming horses as a teenager, about what it was like barreling across the scorching California desert in a beat-up Volkswagen, about the time she dated an opera singer, and the day she shot a wild turkey on her grandmother's land and took it home to butcher for dinner. She had a sharp and dry sense of humor and could deliver wisecracks that called to mind the Bette Davis character in *All About Eve*. Sadie told me that when she came out of the closet she "heard the door slam." And she showed me her poetry, published in obscure journals that I had never heard of, as well as the poem she was then working on. I found her writing powerful, incredibly lucid, and very moving. I was in love, and it felt wonderful. And the person I was in love with was, I felt certain, a brilliant, beautiful, and strong woman.

But there was a whole other side to Sadie that was soon to emerge. One Saturday night in late November, after maybe our third or fourth date, and after I hadn't seen her for a while due to pressing schoolwork, I took the train from Tarrytown into the city, then caught the No.1 subway all the way down to Christopher Street. A gay women's dance would be taking place in one of the student halls at NYU and I was to meet Sadie there. I made my way towards Washington Square through throngs of students noisily enjoying their weekend until I located the venue. At first I could see no trace of Sadie anywhere. I waited over half an hour and began to worry that she may have forgotten our date. But I couldn't bring myself to leave just yet. Another half hour elapsed and then I thought I saw her approaching me as I stood sipping a glass of wine.

Could that really be Sadie? She was walking unsteadily and calling out my name in a slurred foolish voice. Her clothes and hair looked unkempt. No doubt about it -- she was plastered. I spotted one of her friends nearby and she came over to me and whispered what a shame it was that Sadie had fallen off the wagon after six straight months of being sober. I soon learned that the big birthday bash Sadie had told me about was actually intended as a celebration of her half-year of sobriety. Her friends had triumphantly planned it, thinking Sadie had turned a corner at last.

And then there was her home, which I saw for the first time that night. She lived in a dilapidated, mostly Hispanic neighborhood on the Lower East Side. Elaborate graffiti covered the walls of buildings; the sidewalks were strewn with dented beer cans, cigarette butts, and piles of dog waste. Fiery Latin music blared from boom boxes and car windows. Peeking into the half-hidden alleys one could see clusters of homeless Puerto Rican men huddled around barbecue grills laden with glowing lumps of charcoal, just trying to warm their hands and bodies in the frigid night air. Sadie's apartment was a narrow dreary affair with a broken-down stove and plaster peeling off the walls. There was a large mattress on the floor and exposed light bulbs hanging from the ceiling which were turned on by pulling a chain. The door to the bathroom was missing and had been replaced by a large American flag hung sideways like a curtain. It turned out that Sadie hadn't sold much poetry lately nor much of anything else and was living on a welfare check.

Sadie was an alcoholic, with a serious addiction. All I wanted to do was help her recover. It would be tragic if all of that passion and intellectual feistiness and talent were to go to waste. But I scarcely knew what I was getting myself into. Because she was seldom in any condition to socialize or go out dancing we usually wound up at her place. We would watch movies on an old black and white TV and order Chinese takeout. We listened to early-sixties Nat King Cole and Johnny Mathis records that Sadie had pulled out of a dumpster, on a portable phonograph a neighbor had given her. One night we watched the 1959 movie *Suddenly*

Last Summer starring Elizabeth Taylor and Katherine Hepburn. It is a strangely disturbing film about a young woman who witnesses the bizarre and brutal murder of her cousin, a closet homosexual, by the boy he was trying to seduce. When her aunt -- the dead man's mother -- finds out that she witnessed the crime she forces her niece to undergo a frontal lobotomy rather than give testimony that would reveal the shocking truth about her son! Sadie told me she had seen the movie half a dozen times and it still sent a chill down her spine.

Her stories started to become morbid and self-pitying. She often asked the guy down the hall, a kindly old black man named Irving, to do her favors like buying her cigarettes or loaning her his kitchen broom. He sometimes came over to keep us company, bringing a guitar he had rescued from a trash heap and lovingly repaired. Sadie had a frayed, torn up sheepskin coat that she loved to wear and refused to throw out. One day Irving took the old garment, sewed on some patches and mended holes, restoring the coat to a respectable condition. How lucky Sadie was to have such a sweet and thoughtful neighbor, but I wondered what she would ever be able to do for him in return.

In the mornings Sadie would send me to the bodega around the corner to buy a bottle of her own version of Thunderbird – *Boone's Farm Apple Wine* -- which she would consume throughout the day. I would be wearing my oversized army surplus trench coat which had very deep pockets. I could fit an entire 750ml bottle into one of them; sometimes I would buy two and walk back from the store empty-handed, but with two swaying bottles of hooch in my coat pockets. I tried to get Sadie to start going to the AA meetings again, but she was feeling guilty and depressed about her relapse and not quite ready to start over.

I probably shouldn't have been surprised when the next time I saw Sadie she was wearing a black eye patch and had bandages on her right hand. One of Sadie's ex-lovers (of which there were many) had warned me that she was more than I could handle all by myself. She told me that the last time Sadie went on a bender she got hit by a car while carelessly crossing the street and cracked four ribs, that she'd gotten into fistfights in bars, both gay and straight, had been banned from *Bonnie & Clyde's*, and that more than once the police had to be called. Sadie, this woman informed me, could easily go into the "DTs" if she tried to stop drinking and could suffer a more agonizing withdrawal than any heroin addict ever went through. When I expressed surprise at her appearance Sadie told me she had tripped going down the stairs and badly bruised her eye and hand. I didn't know whether to believe her or not. She wanted me to accompany her to a local walk-in health clinic where she could get some Darvon for pain relief, all paid for by Medicaid.

In spite of everything, I was determined to see her through it. I felt I was demonstrating my love and loyalty by sticking with her throughout her time of misery and desperation, even as her other friends were abandoning her. I am witnessing firsthand, I told myself, the proverbial plight of tormented genius. I thought of F. Scott Fitzgerald, Dylan Thomas, and the beat poets of the fifties. Sadie became a romantic figure to me, like some anguished character in a Eugene O'Neil play. I took three weeks off from college to spend more time with her, time I could afford to take only because I was doing so well academically.

So I became her constant companion, nurse and confidante. I made her chicken soup and soft-boiled eggs. I bought a book about alcoholism for my own guidance -- it said heavy drinkers often deplete their stores of B vitamins, which had to be replaced to maintain health. So I trekked over to the nearest health food store and stocked up. Irving came over often, strumming his guitar and singing ballads or old blues songs. Occasionally a song would make Sadie get all sentimental and teary-eyed.

But all of my romanticizing and Florence Nightingale role-playing came to a screeching halt one freezing December night. The local bodega had to close for repairs after somebody tossed a brick through its window, so I had not made my usual trip there that morning. Around midnight Sadie suddenly realized she was all out of both beer and *Boone's Farm Apple Wine* and said she'd get very sick if she didn't get something soon. She wanted to go out and look for another bodega or liquor store. I was reluctant because it was so cold outside, but I couldn't let her go out there all by herself. So we bundled up and hit the streets. We couldn't find any store that was still open at that late hour and Sadie began to get agitated.

Then, after walking around for nearly forty minutes with no luck, Sadie spotted something gleaming under the light of a streetlamp. We went closer. It was a giant bottle of *Lavoris Mouthwash*, about a third full. I couldn't believe my eyes when Sadie greedily picked up the bottle and began to guzzle down the bright green liquid. On the way back she did something still more shocking. Saying she had to pee and wasn't able to wait till we got home she squatted down in the middle of the street, unzipped her pants and pulled them down just far enough to allow her to piss all over the street. At least two people saw her.

After that sordid episode I thought I should call a doctor or take her to the hospital emergency room, and then just head back home to the dorm. But I wasn't quite ready to leave her. As it happened, only a day or two later Sadie got a long-distance phone call. Two of her good buddies from her political activist days who lived in upstate New York were driving down to Manhattan to visit friends. I was tempted to grab the phone and tell them Sadie was sick and couldn't see anyone, but I resisted. When Lynne and Butter got to the city and saw the condition Sadie was in, they immediately insisted that she go back home with them and dry out in their house for a few days. There she could find some peace, quiet, fresh air, and no liquor.

They invited me to come along. Although I really should have been getting back to school, I agreed to go upstate with Sadie. Lynne and Butter were a devoted lesbian couple who had purchased an old farmhouse and a piece of land in rural Kingston, New York. They had chickens, a cow, and a barn. Their home was sunny and spacious and filled with an eclectic mix of furnishings and "feminist art." As soon as we arrived they set Sadie up nicely in an upstairs bedroom that they seldom used.

By now it was about ten days before Christmas, and I helped Lynne and Butter put up and decorate their Christmas tree. One of the high points of my stay was getting to drink raw milk -- milk that had just been pumped from the cow and was neither pasteurized nor fortified with artificial vitamins. It was silky, amazingly fresh, creamy -- in fact, it was sublime, if such a word can be used to describe plain old milk.

Sadie began a slow recovery. Her ex had given me medicines -- painkillers and sedatives -- to help her get through the detox ordeal. But now I began to feel anxious about being away from home for so long. Surely my family would expect to see me for Christmas. I had not called home once and, if they had tried calling me at college my parents were probably worried sick wondering where the hell I could be.

So, after three days in the farmhouse, even though she begged me to stay, I left Sadie safely in the hands of her two caring and competent friends. I packed what little I had and left, wishing all a beautiful Christmas. There were no buses or trains available in the immediate area. The only way I could get back to New York was by hitchhiking, so I chanced it. After twenty minutes of holding out my thumb someone pulled over and let me get in his car. He was on his way to NYC as well, so I got a ride all the way home.

Despite all I'd been through with Sadie, I still loved her and wanted to be with her. I was proud of myself -- I didn't just give up and run like any other woman (or man) in my situation would have done. I had proved my love. Since it was only a week before Christmas I decided not to go back to the college campus but to head straight for my parents' home after I was dropped off in the city. As I approached my mom's house I could see the pretty Christmas wreath hanging on the door and it gave me a warm and fuzzy feeling. I began counting how many shopping days I had left to buy and wrap gifts for my parents, siblings, and grandmother. I was happy and felt that the holidays this year, with or without green butter cookies, would be very special.

Then it occurred to me that I must look awful. After weeks of trudging through the Lower East Side, my army coat had dirt stains at the bottom and two buttons missing. I had worn the same two outfits the entire time I was with Sadie, had taken only four real baths, and my hair was practically in dreadlocks. My hair does have a natural spiral-shaped wave to it and even though I had washed it twice I had not pulled a comb through it. So it fell in twisted strands like the head of a mop. And I probably reeked of cigarettes. If I harbored any doubts about whether I really looked all that bad, they vanished the moment my 13-yr-old sister answered the door. Making a face as if she had just been presented with a bucket of horse droppings, she let me in without saying a word. Then she went as far towards the other side of the house as she could get.

After the holidays I knew I had to get back to school and make up some of the work I had missed, including some final exams and a term

paper. Then I had to register for classes for the Spring semester. I called Lynne and Butter to find out how Sadie was doing and learned that she would be staying with them for several weeks of rehab. For a while, schoolwork provided the perfect distraction from the worrisome thoughts running through my mind regarding the dire situation with Sadie. Did our relationship have any future, given her sorry condition? Had those ex-lovers of hers who gently tried to warn me that I might be getting in over my head, been right after all?

But I just didn't want to let go. If anything, the sad and unsavory aspects of her life only endeared her to me more, made her seem heroic and legendary. She was the struggling artist, a soaring free spirit who could not be captured in the jar of conformity. And like so many highly gifted and extraordinary people, she suffered from a tragic flaw -- but not necessarily a fatal one. Not if she had the right person in her life, the one with the patience, foresight, and wisdom to see her through the crisis, the one who truly understood. And that person, I was sure, could only be me. So I vowed to be there for her every step of the way through her recovery, giving active help and encouragement or just quiet support from the sidelines -- however she wanted it.

But after five weeks had gone by without a word from her, not a phone call or even a postcard, I felt hurt and confused. I didn't want to intrude in any way or violate the private space and solitude she needed for healing. But by now her silence seemed strange. I called Lynne in Kingston and asked to speak to Sadie no matter what state she was in. When she got on the phone she sounded weak and tired, but happy to hear from me. She said she was coming back to the city in a few days, and that she planned to begin attending Alcoholics Anonymous meetings on a regular basis. I reminded her that it was a brand new year and things could only get brighter from this point on. "See you back in the city real soon, babe," I said as I hung up the phone.

About a week later we met in Washington Square Park. Sadie was wearing dark glasses and seemed cool and distant. She said very little and at one point pulled a slender neatly rolled joint out of her bag and lit it up -- a safer way to get high, she said. She asked me how I was doing with my studies at school, almost with the tone of an older sister or parent.

Eventually the conversation got around to "us" and where we would go from here. She was blunt and honest.

"I can't be involved with anyone right now" she said, without any drama or apology. "I have to take care of myself first. That's the only relationship I can handle these days."

I hoped she meant only that she needed a bit more time to get it together before we could be a couple again. But the next thing Sadie said made it clear she meant no such thing. She told me she was planning to move back to Springfield, Missouri and stay with her grandmother for at least six months, where the only company besides Grandma would be a few hens and maybe a goat.

"Then" she continued, "who knows where I'll go. I've got some old friends in Kansas City, and Santa Fe too. I think I'm about done with New York. But I have to say" she remarked in a gentler voice, turning to face me directly, "that you were one of the best things I'll remember about it, and I really want to thank you."

Ah-hah. So the free spirit was about to fly the coop! I may have been one of the best things she would remember, but still not good enough to make her want to stay. I was blindsided by her startling announcement, genuinely surprised. Then I felt betrayed. After all my caring and devotion and fierce loyalty, all those bowls of chicken soup and late night runs to the bodega for those bottles of *Boone's Farm Apple Wine*, after all the squalid shit I'd been through with her. How could she cut me loose so easily?

Back at school I could barely concentrate on my classes. I felt like an aggrieved party desperately seeking redress, a victim of a terrible injustice. I couldn't accept being tossed aside like an old pair of shoes while Sadie flew off to brave new horizons. In a moment of delusion I imagined I could change her mind. Sitting alone at the desk in my private dorm room I tried to gather my thoughts and feelings and then began writing her an impassioned love letter. I poured out my heart and soul onto a piece of pale rose-colored stationery. I made sure to throw in some twenty-dollar words and a few literary references in order to exhibit my refined intellect. "I may be only 19 and may never have published a poem," I wanted to express to her, "but I'll have you know, my dear, I am no stranger to the world of arts and letters."

I got carried away, using my best handwriting, wielding an expensive calligraphic fountain pen that I only took out on special occasions. I told her I knew she could slay the evil dragon of alcoholism once and for all if she put her mind to it. And that I would be her faithful servant, cheerleader, and coach throughout the entire trial by fire, if only she would let me. I continued my passionate pleading, attempting poetic flourishes and heartstrings-pulling prose. The letter ran to almost fifteen pages. After reading and rereading it at least ten times I put it in a fancy envelope, sealed it with some sealing wax I had purchased at a novelty store, put it in the mail and went back to my dorm with a sense of satisfaction. I then waited in delicious anticipation. Surely, a letter such as that could not fail to impress.

But ten days later there had been no reply. Two more weeks passed and still no reply. Nor was the letter returned to me marked "Undeliverable," indicating the person had moved away. Spring semester came and went without a peep from Sadie. As summer break approached, I finally faced the truth. Sadie was probably hundreds of miles away by now and living a whole new life on her own terms. I had become just another footnote in her rollicking life storybook. Well, good luck Sadie, I thought, before dissolving into tears. May you find your own peace. As for me, it was back to being all alone again.

9
A Motley Crew

THE FALLOUT FROM the abrupt unexpected end of my relationship with Sadie might as well have been caused by the eruption of Mount Vesuvius -- that's how devastating it was for me. After handing over my heart -- most emphatically in that last desperate letter -- she had sent it back to me covered in smoke and ash. I felt myself slipping into the quicksand of depression once again. But the constant distraction of classes and studies and my determination to maintain my GPA helped to hoist me out of the swamp. As I shifted my focus from a doomed love affair to the musings of Soren Kierkegaard and the dark romanticism of Nathaniel Hawthorne, my mind got engaged and my mood lifted. Besides, I was surrounded by women. Who knew? Maybe I could meet someone at school -- although the odds were not in my favor at a small Catholic women's college. Any fellow student who had gay or bisexual leanings would likely have gone out of her way to suppress or hide them. Over time however, I did manage to gather around myself a small cohort of dear friends, each one unique and special in his or her own way.

In the fall of my sophomore year I signed up for a course in Eastern Philosophy. This was a bit of an indulgence. I knew that nothing I learned in such a class would help to open any lucrative career doors, but it was a subject I had a special fondness for. While many would regard posing questions such as: *What is Time? Why is there Something rather than Nothing?* to be a colossal waste of time, I just had a natural bent for it, along with the belief that the eternal questions, however elusive or cliche, really mattered.

My professor was everything a "Doctor of Philosophy" should be -- absentminded, hair too long and slightly frazzled, dressed in some nondescript bohemian sort of garb, and with a peculiar way of pacing about the room and gesturing with his hands as he underscored a point. I loved him. His name was Lance Norton and his class soon became my favorite. It was not long before he and I were on a first-name basis. His wife also worked on campus as an administrator and the three of us, Lance, Shannon, and I, got to be good friends. The childless couple lived in a ramshackle farmhouse in the country, about a forty-minute drive from campus, which they shared with ten or eleven cats of varying types and colors. Fond of entertaining, the couple often hosted "Chili Parties" for a select group of students. Lance had a special chili recipe of his own invention which called for a pint or so of *Guinness Stout* as a key ingredient. We would all line up with outstretched clay bowls and he would ladle the savory slop out of a twelve-quart stock pot. We'd each grab a chunk of still warm cornbread baked up by Shannon. Then we would all sit on the floor and discuss such imponderables as what the word "meaning" -- as in *"the meaning of life"* -- really *means.*

Then there were Robin and Sophia Tia -- the first, a punk rock devotee from Bridgeport, Connecticut who had cropped her hair and dyed it purple before it became fashionable, the second, a vegetarian pothead with a fetish for '60s-era hippie beads and Janis Joplin. Because they were fringe-dwellers themselves they accepted me without question and were not put off by the accoutrements of weirdness on display whenever I walked into the cafeteria to meet with them -- army trench coat, bandanna around my head, sullen monochromatic speech, nothing but a large soup platter of plain yogurt mixed with butterscotch sauce on my dinner tray every evening. There was Audrey, who liked something I had written in a Creative Writing class and introduced herself to me.

Perhaps my closest friend at the time was Peyton. She came to Marymount in the Spring semester of my freshman year. Aiming towards a Master's Degree in Psychology, she had heard about the excellent Psych program at the college and had enrolled to earn the additional credits she would need to apply to grad school. Although there appeared nothing in the least freakish or off the beaten path about her, she seemed to take a curious interest in me.

One day there was some sort of happening going on in our wing of the dorm. All I remember is everybody congregating in the hallway and a senior classman named Lucy Farley, an art student, walking up to me and telling me she would very much like to do my portrait. I suppose Lucy saw something intriguingly odd in my dress or appearance that she thought would be interesting to try to capture on a canvas. At some point Peyton inserted herself into the conversation and before I knew it, we were all conversing like old friends. I was surprised that she did not eye me strangely or keep a certain distance as if afraid she might catch something -- the way so many of the "mainstreamers" unconsciously did upon encountering a soul who was obviously and defiantly marching to a different drummer.

Peyton seemed genuinely interested in what I had to say, and I could sense that she would be neither shocked nor rattled by any dark secret I might choose to reveal, such as having undergone electroshock therapy two years earlier. I don't remember if Lucy ever did draw a portrait of me, but I do recall Peyton and I speaking at length that first day. I soon began to feel very comfortable in her presence and welcomed her company and conversation. I could detect in her a keen intellect that was not straitjacketed by convention, as well as a spirit secretly drawn to the subterranean realms and unafraid to discover what might be lurking there.

After a while I felt emotionally safe enough with Peyton to share the intimate details of my love life, all of which revolved around my recent ill-fated affair with Sadie. But I held back a bit, not exactly sure how she would react to the gay issue. The women's movement was then in full swing, particularly on college campuses all over the country. Many if not most female students were swept up in liberation fever and fully committed to the goals of the movement. But there were also a certain number of straight women who bought into the notion, which had lately gained great currency, that *"most of those women's libbers are a bunch of man-hating lezbos."* It could be a touchy subject, so I thought I'd just keep a low profile for the time being. But then things took a very interesting turn, and it was no longer a question of how long I should wait to "come out" to Peyton, but how soon.

Peyton had a friend whom I will call Julia. At first, I assumed the two of them had been friends for a long time, as they seemed to have an easy familiarity and a sisterly kind of affection between them. Plus, they were almost always together. Then Peyton informed me that, in fact, she had just met Julia and there had been a kind of uncanny instant attraction. I had first noticed Julia while walking by the dorm room I used to share with my former roommate, Candy. That was before a certain mini disaster involving me and a bottle of tequila sent poor Candy running for cover. I happened to glance into the open room and was surprised to see a very attractive willowy blonde who appeared to be a few years older than most of us. Someone said she was studying to be a psychiatric nurse and, like Peyton, would be there only long enough to complete certain required courses.

Julia had a sultry voice, a soft swaying gait, and an air of mystery that seemed deliberately cultivated. She also had at times a coy, teasing manner that suggested she knew how attractive she was and would use it to her advantage whenever it suited her. But she was no floozy; this woman had class and intelligence, with a touch of street savvy. I remember thinking that this was the kind of woman who could drive a man crazy if he let himself succumb to her seductive wiles. As it turned out, men were not her only victims.

A red flag went up in my mind as I observed the kind of rapt attention and perfumed flattery Julia would sometimes lavish on Peyton. As I got to know both of them better there was no escaping the idea that Julia simply enjoyed *flirting*. For her it was one of the social graces, a lubricant to be liberally applied to ease the friction, smooth the edges, of interpersonal relations. It was also a political tool she skillfully deployed to get others to do her bidding -- and love doing it. I didn't see any real malice in it; I think she did it more to amuse herself than anything else. She practiced her finely honed techniques on me as well, and I can't say I didn't enjoy playing along.

Julia was nothing if not desirable. But as long as you took a whiff of her clever potion without letting it go to your head, it was all pretty harmless. But alas, my poor friend Peyton was not only inhaling deeply but appeared to have swallowed some of the poison beverage! As far as I could tell Peyton was perfectly straight and into men. Although she didn't seem to have a steady boyfriend, I had met several of her handsome dates. But when I saw her strumming her guitar and singing a plaintive tune she told me she had written for Julia, when I heard her wax lyrical about Julia's maddening charms, when it seemed she could barely carry on a conversation without mentioning Julia's name several times, I realized something else was going on.

This seemed the perfect time to broach the subject that could no longer be ignored. "*I do believe you're falling in love with her, am I right?*" I said to Peyton, or something like that, one night when we were in my private dorm room. That turned out to be the beginning of a voyage of self-discovery for Peyton in which she came face to face with feelings, desires, and aspects of her sexuality she didn't know she had. When I confided to her about my own like feelings and assured her that they were neither uncommon nor unnatural, it helped to forge a deeper bond between us and bring our friendship to a new level of intimacy. Some of my fondest memories from my time at Marymount College were of times spent staying up until the wee hours stretched out on the bed amidst clouds of cigarette smoke, engrossed in deep conversation with Peyton -- sometimes in my dorm room, sometimes in her bedroom at the funky Victorian-style wood frame house where she rented an off campus apartment.

One of the cruelest tricks fate ever played on me happened just before the summer rolled around. It was as if some evil space alien had swooped down in his flying saucer and abducted all of my friends, leaving me alone on a desolate nuclear-scorched earth. Unbelievable as it sounds, by the end of my sophomore year *every single one* of my buddies had split the scene. Robin was dropping out of college to spend more time with her boyfriend who was trying to start a punk rock band. Sophia Tia had enrolled in the foreign student exchange program and was looking forward to an exciting year in Italy. Professor Lance Norton, despite having been warned several times, had yet refused to alter his unorthodox teaching methods (including inviting students over for "Chili Parties") and was summarily dismissed. His wife Shannon, also a good friend, of course left with him. My friend Audrey, who had seemed deeply troubled, had spent a few nights with me during which she "confessed" that she thought she was bisexual and was very confused about it. One day after she had stayed overnight at my place, I woke up to find her gone. But I discovered a hypodermic needle and a tiny glassine bag discarded in the bathroom and knew that Audrey needed to be in a rehab, not in school.

And Peyton, my closest friend? She had moved to Pennsylvania to pursue her Masters degree in psychology at Duquesne University in Pittsburgh.

And so, just like that, I was flying solo again.

10

How I Spent My Summer Vacation

I DON'T KNOW what I was thinking. I had pictured a lovely summer in the mountains, breathing pure air, taking serene walks in the woods, skipping stones across the lake. I had just completed my sophomore year of college and was hoping to find an interesting summer job. Preferably one far from home. I was still reeling over the disappearance of all my college friends and the breakup with Sadie the year before. I desperately needed some sort of major diversion. And so I was thrilled to have happened upon the perfect solution. Could I really have been that naive?

When I spotted the newspaper ad carelessly pinned to a bulletin board in the student mail room, it caught my attention immediately. It had been placed by an agency that specialized in recruiting help for hotels in the Catskill Mountains. That region in upper New York State, often referred to as *The Borscht Belt,* had long been a world-renowned Jewish resort destination. The area drew thousands of vacationers every summer and went into a kind of hiring frenzy as the big season approached. According to the ad there were hundreds of good jobs waiting to be filled by college students as reservation clerks, waiters, waitresses, receptionists, kitchen help, and so forth. Free room and board would be provided. Wow, I thought. So I called for an appointment and registered with the agency. Within less than a couple of weeks they told me exactly where and when I was to report for work.

Almost from my first day on the job at a shoddy looking retreat called *The Vegetarian Hotel*, I knew I had made a big mistake. But it was too late. My folks had just driven a hundred miles to drop me off here and they were not planning to pick me up again till summer's end. I took all my luggage and belongings out of the trunk of Dad's car, gave both of them a hug as they wished me good luck, and watched wistfully as they turned the car around and drove off. I took a deep breath and walked towards the front lobby of the hotel.

The first clue as to what I had gotten myself into came when I was shown where I would be lodging. A short balding man with a huge ring of keys hanging from his belt emerged from behind the front desk and led me up a flight of rickety stairs to a dusty, airless "room" in an unfinished attic. The cramped space, illuminated by a shaft of light that poured in from one tiny window, was cluttered with junk: discarded lamp shades, broken fans, parts of a vacuum cleaner, and in one corner, a stack of *Sears* Catalogs from the late 1940s. I was to sleep on a lumpy cot shoved against one wall, put my things in a wobbly chest of drawers most of whose knobs were missing, and bathe downstairs in an old-fashioned deep kitchen sink -- the kind of sink you would have found in a turn-of-the-century tenement building on Orchard Street or Delancey Street on New York's Lower East Side. A rack of metal hooks nailed to the wall would serve as my clothes closet. I quickly learned that the waitress and lobby desk jobs were reserved for those with experience and references. For me, the only job available was that of chambermaid. In other words, I'd be scrubbing toilets. But before starting on that, Virgil, the man with the keys and the hotel manager ("Virge" for short) wanted me and another chambermaid to do a special project.

Our first job assignment was to renovate and freshen up a dumpy seven-room cottage that the hotel kept on the premises to house musicians. Every summer the same band came to perform at the resort and the band members stayed in the cottage; for the rest of the year it stood vacant. Virge escorted us to the place, which was located in the woods a few hundred yards behind the main hotel building. We took a first look inside the abandoned guesthouse. What a sight! The rooms were encrusted with cobwebs, the cheap linoleum floor marked with dirt tracks. Insect carcasses, empty food containers, cigar butts, and other assorted trash were strewn all about. The refrigerator was blemished with streaks and sticky handprints on the outside, dark green patches of mold on the inside, and the oven looked as if it had never once been cleaned. A couple of the windows were cracked and would have to be replaced; others were clouded with bird droppings and grime. There were dead mice and a broken whiskey bottle in the bathtub. The toilet was filthy and crawling with ants.

Fixing up this place would require backbreaking labor. I was appalled and angered. How dare they expect us -- for the pitiful salary they were paying -- to take on a job like this! I just looked at Dottie, the other chambermaid who had come on board two days before me, and we both shook our heads in disbelief and disgust. The unpleasant task took us several days and I was a few pounds lighter after it was over. I actually looked forward now to cleaning guest rooms.

But that occupation soon became odious as well. Virtually all of the guests staying at *The Vegetarian Hotel* were senior citizens, many quite elderly and not in the best of health. I began to feel more like a nursing home attendant than a hotel maid. My duties included having to change urine-soaked sheets, wipe up traces of vomit or blood in the sink, carefully avoid vacuuming up dropped pills, and tossing aside pieces of yellow-stained underwear in order to make the beds. In spite of all that I gave every guest room the best cleaning I possibly could. A few good tips could go a long way towards making up for my paltry wages. I had to remind myself why I had come all the way up to the mountains -- mainly to get my mind off Sadie. Instead, I found myself thinking about her more than ever. Her dingy East Village flat with a curtain for a bathroom door and a long chain suspended from the ceiling that you had to pull to turn the light on seemed like a room at the Waldorf compared to this place.

As the summer progressed I became increasingly frustrated with life at *The Vegetarian Hotel*. One problem was the food they gave us -- totally different from what the guests were given. In the dining room fancy fruits and salads were served, along with garden-fresh vegetables, since the allegedly much healthier fare was the key selling point of the hotel. But not for the peons who did all the dirty work. Our meals consisted of rice, beans, and watered-down *Wheatena* -- no meat allowed, not even for us carnivores, not even cheap hot dogs. We were allowed only twenty minutes to eat and then had to rush back to work. If we showed up even five minutes late for the start of a shift we were severely scolded. I wondered why none of the other workers ever complained. One day I got into a screaming match with Virge and wound up getting fired. I immediately went back to the agency and asked to be assigned to another, better hotel.

The next place I landed at was larger and more modern, had a nicer clientele, and I got to lodge in one of the smaller guest rooms. I decided this time to seek out allies among my fellow oppressed workers. If I had a couple of friends, perhaps together we would have more leverage when dealing with management. I quickly hooked up with another chambermaid whose name was Louise. She was big and fat and well into her forties, but she had as much stamina as any of the younger staff. She also had a car, which was convenient for driving into town to pick up items we couldn't get at the hotel, not to mention taking long joyrides on our off-hours just to alleviate the boredom and drudgery.

Then I noticed Al. One day I happened to spy this cool-looking black dude with dark glasses calmly peeling onions in the hotel kitchen in a sort of Zen-like trance. I had to walk through the kitchen every morning on my way to the maid's supply shed and there he would be, sitting on a wooden stool letting tissue-thin strips of brown onion skin drift into a bucket. He must have noticed me too because once when I was passing by he stopped me, handed me a sheet of paper, and told me it was a poem he had written about me. It turned out the guy was a self-proclaimed poet and philosopher. I was amazed when, in casual conversation at the dinner table, he began quoting famous philosophers like Hegel and Schopenhauer. Philosophy, of course, had been one of my favorite subjects during my freshman year of college. It was more than amusing to think that here, of all places, I would run across someone who seemed to enjoy it as much as I did. He asked me if I would like to go out with him the next time we both had the same day off and I accepted. We found a local bar and hung out all day talking.

I had waited for months, given her all the time she needed; still Sadie had never answered, nor even acknowledged receiving, the fifteen-page pleading letter I had spent hours composing. I had heard not a word from her. Rumor had it she was back in her childhood home, and apparently had no qualms about burning all bridges behind her. Now, here I was with a man who had already honored me with a poem. It was gratifying to picture Sadie looking on in shock and jealousy as Al came on to me. "It's *her* loss," I said to myself with satisfaction. I would rather be with someone who wants *me*, I thought as I handed Al the keys to my hotel room.

Our first night together was a dizzy tilt-a-whirl ride much enhanced by the thrill of secret trysts and some good weed. It was the first time I'd had sex with a man in over two years. Suddenly I started paying more attention to my appearance and wished I had brought nicer clothes with me from home. Al and I began spending our days off together, taking cab rides into town. He had some buddies in the hood, knew where the best nightclubs were, where to get liquor and drugs, where to get deep-fried catfish and grits. Soon he was sneaking into my room almost every night and some of the hotel staff began to take notice. That included Louise, who seemed a bit scornful and disapproving, perhaps resenting the fact that I was getting something she wasn't. At last, she ratted us out to Flo and Sam, the couple who managed the resort, and we were both fired on the spot.

We wound up at the *Tamarac Lodge,* a much fancier, more upscale hotel than either of the previous two. In fact, the place had a sort of wild party/Spring Break feel to it that did little to discourage my own delinquent behavior. One weekend the hotel played host to a popular "Swingers" club – a hot new trend involving partner swapping and group sex that had emerged in the early seventies. Oh-My-God!! Down by the indoor pool all of us hotel workers had ringside seats and boy, did we get an eyeful. Naked bodies of all shapes and sizes could be seen frolicking in the water. Young couples were screwing right out on the pool deck. Partners were exchanged as if it were a square dance and people took turns performing sex acts on one another. We could hardly believe our eyes. To me it was both shocking and hysterical, as I realized how absurd and undignified people look while having sex. No wonder most of us have such a hard time imagining our parents doing it.

It was so easy to just fall into the spirit of the day and give myself over to heedlessness and hedonism. It lightened the workload, relieved the monotony, and made me feel less alone. And the ever present availability of good quality weed tended to put everything on a higher frequency. I seemed to be acting out a kind of rebellion against a cruel fate. The fate that had decreed I would be spending a beautiful summer in the mountains not strolling arm in arm with a sober, smiling, rehabilitated Sadie, but instead changing stinky sheets and cleaning toilet bowls. After Al (who got caught with a small bag of cocaine and was fired) there was

Wayne, then Franco, then Gary, and even a cute Jewish seminary student I met while out walking as he was coming home from yeshiva. We did it right there in the woods.

But all the while I could feel something in myself unraveling. Oddly, the more profligate and wild my behavior became the more depressed and full of rage I got. I glared at my image in the mirror with profound disgust. Why was I debasing myself in this way? What did I think I was doing or trying to prove? Was it all because Sadie dumped me? Because my twisted, neurotic needs demanded such an outrageous outlet? Because I was just a hopeless fuck-up? I couldn't tell, and that made me even angrier.

After a while I began to take some of this anger out on the hotel guests. One morning I spotted something slender and shiny wrapped around a tree limb. It was a garter snake with a pretty yellow stripe down its back. Knowing they were harmless (from my days in south Florida) I picked it up and let it slither in my hands. Then I casually strode into the main dining room of the *Tamarac Lodge*, serpent dangling from my hands, and made a point of parading slowly past the diners hunched over their breakfasts in a little game of "show and tell," just to creep them out.

Although I was still doing a stellar job of cleaning rooms, making sinks and mirrors gleam and sparkle, I was becoming less tolerant of especially demanding guests. Like those bugging me for supplies -- soap, shampoo, towels -- even though I'd just restocked their rooms the day before. There was this one haughty well-heeled dame, probably in her late fifties, who was particularly annoying. She insisted on things the hotel did not provide -- like shower caps and hair spray and hypoallergenic soap -- and always seemed to have some complaint about the way I did her room. She also had a nasty little dog. It was one of those yapping terrier-type lap dogs, high-strung and nervous with an incessant, screeching bark. She called it "Mister."

One early afternoon she confronted me in the courtyard to bitch about something or other, Mister at her side. The dog was adorned with a rhinestone collar and tiny blue ribbons somehow fastened about its ears. As she voiced her complaint the dog began to bark hysterically at me. She pretended not to notice. Mister was barking so shrilly I could barely hear what the lady was trying to say. But strangely she did nothing, not even so much as say to the creature, *"Now there, calm down Mister, calm down sweetie."* What the hell was she -- fucking deaf?

At last the screeching canine, all worked up at the end of his long leash, leaped forward suddenly and bit me hard on the ankle, drawing blood. Ouch!!! Amazingly, not only did this snobby bitch do nothing to restrain him but she actually laughed, quipping something like "*Oh yeah, he's a feisty little biter, that one.*" Oh really? Apparently, the sight of her spoiled mutt taking a bite out of some lowly maidservant wearing a white uniform and toting a mop around was occasion for amusement. Needless to say, I was furious. And bent on revenge.

After my ankle stopped bleeding and I was able to slap a bandage on it I went out to finish cleaning the rooms. It was a scorching hot day and most of the guests were already at the outdoor pool. Later that evening there was to be some top-drawer entertainment in the main lobby. Pets were not allowed near the pool or in the hotel ballroom, so Mister would spend the rest of the day locked up in a room. A room to which I had the key. "I'll fix your goddamned little mutt," I thought. As soon as Mister's mistress was well out of sight and most of the guest rooms were empty, I unlocked the door to her room.

The dog began barking at once. But there was no one around to hear him. I immediately chased the animal around the room until I backed him into a corner. I'd brought a broom handle and, raising it triumphantly, I struck him several times about the face and head. I wouldn't have thought it possible, but Mister's high-pitched shrieking had actually risen an octave as he sat cowering pathetically in the corner. The deafening shrieks were making me crazy. I tossed aside the broom handle and began kicking him in the face as hard as I could, not caring if I knocked his eyes out. I may, in fact, have dislodged a tooth or two. Soon the shrieks turned into whimpers and cries of pain as Mister, bruised and battered and in fear for his very life, began to shrink into a quivering ball in a gesture of defeat and surrender.

I let up, stepped back, and he instantly scrambled to get under the bed, limping slightly on one paw. I let him stay there, feeling he had been punished enough. I left the room, walked back across the courtyard, and opened the door to my own room. The minute I closed it I collapsed on the bed in a flood of tears and convulsive sobs. My God, I might have actually killed that stupid animal! How could I be capable of such spontaneous violence? What was happening to me? I had come to the mountains to get my mind off a broken love affair and find a bit of peace. How had it all turned into such a gruesome nightmare?

Eventually, my nightly visits to my latest boyfriend's room were discovered and, for the third time that summer, I got fired. Then I began missing my periods. Of course, in my deranged state of mind I had used absolutely no protection. I went to a women's clinic for a test and my worst fear was confirmed. At the tender age of 19 and with two years of college left to complete, I was pregnant! I could not even be sure who the father was. The baby might come out white, black or Latino. And I could not imagine a more unfit mother than I would have been at that time. And so because every child deserves to be loved and wanted from day one, and not to be shuttled from foster home to foster home, I decided the lesser of the evils would be to have an abortion. I wanted to do it as soon as possible, while the developing embryo was still smaller than a grape.

So I returned to New York and had the procedure done immediately. I never told my parents or anyone else. It cost $300 -- just about what I had earned the entire summer, minus the money that Louise had stolen from me (which I did not realize till after I left). By summer's end I was an emotional wreck with a dirty little secret to conceal and not a dime left in my pocket. I no longer knew who or what I was. Sadie didn't matter anymore. Sex didn't matter anymore. Love didn't matter anymore. Gay or straight didn't matter anymore. Then just what *did* matter? I had no idea but knew I would be spending much of the next school year trying to figure it all out.

11
A Scarlet Letter

THE LEAVES WERE turning to rust and my summer vacation from hell was safely in the rear-view mirror, but I was still not quite myself. My mind felt bruised, all black and blue, and I tried desperately to reassess my situation. I finally decided I should focus solely on my education and shut out everything else. I needed to stop thinking about Sadie, stop worrying about how to meet someone new, stop making expensive trips to the city to hang out in divey smoke-filled bars where no one noticed me anyway. For a brief period after the breakup, I had gone into the city regularly to visit some of the old haunts and reconnect with Sadie's friends and exe's, mainly to pick up news about her. I heard she had moved back to her hometown of Springfield, Missouri, where her only company was her poetry books and a few farm animals. I was finally resigned to losing her, and beginning to accept that for the foreseeable future at least, I'd be going it alone. Indeed, with my typically moody and morose expressions I probably pushed people away without meaning to. So I resolved to replace bars and clubs with the campus library.

But it wasn't long before I felt abandoned and alone and knew that academic striving would never be enough to fill the void in my life. Some sort of change was in order. I began applying to other colleges, thinking I ought to transfer to a much larger school, preferably in an urban setting. I set my sights on a few well-regarded universities within the five boroughs of New York City. There, among a far more cosmopolitan, sophisticated, and diverse group of people I felt sure I would have better luck making social connections. And there would certainly be a lot more gay people within reach.

I got accepted by Fordham University, which had a large coed campus right in the heart of the Bronx, just across from the famous Bronx Zoo and the New York Botanical Gardens. A whole new environment -- just the medicine I needed, I thought. So, with Fall classes soon to begin

I packed my bags and moved out of sleepy Tarrytown to head for a school within a ten-minute walk of the hospital where I was born. I left Marymount without regret and without looking back, convinced I was taking a bold step forward. But in fact, it was a rash, ill-thought-out decision and I paid for it dearly.

As a transfer student I did not have much choice in living quarters and was told I would be housed with other juniors in an off campus residential tower owned by the university. The high-rise contained a number of three-bedroom living units that accommodated six people. They assigned me to a suite where six students had roomed together since freshman year, but one of the girls had left school, making a bed available. I instantly felt at a disadvantage to be moving in with a group of girls all of whom had known one another for two years. I was the stranger, the new kid on the block -- not a role I embraced with enthusiasm, given my history.

My new suite mates were a curious bunch. There was big, bright-eyed Gail from Chicago and her roommate, a chatty type named Lindsay from Scranton, Pa. Both gals were majoring in "Communications" and had come to New York with fond hopes of one day landing a job with a TV network or radio station. There was pretty blue-eyed Maude from South Carolina with her teased beehive hairdo and fetching Southern accent. Her roommate, in sharp contrast, was a small nerdy looking brunette who wore thick horn-rimmed glasses. Her name was Ellen and she had come all the way from Tacoma, Washington. Maude was majoring in fine arts and I don't recall what Ellen was studying. My own roommate was a staid, serious, somber looking gal named Alice. She planned to be either a CPA or a pharmacist and took a lot of math and science courses.

The apartment suite itself was pleasing in a *Holiday Inn* sort of way, with framed prints on the wall, beige carpet and drapes, minimalist furniture. Plenty of sunlight streamed through large windows, filtered by attractive vertical blinds. There was a cozy living room and dining area and even a fully equipped modern kitchen. Gail and Maude both felt fully at home and took turns cooking most weeknights, with everyone pitching in a few dollars to buy groceries. But there was also the college cafeteria and a slew of fast-food joints just a block or two from campus. I had to admit it was a pretty nice setup. If only I could feel that I belonged there.

A few days after I got settled in, my mom called to ask how everything was going. I told her the truth. The apartment was lovely. My new roommates -- all five of them -- were just as nice as they could be. What I didn't tell her was how much I detested the entire situation. I just didn't see how I could function in such an environment, or easily relate to this odd collection of characters from all over the country. I could not imagine myself, say, sitting down to dinner with all of them and taking part in their inane conversations, which always revolved around trivia and pop culture. I mean, in Maude and Ellen's room there was actually a big poster of "John-Boy" from the TV series, *The Waltons* pasted on the wall! Whereas, I would have preferred discussing weighty current topics like the war in Vietnam, the Watergate scandal, nuclear disarmament, and whether religion had become obsolete, all they wanted to talk about was college football, their boyfriends, horror flicks like *The Texas Chainsaw Massacre*, and which franchise made the best hero sandwich, *Subway* or *Blimpie's*.

Lindsay was super social and was always inviting people over. Gail, who loved to eat, was forever unloading groceries with one hand while grabbing the phone in the other to gab with her friends back in Chicago. There were occasional little disagreements about telephone bills. Maude always seemed to be redecorating the suite and Ellen, who had a state-of-the-art hi-fi system in their bedroom, had something spinning on the turntable almost every waking moment. Her tastes ran to The Captain & Tennille and Olivia Newton-John, whereas I would rather have listened to Barry White. And the kitchen always smelled like *Kraft* macaroni and cheese.

I had no real privacy, whether to study, to simply relax, or to write in my journal. Alice was quite the homebody and loved to sit at her desk reading when not in classes, while I would have so much preferred having the room to myself to just chill or tackle heavy homework assignments. I began to pine for the private room and those handpicked buddies I'd been lucky enough to have at Marymount College, which in hindsight began to seem like an idyllic Eden compared to where I was now. I spent increasing amounts of time in the Fordham library and the student lounge just to get away from my suite mates.

It wasn't that I never made any attempt to be sociable, to sit on the couch in the living room and chat about various campus goings-on or a home game or the courses we were taking. A couple of times I went into town on shopping sprees with Maude or out for burgers with Gail and Lindsay. Alice was having some boyfriend problems and I tried to listen sympathetically, even to offer some sage advice. But basically it was hopeless. I had nothing in common with these people and considered it sheer punishment to have to be in their company for any extended length of time. Inside my head I could hear my mother's disdainful voice: *"I'm not surprised at all - I always said you were an antisocial snob."* Okay, maybe she was right after all. But I just had nothing to share with these girls, nothing, I felt, which they would want or could appreciate.

As fall turned to winter my moods became blacker, my facial expressions more sullen, and I barely spoke to anyone. Several weeks earlier I had read about how the Pulitzer Prize-winning poet Anne Sexton had locked herself in her garage, turned on her car's engine, and snuffed out her earthly existence. Anne suffered from manic-depression for most of her life and spent years in therapy and mental hospitals. Much of her poetry dealt graphically with her own struggles against her illness, and images of death, sickness, and loss are constantly recurring themes. Friend and fellow poet/writer Erica Jong wrote a moving memorial tribute to Sexton in *The New York Times.* But something she said there really made me do a double take:

"but it seems to me that Ann Sexton killed herself because it is just too painful to live in this world without numbness, and she had no numbness at all. All the little denials, all the stratagems of not-feeling by which most of us endure from minute to minute were unavailable to her..."

That quote struck me as topsy-turvy and disturbing for it implies that *"numbness"* and *"stratagems of not-feeling"* were normal desirable traits that most of us would not be able to live without. Yet precisely the opposite was true for me. To be healthy and whole is to be fully open to one's feelings be they painful or joyful. To anesthetize oneself in order to avoid pain is a form of playing possum -- acting dead so as to avoid being killed. "Playing dead" as a habitual response to life's threats ultimately becomes no different from actually being dead.

The times that I have felt the most despondent, the most suicidal, were not so much times of searing pain or inordinate grief as they were of utter emptiness. Of a sense of *not being there*, of having been erased, of not being part of life but somehow abstracted out of it. A sense that where there should have been a living breathing feeling human there was only a shadow, a ghostly presence cold and cutoff from life. I became depressed and suicidal precisely because I felt *dead already*. In other words, being *unable to feel* was far more "painful" than pain itself.

At that time I was still under the delusion that all that stood between me and happiness was a new circumstance -- a new friend, lover, school, place to live, etc. If only I had that, *then* everything would be different, *then* my life could begin. So I told myself that if I could just meet some other gay people on campus, I might find relief from my constant submersion in a straight conventional world that I couldn't fully relate to. I tried to find out if there was some kind of gay student union on campus, as there were in many large urban universities. But of course there was no such thing to be found at the Jesuit-run Fordham U. My journal entries became increasingly bleak and despairing, with a focus on death:

October 4, 1974

Nothing is new under the sun. It's still the same dull tragicomedy. You're born. And you die. Whatever happens in between doesn't matter. You see, everything is equivalent. The great leveler, Death, makes all things equal. The Queen of England, the street trollop -- all the same in the end. Food for maggots. Why even bother?

I am sure the only thing that kept me from being preoccupied with thoughts of suicide was my academic work. My courses were very challenging and I had tons of reading to do, especially in my history and literature courses. One professor even began his Medieval History class by announcing: *"I just want to inform everyone so that no one will be disappointed -- I have been teaching this course for 14 years and I have never given an 'A' for a final grade."* So I tried to submerge myself in my books and avoided spending any more time in the suite than I had to.

By now there was no doubt that my suite mates viewed me as some sort of weirdo. I shuffled about quietly, except for the constant blowing of my nose in response to sinus congestion that I'm sure was psychosomatic in origin -- a nervous habit. I was rarely seen in the common rooms and other than taking out my own garbage, did not participate in any household chores such as grocery shopping or vacuuming the living room. Since I never ate or entertained in the suite, I thought that was fair enough. But one day Maude baked up a batch of delicious smelling brownies and I had to debate with myself whether or not I had the right to sample one, so estranged from the group had I become by then. I was sinking into a morbid and ugly state of mind and there was nothing I could do to reverse the process. I knew something would have to give soon, and it did. It all began with a letter.

My second cousin Sydney was what you might call the "black sheep" in my mother's family. About ten years younger than my mom, she always seemed more like an aunt than a cousin. The first and only one of the family to leave home *not because* she was getting married, Sydney lived alone in a walk-up building on one of Greenwich Village's most charming blocks. She worked at a law firm by day but in her spare time she was a writer, painter, and antique collector and a total nonconformist. She and I had formed a kind of bond when I was about seventeen because she could identify with me and immediately perceived that: *"Your mother just doesn't understand you."* We had engaged in some long and serious talks, and we began to correspond regularly when I went away to college for the first time. We both had a passion for long, detailed, overly verbose letters and I was in the habit of keeping all of hers.

The summer just past had been particularly traumatic for me. The whole Catskill Mountains nightmare lingered well into the fall, and I needed to unburden myself of the toxic memories. I could think of no better way to do that than to pour the whole torturous tale onto paper in the form of a letter to Sydney. Her response came in late September after I was well settled in at Fordham with my new suite mates. I valued her kind insightful words and kept her letter in my bottom drawer by the bed so I could take it out and reread it every now and then. One rare day when I had the room all to myself, I had taken it out to read once more. Then, suddenly remembering I had a late afternoon class, I rushed out, leaving the letter, still open, on my desk. After the class ended, I went out to get something to eat and sat in the student lounge for an hour before returning to the suite. Everyone was home except Alice.

As soon as I spotted the letter lying open on the desk a shudder went through me. *Oh shit! Had any of them seen or read it?* Sydney's letter to me, long and thoughtful, made specific reference to some pretty personal stuff, like the calamitous affair with Sadie (a name that could not be mistaken for a man's), my stint in a psych hospital, the abortion, and that violent incident involving the little terrier, "Mister." It must have been about forty minutes later when Alice came back, entered the room, and shot me a strange glance. Then, when everyone finally went to bed, she went into Maude and Ellen's room. I felt sure she must have read the letter, which I'd put out of sight. I decided not to confront her or make any mention of the letter.

The next day I did not see her in between classes, but at night she was at her desk studying as usual. We exchanged pleasantries but nothing of substance was said. And that night, she again grabbed her blankets and went into Maude and Ellen's room to sleep. I felt quite uncomfortable but could not get up the nerve to say anything. "My God," I thought. "Obviously she read Sydney's letter and now she thinks I'm some kind of psycho dyke who might attack her at night!"

I knew Alice must have told the other girls because they all began looking at me strangely. Then one night all five of them gathered their sleeping gear and marched out of the suite. By now I felt ashamed, confused, and incensed. When they tried to pull the same stunt the following night I had had it and demanded to know what was going on. Alice finally spoke up. She said she knew she shouldn't have, but the letter was right there on my desk, open, and she couldn't resist the temptation to read it. And having read it, she decided she no longer wanted me as a roommate and felt she ought to "warn" the others. Then Gail spoke up and said they were all going to the student housing director the next morning to ask that I be removed from the suite.

Maude elaborated further:

"It's obvious you don't want to be here. You never have dinner with us, barely speak to us, and you won't even pick up the phone when it's ringing. If you do have some sort of...whatever...emotional or psychological problem then maybe you should try to get help."

The others all chimed in. "You never even sit out in the living room -- it's like you're trying to avoid us," offered Ellen. Lindsay added, "You don't help with any chores. We're all living here and everyone should share in the housekeeping." And then a little bombshell from Gail: "And don't think it's about you being gay or bisexual or whatever you are. That's your business. It's just that you act so weird and unsocial and you're so quiet, you can't blame us for being a little suspicious." And, finally, from Alice, "And I think anyone who would hurt a little dog...that's not the kind of person you… I mean… that tells me there's something really wrong. . ."

As I stood there dumbfounded listening to all of this it was like a trip back in time. I was ten years old all over again and there was my mother standing in front of me loudly detailing my every fault. I knew there was no point in trying to defend myself. Because everything they said was true. I felt like saying, "Okay, yes, I plead guilty. So sentence me." My pride was telling me not to give in without a fight but that was just a knee-jerk reaction from my reptile brain, sounding the alarm that I was under attack and should fight or flee. But it seemed pointless to attempt either.

I hated Alice for reading the letter and broadcasting the most painful intimate details of my life as if I were some curious specimen in a glass jar being passed around for examination in a zoology class. But I had only myself to blame, and it was just as well. The next morning there was a group meeting with my five suite mates, the housing director, a campus psychologist, and a student counselor. It was agreed that, as I did appear to have certain "issues," I would begin regular sessions with Dr. Broderick, the university's clinical psychologist. The girls would remain in the suite and I would be placed in a private room in a much older dormitory on the main campus.

Despite the offer of the private room, I was so shaken by the entire episode, my self-respect so shattered, and the sense of mortification so keen that I vowed to move back home rather than anywhere on that campus. My grandmother lived in the downstairs apartment in the two-family house my parents rented. I could sleep on the couch there and set up a bridge table for a desk. I wouldn't even have to go upstairs and encounter my mother if I chose not to. I could prepare my own meals in Granny's little kitchen. So I moved off the Fordham campus and spent the next year and a half as a commuter student, taking the train to school and leaving the grounds the minute my last class of the day was over.

For about the next six months after that incident, I did have weekly visits with Dr. Broderick, the closest thing to a shrink on the campus. Most of those sessions became opportunities for me to vent outrage at how bad the world was treating me and to lash out at my mother. Dr. Broderick considered it his job to build up my "self-esteem" and act as lifeguard when it looked like I might be drowning in self-pity. Outside of school I was a virtual recluse, spending hours holed up in Gran's apartment poring over books and papers. I had no social life, no friends except Granny. But at least it paid off academically. I just missed a 4.0 GPA by a hair (differential calculus did me in) and graduated Fordham College *summa cum laude*. Even my mother was impressed.

And--oh yeah--that history professor who had solemnly announced at the beginning of his first class that he hadn't given an "A" for over a decade? Well, from now on he was going to have to find a new opening line.

12
West Side Story

I'M SITTING AT my desk at work staring at the blue and white paper cup I have just drained. There's the familiar image of three golden steaming coffee cups flanked on either side by an ancient Greek urn, and floating right above, the words, printed in a blocky Greek style font: "*We Are Happy to Serve You.*" The identical cup can be seen on a number of other desks in the office. Indeed, it had become so much an emblem of New York City back in the pre-Starbucks age that the producers of *Law and Order*, filmed on location, ordered them by the hundreds to have available on the set at all times. So here I was, one more indistinguishable city office worker, and this, apparently, was my answer to the age-old question: *So what do you want to be when you grow up?* How exactly had all of this happened, I asked myself as I crumpled the cup in my hand and tossed it into the trash bin.

Today I have to wrap up my review of those shopping center leases and write out a report for the lawyers. Equitable Life Assurance, my employer and one of the nation's largest insurance companies, was in the lucrative business of funding huge construction projects and shopping center developments. It was a way to put to work the hundreds of millions of dollars in insurance premiums they collected each year. But it had its risks. If a real estate developer was ever to default on one of our loans we could wind up being the owners of some strip shopping mall in Cincinnati or Cedar Rapids or Corpus Christi, and therefore the landlord of every *Victoria's Secret*, *Foot Locker*, and *Gap* store on the premises. It was my job, as the only paralegal in the Real Estate department, to go over each and every store lease with a fine-tooth comb just in case there was anything there that we wouldn't like if we ever had to take over the property.

And I had better get it all done before Anne Fikkert, the gal who sits in front of me, comes back from her extended lunch hour. She always comes back slightly soused and spends the rest of the afternoon on the phone, talking loudly and foolishly to her sister in Florida. She doesn't care since she has given the company 45 years of service and will be retiring next year. I actually like Anne a lot. She can be quite funny and she tells some pretty good stories. I especially like the one about the time she met Fidel Castro in person when he came to speak at the United Nations and how handsome she thought he was. Anne herself, tall, slender, and shapely, with finely chiseled features and lovely blue eyes must have been something of a knockout when she was in her twenties. I will really miss her after she leaves.

I keep thinking about what Professor Engel said to me at the graduation party. All seven of us who had managed to survive the grueling Paralegal Studies Program at Long Island University in Brooklyn gathered together at a student's home for a final self-congratulatory bash. At one point the good Professor took me aside and said, in a quiet voice, *"If you want my advice, don't get a paralegal job, just go to law school. You've got the ability and the brains. Why waste your life doing some lawyer's grunge work for one-quarter of the pay?"* I had graduated at the top of the small class and Professor Engel had been quite impressed with my work. But law school would have meant not only putting off getting a job, but also remaining at home -- with my parents -- for another three years. This seemed intolerable to me at the time.

I had never wanted to be a paralegal. As an English major I'd always planned on a job with a major book publisher, newspaper, or ad agency -- New York was brimming over with them. So, with my Fordham degree in hand so to speak, I began canvasing Madison and Fifth Avenues and other sites of the publishing and advertising industries, showing up at as many as a dozen companies in a single day. But to my great chagrin, I could never pass the entry-level typing test that ALL of them, without exception, required! A rookie employee was always expected to start in an assistant "gal Friday" type of position; however, one could move up very quickly if they demonstrated the talent and willingness to work. But no one had told me this when I was struggling with my typing class in high school and barely getting up to a respectable 35 words per minute.

So it was out of desperation more than anything else that I enrolled in a six-month paralegal training course, after reading an article which claimed that this was a hot new career field. The program was kind of like an army boot camp without the dirt or the grunting, requiring hours of hard labor in law libraries doing research and writing legal briefs. After earning my certificate all I wanted to do was get a job, make some real money, and move out of my parents' house ASAP. I knew I probably could do well in law school and that I might be shortchanging myself by settling for a career as a mere legal assistant. But how could I put my whole life on hold for three more years? It might have been different if my mother and I got along, if I could confide in her, if she were comfortable with my nonconformist lifestyle and unorthodox sexuality. But she would not and could not understand or empathize. Residing under the same roof with her was like getting stranded in enemy territory -- it was only a matter of time before I'd be captured or killed.

Now, gazing absently at the foot-high stack of retail leases on my desk, I realize with dismay that four years have elapsed since I received that well-intentioned advice from my professor. After tossing the coffee cup, I tear open the unused cellophane packet with the two sugars and drop them into my bottom file drawer. I had long ago stopped stirring sugar into my coffee because it aggravated my hypoglycemia. But I couldn't seem to throw the perfectly good sugar packets away.

Over the years I had noticed that mild "obsessive-compulsive" tendencies were creeping into my behaviors. Like fleas on the family dog, they seemed to have been carried in on the back of my depression. These little quirks ranged from the bizarre to the merely disruptive, but I found myself unable to stop doing them. For example, I could not turn a light switch on or off without having to tap the switch plate immediately afterward. Nor could I put on a pair of shoes without turning them upside down and shaking them vigorously (so any specks of gravel or sand would fall out). And now I found myself unable to discard the sugars -- even though I had absolutely no use for them -- and had taken to storing them in my desk. There were probably hundreds in there by now. Where will I put them when the drawer fills up? I don't have a clue.

At least there is one thing to celebrate. When the clock strikes five, I won't be running for the subway or commuter rail train like the rest of my coworkers. I get to walk home. Ever since I'd been old enough to ride the New York City subways, I would unfailingly get this rhapsodic feeling every time I ascended the stairs to exit the station at 72nd Street and Broadway. One of the first things to catch my eye was the tall white statue of Giuseppe Verdi, renowned composer of *La Traviata* and other famous operas, standing in the small park in the square named after him. Then, looking up toward the expansive sweep of Broadway, which curves gracefully at that point as it continues to veer west in open defiance of Manhattan's street grid, my eyes would feast upon the soaring, majestic facade of the *Ansonia Hotel*.

The antiquated looking edifice always reminded me of a luscious cream-colored wedding cake with all of its fussy rounded towers, scrolls, cornices, parapets, lacy ironwork, and the gargoyle-like figures leering over the doorways. The ornate decoration was typical of the Beaux-Arts style, a school of architecture popular in the late 1890s when construction of the *Ansonia* began. To me the building reeked of sophistication, European decadence and Old World charm. Walking up Broadway, with the *Ansonia's* towering eighteen stories shadowing my every step, its imposing mansard roofs and corner turrets in my peripheral vision, I felt like I was inside an elegant sepia-toned picture postcard of yesteryear.

This was the Upper West Side, my favorite part of the city. While others preferred the crooked streets and bohemian atmosphere of Greenwich Village, long known for its colorful collection of starving artists, political radicals, and unapologetic drag queens, I favored the more civilized environs of New York north of 59th Street and west of Central Park. The neighborhood, just above the theater district and near Lincoln Center, took its peculiar tone from its large population of musicians, actors, dancers, aspiring opera singers and other devotees of the performing arts. It also contained some of the city's loveliest architecture with whole blocks full of handsome brownstones, quaint row houses and well-preserved prewar apartment buildings. There were some arresting churches and synagogues as well.

From the day I began my humdrum nine-to-five life I had been planning my breakaway from my parents. Within weeks of earning my first paycheck I set about earnestly looking for a place in the city. On my modest salary I knew I could afford only the most humble of dwellings, perhaps a studio on a third-rate block, but I was determined. Weekends were spent walking through various parts of Manhattan, checking out neighborhoods, making notes, taking down names and numbers of management companies and real estate agents, seeking out the supers or janitors of desirable looking buildings to ask if there were any vacancies, or would be soon. I consulted the massive *Apts to Rent* section of the *Village Voice* classifieds.

But after months of fruitless searching during which I was shown the most unbelievably shabby hovels, including one walk-up with the radiator situated not against the wall but smack in the middle of the living room, and another place that didn't have a kitchen, I was getting discouraged. Then one day I came across an ad shouting:

Large Beautiful Newly Renovated Apartments
Rehabilitation Project.

The address of the building gave one pause. It was located in the low 100s just off Central Park, a section notorious for crime and drug dealing. Out of curiosity alone, I decided to at least go have a look.

The landlord's rep explained that his boss had an ambitious plan to "turn the neighborhood around" by buying up and demolishing old decaying houses or gutting the interiors and putting in hardwood floors and brand new appliances. These improvements would attract a higher class of people to the neighborhood and eventually chase the lowlifes away. I stepped into one newly finished apartment and was startled at how spacious and bright it looked, with a shiny new stove, modern refrigerator, gleaming counters. The walls were freshly painted and there were several closets. A decent-sized bathroom with clean new fixtures. Then I asked what the rent would be. I was shocked when he recited a figure that was less than half the rent of some of the dreary dumps I had been looking at for weeks. Not sure I had heard it right, I asked him to repeat it. He did.

I left feeling confused and anxious. The street directly in front of the apartment building was pleasant enough, but up the block towards Manhattan Avenue I could clearly see dope dealers and users gathered on stoops, and other unsavory characters lurking about. Several of the other houses were burnt-out or had windows boarded up. There was trash everywhere and a look of desolation and abandonment. But -- the apartment I had just seen was so nice! At the rent I had just been quoted it would be a steal. And what if this landlord meant business and truly intended to buy up and renovate real estate until the block was totally "gentrified." I could be one of the first pioneers to move into a block that one day would be highly desirable and pricey to boot.

Plus I was in my early twenties and my declaration of independence from Mom and Dad was long overdue. After anguishing over it for two days I decided, oh what the hell, called back the phone number on the apartment ad and asked if the place I had seen was still available. It was, so I put down a deposit equal to the first month's rent. I then boldly announced to my parents that I had found an apartment and would soon be moving out.

Fast forward to a Sunday night about a week later. I'm sitting in the back seat of the car, my dad at the wheel with Mom beside him, driving down Central Park West, both of them eager to see their daughter's new digs in the city. As we turn onto 103rd Street and slow down to look for the house I watch their expectant faces turn into masks of shock and disbelief and instantly know I've made a mistake. Mom blurts out, "*YOU gotta be kidding*!" while my dad turns around incredulous, as though he wanted to see if this was meant to be some kind of a prank. I even detected a hurt look on his face, as if he had been deeply insulted.

In truth, my father was horrified that I would even consider living in such a place. "*But"* I insisted, *"It's going to get better! They're cleaning it up."* My mom was shaking her head as if she couldn't believe they had driven twenty-five miles from Westchester and missed an episode of *Dallas* to see something like this. And I had to admit, the place did look a lot spookier at night. Then we heard two men down the street arguing loudly, shouting obscenities. A drug deal gone bad? After we got home Dad said he would be worried to death if I moved into that apartment and begged me not to, even offering to reimburse me for the deposit I had paid and would not get back.

When I called the building manager the next day to explain why I couldn't take the apartment, he was sympathetic. He told me his firm managed several residential buildings on the Upper West Side and he would put my name at the top of the list should any vacancies come up. Sure enough, one day about six weeks later I received a call at my office.

A studio apartment had become available in a four-story brownstone on a lovely tree-lined stretch of West 77th Street, between West End Avenue and Riverside Drive. The rent was reasonable and he would give me credit for the first month's rent because of the deposit I'd had to forfeit. It sounded too good to be true. I took the apartment sight unseen.

So -- now I could actually walk to work. I loved living in what I considered the most European, most cultured, and yet -- in its own special way -- the funkiest part of Manhattan. It was a delight to shop at the *Fairway* market with its sawdust-covered floors, gorgeous produce artfully stacked in wedge-shaped heaps and a cheese section that could rival anything in Paris. I liked gazing at the ceiling in *Zabar's,* the legendary Jewish deli -- from which hung copperware, baskets, ladles, and other kitchen utensils -- while waiting for my number to be called at the takeout counter. Walking home from *Zabar's* down Broadway I could often hear the warbling of some aspiring soprano six stories up, probably preparing for an audition at the Metropolitan Opera, just a few blocks away.

Yet, perverse and contrary as it seems, there were times when all of this richness and character and "local color" only made me more depressed. A part of me always wanted to look on the dark side, to find the tarnished tin lining of every seemingly fortuitous situation. I knew with every fiber of my being that all things led ultimately to the graveyard, that God, or Fate, played a cruel joke on all of us by rigging the game to ensure that whatever we loved we would lose. Whether that was just my temperament or the symptom of an emotional illness I had no way of knowing.

Even worse, whatever the splendors of my new neighborhood, I had no one to share them with. Strolling down Central Park West on a balmy night, the sight of shimmering moonlight filtering through the trees brought a tinge of sadness and a reminder of how alone in the world I was. To be in the presence of beauty that I could neither possess nor share engendered only a feeling of loss and mourning. All I could do was sigh and slowly walk back to my studio, to seek solace in a book or put on a favorite record. Okay, I would think, so now I had a decent job and I had my own place, right in the heart of the city. So why wasn't I happy?

13
The Beat Goes On

BY THE TIME I moved into my modest studio on West 77th Street off Riverside Drive I was resigned to being a loner. Peyton had long since married and moved to Charlotte, North Carolina where her husband had an important job with IBM. Maxine, an unconventional character from work who had latched onto me probably sensing a kindred spirit, was my only good friend who was close by. I dated neither men nor women and wondered if I would ever have a love life again. But I wasn't sure if I cared. There were other distractions to tempt and charm and inspire one's imagination.

It was the beginning of the post-disco era. The crowd-pleasing *Saturday Night Fever* craze had turned into a parody of itself and serious dance music had moved underground. Hot new clubs were springing up all over Manhattan. And the best of them, as everyone knew, were gay. The gay clubs had the best music, the fiercest sound systems, and the most dance-crazy patrons. Most had opened for business without bothering to incur the expense and delay of applying for a liquor license. So at the "bar," the only drinks served were soda and fruit juice. But nobody minded. The gay dudes came to party all night long, not to get stinking drunk and make fools of themselves like at the straight clubs, where most of those actually on the floor dancing were the women. Besides, there were other ways to get high.

A music fanatic from birth (or even from the womb -- Mom was an avid record collector and would-be songwriter who, in between household chores, could often be found picking out tunes on the piano that was a constant fixture in our living room), I could not help but be captivated by the infectious jungle rhythms of the new dance music. It was hypnotic -- once you surrendered to the beat you were put into a trance, made even sweeter by the syrupy prerecorded string sections from the New York Philharmonic that were dubbed onto the original tracks to heighten the sense of enchantment. And dancing in a packed dimly lit space to earsplitting music was something one could do all alone without feeling the least bit self-conscious.

So, with almost a dozen dance clubs less than a ten-minute subway ride away, I became a frequent club-hopper. The names of these trendy haunts were designed to evoke images of a child's garden of delights or otherworldliness or even heavenly transport -- *The Saint, Le Jardin, Moonshadows, The Limelight ,The Fun House, Infinity, Sanctuary, The Ice Palace.* But some were downright raunchy. There was one place that would not win any prizes for subtlety. The gay club, *Crisco Disco,* was located, appropriately enough, in the meatpacking district. Upon entering the dark passageway into the club, you were confronted by a huge replica of an open can of Crisco Shortening, at the time a cheap and popular alternative to K-Y Jelly. It was all just one big fantasy trip. I could show up on a Friday or Saturday night at one of these pleasure havens, unknown and unseen, and get lost in the strobe lights and industrial strength sounds. Of course, getting down with a bunch of half-naked sweating men checking out each other's biceps wasn't going to do a thing for my sex life, but half the time I was too stoned to care.

By that time I had become a devoted weedophile. Pot, grass, 'ganja' -- call it what you will, marijuana had thoroughly replaced tequila and other "spirits" as my consciousness-altering drug of choice. At the time, Bryant Park, the expansive stretch of green directly behind the New York Public Library on Fifth Avenue, was a known soft drug bazaar, catering to the office worker set. I would drop by on lunch hours and pick up a nickel or dime bag of pretty decent quality weed. Not only did the cannabis seem to poke big holes in the heavy black shroud that was my depression, much as alcohol had done, it also triggered fascinating streams of thought which would pour out at blazing speed in kaleidoscopic patterns that recreated themselves from moment to moment. As if new possibilities were endlessly being spawned, with not the slightest pause to let a note of despair sneak in.

While stoned I felt I could glimpse great truths in rapid-fire bursts of insight, solve centuries-old quandaries, undergo a do-it-yourself psychoanalysis in the space of two minutes more accurate and revealing than Freud himself could have provided. And while other people marveled at how great junk food tastes when you're high, or how every conversation dissolves into hysterical laughter, for me it was the music, the way it felt and sounded. As the high reached its peak I would literally crawl into the space between the beats, time would be suspended and I would live there, at the center of gravity, while the melody swirled about me and the incessant rhythm, as urgent as war drums, held me spellbound. Voila! I was one with the universe! Nothing else mattered. And, so bewitched, I could dance for hours on end with the blind fervor of Gregorian monks chanting sacred verse.

But eventually this began to wear thin, and I came to feel that I was becoming too isolated, too self-absorbed, too cutoff from humanity. I was meeting no one, and even though I spent nearly every weekend "partying" I essentially had a nonexistent social life. I would have liked to meet some gay women, who rarely showed up at the gay men's clubs. But by that time I was virtually done with the dyke bar scene. Most of those places were dark cramped holes in the wall where, if you could find a few feet of available floor space you could dance to second-rate music in a dense fog of tobacco smoke. The nicest bars were always closing down on short notice. Not surprising, since most were owned and operated by low-ranking mobsters and other shady characters who often used them as fronts for dope dealing or money laundering. So what was one to do? Usually I decided the best thing to do was go home, turn up the stereo, roll a joint, and ruminate on it for a while.

Sometimes, in order not to feel so alone and unsocial, I would ask Maxine to accompany me on some of my clubbing expeditions. Maxine was a rare bird who had a penchant for all things weird, offbeat, and off-the-wall. She would be the first to try, say, roast giraffe, or volunteer to get up on the stage at a magic show, and was always first in line for the latest thrill ride at the amusement park. She thought nothing of taking a six-hour bus trip to visit an ostrich farm or a haunted mansion, would travel hundreds of miles for the privilege of stepping into a bat cave or riding in a hot air balloon, and would eagerly sign up for a guided tour of the *Hormel* factory to see how they actually made SPAM.

Maxine was a sensation seeker and experience collector, assembling a living scrapbook of indoor and outdoor adventures. She recognized me immediately as a fellow maverick and offered both friendship and nonjudgmental understanding. She was basically straight, although perhaps a bit "bi-curious" to use today's vernacular. Although I wasn't attracted to her in that way, I was more than happy to expose her to a healthy Dionysian slice of life and give her some racy material to paste into her scrapbook.

So one day I took her to what was probably the hottest club in the city after *Studio 54* -- a club where, unlike 54, you didn't have to queue up behind the red velvet rope and hope the promoters thought you were gorgeous enough or looked cool enough to let in. It was the black gay mecca way down in the West Village called the *Paradise Garage*, where nobody cared what you were wearing. Literally set up in a converted truck depot, the place boasted the loudest sound system and most turned-on dance crowd in the northeast, if not the nation. It was a private membership club and if you were not a member, you had to know one to get in.

Greg, who worked in the xerox copy room in the law department, was a very outgoing, good-looking black guy who had a "secret life." He held a membership at the Garage and one day he invited me to come on down, and bring Maxine too. I told her to brace herself for a once-in-a-lifetime experience -- even for her. It began as soon as one stepped into the nondescript building on King Street. You would walk up this huge long ramp and then step out into a dreamscape of swirling light and color. There were several tiers; a lower level resembled a high tech penny arcade with flashing videos playing and game machines. There was a punch bowl room where you could chill out with a nonalcoholic drink or grab a banana.

Upstairs on the main dance floor was where all the madness happened. Hundreds of ecstatic, writhing, glistening black bodies dipping and swaying to a deafening "Da-DUM Da-DUM Da-DUM" that went right through your spinal cord and seemed to make the whole dance floor gyrate and convulse. A writer for the *Village Voice* once likened the Paradise Garage to "*Africa before the white man came*." Even Maxine was a little intimidated, but after a while we got loose and joined the fun. There were a handful of women and whites there who were friends of members or simply knew where the action was. The crowd whooped and hollered whenever legendary house DJ Larry Levan spun a favorite track, which was often, and many of the feverish dancing patrons would not have dreamed of leaving before sunrise.

I returned to the Garage a couple of times with Greg, and once with my artsy cousin Sydney, who, though straight as an arrow, loved both dancing and the gay culture and had managed to get herself a membership. But after a while the place became too popular and too crowded, and I began to fear that excessive exposure to 120-decibel noise would leave my eardrums permanently damaged. At length I decided it was time to dial down the solo partying and pot smoking and seek a quieter, more sober way to spend my weekends. But my solitary strolls down Columbus Avenue on warm summer nights, the soft glow of the streetlamps wrapping everything in a romantic haze while happy couples walked hand in hand or sipped wine at the lively sidewalk cafés, only made me feel lonesome and very single. Maybe, I thought, it was time to make a concerted effort to get some kind of a "social life" going. The problem was, I knew no more about how to do that than I knew how to skin a rhinoceros.

14
From Church Basement to Sugar Hill

ANNE FIKKERT JUST returned from lunch. I can hear her joking with somebody out in the hall. She is pleasantly, charmingly inebriated, not enough to be falling down or talking funny, just enough to be cheerful and feeling no pain. As soon as she gets back to her desk I know she'll dial the phone and call her sister in Vero Beach, Florida. Sometimes I get a good dose of comic relief listening to her, which certainly helps to alleviate the tedium here. And today, a Wednesday, is particularly boring. An outside law firm that Equitable retains for major real estate deals was supposed to ship over a packet of about 85 retail leases. Part of a deal for a new shopping mall in Dayton, Ohio that we were financing. My work would be cut out for me the rest of the week and the next. But the shipment never arrived, and as it happens, I have little else to do.

So I fall into a reverie trying to imagine what will happen tonight. Because today after work I am headed for church. Not for any religious services, mind you. I had read about some organization called GWA in a local gay newsweekly. The acronym stood for *Gay Women's Alternative.* The idea was to have a special place for women who were tired of going to bars, cheap dives, and dance clubs as the only way to meet each other. The group held its weekly get-togethers in the basement of the Universalist Church on 76th St and Central Park West, about five blocks from my apartment. I had decided I ought to check it out. So, walking around my desk I start organizing files and cleaning out my in-box until the clock strikes five. Then I take a deep breath, grab my briefcase, and walk out to the elevator bank.

I walked up Avenue of the Americas till I got to 59th Street, then turned left towards Columbus Circle and headed up Central Park West. As I approached 76th Street the church building came into view. It was striking-- an impressive sand-colored structure with severe arched doorways, a huge stained-glass window and adjoining tower built in the

Gothic Revival style. It stood in stark contrast to the Neo-Renaissance flavor that was so much in evidence along Central Park West. But it was still early; the GWA meeting would not begin until 6:30 pm. So I walked towards Broadway to my favorite Cuban-Chinese eatery, *La Caridad.* The place was celebrated for its "cafe con leche," a kind of poor man's cappuccino. They made it strong and it always hit the spot. I found a small table, ordered a cup and lingered awhile, mulling things over as I blew across the surface of the piping hot brew to cool it down. Then I left, a bit revved up from the caffeine, and walked back to the church.

I entered the Universalist Church through its heavy wooden doors and found my way down to the basement, a cavernous space with dozens of folding chairs set out, arranged in neat rows. There were maybe thirty women sitting or standing around. I noticed a table laid out with a coffee machine and paper cups, bottles of soda, bowls of chips and other refreshments. I immediately saw that most of the women were well over thirty-five, although a smattering were in their twenties. I picked up the program announcing tonight's event. A well-known feminist author was to appear, reading aloud from her published work, after which there would be a question-and-answer session.

I took a seat, watched, and waited. The featured guest was apparently late, so I thought I'd wander over to the refreshment table, even though I didn't want anything. There was a woman, about thirty-seven or so, heavyset with dark curly hair, pouring herself a diet coke. She smiled at me and asked if it was my first time here. I said yes, and she said it was her third time and she found it really interesting. Her name was Blanche.

The guest finally arrived and read selections from her book, the audience enthusiastic and attentive. Afterwards, Blanche and I talked. She was a French teacher, divorced, with two teenage boys. She told me she had never realized her lesbian leanings until just two years ago and had recently "come out." Really, I said, surprised. I couldn't understand how someone could go for so long not knowing they were gay. She then told me she'd become romantically involved with one of her students and wasn't sure how far to carry it. Other women gathered around, and I chitchatted a bit with a few of them. Everyone was warm, friendly, appreciative. I left the basement of the church feeling I had discovered a hidden sanctuary away from the all-too-familiar bar scene of hard liquor, reeking cigarette smoke and deafening music.

The next time I attended there was a huge crowd, close to a hundred people. The guest was a lesbian sex-therapist whose presentation was to include slides and graphic illustrations. On a small screen at the front of the room I could see a vivid drawing of a woman who appeared to be masturbating, above a caption which read: *The G-Spot -- Is it real, and how do we find it?* I heard some embarrassed titters among the assembled women, as well as some naughty, knowing laughter. I looked around for Blanche. Surprisingly, there was no sign of her tonight.

During "intermission" I scanned the crowd, trying to find someone I wouldn't feel too shy to go up to and start a conversation with. I found myself strangely unable to do this. Many of the women there were already "coupled." Sometimes I'd see someone standing alone looking nervous like me, but rather than take a chance and approach them in a friendly manner I'd find myself wondering what was wrong with them. Something must be, or they wouldn't be standing there like that, looking lost.

There it was again. Recoiling from what was the equivalent of a store window reflection of myself suddenly glimpsed while walking down the street, I only wanted to hide. I was slipping back into that dark place in my mind where I could only look out at the world, baffled and scared, cowering behind that peep hole from which I could see everything that was going on, but no one could see me. That way I was safe, but also a prisoner, trapped in my own silent dungeon. Maybe it was "social anxiety," a term then being bandied about by dime store psychologists and self-help gurus. Or maybe it was simply because I could not face the reality that, at 28, this was what my social life had been reduced to: looking for love and friendship among a bunch of giggling middle-aged lesbians craning their necks for a better view of some dirty pictures.

Over the next two months, the basement of the Universalist Church became like a home away from home. I attended the GWA meetings regularly, enjoyed the presentations, sometimes even stood up to ask questions or make comments. I stuffed my face with corn chips and wheat crackers, washed them down with cherry soda, and made pleasant small talk with some unusual and fascinating women. Sometimes a group of us went out for dinner or drinks afterward and continued conversations inspired by something a guest had said or presented. There was a feeling of what I would call "solidarity" and it was comforting. But in truth, I was no closer to finding a true friend or lover than I was when I first walked through those massive arches.

One time, while listening to a community activist give a talk, I noticed an attractive slender black woman casually stroll into the room and place a small stack of flyers on a table near the entrance, before disappearing in a flash. On the way out I picked one up and read it. It announced a "*Let's Get Acquainted*" party for women, to be given next Saturday night at an apartment on Park Avenue. All were welcome -- just show the flyer at the door. Signed, "Jackie." Whatever misgivings I might have had about walking into some stranger's party gave way to sheer curiosity. I decided right then and there that I would go, and carefully folded the flyer and slipped it into my coat pocket as I left the meeting.

The following Saturday night I arrived at a swanky Park Avenue high-rise that had a uniformed doorman. I had to sign in at a reception desk while a security guard telephoned upstairs. I told him I was a friend of "Jackie's" and had been invited to a party. As the guard let me in I headed for the elevator, suddenly struck by a fear that I might run into another GWA member also going to the party. That would make me feel a bit, well...embarrassed. But why? I asked myself with confusion. Was I wearing a sign proclaiming: "PATHETIC, SOCIALLY INEPT & LOVE-STARVED -- WISH ME LUCK AT THIS PARTY"? Maybe not, but somehow I felt as if I were. Luckily, no one else was in the hallway as I approached the apartment door and knocked three times. In a few seconds the door swung open and a half naked woman -- the same one who had left the flyers -- answered wearing absolutely nothing above the waist but a few striking pieces of Maasai warrior jewelry. I stared in wonder at these huge brightly colored elaborately beaded collar necklaces with dangling leather strands capped with cowrie shells. Talk about daring!

Inside was a large comfortable apartment with ultramodern furnishings. Several women were sitting on a sofa holding paper plates, munching on celery sticks with hummus dip and other hors d'oeuvres. There were open wine bottles and a stack of blue plastic cups next to them on the kitchen table. Another group of women were gathered around a coffee table, apparently gawking at some rather arresting merchandise. As I got closer I could see a colorful array of sex toys – vibrators, dildos of every size, shape and color, scented lubricants, butt plugs. Ah-ha, I thought, this Jackie is a sharp article, a budding entrepreneur hosting her own kind of Tupperware party. Clever, indeed.

I wandered about, poured myself a cup of white wine, and watched as new arrivals entered the door and exclaimed their shock at Jackie's strange attire. Soon a rather diverse, racially mixed group crowded the apartment, a weird assortment of characters that seemed to fit no particular stereotype. I was intrigued and curious. My God, who were these people!

Someone shouted to turn the music up and several women began to dance. Jackie came by and said that if I didn't feel like dancing there were "movies" in the next room and she pointed the way. I entered a semi-dark bedroom where a large-screen TV was showing porn flicks. A few enthusiastic viewers were sitting on the floor, sipping wine and laughing. Shyly, I made my way over and sat on the floor a few feet away from the others. I poured myself more wine, hoping it would loosen me up, and focused on the TV screen. A luscious blonde was about to go down on a hot-looking brunette, and I heard someone shout: *"Shit -- that ain't no way to do it! If my girl ever did me like that ..."*

I noticed two empty bottles of chardonnay in the corner and then saw Jackie marching in smiling, carrying two fresh ones. As I tried to decide whether or not I was getting turned on by the porn, I felt a hand on my shoulder. A lovely woman who looked like a model said in a distinct Russian accent, "Hi, I'm Oxana, what's your name?" I told her and asked if she knew Jackie. Refilling her blue cup to the brim with wine she remarked casually that she owned the apartment and was Jackie's "sponsor" in the sex toy business. This, she said smilingly, was the third party they had hosted here.

After a few more sips of chardonnay and a few more minutes of graphic porn, Oxana put an arm around me and said, "Can I kiss you?" Flushed with wine, I mumbled, "Sure" and the next thing I knew her tongue was in my mouth and her hand under my bra. I glanced around quickly and noticed there was only one other person in the room, sitting on the bed grinning. Uh-oh, I thought, is this gal planning to start a little orgy right here in this room? Despite having slept with Sadie, I was hopelessly inexperienced sexually when it came to women, being quite unfamiliar with some of the "techniques" I had seen demonstrated in that sex-therapist's slide show at GWA.

I could picture myself fumbling around awkwardly to everyone else's amusement. Besides, this was not exactly my idea of romance. Maybe I was even a bit of a prude, who knows, I thought. But I felt uncomfortable and began to squirm away slowly from Oxana's embrace. "I don't know -- I'm really shy," I protested feebly, thinking what a fool I must be to turn down such a delectable creature, one who could have had men lined up around the block. At length she just smiled and said in her adorable accent, "That's okay -- I didn't mean to make you nervous or freak you out," and I took the first opportunity to slink out of the room.

Back out in the living room several women were purchasing vibrators and Jackie was passing around a notebook, asking everyone to write down their name, address, and phone number to be placed on her mailing list. This way, she said, we'd never miss an invitation to one of these hot parties. I signed the book and passed it to the woman next to me, someone whom I had not noticed before. She seemed to be in her early fifties, tall, well-figured, with long flowing red hair of exactly the shade I loved best. For some inexplicable reason I had always had a thing for women with dark red hair -- not the carrot red that usually went with freckles but a deep copper-toned hue that evoked New England autumns and Irish Setters.

Suddenly the woman looked up at me and said, "Oh -- you live just two stops from me on the number one train. I'm on the west side too, near Ninth Avenue." I was glad for the convenient conversation starter because I was trying to decide how much longer I should stay, having already downed four cups of wine and noticing that no one else was leaving. As we began talking, I detected a very peculiar sort of accent, not one immediately recognizable like Oxana's. I asked her where she was from originally and she explained that she'd been born and raised in northern Virginia, but had moved with her family to Boston at the age of 13. There she studied music, seriously took up the cello, and eventually joined the Boston Symphony Orchestra as fifth chair. Then, after she married, she and her husband moved back to Virginia to raise a family. Indeed, there was the oddest blend of genteel Southern drawl and Boston Brahmin in her speech.

Her name was Lorraine and she had recently moved to New York to embark on her new "fresh-out-of-the-closet" life. She had finally divorced her husband of 22 years and relished the prospect of playing the field in an exciting city like New York. She seemed surprisingly ebullient, brimming over with self-confidence, looking forward to a brash new adventure. There must, I thought, be a condition that was the opposite of depression, a perpetually euphoric state that stubbornly resisted pessimism and gloominess no matter the situation and some folks were lucky enough to have been born with it. After chatting a bit, Lorraine said she had to leave to go meet some friend, but would like to exchange phone numbers; maybe we could get together some night after work. Sounds good to me, I thought. Lorraine seemed like someone worth getting to know.

After a while a few others left and the party started to wind down. A black girl named LeShan, one of the women I'd seen watching the porno flick, and a couple of her friends invited me to go out with them to some bar in the Village. LeShan was one of those people who had the uncanny ability to throw together an outfit out of seemingly incongruous elements and make it look smashing. She had on painter's overalls, a red satin blouse, motorcycle boots and a Dutch Boy cap. "The night is still young," she intoned with a sparkle in her eye. I thought, why not, and tagged along. We went to a place near the #1 subway station on Grove Street called *The Duchess.* The joint was rocking. No room at the bar, and the tiny dance floor was packed. I danced a bit, mainly to test my coordination to see how drunk I was.

All the wine had actually made me more tired than drunk, and I felt like crashing on a couch or a cushion, but there were none. Someone finally got off a bar stool; I grabbed the spot and ordered a ginger ale.

After a few minutes I noticed a woman two seats down staring at me. She was honey-colored and very exotic-looking, like some foxy Creole gal you might have found hanging around a nineteenth century New Orleans brothel -- a few drops of African with a touch of Native American and a good dash of French, with soft green eyes. When the person sitting between us left the bar, she sidled over and sat next to me.

She offered to buy me a drink, which I politely declined. LeShan and her friends were nowhere to be seen and it was getting pretty late. The dance floor was starting to clear out. She asked me to dance, saying she'd been dying to dance all night, but the floor had been way too crowded. "It's actually a lot better on a Monday night," she said, indicating she was a regular. She was also a great dancer, and I seemed to have gotten a second wind. We danced until closing time, when the DJ put on a sweet slow jam to end the night. While dancing close I began to feel her lips caressing my neck and ear. Suddenly she stopped dancing, pulled my face towards hers and began kissing me like there was no tomorrow. It seemed pointless to resist, so I made out with her until the song was over. She whispered, "Come home with me," as we were both walking out the door. After what had just happened at Jackie's party, I felt like I'd be a sap to blow it again.

She was not quite the beauty that Oxana was, but she was alluring and sexy in her own right. Besides, it was too late to go home alone anyway, or so I told myself. As we got out on the street, the woman told me she lived in a restored row house on St. Nicholas Avenue in Harlem, in the famous section of the neighborhood known as Sugar Hill. That was the place where legendary African American artists such as Cab Calloway, Langston Hughes, and Duke Ellington had once lived.

We hopped into a cab and sped uptown. The building was handsomer and in better condition than the brownstone I lived in. We walked up two flights of stairs to her apartment. The first thing I noticed was that the walls were painted hot pink and there was a gigantic cushy looking pink couch right in the middle of the living room, in sharp contrast to the drab hardwood floor. She headed into the kitchen and offered to pour me a drink. Although I didn't really want one I said thanks and she took out two glasses, filling them with vodka and what looked like cranberry juice. Then she came out with the drinks and plopped down on the couch. She reached for my hand and pulled me down beside her. As I took a sip of my drink, she stared at me for a second.

"Yeah, I see it now, you look exactly like one of my exe's -- she came from Lebanon," she said. "I thought you reminded me of her but I couldn't be sure in that dark bar."

I didn't know quite what to say and nervously began thinking up things I could ask her about, assuming we were going to have one of those perfunctory cocktail party conversations in which people exchange trivial personal information that no one will remember afterwards. But before I could even frame a question, she began unbuttoning her blouse and unzipping her jeans. Meekly I began doing the same, thinking, "Right here? Right now? Why -- we haven't even stepped into the bedroom yet!"

Suddenly she began breathing heavily as she tossed her bra aside and slid off her pants, keeping on her briefs. Before I was even half undressed she pinned me down against the full length of the couch and began thrusting her pelvis against my hip and upper thigh, making rhythmic rocking movements as if imitating a man, which got faster and harder by the second. At length I realized that this was how she was going to get off. Sure enough, there soon came a deep moan and then a quick little gasp as she arched her back, and then it was all over. She just looked at me with a smile that seemed to say, "Thanks -- I really needed that," and began slowly putting her clothes back on.

I just lay there in disbelief and confusion. She vanished for a few minutes, then came back with a pair of sheets saying I could sleep on the sofa until morning and then let myself out. With that, she disappeared into her own bedroom and shut the door. Since "morning" was less than an hour away, I set the sheets aside and got fully dressed. Then I wandered over to the window half in a daze. I waited there until the first light of dawn, then quietly left.

Upon getting back to my own apartment I flung myself down on the bed and just slept away the entire Sunday. I woke up with a terrible headache, wondering if last night had really happened or if I'd only dreamt it. How absurd it all was!! Jackie's crazy party. The sex toys, Oxana. And that wild woman from the bar -- I had never even gotten her name! And besides, wasn't the *Slam, bam, thank you ma'am* approach exactly what feminists always excoriated men for? In my search for someone to replace Sadie it looked like I was being forced to choose among several unappetizing alternatives: dowdy-looking librarian types with short hair, glasses and no makeup (like most of the women at GWA), barhopping butches and bull dykes who could always be found around the pool table showing off their tattoos and smoking their unfiltered *Camels*, or kinky pseudo-chic sex fiends like Jackie, Oxana and the Creole babe from last night. God -- maybe I'd be better off if I just tried to go straight!

15

Belly Dancing in Bloomingdale's

FOR THE NEXT two weeks I stayed away from the Universalist Church and the GWA crowd. But then, one Friday at work I got a call from Lorraine, the older woman I had met at Jackie's party. After reminding me who she was she asked if I felt like stepping out that evening and maybe having a bite; she mentioned some greasy spoon she knew of, located about halfway between our two apartments. I had nothing else planned and remembered being intrigued by this tall redhead who told me she used to play cello for the Boston Symphony. So I replied, "Sure, why not."

At the diner we ordered burgers and I asked her how she wound up in New York. She said a good friend of hers who had lived in the city for twenty years recommended Lorraine for a good-paying executive secretary job at a Wall Street firm, because she could type 90 words a minute. "I can't type to save my life," I told her, looking at her fingers as I said it. She had lovely hands, perfectly shaped, the fingers long, slender and smooth, capped with oval fingernails painted with a pale peach polish.

As we were leaving the diner she asked me if I would like to see her apartment. She lived in the northwest corner of Hell's Kitchen, that gritty neighborhood on the edge of the theater district known for its rough and tumble history of rumrunners and Irish mobsters, as fondly depicted in the colorful short stories of Damon Runyon. Her brownish-gray tenement building appeared seedy, even forbidding at first. The dull glow of the streetlamps barely lit up that side of the block. I wasn't sure what to expect as I walked in. The hallway was eerily quiet. We went one flight up and then Lorraine took out a set of keys and carefully opened the three locks on her door and we entered her very modest studio.

Ah...what a difference a little decorating makes! I was blown away by what she had done with such an uninviting space. There were Chinese paper lanterns and fringed curtains and attractive vases full of fresh flowers. Brightly colored artwork adorned the walls. She had a beautiful mahogany sleigh bed with a scrolled headboard. My own place, almost half again as large, was drab and pedestrian in comparison. I went home pleased, feeling that if I hadn't met a romantic prospect yet, at least I've made a fine new friend.

The following Wednesday night at GWA, I spotted Lorraine talking with a small group of women by the refreshment table. I had told her about the meetings at the Universalist Church and was delighted to see her there. I also saw Blanche, the curly-haired French teacher I had met my first time there. I took a seat and everyone settled down for a screening of the 1931 German film *Madchen in Uniform*, a cult favorite among lesbians since it was one of the earliest movies to deal openly and sympathetically with the subject of female homosexuality. After the screening I walked over to where Blanche and Lorraine were sitting and heard peals of laughter. Apparently, Lorraine was telling a funny story with that odd but endearing Virginia/Boston accent of hers.

Then I noticed a young woman I had never seen there before. She had sleek Scandinavian looks with platinum blonde hair and an apricot complexion -- and, wow, what must have been a 38 D bra size! She seemed to be with Blanche, hanging on to her every word whenever she spoke. I soon realized that this must be the student Blanche had confided to me about with whom she was having an affair. Then Lorraine suggested the four of us go out for dinner. Blanche knew of a great Italian restaurant in the upper 80s off Columbus Avenue. So out we went, Lorraine, myself, Blanche and her buxom blonde, whose name was Kirsten.

At the restaurant we ordered a bottle of the house wine and the waiter brought over a basket of still warm, fresh baked bread. Lorraine seemed to be in an exceptionally lively mood, because she monopolized the conversation at once. Apparently, after a few glasses of wine she became very animated, much like Anne Fikkert, my talkative oft-tipsy coworker. She was chattering on about all sorts of things, her former husband, her 19-yr-old daughter, her ex-girlfriend ("Don Rose"), her years in boarding school, her career as a musician, her shrink -- and all at a dizzying pace. It was as if someone had turned the screw to the max on a windup doll and then released it. After a while I could barely trace out the meaning in the nonstop barrage of words:

"After I found out that Don Rose was seeing Phyllis on the side, I gave her an ultimatum. Either break it off this weekend or I move out, taking the Cape Primrose AND Chairman Mao (that was our 3-yr-old Pomeranian) with me."

"Then Winston (my husband) says 'I'm not giving you a divorce until Brook is at least 16, but from now on we are sleeping in separate beds.' Well, that was fine with me; I went out and bought myself a heated waterbed..."

"Don Rose was on the phone with Trudy -- she was the Sutherland's nanny -- and I picked up the extension and she was going on about how they'd ordered this hand-carved bathtub made from Rosa Aurora stone imported direct from Portugal."

"I had just gotten off this macrobiotic diet -- you know, the one where you have to do 'colonics' with a coffee enema? That was when I was teaching belly dancing at Bloomingdale's and I had to drop a few pounds to fit into that glittery outfit."

As I sat silently eating my penne alla vodka I began to wonder if Lorraine was just a flaky dame who liked to tell tall tales, spun from the silken threads of an overactive imagination, like one of those neurotic types with a repressed need to be listened to. *Mommy! Mommy! Listen to me! Please LISTEN!!* Then again, everything she said may have been perfectly true and this was just her way of reaching out and making friends. Who knew -- but really, *belly dancing in Bloomingdale's*? Perhaps there had been some sort of Middle Eastern clothing line introduced and the belly dancing lessons were part of some over-the-top fanciful promotion -- not exactly unheard of at a trendsetting store like Bloomingdale's.

Ever since that day at the restaurant I began to be fascinated by Lorraine and eager to know what made her tick. She seemed quite interested in me as well, calling my office several times a week. We started going out together -- dinner, movies, museums, chamber music recitals at nearby Carnegie Hall, expositions at the New York Coliseum, Shakespeare-in-the-Park, and other attractions. The more I got to know Lorraine the more eccentric she seemed, and the more I was charmed by her. For example, every time we went to a cafe, restaurant, or diner she would unfailingly order a glass of *Dubonnet Rouge* after dinner, a kind of port wine. I couldn't stand the stuff -- sickeningly sweet and "fortified" with brandy or some other hard liquor -- but Lorraine couldn't get enough of it. As the alcohol took effect she became mellow and a faraway look came over her face. Her robin's egg blue eyes sparkled with whimsical lights that beckoned you to enter some magical storybook world that only she had the keys to -- even dared you to resist. Looking at her facial features it occurred to me that she must have been drop-dead gorgeous when she was in her late teens and twenties.

She told me she married only because of her family and social class; it was expected, practically obligatory, and she wanted to keep up appearances. Her husband had built up a successful lumber business, and the two of them had an understanding. All throughout their marriage, Lorraine pursued her unorthodox lifestyle in the "off-hours," partaking in a number of torrid love affairs with women, always planning to leave her husband as soon as her kids were old enough. Her life story intrigued me, so far removed was it from anything I had ever known. Lorraine appeared to me like some character sprung from the pages of a wild racy novel, somehow larger than life. With a bit of surprise, as if caught off guard, I found myself becoming smitten, drawn unresisting into her magnetic field, against my better judgment.

One day she called me and said that she had been talking to Carol, a gay woman she had recently befriended at work, only to learn that Carol was a violinist attending the Juilliard School of Music. Carol's girlfriend, also a violinist, played in the Philharmonic at Lincoln Center. The two of them were throwing a "gay musicians' party" at their spacious apartment in the storied Dakota -- that famous Gothic-looking apartment building now remembered chiefly as the place where Beatle John Lennon was gunned down the year before. They were inviting all the musicians and theater people they knew. There would be live impromptu performances, including some original compositions presented for the first time. Lorraine was welcome to bring her cello and join in. Of course, Lorraine had not brought her cello when she moved to New York -- it had been many years since she'd played professionally. But, she told Carol, she would be delighted to just listen to the music and meet new people. Could she bring a non-musician friend along? The answer was yes. I had to hold the phone receiver an inch or so away from my ear -- never had I heard Lorraine sound so excited. Of course I agreed to go.

Carol and Brett's apartment was one of the largest I had ever seen. The ceilings were fourteen feet high and there seemed to be a working fireplace in every room. The gathering of musicians, at least thirty of them, both men and women, was impressive and even gave me a tinge of pride. Where would New York's "culture," its Broadway theaters, art scene, symphony orchestras, haute couture fashion, dance and the performing arts be without gay people?

A sumptuous buffet spread was laid out in a kitchen twice the size of my whole apartment and everyone was happily milling about, chatting, helping themselves. I talked to several friendly looking people, beginning every conversation with, *"I'm not a musician, I don't play an instrument, but..."* I thought about the clarinet lessons I had taken as a child from the third through the seventh grade but figured it would be foolish to mention that. My mom had played the piano when she was a teenager; there was a piano in every house we ever lived in. While I myself didn't really take to piano lessons, I had certainly inherited my mother's love and appreciation for music of all kinds.

As for Lorraine, she was acting like a kid in a candy store. I watched her having lively conversations with every woman in the room and occasionally taking down phone numbers. Wow, I thought, she is really on the make! I wandered about the crowded room trying to keep a smile on my face and a drink in my hand, looking for an attractive woman about my age. Whenever I spotted one standing all alone, I tentatively began to move in her direction, then stopped, telling myself it wouldn't matter -- she was probably already "taken," her partner either couldn't make it to the event or else was in the bathroom. Despairingly I wondered why I always had to sabotage myself in this way. Was it a "will to fail" or a need to punish myself for already being a failure?

While ruminating thus, I noticed a few people picking up violins, violas, and, yes, a cello. A quartet, including Carol and Brett, was about to perform a piece by Debussy. The acoustics of the apartment must have been excellent because the music sounded superb. Someone took a seat at a beautiful Steinway piano and a Chopin nocturne followed. Then a man holding a silver flute and accompanied by a female singer introduced a song he had just written as part of a score for a new Broadway musical.

For some reason, I began to feel sad. I looked around and there was Lorraine chattering away at some woman with thick black glossy hair combed into a pompadour -- the gal reminded me of Elvis. I started feeling pangs of jealousy. Why was she ignoring me? I don't think she had even looked at me in over two hours. The pangs were followed immediately by twinges of guilt and shame. What right had I to harbor such feelings about Lorraine? She was my friend -- I should be glad to see her enjoying herself and meeting women. Besides, this was ridiculous -- she was way too old for me, almost old enough to be my mother.

But rationalize as I might, I could not deny my growing feelings of jealousy, possessiveness, and sheer infatuation with Lorraine. It was silly -- like having a crush on a schoolteacher. Wasn't I beyond that stage? But then why was she leading me on? Why did she want to go out with me all the time? Why did she *always* insist on paying for everything -- movies, dinner, museums, whatever -- despite my vigorous protests and shoving of cash across the table? Why did she *always* kiss me goodnight full on the mouth -- what was that all about (not that I'd ever tried to stop her)? Why did she gaze into my eyes with that, well, *look* sometimes, or was it just my fevered imagination? Why did she call me nearly every other day? Why did she pronounce my name in such a fetching, almost sensual way that always sent a little shiver down my spine? And only last week she actually asked me if I wanted to go on a vacation trip with her to Cartagena, Columbia for two weeks -- just the two of us. She said she had come across a great package deal in the Travel section of *The New York Times*. I would not have been able to get the time off from work, so it was out of the question. But just imagine if we had gone.

I wrestled with my incessant thoughts and feelings about this woman, tried my damnedest to swat them away as if they were a swarm of gnats, but they wouldn't leave me in peace. I considered just avoiding Lorraine for a few weeks, making excuses every time she asked me out. But then how would I explain it to her? Or maybe I should just confront her directly and declare my feelings. But the mere thought of doing that made me cringe in embarrassment. Then I decided I would try to focus on her flaws and shortcomings, the things I didn't like about her, in the hope that my affections would wither away. But damn it, the very traits, mannerisms, and behaviors that most ticked me off about her also, perversely enough, made her even more irresistible. They seemed expressly designed to irk me, the better to underscore my helplessness. I was caught in the tender trap. At last, I felt I had no choice but to let things run their natural course, come what may.

About three weeks after the musical soiree at Carol and Brett's place, there was another festive happening. *Gay Women's Alternative* was celebrating its tenth anniversary. Everyone was encouraged to bring blankets, wine, and a homemade dish for a potluck picnic in Central Park, right across from the Universalist Church. It was mid-May, the days were growing longer and the air was sweet and cool. About thirty-five women showed up for the Saturday afternoon picnic. Our party consisted of Lorraine, me, Blanche, Kirsten, and a visiting couple, Lucy and Eileen, who owned and operated a bed and breakfast in Provincetown, Mass. They had brought an enormous picnic basket filled with summer sausages, sparkling wine, wheat crackers, brie and goat cheeses, and fresh melon. We spread a beach blanket over the grass in a nice sun-kissed spot and everyone sat down to enjoy food, conversation, and the heady spring breeze.

Lorraine was in her element and it showed. She fell effortlessly into her life-of-the-party role, entertaining us with an outlandish story about the cousin of one of her ex-lovers in Virginia who claimed to be a medium. About a month after Lorraine's mother died of a mysterious illness in 1966, this fellow had conducted a séance in some abandoned opera house and had received two cryptic messages purporting to be from the dearly departed. According to Lorraine, when the medium relayed the messages it turned out they contained certain details about her mother's life that this guy could not possibly have known. Ever since that day, Lorraine told us with a grave tone, she's had a keen interest in and appreciation for the occult and paranormal phenomena like ESP and telekinesis.

After several hours of listening to Lorraine's tales, the food and wine finally ran out. A stiff west wind was starting to put a chill in the air. It was time to leave. But as we were packing our gear, Lorraine, somewhat giddy after all the wine and storytelling, suddenly exclaimed:

"Hey guys, any of you have plans for tomorrow night? My friend Carol at work told me about this really neat restaurant just nine blocks from here that serves great food and has pictures of naked women all over the walls. How about we all go and check it out?"

Everybody laughed and I said, "Watch out honey, I think all that *Asti Spumante* went to your head. If there is such a place, it's probably somewhere in Times Square near Eighth Avenue, not around here."

Lorraine insisted she was not joking. Blanche demanded to know the name of the restaurant. Lorraine said she didn't know exactly, but could look it up at home. More laughter, as Lucy and Eileen hailed a yellow cab to take them to their hotel in Gramercy Park. Blanche, who had brought her own car, popped the trunk and began loading it with the blankets, empty food containers and wine bottles. Kirsten turned to Lorraine and announced, "Okay -- you go look it up and call us tomorrow -- we're game. If it's real you got a deal!" Lucy and Eileen nodded in agreement before stepping into the cab. Lorraine and I began to walk home.

I looked at her and said, "What's gotten into you, are you having lucid dreams or something? Naked women on the walls? What is it, some strip club?"

"No!" she yelled, almost angrily. "Listen, I'll go home, get the name and number of the place and call you. If you still don't believe me you can call them up yourself."

That sounded reasonable so we said goodnight as we turned onto Broadway and went to our separate apartments. Sure enough, about an hour later the phone rang.

"It's called *Cafe de Artistes*," she said, "and it's on West 67th Street."

The next morning I called Lucy and Eileen; Lorraine called Blanche, and we all agreed to meet in front of the restaurant at seven o'clock that evening. When I walked into the place, I could not believe my eyes. Huge murals depicting nude women frolicking in the woods were on every wall, gorgeous nymphs cavorting in the water, lying stretched out on rocks, pushing each other on swings that hung from tree branches. Beautiful naked women romping around together in a sylvan paradise! We all stood there staring with our mouths open. Lorraine exclaimed, "Wow -- it's even better than I thought!" As the waiter happily pointed out, the murals had been painted in the 1930s by Howard Chandler Christy, a renowned American artist and illustrator.

He showed us to a large round table with a beautiful flower arrangement in the center. Everyone was delighted over the murals and couldn't wait to spread the word. We ordered, and someone began talking about the "palimony" lawsuit that had been filed against tennis great Billie Jean King by her live-in girlfriend. I glanced across the table and Lorraine seemed to be deep in some private conversation with Blanche. A quiver of jealousy rippled through me. Was it possible Lorraine was stealthily making a play for Blanche, hoping to entice her away from her starry-eyed student?

Probably not, I thought, remembering the last time we had all gone out together and Blanche left the table to make a phone call. The pay phone was located by the restrooms and Blanche had apparently been speaking French because after Lorraine returned from the ladies' room she whispered to me, "I don't have the heart to tell her, but she speaks horrible French." It occurred to me that this was just one of many similar barbs she had leveled not only at Blanche, but at and about other people ever since the two of us had started hanging out together. Lorraine had a nasty side to her and I berated myself for having fallen so easily under her spell.

But as it turned out, I was soon to be delivered from my predicament in a most unexpected way. The last of the "good times" I would ever share with Lorraine was on the occasion of New York's annual *Gay Pride March*, the colorful street party commemorating the famous Stonewall uprising. That fabled event took place in 1969 when a cohort of drag queens, cross dressers and other "queers" made up their minds that they were simply not gonna take it anymore.

During a routine police raid on a popular drag hangout called the *Stonewall Inn,* the beleaguered patrons for the first time actively resisted, throwing bar stools, breaking bottles, tossing trash cans through the plate glass windows, and creating a rollicking riot that made national headlines. Finally, a spotlight was being cast on the plight of an oppressed group who up until that time had been all but invisible. Ever since then, on the last Sunday of every June, their brave defiance has been celebrated in a grand march down Fifth Avenue, a boisterous, rainbow-colored parade which over the years came to rival both the *Macy's Thanksgiving Day Parade* and the *St. Patrick's Day Parade* in crowd enthusiasm and attendance.

That summer a small group of women who had been instrumental in the founding and success of GWA planned to march under their own banner. The rest of us planned to show up and cheer them on. Lorraine and I, Kirsten, and Blanche arrived early and staked out a great viewing spot on Christopher Street. It was my first Gay Pride Parade and I had brought my camera. It went on for hours. There were marchers of all ages, races, and nationalities. I saw a contingent of "Native American Gays and Lesbians" in full regalia with feather headdresses and buffalo skin skirts, a group of Brazilian gays swaying to a samba beat on an elaborately outfitted float, gay folks in native garb from Taiwan, the Philippines, South Africa, New Zealand, and half a dozen other places, men decked out in outrageous tropical bird plumage that made them look like huge open fans, a posse of women dressed in gowns and high heels holding signs reading *Femmes Rule*, a gay male baton-twirling squad, a "bondage and discipline" float carrying guys and gals in black leather harnesses and metal-studded bracelets brandishing whips, and a group of proud "Parents of Gays" marching to show support for their gay sons and daughters, and much much more. Lorraine, who had never seen anything like it before, was mesmerized.

After the parade everyone flocked to a lively street festival where dozens of vendors were selling or giving away everything from Belgian waffles to condoms, along with rainbow t-shirts, hats, flags, buttons, and other gay-themed merchandise. The late June sun blazed down on us without mercy as we made our way through the packed streets mopping the sweat from our brows and seeking refreshment. And like an oasis in the desert, the sight of sturdy wooden barrels packed with ice containing dozens of bottles of beer available for a buck led to exclamations of joyful relief. Ahhhhh...boring old *Budweiser* never tasted so good!

There would be a host of post parade dance parties at various clubs in the city, as well as a fireworks display on the piers overlooking the Hudson River. Lorraine wanted to go to a special event for women to be held at a nearby church-turned-disco called *The Limelight.* Blanche and Kirsten were tired and wanted to go home, but I told Lorraine I'd be happy to dance the night away -- after all, Gay Pride Day came but once a year. We bid our friends goodnight and headed over to the site, normally a straight dance club, but gay for tonight.

Once inside the club, in the midst of flickering strobe lights and lavender clouds of perfumed mist churned out by a fog machine, I found myself dancing with a number of delirious looking gals with whistles hanging around their necks which they blew at certain climactic moments in the music. Others were shaking tambourines. In between dances, I downed several more beers until I got a pretty good buzz on -- enough, I hoped, to keep my spirits aloft for the rest of the night.

For a while I lost Lorraine in the crowd but found my way back to her just as the bash was starting to wind down. As usual at that time of the night, the DJ put on a slow, soulful ballad and Lorraine and I danced close. It was slightly awkward since she was several inches taller, but I nestled my head on her shoulder and could feel the smooth skin of her neck against my cheek. The heat and humidity had amplified the natural wave of her hair and she was wearing this wonderful Egyptian cotton blue plaid shirt. It was actually a man's shirt, but she had the first three buttons opened, revealing her creamy skin and just a touch of cleavage, making her look more "femme" than if she'd been wearing a dress with ruffles and frills. To me she looked as sexy as I'd ever seen her and my body, loosened up by alcohol and the infectious nonstop pulse of the music, responded, the tingling of tiny bells spreading rapidly throughout my groin.

In my half-drunken haze, I resolved that if anything carnal was ever going to happen between me and this strangely alluring creature it would have to be tonight. As we danced my hands gently explored the contours of her back and shoulders. I ran one hand through her rust-colored locks and tried to determine whether she was squeezing my waist just a tad more tightly than at other times we had danced close. Both of us were wasted and in a devil-may-care mood -- so why not go home together and see what happens. I clung to her greedily as the DJ spun another oozy jam and a faint whiff of patchouli made its way to my nostrils. Dare I plant a soft quick kiss on her neck? Slide a hand gently under her shirt? But before I could decide on my next move everything stopped.

The next thing I know I'm sitting in a nearly empty subway car dazed, dizzy and looking down at a foul-smelling lumpy yellowish glob that looked as if someone had opened a can of Campbell's Chunky Gumbo soup and emptied it on the floor. I was aware of a tender but firm touch on my back. Lorraine was smiling at me, saying,

"Don't worry -- you just got a little sick that's all, probably from drinking on an empty stomach."

"Oh...God" I stammered.

"No, it's nothing. I'll take you home, give you a couple of Darvons, and you can sleep it off on my couch," she said with a warm motherly tone.

Soon we were in her apartment and Lorraine brought over a pillow and gently tucked me in on the sofa with a light blanket. At that moment I wished I could just vanish without a trace and in such a way that anyone who had ever known, seen, or had anything to do with me would have no memory of my existence. Thankfully I had little time to dwell on these despondent thoughts. Thirty seconds after Lorraine shut the light and wished me pleasant dreams I was out cold.

After that embarrassing incident, I resolved to stay away from Lorraine and the whole GWA scene at least for a while. I took up Maxine's offer to accompany her to some airfield in Pennsylvania where she was actually going to try her hand at hang gliding for the first time. She wanted me there to take a bunch of pictures and give her moral support. Now *that* was pretty exciting.

I stopped going to the Universalist Church or to any of GWA's events. Whenever Lorraine called I would tell her I was under a lot of pressure at work and wanted to reserve nights and weekends for relaxing at home. I went to movies and museums by myself. But I was not lying. I really *was* under pressure at work -- the pressure came from constantly thinking about Lorraine. In her absence I had created in my mind an idealized, almost iconic version of her that followed me around like a shadow. There she was, copper tresses falling carelessly about her face, lighting another Newport with a knowing gleam in her eye, blowing smoke rings toward the ceiling and pretending she didn't have a clue about the effect she had on others. She exuded sophistication, wit, and a soft understated kind of glamour that didn't depend on clothes or trappings but radiated from within, as if hardwired into her genes. And I believed that she belonged to me by virtue of some infallible law I couldn't quite define. I wanted to say to Blanche and to those women at the musician's party to whom she'd passed out her phone number and to anyone else who may have been charmed by her stories or her singular accent, *"Hey, hold on a minute,* ***I*** *saw her first!!!"*

I had been given my own office, but unlike the attorneys who generally kept their office doors open, I took advantage of the opportunity for total privacy and kept mine closed most of the time. I relished the chance to sequester myself when needed so that I could dwell in silence and solitude on whatever was racking my brain that particular day. And on most days an endless parade of thoughts and concerns frenetically danced and pranced their way through my mind like costumed revelers at a Mardi Gras festival.

So now I had even more time to fixate on Lorraine, who by now had taken on the attributes of a phantom, distorted and blown out of shape by my wayward imagination. My actual recollections of our time together were tossed into a blender with my delusional hopes and my irrational fears, to stir up a strange brew of memories and longings that was at least two steps removed from reality. I was playing a dangerous trick on myself that could only signal trouble down the road.

I sorely missed painting the town red with Lorraine, missed her humor, her unsinkable optimism, even her ceaseless chatter which would have been grating coming from any other voice, but not from hers. Lorraine's voice had a mellifluous singsong quality that avoided sounding dumb or syrupy only by virtue of its perfect diction. Her words did not spill over or slide into each other but came out crisp and clear, evidence of what used to be called "good breeding." I also missed that insatiable childlike curiosity of hers that made even the most prosaic activities seem fresh and new. Lorraine, more than anyone I knew, could make the "been there, done that" stuff worth doing again.

My attempt at an out of sight/out of mind approach to help me forget about Lorraine seemed to be failing miserably. After about six weeks all my resolve crumbled, and I found myself picking up the phone to call her. After all, I thought, I wouldn't want her to think I had just blown her off without explanation after she had been so good to me. So, violating my self-imposed moratorium I went ahead and called her at work. Let's catch up a bit, I suggested. I proposed meeting later that night at our favorite diner on 57th Street, two blocks from her place. She sounded as buoyant as ever and said she was so glad I had called -- she had a lot to tell me.

Sipping her glass of *Dubonnet*, Lorraine told me first of all that Blanche had finally broken it off with Kirsten. Kirsten's mom had somehow gotten wind of the situation and gone straight to the head of the Languages Department demanding that the "deviant" French teacher be formally disciplined. Then Lorraine told me she had discovered a new hangout for women in a section of town that would later become the artsy neighborhood known as Tribeca (for **Tri**angle **Be**low **Ca**nal Street). She gave me the address and we met there the following Friday night.

The place, whose name escapes me, was a kind of cross between a bar and a café. No hard liquor was served -- only wine. No live DJ, dance floor or pool table either. There was a beautiful old-fashioned Wurlitzer jukebox loaded with oldies from the '50s and early '60s, designed to appeal to older gals who preferred not to have their conversations drowned out by blasting disco music. The walls were decorated with pieces by local women artists and were for sale. Coffee and tea were served along with wine, as well as light snacks and pastries. The place had a relaxed feel and we spent at least two hours there talking and sipping coffee. It was a clear star-studded night and I walked back to my apartment feeling good, little knowing I had just had my last ever date with Lorraine.

I went to the next GWA meeting, not having been there for almost two months, and saw her there, chatting with two newcomers to the group. I noticed she was looking a little more dressed up than usual. Most Wednesday nights Lorraine came straight from work, wearing a conservative pants suit or plain dark skirt with a blazer. But tonight she was dressed in a beautiful billowing silk blouse with a simple Japanese print, and very sheer, baggy Arabian-style "harem pants" that on anyone else would have looked like a gaudy outfit for a costume ball. On Lorraine it looked as natural as if she were born wearing it. It blew me away -- but, what was the occasion?

After the program I walked over to say hi. Lorraine introduced me to her new friends, two fashionably dressed businesswomen in their late forties. She told me that they were all headed down to the new cafe near Hudson Street, where they would be joined by the newly single Blanche -- did I want to come along? As it turned out, I had to get to the office extra early the next morning to tackle some assignments I had neglected. I also felt a bit out of place. It was great that the older gals finally had a nice place to repair to; perhaps it was time I started looking for friends my own age. So I wished them well and left.

About two weeks later Lorraine called me at home sounding all excited -- even for her.

"Guess what happened?" she said.

"What?"

"I met someone."

"Oh?...Where? At that new cafe?"

"Yes! She was just standing by the jukebox when I walked in, almost like she had been waiting for me."

"Hey -- not bad. You guys hit it off right away?"

"Oh God yes! We just clicked immediately. I felt like I'd known her all my life."

There was no denying the unmistakable sound of heartfelt gratitude in her voice. I could detect that rare tearful tremble of relief that comes when a long-cherished dream at last becomes true. Wow. I couldn't help but feel happy for her even as I felt my own heart sinking.

Lorraine gushed on. "When she played *Daddy's Home* by Shep & the Limelights I knew we were meant for each other. So I walked over, and we started talking. She lives in Jersey City, just broke up with her partner of eleven years. Imagine that! Eleven years! That's how long I was with Don Rose."

"No shit...what's her name?"

"George -- she told me her father named her after the famous English woman writer George Elliot, you know her?"

I did indeed know who George Eliot -- aka Mary Ann Evans before she adopted her pseudonym -- was. I had written my senior thesis on her magnum opus, the novel, *Middlemarch*.

"So," I said, "did you guys go out again?"

"Yes! She took me to the most wonderful Southern restaurant on Charles Street, *Horn of Plenty*, I think it was called. You would have loved it, Vicki (and she pronounced my name with that sultry lilt that always sent tingles down my back). I just can't wait for you to meet her..."

So we set up a time and place to meet. When the day arrived, I tried to picture what George would be like. Highly educated, probably. A bit more conservative than Lorraine, quiet, nice-looking with stylish hair and inconspicuous but expensive earrings. A businesswoman type, I felt certain. I was to meet them in front of The Palace Theater at about 6:30 pm, a fifteen-minute walk from my apartment. George had managed to get tickets to the Broadway show, *Woman of the Year*, starring Lauren Bacall. Great seats -- fifth row, orchestra center. I'd meet them there and chat for a bit before the two of them went to grab dinner before showtime at eight.

As I walked down Broadway and approached 47th Street I took a deep breath. I struggled to summon up an expression of happy satisfaction on my face, congratulatory delight. Wasn't I happy for my friend? Yes, of course, but the happiness was adulterated with a perplexing mix of feelings and emotions. Such as a bit of shock, sadness, anger, a sense of betrayal, a feeling of having been tricked. "*Grow up. Get over it*!" I chided myself, as I forced a smile.

Right away I spotted Lorraine standing under the marquee, looking lovely as ever. And then -- immediately to her right -- there she was. With a soft black fedora atop her head, "George" was even taller than Lorraine. She was dressed in a man's worsted wool suit with four-inch lapels and mother-of-pearl cuff links. "George" had on a vest to go with the suit and sported one of those big watches on a chain like old-time railroad conductors used to wear. "George" had short brown hair slicked back with hair gel and a pair of glossy dark brown Oxford shoes to match. I could have sworn I picked up a whiff of *Old Spice* aftershave lotion.

I was dumbstruck, speechless. I glanced over at Lorraine and the look on her face was, with no exaggeration, like that of a five-year-old seeing Fourth of July fireworks for the first time. "Victoria, I want you to meet my good friend and partner in crime," she said, beaming at her new lover and introducing me.

I approached "George" and extended my hand, and it was all I could do to keep from saying, "You're a very lucky guy." I had to admit, they did make a handsome couple. I mumbled some meaningless pleasantries, made an excuse that I was expecting an important phone call and had to get home, and then took off, walking back up Broadway as fast as my feet could carry me. My eyes filled with tears, but I truly don't know whether I was laughing, crying, or both. I got into my apartment and slammed the door, feeling as if I had just witnessed something unspeakable that I must not reveal to anyone. I shook my head in incredulity, doubting I had really seen what I thought I had seen.

No, it can't be! Lorraine could not be "leaving me" for that comical creature who just stepped out of a vaudeville show. Somebody -- God, maybe? -- was playing a cruel prank on me. I sensed the beginning of a headache and swallowed a small handful of aspirin. All I wanted to do was go straight to bed and into a deep sleep and hope somehow I would wake up and find it was all a bad dream.

Of course, no such thing happened. I woke up with a headache still, dazed and confused. It just didn't make any sense. Here was Lorraine, a beautiful, intelligent woman who had been a wife and a mother. How could she -- why *would* she, settle for a male impersonator when she could have the real thing? I thought being gay meant you were attracted to your own sex, attracted to *women*. Was this role-playing thing some kind of a game, a pose adopted for public consumption? Did partners ever switch roles? Trying to imagine George wearing a house dress made that seem unlikely. So did this mean that if I wanted to attract women like Lorraine I'd better cut my hair off and don a top hat and tux, I mused, picturing Marlene Dietrich performing in that famous "queer" scene from the film, *Morocco.*

Then it hit me that these questions did nothing but reveal my complete ignorance, expose my pathetic lack of life experience for which, at age 28, there seemed to be no excuse. Lorraine must have introduced George to all her other friends -- Blanche, Carol, Lucy, etc. Surely none of them had shown anything like my shock and surprise. How could I have become so divorced from everyday reality? What kind of fantasyland was I living in anyway?

For the next several days I retreated into my solitary cave like an injured lioness quietly licking her wounds away from prying eyes. At work I kept the door to my office closed, spent lunch hours taking lonely walks in the park, wouldn't go out with Maxine, barely spoke a word to anyone if I didn't have to. Needless to say, I stopped going to the GWA meetings. I couldn't bear the thought of seeing Lorraine with George.

As it turned out, I needn't have worried. Not two weeks after the night of my rude awakening, Lorraine called me -- that same Christmas morning glee in her voice -- to announce that she was giving up her apartment in Hell's Kitchen and moving to Jersey City with George. They had found a sunny duplex with a river view that rented for less than Lorraine's studio.

"That's wonderful," I said, feeling awful. "When are you leaving?"

"This weekend. I'll send you a postcard with my new address and phone number. You've got to come and visit us."

"Yeah -- we're gonna have to throw you guys a big housewarming party," I said, knowing I would never call or visit. Lorraine had already become a part of my history, even before I hung up the phone.

16
Anger Management 101

THE BIZARRE AND ridiculous way the Lorraine affair ended was devastating for me, much as I tried to pretend otherwise. Not only had the romantic bubble I had foolishly blown up around her burst, but I had lost someone I considered a good friend. I fell into a tar pit of depression and denial. And then an all too familiar pathological pattern began to unfold. I became consumed with unfocused anger, a generic free-floating anger that wanted to lash out at nothing in particular. It was the kind of random rage that seemed to be the flip side of my deep blue depressions, and it was always a coin toss as to which emotion would take center stage. Sometimes I wanted to curl up in a corner and disappear; at other times I just wanted to break things. Confusion and anxiety set in like a viral infection. I thought it might be time to seriously consider seeing a shrink again, if only to get a prescription for Valium to take the edge off. But my insurance wouldn't cover it and I just couldn't see throwing hard-earned money at someone who would charge upwards of eighty dollars per fifty-minute "hour" to listen to me vent. It all seemed hopeless.

I began to entertain thoughts of suicide. One day I took the elevator all the way up to the top floor of our office building to see if there was any way I could gain access to the roof. I went to the library for information about lethal poisons, hoping to find one that was fast-acting, foolproof, and relatively painless. I pondered the best way to go about making that final exit. The easiest way was probably the pills and booze route, very popular with women and celebrities. But, I thought with a twinge of horror, what if it didn't work all the way and I wound up in a vegetative state with irreversible brain damage, like that poor Karen Ann Quinlan?

Then a still worse thought occurred to me. I fast-forwarded to the scene at the funeral parlor. No doubt my mother would go through the closet in my old bedroom and pull out some awful dress that I hadn't worn since junior high school and hand it to the undertaker to put on my corpse. There I'd be, lying in the coffin with my hands gently folded, cradling a strand of rosary beads and wearing something that I. . . well. . . *wouldn't be caught dead in!* Picturing such a scenario gave me a jolt. Ugh!

My perpetual anger began to affect every aspect of daily life. I had arguments with my neighbors. A colorful, eccentric couple in their late forties with no children lived in the apartment directly behind mine. They seemed to be throwbacks to the 1960s, caught in a time warp, he with his long hair and stoner look, she with those *Make Love Not War* buttons pinned to her handbag and her Che Guevara t-shirts. They didn't seem to have regular jobs and came and went at all hours of the day and night. Unlike the other tenants in our brownstone, we entered the building through a separate side door. A heavy outer door led into a narrow vestibule. Our respective apartments were located on either end of that hallway, mine closest to the door. Both my neighbors were in the habit of leaving the outer door swung open. I knew they did it to get more air into their place. I didn't really mind; we lived on a very safe block. But when the weather began to get frigid it was another matter.

The small radiator that heated my studio was sputtering and inefficient. On cold windy days the icy drafts coming in through the hallway nearly canceled out whatever modest amounts of heat I was able to get out of the stingy, clanking piece of junk. I had phoned and written to the landlord, repair men had visited, all to no avail. The thing needed to be replaced but that task apparently was not on my landlord's to-do list. So when the chilly winds of late autumn arrived, I asked the neighbors if they would kindly close the outer door when they came inside.

But old habits die hard and time and time again, whether they did it inadvertently or just didn't care, they'd leave the door wide open at night. I went to them again and pleaded, pointing out how cold it could get in my apartment. Still no use. So now I had to get up whenever I felt a draft and go outside to pull out the doorstop and close the door myself, sometimes in my pajamas or bathrobe. I became increasingly pissed off. I made a point of listening carefully for one of them to come home, then waiting for the reassuring thud of that outer door being shut tight. I almost never heard it. So I would have to run out there, slam it shut as loudly as I could, and yell after them: "Hey, I asked you to shut the fucking door when you come in!!!"

Other times, thoroughly exasperated, I'd rap repeatedly on their apartment door saying, "I don't understand why you guys keep doing this. I asked you in a nice way." They would mumble something about needing fresh air. "Then open your windows, goddamn it!" I would scream. This only made matters worse because now, whenever I angrily slammed the door shut one of those nut jobs would actually come out and open it again, even if it was freezing outside. Then I would have to go shut it again, shouting obscenities at the top of my lungs. This sick and ugly game went on for the entire winter. How we all escaped without bloodshed or broken bones God only knows.

Things came a lot closer to actual blows with another neighbor -- "neighbor" in this case meaning only a fellow neighborhood dweller, not someone living right next door. There was a laundromat called *The Soap Opera* that I always went to because it was three short blocks from my apartment and open until midnight every day. I liked taking my dirty load in on a Friday night about 10pm, not exactly prime time for doing laundry. Come in at ten on a Saturday morning and you faced a mob scene. Fourteen washers and fourteen dryers roaring away at full blast, little kids running up and down screaming and knocking over laundry baskets, the constant "chink chink" sound from the change machine that swallowed dollar bills and spat out quarters. Every available table taken over by hands busily folding sheets, fluffing underwear, shaking lint off freshly washed jeans. It was impossible to read a book or carry on a conversation amidst all the frenetic activity and noise.

But Friday nights were quiet. Sometimes I would be the only one there; more often there were one or two others I considered "regulars" because I saw them so often. Like me, they preferred to avoid the hustle-bustle. As the *Thank-God-It's-Friday* night drama played itself out on the crowded streets, I could sit in my cheap plastic chair behind the window, peacefully reading or writing, oblivious to the commotion outside. Or I could just stare idly at the tacky Chinese calendar on the wall or the lopsided clock that was always three minutes slow, or smile at the sign that read: *Children Not Permitted in the Dryers at Any Time.* There was even a small bathroom in the back. The laundromat was a homey nonthreatening kind of space and I saw it as a kind of temporary refuge from the world -- a world I'd never asked to be born into.

One night I walked in and noticed two new faces at the laundromat, a twenty-something couple I had never seen in the neighborhood before. They had an unappetizing appearance. The guy was unshaven, wearing stained khakis and a leather jacket with a torn collar; the gal was heavyset and her manner of dress in exceedingly poor taste. She was wearing pink polyester stretch slacks that were two sizes too small, fake nails that resembled claws, hideous hoop earrings, and a chintzy gold blouse that perfectly matched her glittery eye shadow. Both of them were loud and foulmouthed. Evidently they'd just finished doing a wash and were loading their stuff into a large drawstring bag to take home. After they left I scarcely gave them another thought.

But the next time I had to do laundry there they were again. Somehow, I felt that my territory was being encroached upon. I had been coming here regularly on Friday nights at 10pm for two years – hadn't I staked a claim to my own little corner of *The Soap Opera?* I didn't mind sharing it with the regulars -- decent folks whom I liked and respected. But I resented the intrusion of these two unkempt strangers. Even worse, they were both smoking, carelessly flicking ashes onto the linoleum floor as they watched their clothes tumbling in the dryer. And then, after dumping the pile on the folding table, the woman put her still burning cigarette between her lips and began folding, every so often raising a hand to snatch it out and flick off the gray column of ash that had formed.

As I watched them, I frowned in disgust. I had given up smoking four years earlier and like many reformed smokers had become far more intolerant of the filthy habit than someone who had never smoked at all. I could not understand how anyone could fold freshly laundered clothing in the midst of that noxious fog. I remembered one time in a hair salon. The girl attending me had a burning cigarette in one hand while combing out my just washed hair with the other. I never went back. Now I walked to the other side of the room, selecting a washer as far away from the offenders as possible. I loaded the machine, slid in my quarters and left, hoping they'd be gone by the time I got back. I walked over to the 24-hour Korean produce market and bought a few things I didn't really need just to pass the time.

I was miffed, feeling I had been unjustly evicted from my private hideaway by barbarian invaders. Suppose those two (where the hell had they come from anyway?) made a habit of doing their laundry on Friday nights? Suppose I had to sit there breathing their smoke and listening to their coarse conversation every time I had to do a wash? While the clothes were washing I could always leave, of course, but I had to go back to take the wet clothes out and put them in the dryer. For me this was something of a production because I had to carefully separate out the items I didn't want to put in the dryer because they might shrink or burn, and the rest of the stuff had to be untwisted and shaken out a bit so the pieces would dry faster, saving me quarters. That could take a while.

Then, one Friday night the thing I most dreaded happened. I had gone to the laundromat later than usual, about 10:45pm, hoping to avoid them. There was no one there and I had the entire place to myself. Good. I did a whole wash, then dumped the wet clothes into the metal basket and wheeled it over to the dryer on the other side. While doing this, I realized that there was another washing machine going, a sudden fast whirring indicating it had just entered the rinse cycle. So there *was* someone else here, after all. I began shaking out my clothes and tossing them piece by piece into the gaping mouth of the dryer. My back was to the door when I heard somebody walk in. I turned around and, lo and behold, it was Miss Manners, this time without her male tag-along. Coming to fetch her sodden wet rags, she already had a cigarette in her mouth and didn't remove it while pulling her stuff out of the washer, apparently not caring whether or not hot ashes fell on her just washed towels.

Unfortunately, the two dryers closest to her were both out of order and all I could think of was, *don't come near me, lady.* But for whatever perverse reason she chose the dryer directly adjoining mine. She had lit another cigarette and clouds of smoke were drifting in my direction. I was horrified at the thought that my fragrant clean-smelling panties and cotton pajamas were about to be polluted by putrid exhaled tobacco smoke. It was too late to move all of my stuff to another dryer, but I had to do something.

So I attempted a polite request. "Excuse me" I said, "but would you mind not blowing your smoke near my clothes, I don't want them to smell like the bottom of a birdcage when I get home, thank you." She looked at me the way one would look at the village idiot after he'd made some grotesque but not surprising outburst. She said not a word and went back to loading her dryer. After shutting it and putting her change in, she stepped back, took another deep drag of her cigarette, blew the smoke upwards and quipped:

"It doan say 'No Smokin' heah, I doan see no sign. If you doan like it you could wash yuh cloze somewheah else."

Standing not more than four feet from me, she kept spewing her poisonous plumes and there was no way to prevent them from wafting over to me and fouling my freshly washed clothes. Since I had made a perfectly reasonable request -- I hadn't asked her to put out her cigarette, only to do her smoking away from my clothes -- I viewed these as fighting words. Enraged, I flung open the door to her dryer, scooped up all her clothes and threw them on the floor.

"There-- how do you like it? Now you can have soiled clothes too!"

"Hey whadda yoo CRAY-zee, lady!?!" she said in indignant surprise, stomping out her cigarette and hastily gathering up her laundry. "They let you out of an a-SY-lum somewhea?"

She picked up her clothes and put them back in the dryer, shut the door, then walked to the back where there was a bench with some magazines, and she sat down. Fuming in my own way, I continued shaking out and tossing articles into the dryer, sorting out those I would let hang-dry at home. After I got done loading the dryer, I took a chair on the other side of the room and waited, too angry to read. After a while she walked over to the dryer and removed her clothes, laying them on the folding table. I prayed she would finish quickly and leave. But she seemed to have tons of socks, boxer shorts, and white t-shirts -- probably her boyfriend's stuff.

When my clothes were dried I decided I'd just stuff everything in my laundry bag and get the hell out of there. I could do the folding at home. But just as I opened the dryer door, as if to deliberately mock me, she whipped out and lit another cigarette. I could swear she was purposely blowing the smoke in the direction of my clothes.

No -- it was NOT my imagination. Just as I was pulling out my favorite pajama top, a puffy cloud of acrid smog drifted over and filled my nostrils. I stuffed the PJ's and all the rest of my laundry hastily into the bag and drew the string tight. Then, without saying a word or even letting out a frustrated sigh, I walked straight back to the bathroom, grabbed the can of Lysol air freshener that always sat on the windowsill, and squeezed off the cap. Then, dragging the laundry bag with one hand and brandishing my fire-ready weapon in the other, I went up to her and pumped three quick blasts of gardenia-scented disinfectant into her face.

"Have a dose of your own medicine, bitch!" I shouted, and stormed out the door. For one diabolical moment I didn't even give a shit if I'd blinded her, but quickly told myself that the most she would have gotten was a burning sting, no worse than getting shampoo in your eyes. As I walked down the sidewalk at breakneck speed she screamed after me,

"I orta call the puh-LEESE on you, you crazy bitch! They shooden let people like you walk the streets. You belong in a fucken cage!"

As I got closer to my block the shouts faded, but their meaning reverberated in my ears. What if she was right?

Later, I brooded over the loss of my Friday night retreat and resolved to tell no one about the incident. I hoped I would never run into that low-life gutter snipe again. What was she doing in Manhattan anyway? On the Upper West Side, no less? Her kind belonged in the Bronx. (Never mind the fact that I was born and raised in the Bronx myself, as was my mother.)

I knew I had to do something, get a grip on my emotions, before things spun out of control. I needed a time-out and some sort of constructive activity to pull myself out of my half-deranged state of mind. Someone at work had told me about The Adult Learning Exchange, a school that specialized in short-term evening courses with a practical "how-to" bent, such as *How to Become a Court Stenographer* or *How to Start a Consulting Firm*. I chose a course in advertising copywriting. It would be taught by someone who had spent over fifteen years working in the industry. While a senior in college and thinking about what I could do with a B.A. in English, the thought of advertising copywriting had come up. But as an ideal career choice, it was a distant second behind editorial assistant for a book or magazine publisher. I dismissed penning ads as just too crass and commercial. Now, I would probably give my left pinky to have a high-paying job at a slick Madison Avenue ad agency.

The class was a useful distraction. Gradually, my mood and outlook became brighter. I looked forward to the future and refused to look back. The past was dead, or so it felt. Little by little the hairy black claws of depression loosened their grip on me. My toxic anger dissipated, and at length I felt ready to look life right in the eye again and say, without trepidation or trembling, "Okay, what's next?"

17
King Tut's Tomb and a Belated Christmas Gift

A COUPLE OF weeks ago, while reaching up to the top shelf in my closet to yank down a heavy woolen blanket, I got struck in the head by a small falling object. When I bent down to pick it up, I was surprised to see a new blank tape cassette in a clear plastic jacket. Only it wasn't new or blank. Turning it over I saw a white label scribbled with black ink; it read: *Astrology Chart and Forecast 1980-1982.* Oh yeah, *that.* About two years earlier I had visited a professional astrologer and self-proclaimed psychic. I had coughed up a hundred bucks for a two-hour "reading." I was not normally in the habit of such extravagances, but Maxine and I had met this fellow while waiting on line to see what was probably New York's most talked about spectacle that year, the King Tut exhibit at the Metropolitan Museum of Art.

The one-of-a-kind show had opened with an unprecedented amount of buzz and garnered worldwide attention. Because for the very first time the entire contents of King Tutankhamen's tomb (excepting the mummified Pharaoh himself) were to be put on public display. The museum had removed much of its permanent collection to make space for the groundbreaking exhibit. Lines to get into the show were all around the block and I had actually taken the day off from work in order to be able to obtain two tickets. By the time Maxine met me after work there was still at least a ninety-minute wait before we would reach the front of the line.

While waiting, we struck up a conversation with the somewhat peculiar looking man standing behind us. He was wearing a baggy, oversized shirt that looked more like a tunic, and a curious crystal medallion hung around his neck. In his hand was a small bible. The man had large luminous cat-green eyes and spoke with a thick Southern drawl. He told us he was an Egyptologist (which surprised me as I hadn't known there was an entire academic discipline devoted to all things Egyptian). He was also a former Baptist minister, spiritualist, and licensed astrologer. He rattled off the names of a few minor celebrities who were his clients (Barry Manilow was one) and said he had a "parlor" on the west side where he conducted his spiritual work. When I asked where exactly, he said it was in the Ansonia Hotel -- the legendary Ansonia, my favorite NYC historic landmark. "Oh, cool," I piped. "I live just a few blocks from there!" As the line slowly advanced, he entertained us with fascinating facts about Egypt and the strange circumstances surrounding the discovery of King Tut's tomb, about astrology, numerology, and other occult matters. The man's name was Charles House.

It must have been about nine months later, near the end of that year, after I had sworn off dance clubs and weed and was feeling bored and adrift, that I remembered Charles House. I wondered what he would have to say if I were to go to him for a reading. If he had famous clients, I reasoned, he must be pretty good; folks with money could pick and choose. He had been so friendly and nonthreatening at the King Tut show and seemed so knowledgeable. Who knows, I thought, maybe he could give me some insight or guidance that I couldn't seem to find anywhere else.

So I scoured all my drawers and dug out the business card he had handed us, called him and asked if I could schedule a reading. First, he would need to know my exact time and place of birth, down to the minute if possible. Then he told me to bring along a blank tape so I could record the entire session and listen to it at home whenever I liked. I fished around for my birth certificate, called him back with the info, and set up an appointment. When I cashed that week's paycheck I painfully withdrew one-hundred dollars. Mr. House gave his psychic readings at unorthodox hours and my appointment was scheduled for 10pm the following Thursday.

While approaching the lobby of the Ansonia that Thursday night I noticed a group of attractive, high-spirited guys and a handful of women starting to gather in front of the side entrance. Only a few years earlier these would have been hot leather-clad young men. Some shrewd entrepreneur had conceived the idea of turning the Ansonia's famous and long-abandoned Turkish baths into a posh gay bathhouse. The new pleasure den was designed to *"evoke the glory of Ancient Rome,"* as claimed in their enticing promos. The finished *Continental Baths* boasted a swimming pool, waterfall, and discotheque amid palm fronds and soft lights, and there was even a special alarm to warn the patrons whenever the vice squad came around. For a short while during the 1970s, when up-and-coming artists like Bette Midler performed in its famous cabaret, the *Continental Baths* was the hottest entertainment venue in town. After it closed, largely due to the AIDS crisis, someone reopened it as a straight swinger's club called *Plato's Retreat.*

When I got to Mr. House's apartment I knocked quietly and looked around. Many of the lavish apartments in the once luxurious hotel had been broken up into individual studios and rented out to all sorts of transient characters, who pursued eccentric occupations and plied odd trades out of their homes. Mr. House answered the door wearing flowing robes, and I could smell the musky aroma of Indian incense. I walked in and he asked me to take a seat on a small sofa. In front of the sofa was a coffee table on which stood a black tape recorder. I took out my blank cassette and slipped it into the recorder. I tried to make myself comfortable on the couch and looked around the studio, noting the swirls of smoke emanating from a ceramic incense burner that resembled a fountain.

Mr. House then moved to the other side of the room and lowered himself onto a cushion. He sat cross-legged, like a Yogi. I watched, intrigued, as he closed his eyes and lifted his hands, palms outstretched and facing upwards, as if to catch raindrops. He said he was going to "invoke the spirits" by a preliminary exercise of chanting and prayer. Going into a trance-like state, he first began reciting Christian prayers, then started repeating certain Hindu chants. I wondered if I should turn the tape recorder on now or wait until the actual reading began. Eventually Mr. House came out of his trance and stood up, offering me a cup of tea. He then cleared his throat, sat down in what looked like an office chair and began talking to me about my horoscope.

First, he showed me the chart he had cast, nicely hand-drawn on a sheet of artist's sketchbook paper. He then proceeded to interpret it. Much of what he told me seemed very general. He said I had a "loaded" ninth house, which indicated a strong interest in "heavy" subjects like philosophy, ancient history, religion, etc. I had Scorpio rising, which meant I was very private and sometimes obsessed with death and the afterlife. He also remarked that not a single one of my planets or luminaries was in an Earth sign, meaning that I was an extraordinarily impractical person, given to fantasy and naive idealism -- exactly the opposite of "down to earth." He said I would have to learn how to rein in my romanticism -- that would be a crucial "life lesson" I would need to master before departing this world.

All of this seemed true enough. But what I really wanted to hear was the two-year forecast. Mr. House claimed to be able to give a fairly accurate prediction of upcoming trends and major events for the next two years, based on your astrological chart and your "aura" as he sensed and interpreted it from seeing you in person. Things like sickness, a job promotion, a new romance, financial reversal, divorce, etc., could be reliably prognosticated within a certain time frame. So I wanted to hear if there was anything I could look forward to.

Now, staring at the tape cassette in my hand, I realized that a year and eight months had elapsed since I'd sat for the reading. The forecast covered two years, so there were still four months to go. I decided to put the tape on again and see if Charles House had foreseen anything of interest for that stretch of time. I loaded the tape and listened. When Mr. House got to the latter part of the second year, one prediction stood out. He said that towards the end of 1981 I was to meet an "older man" who would be instrumental in helping me grow in wisdom. This man would befriend me in an unusual way, and would have a strange tale to tell which would affect me deeply and have a "strong consolidating influence" on my life. Hmm. I rewound the tape and placed it back in its hard plastic case.

As the days grew shorter and the holidays approached, New York City as always became the most wonderful place to be: Festive lights along Fifth and Park Avenues, the giant tree at Rockefeller Center thronged by picture-snapping tourists, skaters whirling about in the sunken ice rink below, lavishly decorated store windows like miniature theaters with their moving puppets and exquisite details, strings of colored lights and little Christmas wreaths festooning the walls of every bar and tavern, beckoning passersby to come in out of the cold, the warm forgiving mood everyone seems to be in. I couldn't imagine being where my younger sister was, in Los Angeles, where it was 80 degrees and the only lights were the headlights and taillights of a million cars. As gloomy and depressed as I often was, Christmastime in New York never failed to release a flood of happy memories, nostalgic thrills, and a sense of well-being. It was a potent elixir that could temporarily block pain and elevate mood.

Christmas Day at my parents' new home in Yonkers was lovely, with Granny in high spirits pounding the beef for her famous "Braciole" dish and later picking up a rolling pin to flatten the dough for her delicious mince tarts. For New Year's Eve I went to a party at some club on the Lower East Side with Maxine, and on New Year's Day we enjoyed a candlelight dinner lovingly prepared by a guy she was dating, at his apartment in Brooklyn. We sipped leftover champagne and enthusiastically toasted the first day of a brand new year that hopefully would bring good things for all of us.

Two weeks later the entire scene had shifted. The streets in front of my brownstone were littered with discarded dried out Christmas trees shorn of all ornaments except for stray strings of silver tinsel stubbornly clinging to the branches. Empty boxes that once were filled with kid's toys or shiny new gadgets and wrapped in bright-colored paper were haphazardly tossed among the trash waiting to be hauled away by the garbage collectors. Only the dull glow of the streetlamps illuminated the block at night. The carols and hymns that I loved to sing along to no longer poured out of the radio or department store speakers. Grim serious expressions replaced smiles and lighthearted banter as people went determinedly about their business wrapped in heavy down parkas and woolen scarves to brace themselves against the stiff Canadian winds. The spell had been broken, and reality was cold, hard and dreary again.

Back in the office at work I stared gloomily at my brand new 1982 desk calendar, its pages opened to January 10th. There were two handwritten entries: *"Meeting with Mr. Stumpf, discuss Belasco lease,"* and *"Call Mom re Uncle Jerry wake."* As I downed the last drop of coffee from my ten-thousandth Greek coffee cup, it occurred to me that I had not even met the "older man" Mr. House had promised. As a matter of fact, a full two years had passed since that incense-filled astrology session and very little in my life had changed, for better or worse.

But then something totally weird happened. For several weeks now I had been taking the bus instead of walking home in the bitter cold. I had suffered a nasty bout of the flu in November and thought I ought to limit my exposure to the elements, at least for a while. So one night while I stood waiting at the bus stop, I noticed a gray-haired man in a trench coat coming towards me. He was carrying a little gold box and came right up to me smiling.

"Here, I just wanted to give you your Christmas present -- I know it's two weeks late, but that's more your fault than mine" he said in a strong Irish brogue as he handed me the gift-wrapped box. "I've been waiting here for you every night for weeks, but you never showed, not until today."

Looking at his face I realized I had seen him several times before, always at this bus stop. He would board the bus after me, and I noticed him because, unlike most of the middle-aged male office workers who rode the bus at that hour he never wore a suit, never carried a briefcase or a folded newspaper. I could tell he was no ordinary working stiff who spent his day shuffling papers around on a desk and then headed home to his wife, dinner, and a TV sitcom. On the contrary, this man had a ravaged, world-weary look that suggested he had been to hell and back and now craved only a moment's peace.

There was one time -- I think it was the day before Thanksgiving -- when he had actually spoken to me, remarking on a thick handwoven scarf I was wearing. *"Now there's a lovely scarf"* he declared. *"I'll bet it's homemade, isn't it?"* he asked with his charming Irish lilt. I thanked him and told him the scarf was indeed homemade, only the maker was not me. Those vivid gold and maroon yarns had been lovingly knitted together by my grandmother. Just then the bus pulled up and our conversation ended.

For the last two and a half weeks I had been engrossed in a key project at work. It was with an attorney for whom I rarely did assignments, and I was determined to make a fine impression. So I had stayed in the office until 6:00 or even 6:30 to make sure everything would get done perfectly before the deadline. That is why I hadn't shown up at the bus stop at my usual time. No wonder the man had not managed to catch up with me until now.

Along with the gift, the man had handed me a business card and then backed away. When the bus came, I got on and sat in the front as usual; he boarded last and headed for the rear. I sat there looking at my belated Christmas present, feeling perplexed and grateful at the same time. What was all of this about, I wondered? Then I looked at the business card which was from some taxi service. On the back of the card the following had been typed:

SMILE!!!!!

I care! Now, I have made your Christmas a little happier!
Give me a telephone call, and add some happiness to mine.

and, signed in ink: "Merry Christmas, Mike"

18
Crime and Punishment

WHEN I GOT home I carefully laid the gold-trimmed gift box -- about the size of a man's wallet -- on my dresser and stared at it awhile. Who on earth would go to the trouble, and why? Finally I began to untie the fancy red ribbon, gently lifted the top of the box and saw, nestled in pink tissue paper, a bottle of designer cologne. I felt slightly embarrassed, even self-conscious. Obviously, Mike had been thinking about me all of that time, ever since I first started appearing at the bus stop. Then came the unavoidable thought: might this be, was HE that "older man" I was destined to meet? Could it be possible? Still, whether predestined or not, the oddness of it all struck me. Here was a man who didn't even know me, didn't know anything about me and yet he had gone out, bought a gift, and waited at a bus stop night after night hoping to spot me just so he could give it to me in person. Why? Who or what was I to him, what did he see when he looked at me?

The following morning, from the office, I called the number on his business card. I wanted to thank him. He said he was surprised to hear from me -- he'd assumed I would never call. When I asked him what had drawn him to me, he told me that he actually didn't like me at first because I seemed so morose and withdrawn. But after that conversation we'd had about the woolen scarf my grandmother had knitted for me he realized, he said in a solemn voice, that there was "a solid gold person" trapped inside of me who desperately wanted to get out. He said he had learned an awful lot about life as a result of some "terrible ordeals" he had been through over the past decade. He was simply glad to be alive and wanted nothing more than the chance to bring whatever little bit of happiness he could to others. Would I like to meet for coffee, or even dinner, one night after work? I agreed to meet him the following Friday.

He met me in front of my office building, and then we grabbed a cab and drove uptown to a favorite haunt of his on Second Avenue. Again,

I took in his appearance and demeanor. He looked to be about 55, tall, raw-boned, powerfully built. A full head of salt and pepper hair, a short tidy mustache, deep-set slate blue eyes that had a mournful, melancholy look. But there was also a steely hard-edged quality that suggested a man who, if you crossed him or threatened someone or something dear to his heart could break you in two without blinking an eye. He could not be called handsome or attractive, but his face was full of character in the full and true sense of that word and not as a euphemistic way of describing an ugly face. It seemed as if a whole multi-volume tome was written on that face and body. I noted the crooked two-inch scar on the right side of his forehead, just under the hairline.

In some ways I had to admit, Mike seemed just a tad scary. But I reminded myself that Charles House had said this man was to be a positive influence in my life. Any instinct I had to recoil was quashed by the idea that I might be heedlessly casting aside my preordained destiny. Over dinner I talked a bit about myself, but mostly I listened. Mike spoke of his childhood and young adulthood in Ireland. He'd been born and raised in County Donegal, famous for its world-class tweed, and he often found himself assailed by rolling pangs of homesickness. He told me he hadn't been back home in over ten years. I learned he had been married and had two teenage kids, but both they and his wife were estranged from him. He sounded lonely and wistful and when he commented that he could sense a certain loneliness in me, I supposed that must have been the source of the attraction. His radar had detected a fellow lost soul. He said I seemed to be "locked up in myself" and he hoped I would allow him to help me emerge from my cocoon.

While listening to his story, I began to ponder what I would or would not reveal about myself. Somehow I resented his perception of my inner solitude. What if I simply wanted to stay alone and content in my own playpen -- just like I did as a toddler? Whose business was that but my own? But then I questioned this feeling of resentment. What was I trying to protect myself from, what exactly? I couldn't say. I decided to carefully cherry-pick what "personal" things I would disclose and which I would withhold. And although I knew that by doing this I would be shutting off any possibility of real intimacy right from the start, I felt I had no other choice. Not, at least, until I knew him better.

We met after work a few more times. What to talk about? Well, for starters there was my frustrated misunderstood childhood. I told him about my exacting and intolerant mother who had constantly criticized me and made me feel "defective." In her unsympathetic eyes, I complained to Mike, I was hopelessly flawed, tainted, like some mismatched pair of socks that winds up in a bin at the 99 cents store. Mike listened with what looked like real compassion. It felt as if I were with a trusted uncle who was able to bridge the generation gap. He asked me if I had ever considered seeing a psychiatrist to help me deal with these "mother issues." I told him I had seen psychologists and therapists over the years, but still felt I hadn't resolved anything. I was surprised when he revealed that he himself had been seeing a shrink. This was because, he explained, he had been through an intensely traumatic experience which had not only left him emotionally scarred, but had cost him much of what he loved in life. Curious, but not wanting to probe, I simply listened with an empathetic ear, waiting for him to sketch in the details at his own pace.

Then, one night after a dinner date, just as we were saying goodnight, he mentioned that he had something important to tell me about his "past" -- something he felt obliged to tell me, and which he sincerely hoped would not turn me against him. He would explain everything at our next meeting. I wondered what it could be, but I still felt confident that no matter what it was I would not be shocked or reject him. I mean, who the hell was a freak like me, a former mental patient, to reject anyone anyway?

I met him in that same Irish pub on Second Avenue where we'd had our first date, a place owned and operated by a dear friend of Mike's from the old country. It was a quiet Tuesday evening. We ordered salads and beer, and then he began his revelation. First off, he told me that shortly after arriving in New York, he had joined the Police Department. After working in uniform for a while he had been promoted to detective, and from there had moved up the ranks until he made it into a very elite squad in the Narcotics Division known as the Special Investigating Unit, or SIU for short. These guys had been handpicked for a daunting task: to tackle head-on the huge heroin trade that had taken over a large part of the city in the late 1960s and early '70s. The Mafia had largely abandoned the drug business and it was being taken over by a new breed of South

American traffickers who were even more ruthless, vicious, and efficient at flooding the streets of Harlem and the South Bronx with cheap smack than their predecessors had been.

The SIU had to be comprised of the most hard-core, street-smart, intuitive and fearless detectives the NYPD could serve up, and Mike was one of them. These men were given wide latitude and discretion in carrying out their mission. They set their own hours, chose their own targets. They always worked undercover, were experts at surveillance and wiretapping, and had direct personal contacts with some of the shadiest, most cunning and notorious criminals on the East Coast. At this point in the conversation Mike's voice changed slightly, assumed an almost pleading, apologetic tone as he proceeded to paint for me a graphic and disturbing picture.

Sometimes, he explained, SIU guys had to bend the rules, sometimes even break them or turn them on their head. They considered themselves nothing less than soldiers fighting desperate battles, warriors in a never-ending conflict that had already produced thousands of casualties in the form of a generation of strung-out heroin addicts in the inner city. These victims were young men and women whose own lives had been destroyed, even as they preyed on others by robbing, stealing, and prostituting themselves to support their wretched habits. And if it was true that all is fair in love and war, then almost anything could be justified if it could help rid the land of the deadly menace of the drug trade. Or at least, so these men told themselves.

But before long things began to get ugly. It started with questionable tactics such as using illegal wiretaps to obtain crucial information not available any other way, and recruiting informants among beaten down addicts and then supplying them with their next fix as reward for their information. It escalated to shaking down low-level drug dealers for money, then letting them go if they gave up the bigger fish they worked for. Soon everything spiraled out of control. Cleaning out the cash from the closets and suitcases of the dope pushers they busted and dividing it among themselves became routine, demanding regular payments from small-time mobsters to look the other way seemed only natural, assembling all the evidence needed to put away an offender, then offering to sell it back to him if the price was right -- no big deal. And perjuring oneself in court to disguise such misdeeds became par for the course.

Finally -- even the unthinkable became standard operating procedure. Stashes of confiscated drugs were supposed to be sent to the property clerk's office and vouchered, held under lock and key to be used as evidence at trial, and then destroyed. But far too often a small amount of the haul was "held in reserve" by the arresting cops, only to wind up being sold back on the street by those same cops, "earning" them thousands of dollars in extracurricular pay.

But the gravy train was soon to careen off the tracks. In 1971 a special federal commission was formed to investigate allegations of widespread corruption among New York City narcotics detectives. The feds were able to find a handful of cops willing to talk in exchange for immunity from prosecution. Over a period of four and a half years the SIU and the entire New York City Police Department were turned upside down as one damning revelation after another came to light. Fifty-two men were indicted in all -- three-quarters of the entire SIU force. At least two of these highly trained detectives, men who had looked human depravity in the face, had stared down the coldest of the cold-blooded perps on the mean streets of New York without flinching, could not handle the shame and anguish of the growing scandal and shot themselves dead.

Eventually the finger was pointed at the three-man team to which Mike belonged. At the time the lead prosecutor was the now legendary former mayor, Rudolph Giuliani, who was Assistant DA for the Southern District of New York. He and other prosecutors offered Mike and his partners a suspended sentence if they agreed to give up the dirt on other cops. To Mike's surprise and disgust, the team leader turned tail and agreed to cooperate fully with the investigation. But Mike swore he would never, ever, rat on a fellow cop, especially his own partners. It was the lowest thing one could do and the most unforgivable. So rather than be a rat, Mike willingly gave up his freedom and was sentenced to ten years in prison, most of which he served in the Federal Correctional Institution in Allentown, Pennsylvania. After serving his time he was released -- and that was a mere six months before he began showing up at the bus stop, on his way home from his menial job at an elevator company.

"So," he said, "I'm a convicted felon, Victoria. I thought it was only fair that you should know. I've been trying to make amends ever since, and I hope this won't cost me your friendship. But if it does, believe me, I'll understand."

Dumbfounded, I didn't know quite what to say and probably mumbled something to the effect that I would have to think about it a bit. When I got home that night my head was swimming with conflicting emotions. This man had gone to prison, had sacrificed ten years of his life rather than do something that violated his own code of honor. Yet he had engaged in stealing, drug running, and had betrayed the trust of the public he was sworn to serve and protect. One could argue that stealing money from dope pushers was doubtless a far more effective way of putting them out of business than allowing them to post bail and abscond or otherwise buy their way out of trouble. Or that using shady tactics such as illegal wiretaps and junkie informants were the only way to ensure that these miscreants would be caught. Were those corrupt cops actually doing a public service? Did the end justify the means when fighting such a hopeless, losing war as the war on drugs?

I couldn't quite sort out my feelings. People were forever rationalizing immoral, unethical behavior by pointing to some greater good achieved. But didn't the old adage, "Two wrongs don't make a right" still apply? What would I have done in Mike's place? It was difficult to judge. At any rate I decided that if Mike had sinned, he had certainly done his penance; he had paid for his crime and I could never reject outright someone I considered a friend just because he had gotten caught up in something he couldn't really control. And I felt there was something noble about his self-sacrifice -- forfeiting his own freedom in order to protect his partners. It would have been an entirely different matter if he'd confessed to being a hitman or a child molester -- I'd have run for the hills. But Mike was made of finer cloth than that. His deeds were the stuff of crime novels – in fact, he told me, a feature-length motion picture had been released only a few years before dramatizing the whole sordid story. It was called *Prince of the City* and directed by Sidney Lumet. And I had to admit the whole thing was kind of exciting, the air of danger and illicit activities did have its strange fascination for me. Tales from the underworld, a taste of the taboo. There was still that "Wow" factor which I was not too jaded or too grown-up to be stirred by.

A few days later I called Mike and told him, much to his relief, that his painstakingly revealed "dirty secret" would not affect our friendship. But even as I put down the phone, something he'd said at dinner the night of his confession was still ringing in my ears. He had said that he had not enjoyed "true sexual intimacy" with a woman since being thrown behind bars. One-night stands, prison sex (usually with transvestites), and assignations with prostitutes did not count, as far as Mike was concerned. Back when Charles House had told me about the older man I was to meet, there was no intimation of anything romantic or carnal.

Yet it now seemed obvious that this would be the next natural step in our friendship. Mike certainly had a kind of animal magnetism, but I did not find him desirable in a sexual way. And as much as I seemed to have flunked out with women, I wasn't quite ready to throw in the towel and attempt to go straight. So now, I felt, I would have to be on my guard. Mike had asked me if I had a boyfriend or had recently broken up with one. He had bought me several more gifts -- earrings, a gold-plated Cross Pen set, a beautiful Irish cable sweater -- despite my embarrassed protests. Pretty soon he'd be expecting something in return.

We continued dating, going to fancy restaurants and bars -- Mike seemed to know maître d's and nightclub owners all over town. He regaled me with stories of big drug busts, turf wars between Latino and Italian mobsters, and the times he'd escaped being killed by the skin of his teeth. I heard about a notorious mobster who went by the name of Sonny Red, so brutal he had once murdered a rival by knocking him down and pounding an ice pick through his chest so hard that it lodged in the floor -- the body had to be pried loose with tire irons. He told me about a colorful character who went by the name of "The Baron," a black ex-gangster turned highly paid informant for the feds who strutted around in full-length furs and drove a parrot green El Dorado Cadillac. I listened wide-eyed, amazed, and Mike was quite gratified at being able to command such rapt attention. There was something undeniably sexy about a man taking a woman on a tour of such dark and forbidden territory. But I was starting to worry about where it would all lead.

One night things got a little hairy when Mike made a move to reach for me and kiss me goodnight on the lips. Though slightly repelled, I somehow felt it wouldn't be fair or right to rebuff him so I didn't. He had been extraordinarily good to me, had listened to me for hours, had never been anything but a total gentleman, and had even risked all by making his grim confession. The whole thing was so frustrating and I just felt sad. Here was an intriguing new friendship with someone who clearly valued me and accepted me just as I was. And according to a highly paid professional psychic, there was a special if mysterious purpose for his coming into my life. But still -- the thought of him as a lover?

Again my head swam and I found myself in a state of confusion and anxiety. Could I really afford to push him away by insisting on keeping things strictly platonic? What if I needed -- spiritually, psychologically, emotionally -- whatever he had to give me? Perhaps if I gave him a chance, he would "grow on me" and the idea of a physical relationship would seem only natural and desirable. But then again, this was not some arranged marriage -- why should I have to force myself?

It all became too nerve-racking for me, and I began to slip into my usual escape mode -- receding into the private chambers of my mind and just going through the motions. If I could not dissuade him from pursuing a sexual affair then maybe I ought to just go through with it, sleep with him once or twice and then make some excuse why I had to break it off. Hell, maybe I could even tell him I was gay.

Something had to give, and one night it did. After much anguished handwringing, one day I just called Mike and told him I needed to talk -- could we meet in a quiet, private place? He suggested I come down to his place of work, a dingy basement office in a parking garage off Ninth Avenue where he worked as a dispatcher for elevator repairs. I also asked him to buy me a bottle of wine because I felt it would relax me. I was torn between wanting to protect my fragile sense of self and my equally fervid desire to be as honest and sincere with him as he had been with me. I hated myself for my peculiar inability to be content and free in my own skin, for always needing to keep my "true self" in hiding. Why, oh why, couldn't I just be spontaneous, just be *with* someone instead of up in that lighthouse watching everything? I agreed to meet Mike after work in front of the Equitable building; from there we could hail a cab to his garage.

When we got there not a soul could be seen walking around and the whole area seemed desolate and abandoned, but then I was in no mood for midtown crowds. We went inside and I sat down in a cheap wooden chair across the room from several metal desks shoved together. Mike sat at one of the desks. I told him the bright overhead fluorescent lights bothered me; he shut them and turned on a small desk lamp instead. I took a few gulps of wine, then a few more, hoping to calm my agitated nerves. Finally, I began my own little "confession." I told him that while he seemed to regard me as a special person, a rare find, I was in fact a waste of his time, a hopelessly messed-up individual with whom he could not possibly consider having a serious relationship.

Mike, you don't understand -- I'm not the person you think you saw waiting at that bus stop. ..I'm not...not...normal. I mean, I'm not like other people. My mom had it right -- there really is something "off" about me. Yes, I am lonely sometimes, I know you picked up on that. But that doesn't mean that I want...or that I'm ready for...I mean I don't think I'm really ready right now for..."

I realized how pathetic I sounded and slowly began to cry. Through tears, I told him I was a misbegotten creature, a warped soul plodding my way along my own crooked path. And that path was a poorly lit narrow road that could only accommodate one. There were some folks, I suggested, who were simply meant to go through life alone. Besides, I wasn't a "real woman" in the sense he assumed, because I wasn't even sure if I wanted a boyfriend or a girlfriend. Imagine that? Sometimes, I haltingly explained as tears kept coursing down my cheeks, I feel like I need another woman to be intimate with rather than a man. Maybe that was because I never had a satisfying relationship with my mother. That is, my mother and I had never truly "bonded," which left me starved for maternal affection.

Throughout my miserable soliloquy Mike sat mesmerized. He just stared at me, taking it all in with a calm, understanding expression on his face, like a kindly shrink. At length he said, "That's okay -- it's okay to cry, Vicki. Cry your eyes out if you have to. I never saw a woman look so beautiful with tears flowin' down her face." This was pronounced with that soft charming Irish lilt which always sounded like poetry to me. As I grabbed another handful of tissues from the box on his desk to blow my nose, I blubbered, "Thank you. Thank you for understanding." I then poured what was left of the wine into my cup and drained it.

My memories of what came next are hazy. I know Mike had his arm around my shoulder as we left the building. Then we were in a cab, and then in the lobby of some tony downtown hotel, like the Four Seasons or the Ritz Carlton. Mike flashed his impressive blue and gold NYPD Detective Shield to someone at the reception desk and next thing I know we're in a four-star hotel suite with a built-in bar and velvet chenille drapes. Needless to say, all of my fears and misgivings flew out the window on a wine-colored cloud and we wound up in bed. I recall Mike being a very gentle and considerate lover, and obviously much more experienced than any man I'd ever been with. But I was too sloshed by then to be very responsive. I had left Mike's drab office feeling acutely uncomfortable -- totally exposed and raw, as if the top layer of my skin had just been sloughed off. And now it actually felt good to have his protective arms around me and to hear his gentle murmurings of reassurance. At least with Mike I could feel, if nothing else, completely safe.

After it was all over and I was back home and sober the following day, I reflected back on the entire scene and became nervous, shaky, and disoriented. I also felt incredibly lonesome. I had crossed a line I'd never intended to cross and now there was no turning back. It was all wrong. The long-awaited friendship with the "older man" that was supposed to enhance the quality of my life had instead brought only pain, confusion, and tears. And now guilt was added to the mix of emotions I felt. I hated myself for "leading him on," that is, for giving a fine, sensitive, compassionate man reason to hope for a kind of intimate loving connection with me that I knew could never blossom into anything real.

And why couldn't it? Because I was abnormal, cold, repressed, and "queer." I never should have accepted his gifts or gone out with him or let him trust me with his midnight confessions -- regardless of what Charles House had predicted at that stupid fortune-telling session. Fuck Charles House! Because of him two innocent unsuspecting people had come together only to hurt each other without meaning to. I had been thrown recklessly into a situation that not only caused me anguish but forced me to inflict pain on another. Shit, man, this whole thing should never have happened.

But it was even worse than this. Because now everything was in question -- my very identity, my integrity as a person. *Who* was that woman Mike had slept with last night? I tried to take a good look at her -- through HIS eyes. She was a shy lonely girl who didn't think very well of herself, a girl who had somehow been hurt in the past and now hid behind a protective shell in order to avoid being hurt again. A girl who was afraid of life and needed someone gentle and understanding like Mike to help coax her out of that shell and show her that life need not be so bad after all. Wasn't that the person he saw? I recalled what he had said the very first night we went out about wanting to "bring me out of myself."

Okay, but was the person whom Mike saw really *me*? I didn't think so. I felt that what I *really* was, was something he couldn't see. It was the old existential dilemma of who or what "the real me" actually was. Not long before all of this happened, I had been reading a fascinating book by the famous Scottish psychiatrist R. D. Laing. Something I read there began to come back to me now with a disturbing sense of recognition. Recalling it, I felt a shiver.

The title of the slim volume was *The Divided Self*, and its author had devoted much of his practice to the study and treatment of schizophrenics. Laing had a unique theory which claimed that full-blown schizophrenia was in fact the end product of a long series of subtle changes in a person's relationship with self and others, and that many individuals with psychological disorders were stuck at various points along that spectrum. One of the earliest stopping places on that long road to schizophrenia was what he called "the unembodied self." This occurs when an individual experiences his true self as being somehow detached from or independent of his body. While his body is out there in the real world, mechanically performing a pantomime of living, his true self exists in a pristine bubble, uncontaminated by contact with mere mortals, not subject to exposure or scrutiny, untested, unchallenged, and therefore full of infinite possibility. Such a sense of detachment and superiority had always been, for me, a form of defense, a protective device similar to a coat of armor.

But Laing had gone on to describe how this led invariably to the next stage, as the person realizes that his or her coping strategy isn't working. I grabbed the book from my bookshelf to find the exact passage:

> The individual who may at one time have felt predominantly 'outside' the life going on *there*, which he affects to despise as petty and commonplace compared to the richness he has *here*, inside himself, now longs to get *inside* life again, and get life *inside* himself, so dreadful is his inner deadness.

As I read those words I thought of how much of my nearly thirty years on earth had been spent in a conjured-up fantasy world that more resembled those tapestries at the *Cafe des Artistes* than anything to do with reality. I'd spent my years in fond imaginings of how wonderful life could be *if only* I had this, that, or the other. Mike was right. I was no less a prisoner than he had been, locked up behind self-made bars. I knew how hyper-conscious I was, how unable to enjoy anything spontaneously, to just let myself go and "get lost" in an activity or experience without the help of alcohol or pot. No wonder I was no good at sex. My relationship with others and with the world itself was always at one remove. Real life, apparently, was just too much for me to handle and now the condition was becoming pathological. Maybe I really did need to see a psychiatrist.

As I began anxiously trying to analyze all of this and determine what it meant, still another sentence from *The Divided Self* caught my eye and cut me to the quick:

> The schizoid individual exists under the black sun, the evil eye, of his own scrutiny. The glare of his awareness kills his spontaneity, his freshness: it destroys all joy. Everything withers under it.

Indeed. And now the promise of a new relationship or even just a new friendship had withered away because of my sickness. After that eye-opening night of wine and tears, I slept with Mike one more time in another fancy hotel room in Manhattan, but without the oblivion caused by alcohol. It soon became obvious to him that the magic he craved was just not there, that his ardent kisses and caresses could not kindle the flames of romance and sexual intimacy he had been missing and yearning for for so long. Mike could see that my heart was not in it, much less my body. We remained friends but went out together less frequently.

Then one day Mike received a letter from a man who had been the chaplain at the federal prison in Pennsylvania where he had been incarcerated. A fellow Irishman, the chaplain had told his recently divorced cousin, a gal named Margaret, all about Mike's life and character, thinking she'd be impressed. She was. Margaret was also originally from County Donegal and she jumped at the chance to be introduced to such an interesting countryman. In the letter to Mike he included Margaret's phone number and suggested that he call her in Minnesota where she now lived alone. Mike decided to call, and soon there was a flurry of letters between them and an exchange of photos.

The next thing I knew Mike was boarding a plane to meet Margaret in person. Evidently, the meeting went extremely well because when he returned, he told me he would soon be moving to Minneapolis! We met one last time for coffee and I bid him adieu and good luck. I sincerely wished him and his new lady all the best and returned to my uneventful life. I breathed a sigh of relief, even if it was suffused with a sense of sadness. It had all been quite an adventure but also a sobering learning experience that I would not soon forget.

19
Sweet Georgia Brown

THE FIRST THING I noticed was the purple eye shadow. A vivid shade of purple with a bit of glitter in it. It perfectly matched the odd briefcase she carried around. A hard hefty metal box that resembled a piece of luggage except that it was shiny and bright purple. She was the new Systems Administrator from Data Processing one floor below who had been sent up to our floor in order to preside over the company-wide conversion to the Wang Word Processing system.

It was the early 1980s and a wondrous new device had arrived on the scene, one that would change the nature of office work forever. It was not so much the machine itself -- versions of the personal computer had been introduced by Commodore, Radio Shack, and others a couple of years before. Rather it was the magical software that came with it. The *Wang OIS* terminal with its built-in word processor made its debut, promising a mini-revolution for secretaries and administrative assistants the world over. The old reliable *IBM Selectric* typewriter was fast becoming obsolete, soon to be relegated to the dustbin of techno history. Likewise, sliding cartridges and liquid white-out would soon be relics of the past, no longer needed in the super-efficient new world of digital word processing.

The entire secretarial pool in our department was about to be turned upside down. Everything would have to be revamped and rewired and a brand new *Wang* machine mounted on every desk. It was a major installation and would be followed by an intensive training program for the secretaries. A huge mainframe computer was to be set up in a separate glass-enclosed room and a “client-server” network would be created, linking every *Wang* terminal to the central database. It had been years since the legal department had undergone such a massive undertaking and we all had to expect some disruption in our daily routines. I was informed that my entire office would be torn down and replaced by two gray cubicles.

As the work proceeded, I wondered who would be occupying the cubicle in front of mine. There had been some talk in the department about hiring a second paralegal, due to the increased workload. But I did not recall seeing any new faces coming in for interviews. One morning I was sitting at my big wooden desk -- all that remained of my lovely private office after they knocked the walls down -- idly stirring a cup of coffee. Waiting for an assignment from Mr. Stumpf and having no other work to attend to, I was watching the workmen put the finishing touches on the cubicle that would adjoin mine. It was almost complete and a fresh out of the box black *Wang* terminal was in the process of being hooked up. I could surmise that my new office mate would not be a typist because all of them worked on the other side of the floor. Nor would she be an executive secretary, as they all sat at desks right outside the offices of the attorneys they worked for.

So I asked someone if they knew who the new workstation was for. "Oh, that's for the Systems Administrator," he replied. "She will be running the computer room and training the secretaries in Word Perfect."

I felt somewhat imposed upon. The space had been vacant ever since the remodeling of the area where the paralegals and legal proofreaders and the rest of us non-lawyers worked. Solid walls had come down, fine old wooden desks were removed, and our modest offices were replaced by drab gray cells the size of toilet stalls, separated by cheesy partitions with the consistency of cork. At least they were perfectly suitable for shoving push pins into, offering the consolation of seeing pictures of your kids, dogs, and last vacation while slaving away at your little counter. As long as the cubicle in front of me had no occupant, I had been able to enjoy a modicum of privacy despite no longer having a door to close.

But now that privacy was about to be invaded, even if for only a few months. I was not happy. Making matters worse, I soon gathered that Ms. Purple -- whose actual name was Roxanne -- was a typical so-called Type A personality – driven, ambitious, always "on." She was also quite the "people person," with a ready 100-watt smile for everyone on every occasion. How lovely, I thought, but it will all be wasted on me. Perhaps when she realized she was sitting in front of an antisocial eccentric she would ask to be transferred to another workstation and I would get my peace and solitude back.

Alas, it was not to be. Roxanne settled into her new home contentedly, pleased that it was only a few yards walk to the computer mainframe room where she would be spending much of her time. She introduced herself in as friendly a manner as possible and asked for my name. My introversion and unsocial attitude appeared to pose a special challenge for Roxanne which she was evidently all too happy to take on. Within a few days of settling in, she made a point of loudly greeting me each morning as I walked past her on the way to my cubicle, as if to shame me for walking in unsmiling and without a word or glance at anyone, as was my wont. Sometimes she would pop in when things were slow and start impromptu conversations, trying to draw me out.

I noted her sweet, crisp, not at all drawly Southern accent. It was subtle but unmistakable. She told me she was a native of Savannah, Georgia, whose family had eventually moved to a suburb outside Atlanta. She graduated from Georgia Tech with a degree in Business Administration. Roxanne had a curvy figure and a penchant for frilly blouses and lacy, Peter Pan collars. Her eyes were oval and hazel-toned, resembling tiny pools of molten gold and certainly did not require so much eye makeup. With her curly light auburn locks and fetching expressions she reminded me a little of Shirley Temple. I could almost hear strains of *On the Good Ship Lollipop* as she approached. Indeed, her rather aggressive and cloying femininity seemed designed to throw my near defiant *un*-femininity into stark relief.

Well, perhaps that's what Roxanne was after, because before long she was asking me why I wore pants or slacks to work every day, never a skirt or a dress. Then there was talk of introducing me to male friends of hers. Would I like to meet a guy, or did I already have a boyfriend? She made teasing remarks about my motorcycle jacket and Timberland boots and noted with approval that I appeared to be a "free spirit." I began to feel vaguely resentful yet somewhat intrigued, maybe even a bit flattered, at all the unsolicited attention.

Roxanne was, to put it plainly, a flirt and a tease. That this was no secret to others became obvious through snatches of inter-office gossip and whispers in the ladies' room. The odd thing though, was that she deployed her ingratiating smiles, honey-toned voice and excessive attentions no less with women than with men. There were echoes of Julia from back in college, but with an added touch of ruthlessness. Roxanne latched onto anyone who could advance her career ambitions and was on quite a track, having already worked herself up via nighttime computer courses from a modest accounting job to Systems Administrator. I was surprised to find her on a first-name basis with the Chairman and CEO of the company, an amiable chap who every so often would appear unexpectedly downstairs in the lobby or on an elevator. She even occasionally went out dancing with one of the company Vice Presidents. Clearly, she knew the game of how to curry favor with all the higher-ups, and I heard someone who ought to know refer to her as "a first-class bullshit artist."

Okay, fine, I thought, but what on earth could she want with me? There was nothing I could do to help catapult her to the next rung of the career ladder or get in good with the company's movers and shakers. That question loomed a lot larger after she did something that both embarrassed and confused me. At our office, whenever it was somebody's birthday, a card would be passed around and everyone -- lawyers, secretaries, even the guy in the mail room would sign it. When that person came back from lunch they would find the birthday card sitting on their desk. A nice gesture of office camaraderie.

So, when my birthday came up about a month after Roxanne came on board I returned from lunch expecting to see the usual envelope on my desk. But there was none. Had they forgotten, I wondered? Then, a few minutes later I see Roxanne hurrying down the hallway with a grin on her face, brandishing a large bouquet of fresh flowers. She headed straight for me and handed them over while intoning in a singsong voice, "Happy *Birth*-day, Victoria. Happy *Birth*-day to you." I looked at her as though she were nuts, wondering how much that cost and whose idea it was. Had everyone chipped in? Or was it just Roxanne's quirky notion? But why...?

After that there were invitations to go out to lunch. That was a nonstarter. My lunch hour was sacrosanct and utterly private. This was my only time to get away from everyone, to seek refuge in the anonymity of city streets and get lost in my own musings. I rarely if ever ate on my lunch hour, usually being satisfied with a cup of coffee, tea, or hot chocolate. But Roxanne didn't seem the least bit deterred by this -- indeed, her little treks to my cubicle for spur of the moment conversation became, if anything, more frequent. I began to feel trapped and wished she would just go away. How much longer, I thought impatiently, would this *Wang* conversion project take?

But short of being outright rude, there wasn't a whole lot I could do about it. One day it was, *OK, if you don't do lunch then how about a few drinks after work?* This sounded even more absurd to me. Not once in almost seven years of working there had I ever gone out for drinks with coworkers. But one evening we had both been working late and were getting ready to wrap it up when Roxanne announced that she would be stopping by the local watering hole with one of the young lawyers in the department. Why don't I come along for once, she implored. I thought -- ah what the hell, let me go just this one time before everyone thinks I'm a certifiable misanthrope, or else so totally bereft of the social graces that I can't even bear to be in other people's company.

Inside the noisy bar the three of us took a table in the back, ordered some food, and I tried to get into the spirit by ordering a glass of wine for myself. Brendan, the lawyer, and Roxanne began to engage in conversation. He was one of the many men who had apparently fallen into Roxanne's cleverly woven web of innocent flattery and flirtation. Fairly young and single, Brendan was something of a rising star in the department, well on his way to a corner office with a view. Perhaps he thought that would impress Roxanne, because he had asked her out a few times and she had mostly declined, offering excuses. Maybe Roxanne had asked me to tag along just so Brendan would have no illusions that this was a "date."

Listening to their talk, I couldn't help but notice what a sharp and breezy conversationalist Roxanne was. She seemed able to converse on any subject, work-related or otherwise: the turmoil in the Middle East, Reagan's tax policies, the film *Chariots of Fire*, the Pope, the "magical realism" of famed novelist Gabriel Garcia Marquez. And she discussed these things in a strikingly intelligent and discerning manner, making interesting remarks and pointed observations. Brendan could scarcely keep up, and eventually he said he had to leave. But Roxanne and I stayed, continuing the thread of discourse. I was surprised to find how many ideas and points of view we had in common and could barely remember the last time I'd had such a stimulating talk with anyone.

Before we left I asked her what she thought of Brendan. Her surprisingly flippant answer was, "I don't date short men."

This lady was a piece of work, alright. As I would walk over to the secretarial pool with some letters I needed typed up, I'd often spot her sitting in the large glass-enclosed room where the massive mainframe computer, to which all the smaller terminals were connected, resided in all of its high tech glory. There all by herself sat Roxanne, eyes intent on a control panel, pushing this button or that to do who knew what. She made a rather imposing presence sitting there in her dark business suit, oblivious to all besides the mysterious workings of the big beeping machine. I began to pay more attention to her as she managed the formidable task of turning all the gals in the typing pool -- most of whom had never so much as sat in front of a computer -- into skillful and competent word processors.

I could see that she was an excellent trainer who knew how to make the learning curve fun and not in the least intimidating. All the secretaries enjoyed working with her. I was impressed at how well Roxanne had mastered this stuff herself, and could sit in front of the keyboard clicking away with ease. The results were impressive -- sharp, professional looking documents that made the older slightly yellowed letters and memos, often peppered with dabs of *Wite-Out* or bits of correction tape to hide typos, look like something dug out of an old trunk. She may well have been a bullshit artist and a ruthless career climber but there was no denying her intelligence, adeptness, and thorough professionalism. I began to suspect that some of the unkind gossip I'd heard about her was motivated more by sheer envy than anything else.

As time passed I had to admit that Roxanne was starting to grow on me, and I could feel myself tentatively beginning to thaw out and open up to her. Her attentions to me did not slacken, despite her heavy workload. During downtimes at work, she would trot over to my cubicle to talk, dragging a chair in. Her conversations also got more personal and revealing. I learned that she had a nine-year-old son but was no longer involved with his father. That only recently she had been dating a married businessman but that he, fearing his wife would find out, had broken it off. That she had something of a "wild side" and had run around with a biker gang back in Georgia for a few years. That notwithstanding her apparent gregariousness and social finesse, she could count on one hand her really "true friends." That she always felt she was searching for some ultimate something, something which despite her seeming successes had eluded her.

At times, while sitting and talking like this she would manage to gently touch my shoulder, tap my knee, or casually slip her hand on my thigh in a pat or little caress, as if to emphasize a point. Sometimes she would notice a necklace or pendant I was wearing and take hold of it, asking where I'd gotten it, etc. Was she actually flirting with me, I thought? Is this just her standard repertoire or was I being singled out for special treatment? Had she sensed something about me, that I was, well, "different"? Slowly, like someone just in from the cold warming his hands by the fireplace, I began to succumb to the warm glow generated by her constant attentions. At length I got up the nerve to return some of these physical gestures, to walk into her cubicle and place my hands on her shoulders with a tiny squeeze, just to see how she'd react. She always reacted with a coy smile. By now I was no longer rolling my eyes at her approach, no longer wishing she would go away.

I became increasingly confused at the same time as I was becoming increasingly smitten. I could sense the same feelings welling up in me as I'd experienced shortly after meeting Lorraine. This was especially so after Roxanne had revealed those personal things to me, unveiling a sensitive, yearning side of herself that I doubted she exposed to many people. I knew she had touched me in a way that completely dissipated all the annoyance, irritation, and resentment I had initially harbored. Despite my attempts to shield it, she had managed to pierce the crusty armor around my heart and get right to the sweet spot. A red warning flag began waving in my mind bidding me to tread very carefully lest I find myself on dangerous ground. But it was too late. I had already begun slipping into the quicksand.

By October, Roxanne, who had been working so hard getting sixteen secretaries successfully acclimated to the Wang Word Processor, was due for some kind of vacation. One day she came running into my cubicle and giddily announced that a friend of hers had just Fed-Exed her a plane ticket to Acapulco where he was staying on business. He invited her to fly out for a week in the sun. Roxanne, as if thinking it might be of concern, made a point of assuring me he was "just a friend" and there was "nothing romantic" involved. The last Friday before she was to leave, she invited me out for a toast to her achievements and a happy send-off to the warm sands and blue seas of the legendary Mexican fun spot.

We had more than a toast. We spent hours talking about all kinds of things and Roxanne revealed more and more of her secret dreams and longings. I was touched by the way she seemed to trust me, to feel she could confide in me without fear of judgment or betrayal. I was probably on my third Tequila & Soda when I found myself placing my hand on top of hers as she disclosed some particularly intimate detail of her past, tenderly caressing it as she spoke. In my half drunken haze I noticed that she did not flinch or squirm or seem the least bit uncomfortable. I excused myself for a trip to the ladies' room; my head was spinning with delight and something like love sickness. Leaving the bar, we hailed a cab to drop her off at Penn Station where she would catch her train back home to Long Island; then the taxi would take me to my apartment on West 77th Street.

As the cab pulled up in front of Penn Station to let Roxanne out, I leaned over to wish her a wonderful trip and give her a quick hug. Though her hand was on the door handle she had not yet pushed the door open nor taken her eyes off mine. After I had said my goodbye she just continued looking at me intently. Did she want to say something else? Or.... Next thing I knew I had moved my face to hers and was kissing her full on the mouth. We lingered a few seconds in what for me was a moment of sheer bliss. Then she smiled at me, said not another word, and got out of the cab. I looked at the cab driver who had a somewhat bemused look on his face. The poor guy -- he's probably thinking: *only in New York,* I thought to myself with a smile.

Roxanne spent that next week lying on a beach, swimming, snorkeling, and sightseeing. I spent that weekend lying on my pullout bed dizzy and feeling that at any moment I could dissolve into slush like a melting snowman, so much had the icy walls of my self-built safe house come tumbling down. I was hopelessly, almost hysterically, in love and it felt wonderful. Time for hallelujahs and prayers of thanks because, after such a long lonely drought the clouds had burst and it was raining like mad. And -- unlike in times past -- the one who's captured my heart feels the same way about me, judging from what happened in that cab.

I was back in the office on Tuesday, having taken a "sick day" Monday, the better to revel in my newfound rapture. For the first time in I couldn't remember how long, I was able to shower my coworkers with smiles and good cheer without having to fake it. A few days later I came back to my cubicle after doing some research in the law library and saw a large postcard on my desk. There was a beautiful photograph of a sunset over the Pacific and on the other side was handwritten: *Having a lovely time. Just wish you were here. Love, Roxanne.* I felt pangs of love and warmth and spent most of the afternoon trying to picture the scene in my mind: Roxanne lying on a blanket next to her friend, or sipping cocktails with him while gazing out at ocean waves, or dancing dirty at some Acapulco disco, all the while wishing it was me beside her instead!

When Roxanne returned all I wanted to do was wait on her hand and foot. I would show up with her favorite tea and croissants in the morning, run errands for her when she was busy and bring her little gifts like stuffed animals and miniature cloisonné boxes. Both of us were swamped with work that fall and she was often away from her desk, but we still managed to get together for an occasional drink after work. Those were long nights of deep discussions and revealing conversations, then walking slightly inebriated and red-faced to the train and kissing goodnight on the platform. No doubt my odd behavior raised more than a few eyebrows among my coworkers, and I did make some effort to keep my feelings under wraps, but it was like trying to suppress a blush. I could scarcely believe that only a few months ago I had almost dreaded the approach of this sweet-talking sophisticated Southern belle with her over-the-top eye makeup, constant chatter, and fondness for teasing. Now I could barely keep from peeking around the partition of my cubicle to see if she was coming by. And whenever she did, we would steal as much time as we could spare to engage in pleasant chitchat, laughter, and gentle ribbing.

The Thanksgiving weekend approached and, while our office did not close on the Friday after Thanksgiving Day, almost everyone including me took the day off as a vacation day. When I asked Roxanne about her plans for the long holiday weekend, she told me that she was planning to come in on Friday to get some important work done in the morning. Given her work ethic I was not surprised, but then she added, "Nobody does any real work after lunch, we just kind of drink and party." "No kidding," I replied. Then she said, "Don't take the day off ... come to work Friday, you'll see."

Sure enough, Friday turned out to be a dress-down, no pressure, kick off your shoes kind of day. Only a handful of people showed up and we all worked steadily through the morning. But at lunch time I went looking for Roxanne and found her in the computer room. Placing my hands on her shoulders and giving a gentle squeeze, I asked her if she was about ready to go out for lunch. She said she'd be ready in a few minutes and told me she had invited a couple of friends from her old stomping grounds -- the Data Processing department on the 34th floor -- to join us.

We wound up at *McCann's*, the nearby spacious bar/restaurant where almost everyone from the office hung out. We feasted on chicken wings, nachos and similar salty fare designed to stimulate thirst and downed numerous beers over a span of several hours. One of Roxanne's friends mentioned that she had managed to get hold of some last-minute tickets to a Rod Stewart concert at Madison Square Garden. It was to be that very night. She had three extra tickets -- enough for all of us. So we decided to head for the Garden. A quick dash back to the office to tidy up our desks and get our stuff, then we hopped on the subway. But when we got to Madison Square Garden it turned out that the seats we had were very high up and behind the stage!

It was hardly worth it. But, what to do? Roxanne suggested we go to a dance club she'd heard a lot about and always wanted to try called *The Mudd Club*. This place was a funky downtown alternative to the glitz, velvet ropes and V.I.P. rooms of better known clubs like *Studio 54*, and it was celebrated especially for its underground and experimental music. Roxanne's two friends decided that back of the stage seats were still better than nothing and went to the concert. That left just me and Roxanne.

However, it was still way too early to go out clubbing in New York. So Roxanne asked me if we could maybe buy a bottle of wine and hang out at my place for a few hours before it was time to go. I was thrilled at the thought and dared let my imagination off its leash. Tonight, I decided, will be the night we finish what first started in that cab back in October. It was only my shyness and fear of rejection that had kept our budding romance from taking the next logical step. But with the help of some adult beverages, trippy music, and low lights ...well, anything was possible.

We hailed a cab and I gave the driver my address. On the way Roxanne wanted to stop and run into the liquor store for the wine as I began to get dizzy with anticipation. When we got to my place Roxanne seemed impressed by the handsome brownstone building, which sat just a few houses away from lovely Riverside Drive, with its expansive park and panoramic views of the Hudson. But when I unlocked my door I felt ashamed of the smallness and drabness of my studio apartment and began to apologize. She cut me off saying she thought it was quite cozy and charming.

She took a chair at the kitchen table while I sat on the convertible sofa. Suddenly I saw her pull a small paper bag out of her purse. She reached into the bag and pulled out two plump, very nicely rolled joints and a cigarette lighter. "Oh!" I exclaimed, surprised. "You brought some weed?" She said she had gotten it from a favorite cousin who had showed up for Thanksgiving dinner the day before. "Cousin Lamar gets only the best smoke. This shit is dynamite."

With that she lit one of the joints, took a deep drag, and handed it to me. "Hmmn," I thought, "if only those corporate suits in the law department could see her now." I tried the grass and it hit me right away. "Wow, this is powerful stuff," I said with a cough. Fifteen minutes later -- or was it just two minutes later? -- we were convulsed with laughter and Roxanne's face and features took on a surreal and dreamy aspect that was a bit startling.

Who is this strange and fascinating creature sitting at my kitchen table looking straight at me with delinquent eyes and a wayward smile?

What was she doing in my life? The wine tasted like candy, and we drained the bottle in no time. Bizarrely, my mind flashed back to the second grade with me and my classmates secretly sampling bits and gobs of that sweet white paste that came in a big plastic tub -- the stuff we used for gluing pieces of construction paper together. It must have been milk sugar we were tasting -- how else to explain the picture of a cow at the top of the glue container? For a while everything became one-dimensional and cartoon-like and painted in bold primary colors. At length, someone looked at the clock on the kitchen wall and, laughing, tried to read what time it was. It seemed like it might be time to head out to the club.

Since we were too stoned to find our way to the precise Tribeca location via subway, we resorted once again to the old faithful school-bus-yellow NYC taxicab. We found the address on White Street and entered the club. The dance floor was packed with swaying body forms and serious reggae music pulsated throughout the room -- a space which resembled a cave lit by torches. Roxanne and I soon lost sight of each other as we squeezed in among the dancers to find a patch of floor space. Immediately guys began asking me to dance and at one point I looked across the floor and saw Roxanne dancing with some dreadlocked dude. The music was mesmerizing and it soon felt as if we were all partaking in some ancient religious ritual, joyfully on our way to ecstatic communion with the gods.

Then I noticed Roxanne coming straight toward me with a drink from the bar, which she handed to me while asking if I was having a good time. I guess she didn't think I was quite plastered enough. I drank the concoction unable to guess what it was made of, not that it would have mattered. Roxanne and I danced together for a while, then another guy broke in and once more she was off to the nether regions of the dance floor. Later on there was a live act, which gave everyone a chance to ratchet down the frenzied motion and stand to face the stage. As I was trying to determine on a scale of one to ten just how high I was, I saw Roxanne moving toward me again, drink in hand. Again, the drink was for me. It occurred to me that I hadn't seen her drinking at all that night other than the wine at my apartment. I took the libation, and twenty minutes later came another, then another still.

It must have been about 4:30 in the morning when we finally left the club. Obviously at that hour Roxanne would have to crash at my place. When I asked her about her son she said he was staying over a friend's home for the weekend. So back we went to my cozy cubbyhole. Immediately she sat down at the kitchen table and removed her jacket, then began removing other articles of clothing. Luckily the apartment was toasty warm and comfy on that windless night, which was not always the case. No need for the heavy flannel PJ's tonight. I hung up my coat and proceeded to set up the convertible bed. As I embarrassingly pulled out the thin mattress I cursed my luck for making too modest a salary to afford even a decent bed, much less a decent-sized apartment. But Roxanne scarcely seemed to notice as she continued unbuttoning her blouse. When she was down to her bra she cocked her head, shot me a teasing glance, and quipped in that subtle Southern accent, "Well, where am *I* going to sleep?"

By now I had stripped down to my bra and underwear and was lying on my back on the mattress. I slid myself over a bit to the far side of the bed, patted the space next to me and said, with a voice that sounded far off as if it were coming from a ventriloquist's dummy, "Well, honey, you can sleep right here next to me." At that, Roxanne's bra came off exposing two ripe globular breasts capped by soft brown nipples that reminded me of rose petals. She got up, breasts bouncing gently, and came toward the bed. She slithered around the side and the next thing I knew this incredible creature was lying flat on her back by my side.

In a moment I was on top of her. Tentatively, shyly, hands and mouth began roaming over her silky body. I planted gentle kisses on every part of her face, stroked the long velvety limbs, kissed and caressed her shoulders and neck and half-whispered *I love you*, trying not to slur those critical words. She squirmed in what I took to be childish delight and her undulating body under mine seemed to respond to my every movement. By turns I sipped slowly on each sepia-toned medallion atop those creamy orbs of flesh. She breathily murmured something which I couldn't make out. I responded with French kisses.

At last my fingers crawled by slow degrees to the outer band of her panties as I looked at her face to gauge her reaction. She looked a bit nervous and hesitant, saying "But Vicki, I've never done this before." So I backed off, secretly relieved because in my besotted condition I doubted my ability to perform. Instead I just laughed, slid over onto my side, reached out and stroked her cheek. She seemed to be speechless but happy and there was this radiant little smile on her face that never faltered. After a while she returned the gesture, stroking my face and looking like a grateful puppy, overjoyed to be so loved and wanted. I kind of wished she would say something more, or even ask a question. But since she didn't I just reached out and held her and we lay there, somewhat exhausted, in a languid embrace until slipping off into slumber.

We didn't get up until about two o'clock Saturday afternoon. We were both pretty hungover, especially me, and Roxanne had to get home to pick up her son. So, amidst all the confusion we set about gathering Roxanne's things; I hastily pushed back the bed and replaced the sofa cushions, then picked up empty wine bottles and burnt-out joints while she showered and dressed. Then it was off to Penn Station to make a 3:49pm train. Just a brief hug and then she was off. My head reeling, I stopped into a *Dunkin' Donuts* on 34th Street for a strong black coffee and bought a box of aspirin before catching the No.1 subway home.

Back at work the following Monday, Roxanne was caught up in meetings. The project of transforming the law department's typing pool into an efficient word processing center was going well, but there were still various logistic and budget issues to hammer out. For a while that week she spent most of the workday on the 34th floor below, where the IT department was, and only appeared on my floor briefly, hard at work in the computer room. I would just sit and stare at the empty cubicle in front of me in despair and longing. We had barely spoken since Friday night. Nor had we gone to lunch or out for drinks after work. I was dying to know what she thought and felt about what had happened. Since she hadn't told me, I was left to my own devices to infer what it all meant to her.

Over and over again I replayed scenes from Friday night in a theater of my memory. The way she had looked lying on the bed next to me, that seeming expression of relief and gratitude on her face, the barely concealed excitement and sense of wonder in her golden eyes, the way she had stroked my arm, held my hand. Then I flashed back to that lovely *Just wish you were here* postcard she had sent me from Acapulco, to the look on her face after the tender kiss in the cab and the way she had slightly hesitated in getting out of the car as if she had expected and wanted me to do it. And then, rewinding even further back: how she had smiled that night at the bar when I caressed her hand as she was revealing personal matters, the bouquet of flowers on my birthday, the constant visits to my cubicle even when I'd shown no interest in engaging in small talk.

There could be no doubt about it now. Roxanne had been mysteriously attracted to me from the very start and was perhaps surprised by the feeling. Now she had come to know herself better, to realize the startling truth as to why past relationships with men had gone sour, why she felt that something had been missing in her life, why there was that subtle simmering discontent even when outwardly all was going superbly, why she was forever "searching." There was no question about it -- Friday night had been a wonderful revelation to her and now, perhaps, she was struggling to process it all. The demands of work had intervened to take her mind off what surely must be disturbing and disorienting. So keeping busy at the job was a needed distraction. Yes, I had rocked her world! And now I just had to give her some time to confront the issue head-on and accept what she had learned about herself. That what she had really always wanted was a woman, and that woman was me!

So I tried to be patient and give her as much time as she needed. But by Friday, an entire week having passed since our intimate encounter without a word from her about it, I couldn't resist calling her at her office on the 34th floor. She was not in at the time, but a secretary took a message. Roxanne did not get back to me for hours, not until a quarter to five, when I was getting ready to leave for the day. When I picked up the phone she sounded tired. I told her sweetly that I had "missed her" all week, and just wanted to see how she was doing. She replied, somewhat impatiently I thought, that she had been overwhelmed with work and hardly knew what day it was. "*But thank God it's Friday, right!*" I said cheerfully, and asked her if she'd like to meet me for a drink afterwards. She said no, she had to work late and offered no alternative time to meet. Seeing that she was clearly exhausted, I had no choice but to wish her a pleasant weekend and hang up the phone. As I did so I felt the slightest chill.

Why, I wondered, had she not invited me to her house for the weekend? Several times in the past she had mentioned how she would love for me to come out to Long Island sometime and see her home, meet her son. Yet weekend after weekend had passed with no invitation. But now -- especially now -- wouldn't she be ripe for the chance to take our fledgling romance naturally to its next stage? You know, to further explore the strange and wondrous feelings and sensations that had gushed forth like a fountain on that magical night? Instead, her voice had sounded dry, bored even. I replayed the phone call over and over in my mind. I could hear no warmth really, no hint of affection or tenderness. Tired or not, is that any way to talk to a lover? In fact, I was forced to admit, the way she sounded it was as if last Friday night had never happened.

I spent the weekend fretting over it, pacing the worn linoleum floor in my studio, and wondering if I should dare call her at home. Did she just need more time? Was it just too much for her to handle? Or was the problem my own shyness? All I wanted to say to her was -- darling, please let's continue from where we left off. Now that you made me love you ("*I didn't wanna do it, I didn't wanna do it…*" as the old song goes) you can't just walk away. But I couldn't get up the courage, just didn't have the nerve. Also, I didn't want to push her. She had a right to sort it all out herself, at her own pace. Still, I wished she would share some of it with me.

I went back to the office Monday resolved not to let a whole other week go by without spending some time with Roxanne, even if it was just over a cup of coffee on a ten-minute break. Roxanne was still super busy and not around much, but I called and left a message saying I needed to talk to her. When she finally got back to me on the phone her first words were, "What was it you wanted to talk about?" and I suddenly felt like someone standing on the sidewalk who'd just gotten splashed by a car careening through a puddle after a heavy rain. "Man, as if you didn't know what I want to talk about!" I thought angrily. But I calmed down and said that since we hadn't talked in a while I thought it might be nice to get together for a bite or a walk or whatever. She agreed to meet for lunch at a local eatery.

Although the place we chose was packed with office workers we managed to squeeze into a pint-sized booth in a corner near the window. After ordering our sandwiches, I looked at her steadily and asked her how the project was going and about other work-related issues. She seemed anxious to vent and I listened attentively. Then there were a few minutes of silence as I looked through the window out onto Avenue of the Americas, watching the tourists flocking to nearby Radio City Music Hall or to NBC Studios for the tour, or even for fine dining high up in the sky at the Rainbow Room. Finally the food came. After eating we ordered coffee and desert and, while sticking a fork into my thick wedge of New York cheesecake as Roxanne gazed calmly out the window, I couldn't resist. And so, feeling the heat rising in my face, I looked right into her eyes and said,

"I really enjoyed that night at the *Mudd Club*. It was wonderful, don't you think?"

I braced myself for her reply. At first, she looked down at the table for a few seconds. Then she lifted her eyes and said:

"Yeah, it's all kind of a blur now, but it was, well. . . I guess you could call it, you know, a pretty interesting experience. It really was."

Then she turned her attention to the slice of key lime pie on her plate and looked away. "Well, would you wanna do it again?" I managed to blurt out without thinking. "Do what again?" she said, "Go to a club? Yeah sure, maybe someday. Right now all I'm thinking about is getting this damn project finished."

Then she began telling me about a new position that had been posted on the jobs bulletin board at work. The IT department, then in the process of expanding and moving its operations to a building across the street from current headquarters, needed a Data Base Administrator. Roxanne said it would be a prestigious position and would mean a nice jump in salary. She told me she was a bit anxious about applying but had made up her mind to go for it.

I listened but could hardly hear anything. So that blissful night was, to her, *all kind of a blur*? And what happened between those sheets merely a *pretty interesting experience*? I was shocked and confused. But wait, I thought -- what about all those knowing looks, the soft touches, the sweet whispers, those tender caresses, what about all that had passed between us during all those weeks and months? The thrilling way she had responded to my lovemaking. Surely she felt something for me, something that would be plain and obvious to any objective observer. Why would she run away from those feelings? She was in deep denial, I concluded. And all of this preoccupation with work and with landing this new job was nothing more than a sublimation of her true feelings, a thinly veiled attempt to harness and enlist their energy and power in the service of her naked career ambitions.

Should I confront her about this, I asked myself. Or should I just wait until she comes to her senses. But my patience was wearing thin, and I wondered how long I could hold out. Very long, as it turned out. Over the next several weeks I tried to recapture her affection by demonstrating just how much I cared. I got my hopes up by imagining that Roxanne's real problem was actually her *own* fear of rejection. In truth, I decided, she felt exactly as I did and was secretly dying to declare her love but dreaded looking embarrassed and foolish should it turn out that I had no such feelings in return.

So I began to practically follow her around. If she was working downstairs I'd go down to bring her tea and croissants every morning. If I spotted her with her arms folded in the icy computer room I'd go in there with a sweater. When she complained about holes in her stockings I'd run down to the five and dime and buy her some new ones. I would pass her little notes of encouragement and support, or to wish her good luck in her job application, or to tell her I looked forward to going out for lunch again. I bought her flowers and chocolates on her birthday.

Roxanne seemed slightly amused by these fawning behaviors but genuinely appreciative. Nevertheless, whenever we went out for lunch the talk was strictly business; there was no more drinking after work and the long-awaited invitation to her home on the Island never came. Over and over in my mind I would run the memory reel again and review all those past scenes, the telling gestures, the body language, the tone of her voice, in order to convince myself that she was as infatuated with me as I was with her. She chooses to suppress and deny it, is all. Someday, I thought. Some day. But what was to be done? I was no psychiatrist or Freudian analyst who could strip away the veils and compel her to face the truth about herself. So in the meanwhile all I could do was wallow in the loneliness of being in love all by myself.

Getting more and more desperate, I debated whether or not to simply force the issue. To insist that she sit down with me somewhere, put all thoughts of work and career out of her mind for the moment, and talk about what was going on between her and me and what it had all been about from the beginning. But if I did that, I knew that even one flippant remark, skeptical glance or a look that said "Where did you ever get *that* idea?" would cut me to the quick. And gradually, bit by bit, even as I tried to keep it at bay, the real truth began to creep out of its hiding place like some nocturnal animal that refuses to expose its face to the light of day.

Roxanne -- "bullshit artist" that she was -- was in no denial whatsoever. She had known all along exactly what she was doing. Adventurous, opportunistic, and always in the market for any knowledge, information, or inside scoop that might somehow prove profitable in the future, she had targeted me in order to satisfy her curiosity. She had sensed what I was and, perhaps somewhat intrigued and somewhat desirous of adding another feather of conquest to her cap, she became determined to insinuate her way into my life and into my affections, using whatever methods or tactics would avail. Highly intuitive and tuned in to people -- the same talents that had allowed her to rise so far in her career -- she knew exactly how to get to me, how to press my buttons and prey on my weaknesses. It took a while, but she masterfully broke down my resistance until I fell into her trap.

Plying herself with liquor and weed in order to loosen any inhibitions that might accompany a novel experience, she came to my apartment that night well prepared. She had asked me to come in to work the day after Thanksgiving with the express intention of going out to get drunk afterwards and then find some way to hang out in the city until it was too late to go back home all the way to Long Island. Indeed, she had already arranged to have her son stay over a friend's house that night. Now it was all too clear. And after the "interesting experience" -- during which she had faked whatever she deemed appropriate in the way of looks or mannerisms -- had run its course, she had one more life event to put alongside riding around with a motorcycle gang, dancing with a company Vice President, and dating a married businessman, to add to her ledger of sophistication and worldliness. Another stamp on her passport to prove how well traveled she was.

And as for me, having served my purpose, having played the role she had cast me in…well... I could now be safely discarded. I recalled with bitterness how, the very Monday after the intimate weekend she had not even looked at or spoken a single word to me, had made no attempt at all to stop by, hadn't picked up the phone. No one could be that busy, no matter how much work there was or how great the demands of the project. Now it was so obvious. Roxanne had sensed my weak spots and vulnerabilities and had stalked me like some jungle prey, then moved in for the kill. Like some perverse fiddler bent on mischief and vandalism she had played my heart strings until I swooned to her tune, bewitched and helpless. Why had I been so blind before to what now seemed as clear as a Montana sky?

Roxanne did indeed get the plum Data Base Administrator position she had applied for, no doubt largely through sweet-talking and sycophantic sucking up to the right people. I came in one day to find her cleaning all her stuff out of the cubicle in front of mine. She told me with a glowing smile that they had given her a beautiful office in the building on Seventh Avenue, the new venue to which the entire IT department was relocating. I said congratulations, wondering if I'd ever even see her again. "Come visit me" she said. Sure thing, I replied, and walked back to my own modest workstation.

Oddly enough, when one of the senior lawyers, who had given over fifteen years of service, announced that she was leaving to start a family, her vacated office was offered to me. For the second time I was to get the private office of an attorney. It happened to be a corner office with not one, but two expansive windows looking out over midtown Manhattan. So, hah - now I had some bragging rights too. It was a generous move on the part of the department and I appreciated it. But I could not enjoy it. Numb with grief over losing something precious that I'd never really had to begin with, I could only go through the motions of working, of striving, of any normal activity, of living itself. I resumed my gloomy pre-Roxanne life in mechanical fashion, on autopilot, and with as little sentiment or emotion as possible.

I sought out odd consolations. As the weather turned warmer, I'd find myself taking long walks in Central Park on my lunch hour, then finding a bench and just sitting in the sun as still as a statue. The intense solar rays penetrating my scalp gave a strange comfort, and the warmth that suffused through me seemed to dissolve all tension and bring a feeling of peace. I would find myself sitting there for hours, not getting back to my office until 3:30 or 4 o'clock. It didn't matter as long as my work got done and handed in on time.

As spring turned into summer these sunbathing sessions became longer and more frequent. On sunny weekends I'd leave my apartment and walk over to nearby Riverside Park carrying a lawn chair and spend the day looking out at the river and soaking up sun rays, as if I were a solar battery that had to be fully charged every day or else it was useless.

After many months had passed, I got a notion to take Roxanne up on her invitation to come visit, and trotted over to the building on Seventh Avenue to see her new setup. I was genuinely startled when I saw her. She seemed to have aged several years and I could see creases and wrinkles on her face that I'd never noticed before. For the first time she actually looked "hard." The shimmery liquid quality of her hazel eyes had turned into a brittle glinting varnish. One of the things I had loved about Roxanne was the way she managed to combine intelligence, competence and driving ambition with an endearing, enticing, almost frilly femininity that never lost its softness. Now that latter quality was clearly gone.

Her desk looked a mess and her high-heeled shoes had been carelessly tossed on the floor alongside her bulky leather bag -- her famous sleek purple briefcase nowhere in sight. The wastebasket was overflowing with food takeout containers and crumpled soda cans. She told me she had been working harder than ever and seldom left the office before 8:00 pm. The salary was very good, but they were making her earn every penny of it. She rattled on and on but not once did she ask me how I was doing or feeling, or if there was anything new with me. In a way I almost felt sorry for her. I left the building thinking that, most likely, I would never see her again. And I didn't.

Eventually I grew tired of my cramped studio and despite how much I loved the Upper West Side and being able to walk to work, I took a large two-bedroom apartment that had become available in a building in the Inwood Heights section of Manhattan, almost at the very northern tip of the island. The neighborhood feel was strictly the Bronx, but the apartment was as spacious as ever I could want. Gradually all thoughts and memories of Roxanne began to evaporate from my mind like snow drifts exposed to a steady glowing sun.

That September there came an excellent chance to hammer the final nail into the coffin of my shattered fake romance. My cousin Sydney had suggested a trip to Europe -- to Italy and Greece in particular. An inveterate globe-trotter, she knew all about bargain airfares, travel agents, tours and package deals. I had never been to Europe and was excited by the prospect. So I requested my two-week vacation and shortly thereafter found myself sitting on a 747 bound for Rome.

20
Trip the Light Fantastic

IT MUST HAVE started sometime last summer, during those bright blue days that found me sitting transfixed on a bench in Central Park basking in the warm glow of the sun, partly as a way to ease my grief over the whole episode with Roxanne. But it was in Rome where it morphed into something like obsessive-compulsive craziness. It could have happened right there at that bustling open-air food emporium near the Piazza Navona known as *Campo dei Fiori* (literally, field of flowers).

It was late September, the fourth or fifth day of our excursion to the "Eternal City" and the morning sun was streaming all over the square. Surrounding us on all sides was a lavish display of ripe fruit, garden-fresh vegetables of every color, spices of every description, a profusion of flowers, and hordes of tourists toting bulging shopping bags. Everything was saturated in light and color. I was looking all around me, trying to take in the whole glorious sight. And that's when it happened. At some point, without any warning, I was simply stunned still, stopped in mid-stride as it were. All of a sudden I was not standing on a cobblestone street amid dozens of folks prowling around market stands voluptuously laden with the bounty of the Italian countryside. Rather, I had dropped into a Renoir canvas and gotten trapped. All I could see were beams of sunlight reflecting off surfaces flat and curved, horizontal and vertical, vibrating madly to the frequencies of all the splendid colors. The ancient, charmingly crooked buildings lining the square were actively giving off warm lovely tones of yellow, rust, peach, burnt umber, cocoa, tan, and gold. And then there were the heaps of color spilling over and out of the market stalls -- the bright reds, purples, oranges, greens. It felt like it was all beaming straight at me, me in particular, commanding my attention, stopping me in my tracks, bombarding my eyes and my mind.

Up ahead I could see my cousin Sydney, my traveling companion, looking back to see where I was. She probably thought I was staring at the brooding bronze statue of the unfortunate Giordano Bruno, which stood somberly in the center of the square, and at which many a tourist's pocket camera were snapping away. According to my guidebook, Giordano Bruno was a sixteenth-century philosopher who went public with some unorthodox ideas that ran counter to the prevailing wisdom of the Church. Such daring defiance reaped its usual reward -- Bruno was denounced as a heretic and burned at the stake in the year 1600.

But I could hardly think of taking any pictures at that moment. While the fishmongers hollered and the strawberry vendors sang out "*Fragole della compagna*!" I somehow felt I could hear the sunlight itself speaking directly to me and I was compelled to listen. I didn't understand what was happening, but it seemed as if time had stopped and I was locked in place unable to take my eyes off the objects in the square. Those ordinary objects now appeared enwrapped in some sort of halo, irresistible and resplendent in the morning sun, suddenly rendered beautiful, sacred almost, and frozen in time.

I didn't know if I was hallucinating or suffering from a mild form of sunstroke. Maybe it was just because I hadn't thought to pack sunglasses for the trip. Sydney had chided me about that when we arrived at the hotel. The Mediterranean sun must be "different" I thought, much more intense, more dangerous. There now seemed to be a subtle but unmistakable "hum" all around me as I continued to stare uncontrollably at buildings, at cars, at people walking or grouped around cafe tables under white umbrellas, at striped awnings gently fluttering in the breeze, at vivid green and purple piles of zucchini and radicchio, at bunches of brilliantly hued flowers everywhere. It was all madness. Was this some sort of revelation? Or were some rogue neurons misfiring in my brain? Spiritual experience or mental illness? I had no way of knowing.

With great difficulty I tore myself away from the scene, caught up with Sydney, and tried to act normal. But the effects of the bizarre experience lingered throughout the rest of our trip. Two days later, on a gloriously sun-drenched afternoon, we arrived at the Vatican. I again became transfixed in St. Peter's Square as I watched a couple of one-horse carriages click-clocking along the cobblestone pavement, the red wooden wheels and the chestnut coats of the animals gleaming and magnificent in their halo of liquid light. Sydney had to angrily tap my shoulder and drag me over to the line of folks waiting to enter the basilica. On another day, at the sprawling *Porta Portese* outdoor flea market my eyes gorged on the riotous and haphazard display of precious "junk": Italian comic books, chintzy Madonna paintings, Mussolini ("*Il Duce*") memorabilia, rosary beads, antiquarian books, 1950s-era TV sets, used auto parts, live parrots squawking "Ciao," tarnished bits of old jewelry, and other assorted kitsch, all glinting and sparkling in the brittle morning light.

It was a riot of light and color which made me slightly delirious, not to mention the accompanying sounds -- the noise of haggling, shouting, and laughter emanating from hundreds of vendor stalls and the jostling about of legions of curious wide-eyed shoppers. My eyes were drawn to an odd-looking bronze ashtray lying on a blanket. It was in the shape of a large seashell, flanked by a curvy, full-breasted, reclining woman clothed only below the waist. She was, in fact, a replica of one of four baroque fountains that adorn the *Church of San Carlo alle Quartro Fontane*, a masterpiece by architect Francesco Borromini. Almost in a trance I reached out for the glistening object, handed over my crumpled lire, and tenderly deposited my shiny new treasure into my purse.

We visited the ruins of the *Casa delle Vestali* (House of the Vestal Virgins). Deserted as the place appeared, the few broken statues that remain standing seemed almost to come to life as the sun, sparkling like a diamond engagement ring, splashed light over the smooth polished surfaces of their block pedestals and their meticulously sculpted flowing folds of drapery. Walking among the weeds, there was at once something utterly desolate about the scene, as if I had just set foot on Mars or some other cold barren planet. And yet there was undeniable warmth, not merely from the solar rays baking into clay and concrete, but from the knowledge that this scene, no matter what took place here thousands of years ago, was somehow blessed or sanctified by this all-embracing, all-cleansing light.

Dusty crumbly ancient history jolted into life by ultraviolet radiation. Or so it seemed as I stared at the silent alabaster virgins. Who knew how many of the chosen young maidens had failed to keep their thirty-year vows of chastity, drenched as they were in the rollicking hedonism and decadence of imperial Rome. Again, according to my guidebook, a cruel and peculiar fate awaited anyone who slipped and was found out

-- the unlucky lass would be buried alive with a lamp and a loaf of bread. Be that as it may, somehow under this enveloping luminescence all was mellowed, all was made right.

One of the last sites we visited in Rome, the soaring interior dome of the *Pantheon*, was breathtakingly beautiful not only because of its precise and perfect geometric proportions but also because its sole source of lighting was a small circular opening in the center of the roof. Through this portal natural daylight streamed and radiated outward in all directions, creating 360 degrees of heavenly perfection. After that it was on to Athens, Greece, where my new fixation with sunlight continued unabated.

We took a side trip to the island of *Santorini*, one of the most picturesque of the Greek Isles, where pastel-colored villages sit atop volcanic cliffs overlooking a deep blue sea. Once again I was in a dreamscape, a gorgeous watercolor painting suspended in time and I was startled by my own reactions. I became obsessed with the piles of bright yellow rope coiled on the docks from which small red, pink, and blue fishing boats set out into the Aegean. I could scarcely take my eyes off the charming island bungalows that looked like they were made of chalk, and the taupe and white donkeys who plodded humbly along the wharf, weighed down with sacks of fishing gear. It seemed as if the whole picture-postcard scene was self-contained, sealed within its dome of shimmering light and color much as a wintry landscape is contained in one of those shake-it-up snow globes. It occurred to me that if light travels 186,000 miles per second, then somewhere across the universe millions of miles from earth, the scene on which I was now feasting my eyes might one day be viewed by a race of space aliens living in a far distant galaxy.

And then there were all those stray cats! Apparently, these islands were once a favorite dumping ground for pet cats who had worn out their welcome. Over the years the feline population had exploded to the point that you couldn't venture very far inland without seeing dozens of them. You would spot them casually strolling about or stretched out languidly on doorsteps or draped over the balconies of homes whose owners were either out of town or disinclined to chase them away. It was not unusual to see as many as eight or ten cats adorning a single house and although some would use the term "feral" to describe these wild self-sufficient strays, the cats of *Santorini* did not seem to be particularly savage. Like me, they were probably dumbstruck by the beauty and tranquility and the chance to have a permanent place in the sun.

So I would just stand there and marvel, watching the cats and the tourists and the fishermen and the seacraft large and small moving on the sun-dappled waters. Everything acquired a purity, an innocence, a sacred splendor while bathed in that virgin light. Plants, people, animals, inanimate objects, all looked as I imagined every new thing must have looked to God on the first day of creation. It blew me away. Why had I never noticed this before? Or was it really all in my mind? No one else seemed to take any note of it.

My reflections led to a studious recalling of all I had learned about light in science classes. How for a long time there was a raging debate over whether light consisted of waves, much like radio waves, or whether it was actually a stream of particles as Einstein asserted based on experiments he had conducted. It turned out that light could be both, or either. It depended on the circumstance. Like water, which could pour continuously in an unbroken flow or come down in a shower of individual raindrops, light, apparently, could take on different forms and manifest in different ways.

This seemed fitting given what an important role the concept of light plays in virtually all major religions. It was the first thing given by the Creator, perhaps before space and time itself. How nice it would have been, I thought, if I were an artist. I could have dragged my oils and canvas right over to this spot where I now stood, set up my easel, and turned my impressions into carefully rendered shapes and forms, translating, via splotches of pigment, what my eyes beheld into images on a flat white surface. It would be an enthusiastic if vain attempt to capture in permanent form what could never be captured, possessed, or even articulated.

But alas, once the European adventure ended and I was back home and back to work these fanciful musings gave way to some real, anxious concerns. For some inexplicable reason I could not shake the idea that the sun, broadcasting its beams of light and clarity whenever I chanced to be outdoors on a clear day was trying to tell me something. Something I needed to listen to. I had hoped the whole bizarre fixation could be chalked up to some weird reaction I had had to the strangeness of foreign lands or the peculiar intensity of the Mediterranean sun. But now I could see that my reaction to the considerably cooler and paler sun of New York City was not all that different.

I soon found myself spending an entire lunch hour standing on the northwest corner of 38th Street and Fifth Avenue watching people passing on the other side of the avenue, waiting for the exact moment when someone would step into a sun-drenched portion of the pavement and be for that brief instant "all lit up" in a halo of white light. At that moment the individual, no matter who they were or what they looked like became something holy and pure, something inviolable and eternal. I would stare at the yellow taxicabs stopped in front of traffic lights, watching them giving off their *deep yellowness* in hot undulating waves, alive and vibrating. Light and color as active, living, breathing agents. Wow! I felt the same way the first person ever to view a drop of water under a microscope must have felt when that obscure smear on a slide was suddenly teeming with squiggling life forms. It was all so uncanny, and so ridiculous too.

For the life of me I could not fathom why I was having this crazed reaction. Again I wondered, is this a kind of mild hallucination, a rare disorder, or a psychotic episode? Before the trip to Rome and Greece there was nothing of the kind. What on earth had happened to me? It was all so freaky I couldn't imagine attempting to tell anyone about it, not even a psychiatrist.

Things began to spin out of control when I found myself feeling a need to actually look directly at the sun, as if doing so would finally reveal the source of the problem, uncover the important message I seemed not to be getting. *What do you want, damn it!!* I would think as I turned around while walking to find the golden tyrant stalking me. Of course the glare was blinding, and I had to shield my eyes at first but before long I was able to stare without squinting until I could discern the round white disc of the sun at the dead center of all that profusion of light. It became one more obsessive-compulsive symptom to add to the inventory of similar OCD tendencies I had picked up over the years.

But in this case the sick compulsion affected my work -- something none of my other OCD symptoms had ever done. I found myself sneaking out of the building on bright days in order to get away from the artificial office lights and experience natural sunlight. These increasingly long spells away from my desk could no longer be explained away as trips to the law library or consultations with attorneys in their offices. I knew I was being watched and yet all I could do was pray for rainy or overcast days to banish all temptation to go outside.

Even worse was the damage I was doing to my eyes. Headaches, a sense of straining to see, and difficulty focusing on text were the first telltale symptoms. Outdoors at night the white lettering on neon signs seemed to spill over into an indistinct smear if I tried to focus on it. The full moon on a clear night looked blurry.

I made an appointment with an ophthalmologist. Embarrassed and unwilling to come clean about what brought me there, I told the doctor I had experienced a couple of bad acid trips. With my fellow spaced-out trippers, I had lain down on a pier and tried to "stare down" the sun, I explained in an apologetic tone. He nodded knowingly, as if he had heard this sort of thing before. He conducted a thorough examination and told me he detected scarring and damaged tissue in my retina. There was nothing to be done about it; it was not correctable with any kind of lens. However, it was confined to a relatively small area and as long as I refrained from my idiotic behavior I should notice only limited interference with my vision. The doctor's parting advice was that I be very thankful I hadn't gone completely blind -- other patients he had seen with similar tales of drug induced sun-gazing had not been so lucky.

The fear of going blind was enough to make me buy an expensive pair of French ski glasses which wrapped around my face like goggles and blocked out the most harmful ultraviolet rays. I never went out on a brilliant day without them and tried to steer my sick compulsion away from the sun itself and towards the light as reflected off objects, the way it had begun. Soon I came to feel like someone in a twelve-step program, patiently wrestling with a stubborn addiction and trying to take it "one day at a time." I never understood what had caused it, had never gotten the "message," whatever it was. The sun god had failed me and I was determined to tame, if not altogether conquer, the dangerous compulsion.

But taming it proved a considerable challenge. Meanwhile, it started getting busy at work. It became a lot harder to slip away unnoticed or return late from lunch. I grew increasingly anxious, almost to the point of panicking, when forced to remain confined at my desk for extended periods. After receiving a couple of warnings, I had no doubt where it was all headed. Still, I was powerless to curb the bad behavior. And sure enough, one afternoon I was taken aside and told that my services were no longer needed. I was out of a job.

21
The Sun God's Revenge

IT WAS THE weirdest feeling, emptying out my drawers at work, clearing off my desk, glumly surveying over seven years' worth of office paraphernalia -- while all around me others went about their work as usual. With the exception of Greg in the copy room and my good friend Maxine, no one came by or said anything to me. After all the fine work I had done for the law department, the countless hours spent doing research, drafting legal documents and briefs, analyzing leases and more, not a single attorney came by to thank me or wish me luck. Who knows what they were thinking. Having been abruptly fired, I had become persona non grata and was shunned. I felt cheated and abused by fate, victimized by a mysterious disorder that had come on suddenly with no apparent cause or explanation. I just wanted to get out of there as quickly as possible. So I chucked everything except a spare sweater, grabbed hold of my shopping bag and headed straight for the elevators, leaving a parting gift for the next person who would occupy my office: a bottom drawer full to the brim with sugar packets. I never took sugar in my coffee but the guy at the deli always automatically dropped two sugar packs encased in cellophane into my little white bag when he handed me my morning coffee, and I had hoarded them.

In a frantic attempt to understand what had happened, to pinpoint the cause of the strange "sunlight addiction," I began making trips to the medical library on upper Fifth Avenue to research various panic and anxiety disorders and the peculiar forms that Obsessive-Compulsive Disorder could take. But I found nothing that seemed directly related to my case. Even among the mentally ill I was a misfit! There was no place for me in the DSM (*Diagnostic and Statistical Manual of Mental Disorders*) -- the bible of the psychiatric profession. The summer after I was fired was unusually blistering and full of sun glare. Here are a couple of excerpts from my Diary for July of that year:

July 13th

The first thing to mention is this horrible fact. As soon as I woke up I saw how BRIGHTLY the sun was shining. Diamond-white, silvery like a shimmering mirror in a sheet of pale blue. I had to look!!! Then I realized that it was exactly a year ago today -- July 13th 1987 -- that I had done the very same thing -- stared directly into the white glaring sun, and then went home and wrote about it in my diary. Swearing, hoping, that it would never happen again. A full year later -- I've learned nothing.

July 17th

Another muggy hazy hot hot day. Mom and Dad were supposed to come over to put up the blinds they bought me at Pergament -- so I tried to tidy up the house a bit, vacuuming here and there.

Yes -- I looked at the sun again. In the morning as usual. I don't know why I keep doing it. I guess because I can't get any real satisfaction out of it. It gives me nothing except its hideous white shimmering glare. It dares me to look at it and then it's just a tease. I prayed to God that I could stop doing this.

Since some kind of severe anxiety seemed to be at the core, I could think of nothing to do but go to a doctor and ask for a Valium prescription. So I did. After several weeks on the medication, I was able to count small blessings. I was no longer tempted to look directly at the sun and made sure to always protect my eyes with very strong sunglasses. But there was still an almost irresistible need to spend as much time in sunshine as possible, no matter the season.

Newly unemployed and free to indulge whims I soon discovered that my new two-bedroom apartment on the far northern tip of Manhattan had a fire escape that was a perfect perch for catching rays. The sun shone on that side of the building all day long and even on a bitter cold day, enough of the abundant heat from the radiator reached out to the fire escape so that I could sit there for hours with only a cloak or light jacket on. So I laid a blanket and cushion over the iron bars to make a comfortable seat and proceeded to turn that fire escape into my private study. I brought out books to read, journals I was working on, my mail, and anything else that involved reading or writing.

Sitting there in my little black cage, suitably proportioned for one person, wrapped in a warm bubble of solar radiance, I felt perfectly at peace. I couldn't fathom how merely being bathed in sunlight, even in the wintertime with no skin exposed as opposed to lying on a beach tanning in August, could infuse me with such a sense of calm and well-being. The effect was almost akin to a drug. All anxieties melted away, all irritation soothed as if by a magic balm. It felt like being in the caress of a warm loving mother in whose bosom all was safe and sound, all cares took flight, and the whole universe screamed the message: *Don't worry -- everything's gonna be okay!* But I was in no mood to analyze and deconstruct, so I just surrendered to it.

One day as I was peacefully sunning myself and writing in my journal, I noticed a police vehicle pull up to the curb on the street below. Several cops got out and appeared to be looking up towards my building. It was a six-story apartment building and my apartment was on the sixth floor. Immersed in my writing, I did not pay much attention; the presence of cops in the neighborhood was, if not an everyday occurrence, certainly not a rare sight. But about five minutes afterwards I heard a loud knocking on my front door. What? It suddenly struck me that someone must have noticed me on the fire escape, thought perhaps I was a burglar or maybe even a potential suicide, and they had dialed 911. I opened the door, assured the cops I was indeed the owner of the apartment and no, I was not thinking about jumping, just catching a few sun rays. They looked at me strangely the whole time, but realized there was no real emergency and simply suggested I find another place to sun myself. I felt slightly shaken and not a little bit angry. What harm was it to anyone if I chose to sit out on my own fire escape? I was minding my business, why couldn't other people mind theirs?

But after that incident, I decided to switch to the roof, a few short steps up from my apartment, where I could bring out a lawn chair and even a bridge table. Up there, without the benefit of heat from the bedroom radiator, I had to wrap myself in several layers of clothing, including scarves and gloves if the thermometer dipped below 40 degrees or so. Temperatures as low as 25 degrees did not dissuade me from enjoying my private rooftop picnic, so long as the sun was shining brightly in a clear blue sky and there was no wind. I had plenty to occupy myself with and gave scarcely a thought to looking for another job. I had pleaded with Equitable to say that I had been laid off rather than fired so that I would be eligible for unemployment insurance and they consented. Considering my low-maintenance lifestyle, those unemployment checks combined with my own savings could easily last me a year.

As winter turned to spring and spring ripened into summer, I began to switch venues from my rooftop to the beautiful park mere blocks from my building -- Fort Tryon Park. This park was, among other things, home to the Cloisters Museum whose prized collection of medieval art brought visitors from all over the city. Lovely wooded trails, flower gardens, promenades and terraces, and vast stretches of green provided a full day's recreation until the sun finally set over the Hudson River. I frequented the park pretending I was retired and enjoying well-deserved hours of leisure and blissful idleness long denied by years of boring soul-crushing labor. Sitting cross-legged on a blanket reading, writing, or watching people pass by was a totally satisfying and stress-free occupation. I gave no thought to the past or the future; the present moment was all.

But every now and then my serene facade got ruffled a bit; ripples of worry and guilt passed through me as I counted down my unemployment checks and watched my bank account shrink ever so slowly. I thought perhaps some part-time work would not cause too drastic a change in my pleasant daily routine. I thought about the hordes of street vendors I used to pass on midtown streets during my lunch hour, peddling everything from handbags to watches to bootleg videos, much of it stolen, counterfeit, or knockoffs of designer and brand-name merchandise. Cash always seemed to be flying from the purses and hands of excited shoppers, usually female, convinced they were getting some super bargain. Street vending seemed like something I could handle.

So I did some research and found a wholesale warehouse in Chinatown where much of this junk could be purchased in bulk, very cheaply. I started out with small lots of costume jewelry, printed scarves, and other lightweight items. I got myself a small fold-up table, loaded the goods into a knapsack, skipped down the steps into the subway station right in front of my building, and took the A train downtown. I would pick out a spot heavy with foot traffic, open up the table, and display my wares as attractively as I could. I was surprised at how quickly small crowds of office workers would magically spring up around my table, eyes wide, fingers grasping, hands dipping into pocketbooks to fish out five or ten-dollar bills. I charged the customer three times whatever I had paid for any given item.

For a while all went smoothly. I experimented with different merchandise, different parts of town. But I was too new to the game to appreciate the risks. One day after I had just set up, I spotted a blue and white van across the street. Out popped a handful of police who headed straight in my direction. Before I realized why they were there they were upon me, asking to see a valid vendor's license. Although New York City's multi-billion-dollar retail industry would like nothing better than to eliminate street vendors entirely, the city fathers are loath to remove so intrinsic a part of the culture and color of New York. So they compensate for the loss of sales tax revenue with strict licensing regulations and fees, as well as substantial fines for transgressors. Upon my failure to produce a license, my goods were quickly confiscated, table and all. I was let go with a warning. Thinking I would be more on the lookout for cops from now on, I chanced it again. But eventually a plainclothes detail caught up with me, took my stuff, handed me a summons, and threatened jail next time. That pretty much put the kibosh on my entrepreneurial pushcart ambitions.

I deeply regretted having to give up a "job" that allowed me to be outdoors in the sun, but money was getting tight and I needed some additional source of income. In the late fall I took a part-time salesgirl job in men's furnishings at *Macy's* department store in Herald Square. With swarms of tourists passing through the giant retail emporium every day, there was no lack of customers. The time moved fast and I was never bored. As the holidays approached, in fact, it was even kind of fun, watching agitated crowds become increasingly hysterical as the number of shopping days dwindled. I would spend the last half-hour of my shift wading through piles of leather gloves, cashmere scarves and argyle socks that the frantic patrons had picked through and heedlessly let fall to the floor. But although I rang up dozens of purchases per day, apparently I was not persuasive enough lauding the virtues of Oxford dress shirts, silk ties and designer cuff links to meet the sales quota my supervisor had set for me. As soon as the holidays ended I was quickly let go.

I then found a position in a call center with the Lou Harris Poll. My job was to call a list of randomly selected telephone numbers all over the country and poll people on their political views -- had they voted to re-elect President Reagan? Or their consumer tastes -- when had they last visited a *Red Lobster* restaurant, was it a satisfying experience, etc. The work itself was not bad. Everyone had to read from a script verbatim without the slightest deviation, so I got a chance to practice my diction and smooth out the edges of my *New Yawk* accent. But what I couldn't hack was the feverish pace. We were expected to have completed a certain number of surveys by the close of every shift and I consistently failed to achieve the recommended volume. I was told I needed to dial the numbers faster, speak more quickly, rush through the questions. But unfortunately for me, my fingers and vocal cords were not up to the task; after about three months I was fired. So that made three times in a row that I had been fired -- a pretty dismal track record.

As another summer approached, I consoled myself with the fact that I had at least earned a decent sum of cash during my several aborted attempts at employment and would not be forced to look for a real job until next spring at the earliest. But I could not be so sanguine about the sunlight problem, or about the eye damage I had already sustained. I still had trouble focusing on text. Frustrated, I went to another eye doctor. He agreed to prescribe a pair of strong reading glasses to make it easier to handle fine print, but cautioned that the injury to my retina was permanent and the best advice he could give was that I prevent any further damage by avoiding the sun.

I felt lost and confused. Leaving the doctor's office, I went to sit in the park and realized the situation was hopeless. The sun in the sky was keeping its watchful eye on me, bidding me be still, its long octopus-like tentacles of radiation reaching out to grasp my head and hold it in a vise. I put on my French ski glasses and refrained from looking at the sky, but I couldn't help wondering where it would all end. It was only a matter of time before I would have to be working in an office setting again, under those awful, antiseptic fluorescent light tubes. If I wasn't given enough latitude to work independently and set my own hours, to sneak outside every now and then without being noticed, it would be next to impossible for me to keep any office job. The only saving grace was the fact that New York weather afforded few brilliantly sunny days. Had I been living in Phoenix or Los Angeles I would probably have wound up in a hospital, a home for the disabled, or even in jail.

It was a problem I would struggle with for the rest of my life. Years later I would read that scientists studying such phenomena as compulsive sun tanning had found that prolonged exposure to sunlight can, in certain susceptible individuals, release endorphins and "feel-good" neurotransmitter chemicals. That bathing in sunshine can trigger surges of serotonin and dopamine directly into the bloodstream. So in a sense, I might have been self-medicating for depression. When many years later I was able to take advantage of the new generation of serotonin-enhancing antidepressant drugs such as Prozac, the sun compulsion became much easier to rein in and control, but it was never to disappear completely.

22
Water Sports

BRIDGETT DANAHER LOOKED so small and so ancient sitting up there on the witness stand. A handsome crown of soft snowy white hair dwarfed a bird-like face. She was well into her eighties and her chalky face was covered with fine wrinkles, hair-thin fissures that gave her a certain dignity and fragility, like a specimen of antique parchment one hesitates to touch lest it crumble into dust. But her lavender blue eyes retained a lively sparkle and her determined voice, with its refined Irish brogue, came across just as clear and striking in that near empty courtroom as a telephone ringing at three in the morning. She was talking about the eccentric antisocial oddball who lived one floor above her and was causing her and her husband such grief. She was talking about me. Bridgett was being questioned by the attorney representing Millburn Management, the company that managed our apartment building.

Attorney: "Please describe where your apartment is located, Mrs. Danaher."

Mrs. Danaher: "We're on the fifth floor, on the east side of the building."

Attorney: "And is your apartment directly below that of Ms. Maiden?"

Mrs. Danaher: "Yes, she is right above us on the sixth floor. I 'm in 5F and she's in 6F, right on top of us."

Attorney: "Mrs. Danaher, how many times have you written to us or called us since January of 1984 to ask that we remove Ms. Maiden from the building?"

Mrs. Danaher: "It must have been at least three times, maybe four."

Attorney: "Can you describe for the court some of the complaints you have about Ms. Maiden?"

Mrs. Danaher: "Oh, where to begin. Loud music, at all hours, ten, eleven o'clock at night. 'BOOM, BOOM, BOOM', going right through our walls! My husband always grabs the broom and starts banging up on the ceiling, but it does no good. And she's just . . .strange . . .In the morning I'll open my bedroom window and lean out to see how the weather is. I'll glance up and there she is standing out on her fire escape all wrapped in towels -- like she just stepped out of the shower!

Attorney: "And how many times have you observed Ms. Maiden like that?"

Mrs. Danaher: "Three times this past year alone. One time somebody called the cops -- they probably thought she was gonna jump or something -- I saw the police cars pull up, a couple of officers walking into the courtyard right up to our lobby."

Attorney: "And have you also had complaints about Ms. Maiden's water usage, Mrs. Danaher?"

Mrs. Danaher: "Oh God! She lets the water run for hours in the bathtub -- HOURS at a time -- we hear it running, in the pipes. And she lets her tub overflow, I know it! There's no other explanation! We've had constant leaks into our bathroom. Our wall behind the toilet is corroded from water damage, the plaster's falling off, and one corner of our ceiling is about to cave in, for heaven's sake!"

Attorney: "Have you ever attempted to speak to Ms. Maiden and tell her that her water usage is affecting your apartment?"

Mrs. Danaher: "We've left notes under her door. We tried calling but she has an unlisted phone number. She's not exactly what you'd call approachable -- in fact, my husband is afraid of her."

Attorney: "Afraid of her?"

Mrs. Danaher: "Because she seems so weird. I see her walking up and down the street at all times of the day. She doesn't seem to work. And -- I mean the fire escape -- I see her out on the fire escape, just standing there staring up at the sky! And that constant running of water -- for hours and hours. Dennis thinks -- and I agree with him -- we think she's in some crazy religious cult or something."

I glanced around the room, thankful that this was not a jury trial. I tried to glean the judge's reaction from his facial expressions, but he maintained a blank poker face the whole time. The questioning continued.

Attorney: "Religious cult?"

Mrs. Danaher: "Not in the true sense of religion, certainly not Christian, anyway, but something that. . . maybe involves drugs or going into trances, or whatever these young people do nowadays. We can't tell. Only a week ago I saw her up on the roof, all by herself, repeating something over and over again, like someone possessed."

Attorney: "Like a chant?"

Mrs. Danaher: "Yes, you could call it that. I've seen TV documentaries about devil worship and satanic cults, young people taking up things like witchcraft. It's crazy, this younger generation -- the drugs, the music. . . the strange rituals. It's frightening."

In a few minutes my own lawyer would put me on the stand to refute some of Mrs. Danaher's charges. And I also had my friend Maxine there as a character witness. But I wondered if that would be good enough. Bridgett Danaher was doing just fine; she was obviously neither senile nor hysterical. Her testimony was even and matter of fact. How would I respond when cross-examined by Millburn's lawyer? How could I convince this judge -- who seemed to be one of those stern no-nonsense, no-pity types that New York landlords loved -- that I was not some nut job or sociopath who wasn't fit to live among civilized God-fearing people like the Danahers?

It had finally come to this. After two years of denials, recriminations, angry exchanges between me and the landlord, and threatening letters back and forth, the management of the building had decided to commence formal eviction proceedings against me. The charges leveled at me were essentially false, but not wholly unfounded. Overflowing bathtub? Never happened. I didn't even take baths, only showers. Standing out on the fire escape wrapped only in bath towels? Maybe once or twice -- but is that any of her business? Chanting on the roof? Well, that was only temporary. But again, what business is that of the Danahers? Constantly running water? Well, okay, I liked to take long showers . . . really long showers. It's like self-medication or something, a natural tranquilizer or anti-anxiety pill. Besides, nothing in my lease says anything about how long I'm allowed to run the water in the sink or tub.

Okay, I'll admit -- it was all an awful mess. But it had happened gradually, in classic boil-a-bullfrog fashion. I swear there had been no malice on my part, no intent to cause any kind of property damage or disturbance to other tenants. I always paid my rent on time, took good care of my apartment, was friendly with the super. I didn't deserve to be evicted. For a New Yorker, eviction can be more of a nightmare than for folks in other parts of the country. That's because in New York the vast majority of apartments in so-called "prewar buildings" were rent-controlled or rent-stabilized. Landlords were severely constrained in how much they could legally charge, and by what percentage they could raise the rent with each lease renewal.

But in recent years the tide had turned somewhat in favor of landlords. Many landlords had been forced to abandon buildings as their taxes and utility costs soared, and in order for the city to attract new development, various incentives had to be offered, among them allowing landlords to charge market rates on the newest apartment towers and luxury condos springing up all over town. Tenants lucky enough to have rent-controlled apartments almost never moved, unless they were leaving town altogether. Being evicted from a rent-controlled apartment meant you were thrown into the free market jungle -- you might have to pay three or four times as much for a comparable apartment in a newer building.

I had reluctantly moved to the Inwood Heights section of Manhattan after two years of trouble with heat and neighbors on the Upper West

Side. I also needed more space, had at long last grown weary of coming home each night to a big walk-in closet. So in January of 1984 I had taken a large two-bedroom with twelve-foot-high ceilings and old-fashioned moldings overlooking Broadway. The six-story apartment building dated back to 1926.

Moving in was somewhat depressing because it felt like I had moved back to the Bronx. Where once I could hear strains of *Madame Butterfly* or *Rigoletto* pouring out of some upper window as I sauntered down my block, now there was only salsa music blaring out of somebody's car radio. Wonderful culinary emporiums like *Zabar's* and the *Fairway Market* were replaced by bodegas that sold day-old bread and cigarettes by the piece, and by a dingy looking *C-Town* grocery store. The antique shops and used book stalls I used to love to browse in gave way to locksmiths, shoe repair shops, and check cashing storefronts. Where once there had been street cafes and quaint little restaurants serving up Szechuan, Northern Italian, or Middle Eastern cuisine, now there was just a greasy Dominican diner, a *Burger King*, and a charbroiled chicken fast food joint called *Pollo Supremo*. I felt like I had been demoted, had clumsily slipped from a world of professionals, artists, and *The New York Times* to a blue-collar world of lunch pails, malt liquor, and the *Daily Racing Sheet*.

About two months after I returned from my trip abroad, I went back to work, having found a paralegal job in a midtown law firm. Once I was back to being a nine-to-five commuter, the limitations of my neighborhood stood out more conspicuously. Arriving home on the A train after a jolting and jarring twenty-minute ride up from midtown, I could barely walk out to the street without letting a sigh of something akin to despair escape from my lungs. And my distress over my unappetizing surroundings was only compounded by a growing feeling of isolation and loneliness. So many people had been in my life in a significant way and then left – my college buddies, Sadie, Lorraine, Mike, Roxanne. I felt abandoned, carelessly tossed aside like torn Christmas wrapping. I wondered if I would ever have a lasting relationship with anyone.

Inevitably I slipped back into depression and felt grateful that I had a job that forced me to spend my time doing something productive. And I had all to do to resist the pull of the sunlight fixation lest I get fired again. And so the stage was set for some disturbing and perverse psycho-emotional play-acting. Needs that could not be satisfied in normal acceptable ways became twisted and warped into strange compulsions, the acting out of which served as a kind of release valve that somehow helped to dispel the awful crippling tension.

My apartment building was remarkably well-preserved and well-maintained on the outside. But the infrastructure was in pitiful shape. Interior walls were cracked, lighting fixtures were falling apart, the elevator kept breaking down, and the pipes were old and tired. The first year I lived there the boiler went on the blink at least two or three times, leaving us to go for days at a stretch without heat or hot water. When the boiler was working and heat was flowing, the radiators made gruesome clanking screeching noises that made your hair stand up and jerked you out of bed at night.

Taking a shower was a frustrating experience. The water came out in a limp flaccid stream that would suddenly turn scalding hot or go ice cold without warning. On frigid winter days when we went without heat, I would have to sit in the kitchen wrapped in blankets and turn on the oven. At length, after pressure from complaining tenants and city agencies, some major overhauls got underway. One day in the middle of February the super announced that the entire boiler and natural gas system were to be replaced, and we would be without heat and hot water for several days. He also said he would see what could be done about the weak water pressure. So I packed a small suitcase and went to stay at my mother's house for a while, commuting to work from Yonkers.

When I returned to my building there was quite a surprise. In the bathroom the small bent shower head fixture had been replaced by a larger sturdier one with more holes and a wider circumference of spray. The first time I took a shower was a revelation. The water came out in a full dense stream that rained down on your entire body. When you turned on the "Hot" faucet the water quickly got hot and stayed that way. It was easy to blend in cool water to keep the spray at just the right temperature. And the pressure! Full and strong, it hammered right into you and made your skin vibrate and tingle.

Moving my body around in the bracing spray, I felt like I was getting a Japanese massage. I could feel the dead skin flakes flying off me and my circulation speeding up. Muscle aches and knots of tension just dissolved in the steady assault of water pellets bursting upon me like rounds from a machine gun. Enough pressure to hose down and clean an elephant. It felt wonderful. I would walk into the shower feeling worn-out, drained, blue and hopeless. I would walk out feeling invigorated, glowing, pink, and primed for action.

It was not long before my stimulating hot shower became the high point of my day. Sometimes I took it first thing in the morning. Sometimes I waited for the afternoon or evening. Sometimes I'd take a shower at midnight, then jump into bed naked, refreshed and smelling of *Camay* soap, and drift into oblivion the moment my head hit the pillow. I scarcely noticed the time passing while I was splashing around in utter contentment. Before the repairs and overhaul I had been in the habit of taking long leisurely showers. I could easily spend a half-hour to 40 minutes under the spray.

But now! I felt like I was undergoing a vigorous water treatment -- something healthful, healing, and mentally uplifting. Even the sound of the gushing, forceful spray was somehow soothing, a kind of white noise that blocked out distractions and provided a protected walled-in space in which to think, breathe, and reflect. I called it a "hydrotherapy session," since it produced the same salutary effects as any good physical therapy.

Over time the showers became longer and longer. On days when I was feeling particularly depressed or needy or frustrated, when my nerves were especially raw, I could stay in the shower as long as an hour, an hour and a half, even two entire hours or more. I just lost all sense of time while the tension drained away in waves, and I felt a sense of peace and well-being very similar to what I felt while sitting in the sun on a clear day. With the new boiler the hot water never ran out, the pressure never let up. I heard no phones ringing, no shouting voices, no shrieking car alarms going off, felt no intrusions from the outside chaotic world. I was in a cozy private retreat bounded by gleaming tile walls and a waterproof vinyl curtain, a temporary refuge from the coarseness of the mundane workaday world.

It was maybe three weeks or so after beginning my daily regimen of long hydrotherapy sessions that I spotted the first note under my door. It was scrawled in a red pen, all in crude, uppercase letters. It said:

WATER FROM YOUR BATHTUB IS RUNNING INTO OUR BATHROOM. WE HEAR WATER RUNNING FOR HOURS. PLEASE BE CAREFUL ABOUT OVERFLOWING YOUR TUB. OR ELSE WE WILL HAVE TO MAKE TEDDY COME UP.

The Danahers

Teddy was our super. I could not understand why any water would be seeping into their apartment. I inspected my bathroom and shower carefully. I had a long heavy shower curtain which I carefully tucked in against the inside of the tub whenever I used the shower. No water splashed out. When I stepped out of the tub, the floor was completely dry. I found a sheet of scrap paper and began writing a note back to the Danahers saying that I had not overflowed the bathtub or sink and suggesting they check their own pipes and look for a possible leak. I went down to the lobby, twisted the slip of paper such that I could slide it into their locked mailbox, and went back upstairs.

But over the next week I got two more notes from the Danahers voicing the same complaint. I made another, closer inspection of my bathroom. I went to the hardware store and bought two fresh tubes of caulking putty which I carefully applied to all the seams around the tub edge or between tiles. I bought a second shower curtain to act as a liner to the first. After taking these measures I felt certain no water was escaping from any fixture in my bathroom onto the floor, and into the apartment below.

But the protests did not stop. Eventually I got a letter from the management company notifying me that the tenants below had been complaining. I knew that the problem had to be within the walls themselves, invisible to me. The pipes in the walls were 60 years old and had never been replaced or retrofitted. For most of that time the water pressure in the building had been relatively weak. But now, with the new boiler and shower fixtures and with my shameless exploitation of the enhanced water pressure, the pipes were obviously being burdened beyond their ability to cope. The strong rushing current of water from my shower must be finding every possible corroded kink or hairline crack in the seams between pipe sections and was somehow spilling out into the walls. Dripping right through the plaster and running down the Danaher's ceiling. I couldn't imagine any other explanation.

But was it really my fault that the pipes had not been upgraded in sixty years? If I was doing nothing careless or negligent in my bathroom, such as letting the sink overflow, why should I bear the blame for what was happening in the walls? Walls and pipes were strictly the landlord's responsibility, not mine. I wrote back to Millburn Management explaining that the only thing I was guilty of was taking long showers -- not exactly a violation of my lease. I mentioned that I was even willing to pay a surcharge for my excess water use, but that the amount of time I spend in the shower is really none of anyone's business but mine. Still, I didn't know what I could do to satisfy the Danahers.

Yes -- Mrs. Danaher *had* seen me on the fire escape wrapped in bath towels. My bedroom window faced east, and often in the early morning I would step out of the shower into the room and be immediately dazzled by a sparkling sun and a clean sheet of blue announcing a beautiful day. I had always thought of the fire escape as a small extension of my bedroom -- almost like a little deck -- and stepping out there to take in the brilliant sunshine and fresh air for a few seconds seemed like the most natural thing in the world to me, even if I was clad only in towels. I would step right back inside, of course, within less than a minute. But, unfortunately, often not fast enough to prevent the nosey busybody below from having the chance to gaze up at me, scrunch her face into a Halloween mask of ugliness, and murder me with her eyes.

On those rare occasions when I saw her in the lobby as I was entering the building, she refused to ride in the elevator with me. She would look at me and avert her eyes quickly, as if I were a living remnant of some bad dream she thought she'd woken up from. I would hear her beneath me, banging up on my floor, whenever I played the stereo. But the neighbors on either side of me -- more likely to be bothered by noise from my apartment than the people below me -- never expressed a word of complaint, so I assumed my volume was okay. But the Danahers were probably the kind that went to bed at 8:30 and were fidgety light sleepers. Just the sound of me walking across the floor, even with my slippers on, probably upset them.

In the courtroom the hours dragged on. After two recesses it was finally my turn on the witness stand. First the lawyer for the plaintiff -- the plaintiff being, of course, my landlord -- would get a chance to interrogate me.

Attorney: "Is it true that you are in the habit of going up to the roof to chant or mouth some odd religious phrases or mantras, as Mrs. Danaher testified?"

My lawyer objected, but the judge ignored it.

Me: "OK -- two coworkers told me about this new spiritual practice they were into. They called themselves "Buddhists," but this particular sect of Buddhism believes in chanting a certain Japanese phrase over and over again -- it's a form of prayer. Just to be a good sport, really -- I'm not into this sort of thing as a rule -- but just to humor them, I agreed to try it for two weeks."

Attorney: "So you went up to the roof of your building and knelt down and..."

Me: "I didn't have to kneel down. You could do it standing up."

Attorney: "So you stood up and began chanting this phrase, out loud?"

Me: "Yes, you're supposed to chant out loud. It's considered more effective."

Attorney: "And what exactly was this phrase, if I may ask?"

My lawyer: "Objection!"

Judge: "I'll allow it."

Me: "Well, it's Japanese. I have no idea what it means. You just say it by memory, repeat it over and over."

Attorney: "And the phrase is...?"

Me: It's. . . um. . . well, it's. . . The actual phrase is -- the way they pronounce it -- goes like this: Nam-myho-renge-kyo.

Attorney: "Excuse me?"

Me: "NAM-MYOHO-RENGE-KYO. Just like that -- Nam-myoho-renge-kyo. Nam-myoho-renge-kyo. You say it over and over."

Attorney: "So you were saying this over and over again when Mrs. Danaher happened to come up on the roof?"

Me: "I don't know. I didn't notice her come up on the roof. But one time I glanced over and saw her with Teddy adjusting a TV antenna. We had experienced a really big windstorm the night before and a lot of people's antennas got all turned around."

Attorney: "And when you saw Mrs. Danaher looking at you, you kept right on chanting?"

Me: "I didn't notice her looking at me, I only saw her out of the corner of my eye. Yes, I kept right on chanting, I didn't want to break the concentration. Why shouldn't I continue? I wasn't shouting, I was speaking low. It was really no one else's business."

Attorney: "And you say this is a recognized, legitimate religion that your coworkers introduced you to? That requires you to chant out loud on the roof?"

My lawyer: "Your Honor, this has no bearing..."

Judge: "Where are you going with this, counsel?"

Attorney: "It goes to the issue of 'continual nuisance', the grounds on which we are seeking to evict the tenant."

Me: (Angrily) "Yes, it's a legitimate religion! In fact, there was a front-page article in the ***Wall Street Journal*** *about it a few months back. And I have a right to practice any religion I want, or chant anything I choose. This is still supposed to be a free country, isn't it?"*

My own lawyer, who was one of the partners in the law firm where I worked (he had agreed to take my case at a reduced rate), was questioning me now:

My lawyer: "Have you ever willfully or inadvertently allowed your sink or your bathtub to overflow?"

Me: "No, never."

My lawyer: "Have you ever allowed water to splash onto the floor while you are showering?"

Me: "Absolutely not."

My lawyer: "Have you ever poured or spilled water onto your bathroom floor as some sort of a cleansing or religious ritual?"

Me: "Of course not!"

My lawyer: "Have you ever had an accident, such as a toilet overflowing, or knocking over a bucket of water while mopping?"

Me: "No, that's never happened since I moved into my apartment, not a single time."

My lawyer: "Do you sometimes take long showers, even up to an hour or more?"

Me: "Yes, I'll admit to that -- they help me with back aches. . . the hot water, that is, and the pressure, too. . ."

When my lawyer called Bridgett Danaher back to the stand, he asked her if I had ever harassed her or threatened her or damaged any of her property. She had to answer no. He asked her if it was possible that the water leakage into her apartment was the result of corroded sixty-year-old pipes within the walls. She had to say yes. He asked her if she had ever approached me in a nice way, in person, to discuss her concerns regarding things like loud music coming from my apartment. She had to say no. My friend Maxine took the stand and testified that she considered me an honest, responsible, fundamentally decent human being who would never cause harm to any other tenant or their property, either willfully or through negligence.

In the end the judge refused to grant my landlord an eviction, but insisted we settle. I agreed to take less frequent long showers and run the water at a slightly lower pressure. I also agreed to pay the cost of installing a sliding glass shower door. Management agreed to commence a major upgrade of the plumbing system, replacing old pipes where necessary.

After the whole exhausting ordeal, we finally got out of the courthouse. I took Maxine out for a drink to thank her for taking a day off from work and spending it in a gloomy courtroom just so she could say some nice things about me. As soon as I got home, I collapsed on the bed. I decided to call in sick the next morning.

As for that chanting business, a new Buddhist fad had developed among New York City office workers, started up by some Korean entrepreneur, I believe. In my office, one of the secretaries and a young intern had gotten deeply involved with it and I had let them take me to a meeting at a "church" that resembled a sports arena. The sight of a few hundred people chanting loudly in unison had been quite startling and pretty impressive. Nothing at all like the monotone hum of parishioners mouthing *Our Father* and *The Apostle's Creed* in the Roman Catholic masses I was used to. So I promised Paul and Barbara that I would try the chanting for two solid weeks. For at least an hour at a time, I told them.

I had two more days to go. The chanting was like prayer. You closed your eyes and focused intently on something you really wanted. It didn't have to be something noble like a more challenging career, or a better relationship with your spouse or your child. It could be something perfectly crass and pedestrian -- like a new refrigerator or mini-van, or to score big at the slot machines in Atlantic City. The intoning of the phrase out loud was supposed to set up a vibration that aligned your desires with powerful forces in the universe that wanted you to succeed. The new "religion" had become so popular that it was deemed worthy of a cover story in the **Wall Street Journal**, just as I'd declared in the courthouse.

The next morning dawned blue and beautiful -- a perfect day to have taken off from work. I thought, why not get today's chanting session out of the way early. So up to the roof I went. I had been focusing on something precious to me that I had recently lost: a charcoal gray wool sweater that my grandmother had passed down to me. It was amazingly warm and soft without being the least bit itchy, and it fit me like a silk stocking. I had somehow lost or misplaced it -- where, I had no idea. On a bus? A park bench? Flung over a chair in the company cafeteria and left there? I had retraced all my steps and had been looking everywhere. I 'd been calling up lost and found departments. Nothing. So I chanted:

"Nam-myoho-renge-kyo
Nam-myoho-renge-kyo
Nam-myoho-renge-kyo. . ."

And over and over again for a whole hour. I couldn't believe people really did this seriously. I couldn't believe Barbara and Paul did it. Yet even the newspaper article had suggested that the chanting often produced results. I'd clipped the piece and shown it to them.

After I was done chanting I went down to the street and decided to go across to the *Grand Union* supermarket and pick up a gallon of *Poland Spring Water.* I thought it would be a good day to start a three-day fast -- another ritual I indulged in occasionally. On the way back up the elevator with the water, the car stopped on the 5th floor. Mr. Castiglione, who lived next door to the Danahers, got on with an unlit cigar in his mouth. He was a retired accountant who sometimes did tax returns for people in the building. While the elevator was stopped I saw Mrs. Danaher open her door to let in Teddy, the super. A piece of her ceiling had indeed caved in, and the mess still hadn't been cleaned up. As soon as she caught sight of me standing in the elevator her eyes turned into daggers of hatred. I truly felt bad about the whole thing. Secretly I vowed to try taking my "hydrotherapy sessions" only every other day, and to turn down the volume on the stereo, but my face gave away nothing.

Again I thought about maybe trying to get some psychiatrist to write me a prescription for an anti-anxiety drug. Just something to help combat the obsessive-compulsive rituals like the two-hour showers and the excessive sunbathing. But somehow, in my lonely, despairing state of mind I felt that much of this was Roxanne's fault, and Sadie's too. I had opened up my heart to them and shared intimacies at very vulnerable times in my life and it was their betrayal that had at length driven me to all of this madness. I was certain of it. My natural desire and tendency to pour out love and joy had been choked off, blocked, forced to take a detour. It had turned toxic and sought expression in bizarre symbolic substitute gratifications.

So thanks Roxanne, thanks Sadie, for turning an already broken spirit into a textbook case of neurosis. Wonder what kind of karma that'll get you. And so, I had managed to keep myself from getting evicted this time -- good for me. But I was far from feeling I had won anything or triumphed in any way. It was a hollow victory that only reinforced my status as an outcaste, a three-dollar bill. And I never did find Granny's sweater.

23
Swinging on a Star

THERE HAD BEEN one advantage to being out of work all those months-- a windfall of time and opportunity with which to explore my new neighborhood of Inwood Heights. Alongside the beautiful Fort Tryon Park with its towering views of the Hudson, there was Inwood Hill Park, which stretched for almost a mile along the riverfront following the abandoned railroad tracks. The neighborhood's population, a slightly incongruous mix of recent Dominican immigrants, hip young refugees from more expensive parts of Manhattan, and an older off-the-boat Irish community gave it a unique flavor.

I began taking long leisurely walks just to observe and take in the vibes, culture, and commerce of an area unknown to most New Yorkers. Eventually, I even got into jogging and I kept it up even after I finally went back to work as a paralegal in a midtown law firm. I began taking daily early evening runs along the riverfront in Inwood Hill Park as a way to keep fit and active after sitting in front of a desk all day. At some point I started to notice a fellow jogger who seemed to come to the park about the same time every day as I did.

He was trim and muscular, with blue eyes and honey-blonde hair. He was somewhat short – maybe an inch taller than me – but well-proportioned and handsome. When we got to talking I learned that he was born in San Juan, Puerto Rico, where his father, an airline pilot, still lived. But he had emigrated with his mother many years before, had gone to college in the U.S., earned a Master's degree in Health Administration, and now had a good job working for the Washington D.C.-based **Centers for Disease Control.** He lived in a fifth-floor apartment directly across the courtyard from mine.

We took some jogs together, although I couldn't keep up with his pace. Alejandro was well-mannered and polite and somewhat studious. His speech had no trace of a Hispanic or New York accent. You couldn't tell where he was from, only that he was educated and well-read. He was my age -- exactly. In fact, his birthday fell on the day before mine in the same year. I liked him a lot and we seemed to click right away. I was surprised to find that he had lived in the building longer than I had, yet somehow I had never encountered him until now. He told me, however, that he had noticed me many times and was curious. To his eyes there appeared something brave, fiercely independent, and even "elegant" about me and he wanted to know more. But there had never been quite the right opportunity to approach me until I started coming to the park. I was taken aback, even a bit startled, to hear him say such a thing. All the while that I was not even aware he existed, he had been watching me and liking what he saw. It was flattering.

The first time I went to Alejandro's place I could scarcely believe that a guy, all by himself, could furnish an apartment so artfully and tastefully. I was even more impressed than I had been when I first saw Lorraine's Hell's Kitchen pad. The theme was Japanese. There was an unadorned white platform bed covered with a snow-white silk comforter, luxurious in its sheer simplicity. A bamboo shoji screen with rice paper panels partitioned the dining area off from the kitchen. In a corner stood a floor lamp with an iridescent glass shade. A hand-painted silk folding screen graced one entire wall, depicting a group of dancing cranes on a gold leaf background. In the living room was a sleek, low-to-the-ground sleeper sofa framed by a pair of black lacquer end tables. And, leaning picturesquely in the crease between two walls in another corner was a beautiful Spanish acoustic guitar. Wow! This guy was a class act.

The first time I spent the night at Alejandro's place he strummed his guitar and sang a few bars of *When Sunny Gets Blue*. He showed me photographs from his many travels. He had spent the year after college graduation touring Southeast Asia with a couple of friends. They had stayed in youth hostels and earned extra money doing odd jobs, including giving English lessons to local businessmen. He spoke fluent Spanish, of course, and a little French. When he returned to the U.S. he began his job with the CDC and, because of his background and ease in international settings he was often given overseas assignments, such as working with the health ministries of developing countries to set up public health surveillance systems, or helping to immunize children in remote rural villages.

Often, while talking about his life and his work, he made me feel quite useless in comparison. What had I ever done to help people in need, or to advance larger universal goals that improved the lot of mankind? What had I ever done to make the world a better place? It was bad enough that he put me to shame when it came to home decorating, and that he could speak two foreign languages. Damn! I thought to myself -- maybe this guy is out of my league. But one of Alejandro's odd jobs overseas had been mixing cocktails in a tiki bar, where he'd earned a reputation for creativity. Those wonderful coconut rum and cherry concoctions he would whip up for me in his deluxe super blender -- drinks with such colorful monikers as *Bahama Mama, Captain Creamsicle* and *Cornholio's Revenge* -- went a long way towards drowning out the inner voice of reproach. There was still time for me to make my contribution to humanity, I would muse, as the alcohol hit me. But right now, it was all about unwinding and enjoying the moment.

After handing me my drink, Alejandro would waltz over to the stereo and put on a Windham Hill tape. I was not familiar with Windham Hill, which was an independent record label founded by a folk guitarist who wanted to bring the works of alternative artists -- those creating what was then called "world music" -- to a wider audience. It was a revelation. The recordings were of the finest quality and the sounds were eclectic, rich and varied, including Celtic harps, jazz guitar, mandolin, and electronica. The music set a mood that was lush, refined, and cerebral. It made me feel, as I sat sipping my second frozen cocktail and relaxing with this cool guy, as if I were slowly ascending to a higher spiritual plane.

And Alejandro had another special talent to go along with his bartender skills. He knew how to cook up a mean batch of "space cookies" i.e., baked confections containing small amounts of cannabis. I would sit in the kitchen and watch with awe as he melted butter in a pan, then added about 4 grams of finely ground weed and let it simmer for about a half hour. As he happily explained to me while standing in front of the stove, he had to do this because the psychoactive ingredient that gets you stoned – THC – is not water soluble and must be infused into a fat or an oil in order to be digested and get into the bloodstream. The result is a high that comes on much more gradually but lasts much longer than you would get from smoking it.

Sometimes a couple of Alejandro's friends came over for a "Space Cookie" social. A few hours later as the pot kicked in we would have marathon discussions about books, film, art, music, and whatever else came to mind. The intellectual stimulation was like electricity coursing through me, while the weed allowed my body to melt into the couch, engendering a perfect harmony of mind, body, and spirit. Think three voices in a doo-wop group striking a beautiful, blessed chord at the end of a song. Maybe life could be perfect. Like a high-potency vitamin and mineral supplement, it seemed, Alejandro was actually good for me, a source of health and well-being. And the whole experience of sex, on his pure cotton futon mattress, took on a new dimension as it moved to a finer, more rarefied meeting ground. In this kind of exhilarating clear mountain air, the dark brooding concerns of the past were simply bleached away, leaving no aftertaste.

An idyllic summer scene: sparkling water splashing over ragged gray rocks, intense quiet all around, a pearly finespun mist overhanging everything, thick brown mud carpeting the ground like dark chocolate frosting spread over a devil's food cake, the pure green organic scent of the air. And it all felt as if we were a thousand miles away from New York City. Alejandro was putting on a little show for two teenage girls who were sitting on a large flat stone by the shore. Someone had tied a long heavy rope to a thick tree branch and he was slowly swinging on it, Tarzan style, back and forth over the pond. Swinging gracefully to and fro, his legs dangling just a few feet above the glistening surface of the water. He looked so cute with his compact, well-muscled body and damp locks of sandy blonde hair fluttering carelessly in the breeze. Alejandro had a huge happy grin on his face and the girls were giggling with delight.

Actually, we were not all that far from the city after all, maybe ninety minutes away. We were in the *Greenbrook Sanctuary*, a nature preserve and geological park in Alpine, New Jersey, one of the loveliest and least known parts of the much-maligned state of New Jersey. In fact, Alpine was home to some of the richest people in America. Alejandro and I had been dating for about a year and a half when he told me about the place and said he had always wanted to visit and to spend a day exploring the pristine grounds. It was a rare treat to be able to escape the constant din and dirty air of the big bad city.

Later on, we trudged through the mud hand in hand up steep boulders and cliffs, slipping and sliding together, high on weed, oblivious to the risks of stumbling and tumbling over sharp-edged rocks. We padded through a field dotted with tiny bright yellow sunflowers. Alejandro stooped down to pluck a few of them and fasten them to the upper-left pocket of my blue denim jacket. We had trekked through several trails, looking for a quiet tucked-away place where Alejandro could set up the new handwoven rope hammock he had brought along. Way out in the thick of the woods we found it. A perfect spot between two sturdy trees. He carefully drove pegs into each tree trunk and suspended the hammock. Within moments we were both lying in it together, swinging gently from side to side like two babes in a cradle. The light drizzle had ceased, the sun had finally come out and it was now warm enough to throw off our jackets. Alejandro loaded a Windham Hill tape into his Sony Walkman, we lit another joint, and then we each grabbed one of the pair of headphones so we could share the music. No one else was around. You might say it was a classic *it doesn't get any better than this* moment.

After our enchanting day at the sanctuary, Alejandro and I boarded the bus back to the terminal on the New York side of the George Washington Bridge. Then we waited for the A train which took us right back to our apartment building. We stopped at our local Latin restaurant, *La Gran Via*, and enjoyed a dinner of fried rice with squid. Then we went to the *Grand Union* supermarket and got a six-pack of cold beer. At Alejandro's place we both crashed on the sleeper sofa, laughing at the ceiling, snapping the pull tabs off our beer cans, and feeling grateful.

The next day, Sunday, we decided to go for a jog in the park. It was a gorgeous early summer day and by ten in the morning the park was already teeming with runners, families picnicking on the grass, kids playing baseball. Down at the far end of the park a group of Dominican men were roasting a whole pig on a spit, Hawaiian style. Hot Latin dance music blasted out of "boom boxes" -- those battery-powered portable stereos with handles that everybody carried around. We turned away from the river towards the foot bridge and climbed the steps up to the thickly wooded hills. We began walking the well-beaten path at a moderate pace, crunching tinder-dry twigs underfoot, inhaling the fragrance of bark and decomposing leaves, watching alternating bands of light and shadow as the sun, playing hide and seek, dappled the forest floor. A Korean family, each member holding a brown paper bag, was carefully picking wild raspberries.

Later that evening, while sampling a fine Johannesburg Riesling and listening to the haunting piano strains of George Winston, Alejandro told me he probably would be going away. The CDC was assigning him to a facility in Puerto Rico, and it would likely be a long-term assignment, at least two years. He was actually looking forward to it, because his dad still lived there and Alejandro hadn't seen him in years. He was also excited about the chance to try his hand at scuba diving again, a hobby he had taken up briefly while on his overseas travels but never had the chance to pursue. He hadn't hinted at anything like this before and I was a bit stunned. When would he be leaving, I wondered aloud? He thought it might be as soon as three weeks from the day. Well at least that would give him the opportunity to accompany me to my cousin's wedding the following Sunday.

Mom and Dad were rather shocked to see me with my handsome date, whom they had never met until then. They may even have gotten their hopes up that their wayward daughter was embracing the wholesome state of "normalcy" at last. And indeed, there's no telling how things might have turned out if Alejandro were not leaving. But three weeks after the wedding, on a balmy Saturday night, Alejandro's mother came from the Bronx to her son's apartment, cooked up a banquet and threw a big going-away party for him to which all his friends were invited. More than two dozen showed up and we laughed and danced and ate and drank till 3 am. Then everyone gave Alejandro a big hug or a handshake, wished him all the best, and left.

Afterwards I stuck around to help him and his mom clean up, and to take one last look at that splendid apartment -- the scene of such gratifying interludes and fond memories -- already partially dismantled. Alejandro was officially moving out on Tuesday. After work on Monday, I was in a state of semi-shock and sadness as I helped him with his last-minute packing, not able to fully process that he was really leaving. Our last night together was sweet and somber, sans weed or alcohol, but not music. Alejandro strummed his beautiful guitar and sang me a Spanish farewell song. Then we dove under the cool white sheets of his sleek platform bed and held each other, skin to skin, one last time. He promised to write and send postcards.

And sure enough, two weeks later there was a postcard in my mailbox with an unfamiliar stamp on it featuring a gorgeous photo of Flamenco Beach, located a few miles east of the Puerto Rican mainland. I almost wanted to jump on a plane. But of course I knew that I wouldn't, and knew that our romance, if not our friendship, was certainly over. A smart good-looking guy like Alejandro was bound to attract legions of attractive women in Puerto Rico and, under the influence of intoxicating tropical breezes and the sounds of surf and salsa, all thoughts of me, I was quite certain, would slowly evaporate over the span of two years.

I suppose it had all been like watching a gripping, unforgettable movie. Captivating, thrilling -- you lose yourself in the story and spectacle and time seems to stand still. Maybe the film has you on the edge of your seat gasping, or in stitches laughing, or in tears sobbing. But then the whole experience comes to an abrupt end and the lights switch back on. The law of gravity reasserts itself and it's back to solid ground and flattened emotions. And whatever may have gotten drowned out in all that Dolby surround sound becomes audible once again.

And for me that was the buzz of the alarm clock going off at six in the morning and the voice of my boss at work chiding me once again for my extended lunch hours. It was back to the tedium of a boring nine-to-five job which didn't pay all that well. Yet another unforgettable person had stepped into my life only to step out again after less than two years. Maybe I was just meant to go solo in life, or maybe I was cursed or being punished for some unknown offense committed in a past life. Or maybe I was just unlucky and there was no rhyme or reason to it at all.

24
Ruffles, Feathers, and Lace

THREE WEEKS SINCE Alejandro's departure and I am back on the unemployment line. Two of the partners at my law firm left to start their own practice, taking many of the firm's clients with them. That led to a round of layoffs which included me and the "Buddhists" Barbara and Paul -- assuring they'd have something to chant about in the future. But chanting is not going to help me find another job, and after weeks of fruitless searching, I am starting to get a little frantic. I take a job as a desk clerk at a posh new office building, signing in visitors, as a security guard at Radio City Music Hall, chasing away ticket scalpers, as a kitchen worker at a boy's prep school, serving ice cream. I take a half dozen four-hour civil service exams to land positions like *Insurance Claim Adjuster* or *Court Officer.*

Finally, one frigid afternoon in February, having just returned from the unemployment office where they'd reminded me I had only three checks left before my claim would be exhausted, I drearily pull out a wad of mail from my mailbox. Riding up the elevator to my floor, I quickly cycle through the supermarket flyers, phone and electric bills, and a picture postcard of the Rocky Mountains from Maxine who had taken a trip to Colorado. And then I spot it. A letter from one of the law firms I had sent my resume to at least six weeks earlier. I'm surprised to see it. I had been sending out resumes with cover letters all winter, but few of the law firms had taken the trouble to write back to me. I'd had to make numerous phone calls just to ensure they had actually received and looked at my resume. Of those who had written back, all had been polite rejections. But for the fact that they had waited so long to send it, I would naturally assume that this is no different. I wait till I get inside my apartment to open it.

But it's not a rejection. The letter says the firm recently expanded its real estate activities and needed to add at least two paralegals to their staff. I breathe a sigh of relief. I desperately need a job. A decent, respectable job, that is -- one requiring a college degree and paying more than minimum wage. By now I was beginning to experience something of an identity crisis. The letter suggests I call to arrange an interview as soon as convenient.

So the first thing next morning I call and we set up an appointment one week from the day -- next Tuesday, at eleven o'clock. I allow myself to get my hopes up and get slightly dizzy with anticipation. I mean, I really, urgently, absolutely, need a bona fide professional type job. However, there is just one thing that gives me pause. Of all the law firms I had written to in the course of my job campaign, none had so impossibly stuffy a name as this one. The firm went by: *Cadwalader, Wickersham and Taft*. Whew! Now this was not your garden-variety WASP law firm handle like, say, *Wells, Larson & York*, but something smacking of powdered wigs, tall clocks with swinging pendulums, and the founding fathers. But, hey, what's in a name, right? I tell myself I ought to feel lucky to have landed the interview.

I spend the next few days going over my old notes and brushing up on my areas of expertise. From the back of a closet I fetch an old textbook I had used when I was in the paralegal training program and begin to review it carefully. I focus on key areas of real estate law that I think would be most relevant to the law firm's practice. I conjure up and recite possible answers to interview questions, speaking out loud in front of the mirror. I call up a few of my references to put them on notice that a prospective employer may be contacting them.

I enlist my good friend Maxine in the effort. Luckily she had returned from her Colorado vacation just in time. I invite her over and we sit down on my living room couch with snacks laid out on the coffee table. I hand Maxine a legal pad on which I've written what I think would be the most challenging interview questions that I might be asked by the attorney who will interview me Tuesday. I've prepared all of my answers and we do a little dress rehearsal.

Later in the evening Maxine calls me to say that she thought I came across very professional, quite impressive. I hope she's not flattering me. I spend the beginning of the next week fidgeting and fussing about the interview Tuesday. I bring my skirt to the dry cleaner, get my shoes polished, and press several blouses and tops, wondering what the weather will be like Tuesday. I call my mother and tell her I've got an interview at a very prestigious law firm. I do more studying, call the woman at the firm to confirm our appointment, and keep my fingers crossed.

Monday night I get to bed extra early and the next morning I'm downtown by 9:30, an hour and a half before the scheduled interview. I find a French bakery, go in and order a cup of coffee and a broccoli-cheese croissant. I don't normally do breakfast but today I feel I might need some extra nourishment along with the caffeine. Finally, I get up and walk all the way down Maiden Lane towards Pearl Street. I locate the building and walk through the gold-framed glass doors. I find the elevator bank and head upstairs to the main reception lobby.

I enter the lobby. Whoa -- what is this? Have I landed on some movie set or what? I look all around in amazement. Everything in the room screams silk stockings and blue blood. There are weighty Renaissance style portrait paintings all over the walls, hung in gilded ornamental frames. I see rich rosewood paneling everywhere, polished to a tee. There's a *Gone with the Wind* type winding staircase, and heavy three-layered velvet curtains tied back with rope and adorned with tassels and ribbons. There are leather armchairs, a settee, an intricately woven Turkish rug. What the hell!

I feel as if I've been transported to a Victorian era drawing room on some grand English manor. Quite a setting indeed, I think. About the only thing missing is an upright *pianoforte* and a few characters from a Jane Austen novel chattering on about foxhunts, private balls, and how lovely the hollyhocks look in Kensington Gardens. I am greeted by a well put together frosty-haired receptionist who reminds me of the Maggie Smith character in the film *The Prime of Miss Jean Brodie,* except she has a proper British, rather than Scottish accent. She is sitting at a preposterously oversized wooden desk. When I tell her with whom I have an appointment she picks up the phone and gestures toward one of the armchairs, indicating that I was to have a seat.

I am kept waiting for twenty-five minutes. Finally, the secretary of the attorney who is to meet with me comes out to get me. She is dressed in some fussy pink garb with a lace front, ruffles, and puff sleeves. I am escorted down a hall to a corner office where I meet my interviewer standing in the doorway. Tall and regal in bearing, this lady is wearing an exquisite satin blouse under a very expensive looking linen jacket, with choice pieces of jewelry in just the right places. I feel slightly intimidated but try to appear and sound as businesslike and composed as possible.

The woman invites me into her office, and I take a seat on a small couch across from her desk. She tells me she works in the Securitization division which is rapidly expanding and in dire need of legal assistants. It turns out that the firm -- riding the wave of exuberance in the financial sector brought on by President Reagan's policy of slash and burn deregulation -- had innovated exciting new forms of securities backed by residential home mortgages. They are particularly interested in me because I appear to be quite conversant with the language of mortgage notes and related documents. There will be tons of paperwork to review, I am told, and they really need someone to go through them with a fine-tooth comb and check for certain provisions or legal terms. I would have my own private office and work with limited supervision.

We stand up and she invites me to follow her for a quick tour of the grounds. I pass by a row of quiet, plushly carpeted cubicles with dark wooden partitions where most of the secretarial staff are housed. I can't get over how extravagantly dressed everyone is. I wonder what proportion of their salary these gals spend on their costly threads. I can hear a dozen keyboards clicking away, but don't feel as if I'm walking the aisles of a typical office typing pool. It feels more like a stroll down the corridors of some upper crust English boarding school. We continue walking, ascend a half flight of stairs and, pausing briefly, she proudly points out the executive dining room which occupies the whole side of the floor. It resembles a super pricey French restaurant with immaculate white tablecloths and fresh flowers on each table.

After the office tour, I meet with two other attorneys, both of whom I will be working with closely if hired. They are only slightly less intimidating than the first. On the desk of one I spy an odd ornament -- what looks like birds under a glass dome. And they are not replicas or figurines. From the colors and texture of the feathers I can tell that these are real specimens -- stuffed birds. I wonder how much that cost and where one would find a taxidermist in New York. The office of the other attorney has some fabric wallpaper with a busy scroll and vine pattern.

The two lawyers invite me into the second office and we exchange pleasantries. Then they let me take a look at some of the actual documents I would be reviewing. They pose some questions to test my knowledge and seem pleased with my answers, nodding at each other and smiling. The job as described appears straightforward, uncomplicated, and manageable enough. When they ask me about salary requirements, I decide to mention a figure near the top of my range. No one raises an eyebrow. Back out in the lobby, everyone shakes my hand warmly and looks at one another with smiles of approval. I am told the attorneys will consult among themselves and that someone would be getting in touch with me in a few days.

I leave feeling strange, as if I've just stepped out of some weird exhibit at a carnival, or like someone had just played a silly prank on me -- like say, leaving a plastic mold fashioned to look like vomit on the chair I'm about to sit on. I'm not quite sure why, but I feel disoriented, off-balance. I find myself thinking, *"Are you kidding? They'll never offer ME this job."* Surprisingly, the thought hits me with a certain degree of satisfaction -- relief, even. But wait! I NEED this job! The nature of the work, the pay -- all appeared perfect. It would be nothing less than a stroke of fantastic luck if they actually hired me. And the interview seemed to have gone so well. Confused at the perplexing mix of emotions I feel, I decide to go home and forget all about it for the time being. The ball is in their court now anyway.

Several days pass. The weekend arrives. I haven't heard anything. That Saturday night I head downtown to meet my friend Maxine. It seemed that Maxine, ever the adventure seeker, wanted to take in a bit of the hard-core punk rock scene in the East Village, and hang out at clubs like *Pyramid* and *8BC*. Feeling I could use a little recreation I had agreed to get together for the weekend. So I meet Maxine on St. Mark's Place and we head for Avenue A. Within the pitch-black walls of the *Pyramid Club* we find a motley collection of humanity: twenty-somethings sporting spiked green hair and bracelets that resemble dog collars, skinny guys dressed all in black leather, nerdy sci-fi types with horn-rimmed glasses, heavily tattooed skinheads, wig-wearing drag queens. We listen to raucous New Wave music and watch self-styled performance artists sing, dance, and act out -- their histrionics just another part of the entertainment.

Later we get brave and walk across blocks of abandoned burnt-out buildings in the notorious "Alphabet City" section as we make our way to the other club, *8BC*. When we get there a British band calling itself "The Vapors" does a number called "Turning Japanese." It's pretty catchy. But then some awful punk band called "Copernicus" takes the stage. We leave after the first set.

The weekend winds down, and already I begin to push *Cadwalader, Wickersham & Taft* out of my mind. By Tuesday morning I get out of bed and realize it's been one full week since the interview and I haven't heard a word. They probably could intuit that I was just not a good fit, I think to myself without any palpable sense of disappointment. "Oh well, back to square one," I mutter under my breath.

One hour later the phone rings. It's the hiring partner at the firm calling to tell me the job is mine if I want it. They offer me the very top of my salary range. For a moment I'm stunned. I mumble something like "oh?" and "thank you," and "I'll get back to you before the end of the week." For the next few days I agonize over it, talk about it with my mother, talk about it with Maxine. Both think it would be a great opportunity for me, too good to pass up.

So I begin trying to picture myself as a valued member of the CWT team, reporting dutifully to that impressive building on Maiden Lane just blocks from Wall Street, a building owned in full by the firm, not merely rented space like the offices occupied by 90 percent of the city's law firms. I envision myself clad in a black London Fog trench coat, carrying a handsome leather briefcase, walking to work each morning, cup of coffee in hand, with passersby from nearby offices just naturally assuming I'm a lawyer or some Wall Street banker. Hmm, not bad, I muse.

But then I throw some cold water on my face. I force myself to remember just how I felt when I was there, right there in the place where I will likely be spending well over eight hours a day, forty hours a week, if I accept the job offer. Uncomfortable visions intrude. I see myself poring through the racks at *Lord & Taylor's* in search of a wardrobe worthy of my new station, eagerly seeking that tag with three different colored slashes of ink through the price, indicating the final markdown. I see myself fussing over my hairdo, wondering if it exudes enough class and refinement. I imagine coming into the main lobby every morning and being spooked by the eyes of all those illustrious forebears staring down at me from those gaudy picture frames. I wonder if my voice would pass muster while on the phone with really important clients -- would I need to get a voice coach to refine my Bronx accent?

And suddenly, like a traumatic memory recovered under hypnosis, visions of the *Katherine Gibbs Secretarial School* flood into my brain. The summer after I graduated college, before I decided to enroll in the paralegal school, I had pounded the pavements looking for something constructive to do with my BA in English. I had hit ad agencies, newspapers, publishing houses, magazines, the broadcast networks – any place where good writing and competent verbal skills would be an asset. In every single case, bar none, I was asked to sit down at an *IBM Selectric* typewriter and take a typing test. As with everyone in my high school, a semester of typing was required for graduation. But I could barely make it to 35 words per minute and passed the course by the skin of my teeth. I was not able to type any faster without greatly sacrificing accuracy. Nervous as I already was about interviewing for entry-level jobs as a fresh college grad, my woeful typing skills dealt the death blow every time I sat in front of one of those dreadful machines. I flunked every single typing test. The smart thing to do would have been to go home and PRACTICE, PRACTICE, PRACTICE -- but whether due to foolish pride, obstinacy, or just plain stupidity, the embarrassing experiences served only to reinforce my resistance, giving me even more of a typewriter-phobia.

After that summer ended, I realized I would never find a suitable job and sunk into a dangerous depression. I refused to get out of bed and moaned aloud about being destined for the poor house, or maybe for a life of crime. My parents, fearing for my sanity, wrote to *Katherine Gibbs*, requesting information and an application for me. The institution, founded in 1911 by two sisters, was originally dedicated to instructing upper middle-class women in the arts of stenography and taking dictation. The school claimed a great track record of success, with virtually 98 percent of their graduates finding respectable, good-paying jobs as administrative assistants and executive secretaries in corporate offices all along the eastern seaboard. My dad offered to pay the full cost of tuition, which I could pay back after I got my first job.

But when I looked through their catalog I was, well, horrified. There, in black and white photos, were the smiling "Gibbs Girls," perched on upholstered office chairs, wearing elbow-length white gloves, steno pad at the ready, cheerfully taking dictation. Then there were the Gibbs instructors -- starched, matronly looking middle-aged women with dour expressions that seemed to announce: "Inappropriate behavior will NOT be tolerated here." I tried to read the boastful descriptions of the top-notch training the school provided, the comprehensive curriculum, the modern facility and equipment, etc., etc. But my eyes were distracted by other things, like their rules and policies. In the classroom, trousers or pants were verboten, scuffed shoes or runny stockings not allowed, poor diction would be pointed out and corrected, poise and manners were expected at all times, and perfectly coiffured hair was a must. What? I couldn't believe my dad was willing to fork over thousands of dollars to put me -- ME, of all people -- in a goddamn finishing school!

On Friday I called back the hiring partner at *Cadwalader, Wickersham, & Taft* and politely turned down the job. I just couldn't do it. My mother didn't understand, of course, but then she had never understood much regarding me. There were times shortly afterwards when I regretted my decision, wanted to kick myself for being a fool, lambasted myself for being so inflexible and unwilling to adjust, to take things in stride. Especially when I so desperately needed a steady source of income. But then I would think of long white gloves and stuffed birds in glass domes and frilly puffed sleeves and all the silly phony trappings of pomp and baronial splendor and it all just made me cringe. And laugh.

The truth is, they would have been crazy to hire me, even if I had accepted the offer. At some point there would have been an embarrassing scene, or I'd have made an inappropriate remark. Some unforgivable blunder in etiquette, some awful social faux pas -- it would have been just a matter of time. Or else, in some devilish satirical fit I might have scrawled some uncomplimentary graffiti in the ladies' room. I probably would have been their worst nightmare. I actually did them a great favor by turning down their job. A lordly gesture on my part. It was the least I could do.

A few weeks after rejecting the job offer from *Cadwalader, Wickersham & Taft* I got a letter from a midtown law firm to whom I had sent a resume nearly two months before, with no response. But the firm had just acquired a new client -- a real estate developer who built dozens of shopping malls from coast to coast. My expertise in retail leases was an asset they suddenly needed. It was a medium-sized firm with four partners and located right near the New York Coliseum in Columbus Circle. When I went for the interview, I found that the place had a really relaxed feel, a certain pleasant messiness. No pretensions, no snobs, no WASPs. Their salary offer was not nearly as much as what I had just turned down. Regardless, I accepted it happily.

25
Saints and Sinners

I DIDN'T THINK I was drunk or anything. I had ordered a vodka and tonic at the bar when I first came in and it wasn't particularly strong. Later I ordered another, and was only halfway through it. That was all. But something weird started happening as she was talking to me. Her face seemed to be morphing into someone or something else. When I first entered the club I had noticed a pretty wavy-haired blonde standing near the bar, looking somehow out of place. Later on, after I had retired to a dimly lit portion of the lounge, I saw her again, looking straight at me with the slightest hint of a smile, and then, seemingly, beginning to float towards me in slow motion. She moved gracefully, her flowing yellow hair cascading sexily about her shoulders. She was wearing some kind of loose-fitting tunic featuring a profusion of vividly colored flowers that reminded me of my great aunt's French country bedspread. Her expression was so serene, so knowing, so self-assured. She seemed to be bearing gifts or good news or some kind of benediction. As she slowly came into view from the far side of the room it was as if I were apprehending a modern-day Demeter, the original Greek fertility goddess, promising a bountiful harvest and blessing the earth with amber waves of grain. She fastened her eyes on me with a laser focus and moved straight in my direction.

But right now I seemed to be looking into the eyes of a precocious, unbearably adorable nine-year-old girl. With her face artfully tilted in a coquettish pose, she kept breaking into these wide effervescent grins, white teeth gleaming, eyes beaming. Her voice was sweet, childlike, and grateful sounding, as if all she wanted to do was talk and was delighted to have found a listener. I was so transfixed by the spectacle I could barely hear what she was saying. There was something about a trip to Israel, about studying acting, a mention of *Our Lady of Peace* Church and someone named Carmen, and something about liking older women. While listening, I wondered which of the two versions of her was the true one, and why she was coming on to me this way. Me, out of all the maybe fifty or more women I had seen at the club so far that night. We were in a beautiful high tech gay disco in the East Village called *The Saint*. Not long before, the club had been wildly popular but had since fallen on hard times after the AIDS crisis so decimated the community. Now the management rented out the venue to private concerns and event planners for special occasions, and this was the Summer Solstice Party for Women.

She still hadn't told me her name, or had she? I tried to settle in my mind whether or not I had come here in the hopes of meeting someone. I think I had just wanted to immerse myself in the atmosphere, reacquaint myself with the vibe. After two years of dating men, never having completely gotten over the emotional devastation that came in the wake of the Roxanne debacle, it seemed it was time to come out of hiding and get back in the scene. Yet when I arrived here I had felt shy, had spent the last hour sitting by myself and staring at the flickering images on the giant video screen mounted above the bar. I had not even gone upstairs to the dance floor. But somehow this mythical creature had spotted me, must have liked something, and walked straight over without the slightest hesitation. In answer to her questions, I had revealed a little about myself, such as my age -- 33 -- where I worked, where I lived, how often I came here, etc. She was seven years younger, did not work, lived in an old walk-up apartment on the Upper East Side near First Avenue, and came here as often as possible. She told me she loved to dance, and suggested we head upstairs.

On the dance floor, she metamorphosed into yet another edition of herself. We moved towards a crowd of women gathered under the club's huge domed ceiling, where all the dance action was. Suddenly, beneath that great rotating mirrored disco ball, in the multicolored strobe lights pulsing to the beat of house music blaring from dozens of embedded speakers, she became a performer, a main attraction. With her svelte, well-muscled, well-proportioned figure, she dipped and spun and gyrated like a professional backup dancer on an MTV music video. Others on the dance floor stopped dancing to stare at her. Amazingly, while a star projector machine just like the kind used to create effects at a planetarium, flooded the dance floor with twinkling stars, her swaying form was instantly wrapped in a halo of shimmer and glitter, making her look like a cross between a rhinestone spangled Vegas showgirl and somebody's fantasy of heaven's gatekeeper.

Then, as quickly as she'd begun, she stopped dancing when the next tune dropped, said she didn't care for the music, and suggested we go upstairs to the third level. The space above resembled a Greek theater and there were seats that looked like bleachers. We climbed up to a spot far removed from the dance floor and sat down. I complimented her on her striking performance, and she said she had once considered becoming a professional dancer. She suggested getting a few drinks; we spotted a wandering cocktail waitress and ordered margaritas. We imbibed, licking salt off the rim of the glass, and talked some more. When the waitress came by again I ordered a second round.

Gradually I became aware of her hands beginning to paw me a little as she told me again how much she was into "older women." While raising my drink to my mouth I found myself shyly slipping the other arm around her shoulder. As the liquor went to my head my hands tentatively explored her lustrous hair and moved about her back and shoulders. Soon we were making out and I was thinking vaguely about how surprisingly strange the night had turned out. I had doubted whether I would even wind up talking to anyone, much less necking like a couple of teenagers in the back seat of a car. I tried to stop analyzing and just enjoy the moment, weird as it was.

All of a sudden, she pulled herself away, looked at her watch, smiled at me almost as if embarrassed, and excused herself to go to the ladies' room. When she came back, she looked different. I couldn't say how exactly. We sat a while longer, finishing off our drinks. We exchanged observations about some of the women there, about the DJ spinning the records, about what a cool club it was and the novelty of seeing it full of partying women instead of bare-chested guys blowing whistles and sniffing amyl nitrate out of little glass vials. But then her face seemed to turn serious, somber even, and she appeared to be deep in thought. A shadow slowly descended over her. For a few minutes neither of us said a word. Suddenly, somehow, the fetching nymphet I had been gazing at in wonder less than a half hour ago was gone, so was the sexy, uninhibited party girl. Nor was there any sign of the wise and brazen Earth mother who had casually swooped down on me like a bird of prey. Just who was this person, anyway?

She looked at her watch again, said she was getting tired and thought she ought to go home. I decided I would leave too. Out on the street, she said she was glad she'd met me and hoped to see me again. Somewhat confused, I asked her for her phone number, but she declined. She said I could give her my number instead. I scribbled it down on a slip of paper and handed it to her. She thanked me, then hailed a cab. And she finally told me her name. It was Mariel.

The next morning I woke up with a hangover and tried to piece together the events of the night before in my mind. Things were a bit scrambled, but the image of Mariel, or rather, the various versions of her that I had glimpsed last night emerged from the haze in sharp relief. I smiled to myself and shook my head. I wondered if she would ever call me. Probably not, I thought -- she seemed a bit flaky. Cute as hell, but flaky. Still, I thought it might be fun to go out with her, a pleasant diversion, something light and refreshing. You know, kind of like a slice of watermelon at a summer picnic. But the whole work week passed, and I heard nothing from Mariel. I had given her both my work number and my home phone number. Then, late Friday night, while I was watching some comedian on Johnny Carson, the phone rang. Surprise, surprise -- it was Mariel.

She told me how much she had enjoyed herself last Saturday night and asked me if I wanted to go out again. She suggested some bar I had never heard of, said a friend had told her about it. She had never been there herself. Was I adventurous enough to try it? Well sure, why not, I answered. We made a date for tomorrow night and arranged a place and time to meet.

Saturday night I met her at the Christopher Street subway station and we found our way to the unknown bar. It was one of those no-name places that make its patrons feel like members of a secret society. A nondescript building entrance with no sign on the door, no awning, no name embossed on the window, no indication other than a street number of where exactly you were. But this particular place was unusually dingy and fly-by-night looking. Walking inside felt spooky with ultra-low lighting and a collection of wisecracking, beefy dykes clad in biker garb moving in the shadows and slumped on bar stools. Dance music spewed forth loudly from a subpar sound system, but only two couples were grooving to the beat. There seemed to be other areas to explore, however, and Mariel and I soon found ourselves on a very comfortable couch in a lounge area in the back, where in other bars one might find the pool table or pinball machines.

It was difficult to get a good view of Mariel's face in the muted light, but it soon became plain that I was dealing with yet another version of this curiously multifaceted woman. For one thing, she suddenly looked much older. The bouncing, wavy blonde hair looked straighter, more severe, like a heavy veil shrouding her face. Her shoulders were hunched, her posture awkward, her face looked drawn, almost gaunt. I couldn't believe this was really the same person I had met at that magical club only a week before. When she spoke, her voice sounded halting, tenuous, as if she were nervous or not sure of what she was saying. She was asking me if I had ever wondered whether life is worth living. It seemed an odd choice of subject for what was, in effect, our "first date." Had she sensed that I was someone who struggled with depression?

After replying yes, I tried to change the subject by asking her about her family background, where she grew up, her ethnicity, etc. She was of Irish/German descent, had been raised as a Catholic, and had grown up in Fort Lee, New Jersey. But it soon became clear that she wanted to talk about other things. Suddenly looking solemn and serious, she told me that there were some unpleasant things going on in her life. She seemed to want to vent, to unburden herself, to pour all her worries and woes into a receptive ear. So I obligingly took on the role. We were pretty much alone, having this part of the lounge all to ourselves, so it seemed the perfect setting for some baring of the soul, if that indeed was what she had in mind.

Mariel told me she was in the final stages of a stormy relationship with a woman she had been living with for almost seven years. This woman had become too possessive, too controlling, and made her feel like a child. She had begun to spend more and more time away from home, and recently had moved into her mother's apartment in the East 60s. But that was no ideal solution either. The apartment was small, and her mother, who was in her mid-seventies, was not in the best of health, having suffered a nervous breakdown only a year earlier. Sometimes, Mariel told me, she felt that her only choices were either to be a marionette doll whose strings were jerked at will by her domineering girlfriend, or a nursemaid slash therapist, for her aging mother.

Life had never been easy for her, she said. The youngest of seven children, she was a "surprise" baby, born when her mother was in her late 40's and on the verge of separation from her alcoholic father. The father, often absent or in trouble with the law, could be violent and abusive while at home and had nearly turned her mother's life into a living hell. The older children, unfortunately, were not much help. One of her brothers took closely after their father and had been in juvenile detention before the age of 14. One of her sisters had run away at the age of 15 and now lived in California with some guy in a rock band. When Mariel was in the tenth grade, their dad up and left, moving in with the woman with whom he'd been having an affair. This forced Mariel to drop out of high school to attend to her ailing mother. She took part-time jobs as a waitress, babysitter, store cashier, or whatever she could find. Eventually, once the divorce settlement came conditions improved somewhat for her mother. It was about then that Mariel met her present girlfriend and shortly afterwards moved in with her at her place in Astoria, Queens. She told me she always regretted never having finished high school.

But alas, this was not the worst of it. Only last December, a few weeks before Christmas, a tragedy struck her family involving her closest sibling -- closest in age, personality, and affection. Her brother Connor, who had been diagnosed with manic-depression and was undergoing treatment, had come to visit his mother for a few days. One afternoon he was found dead in the narrow alleyway that adjoined the apartment building. He had either fallen or jumped from the bedroom window of their eighth-floor apartment. Connor had just started a new medication, and no one knew whether the side effects of the medication had caused him to become dizzy, lose his balance and fall out the window, or whether the meds failed to alleviate, perhaps even worsened his depression, causing him to abandon all hope and take the only way out he could see. In the weeks prior to the tragedy, Mariel told me, he had often sought her advice and counsel.

But Mariel disapproved of Connor's drug use, particularly his affinity for pot and mild hallucinogens like mescaline. She urged him to seek professional help for his bipolar disorder, but he turned away from Western medicine and the psychiatric establishment, instead seeking refuge in Eastern religion and practices like yoga and meditation. It had led to many arguments between them. So now she felt overcome with guilt, a deep sense of loss, and anguish over a world in which good, sensitive, seeking souls like Connor had to be sacrificed. Once or twice while relating her tale she had paused to say she didn't really know why she was unloading all of this on me. Only that she had sensed, somehow, that I was someone she could trust, someone who naturally "understood" such things.

I had been watching her closely all throughout her heartfelt outpouring, and continued to be amazed at how this person, who spoke in a plaintive, cracking voice and seemed at times on the verge of tears could possibly be the same person who last Saturday night was a sexy sparkling siren, an angelic acrobat gyrating in rapture before a crowd of stunned onlookers. If I had to describe her right now, I thought, with her bent shoulders, strained expression, haggard look, and limply hanging hair, it occurred to me that the term that would most capture her essence was: *dilapidated.* Images from those familiar black and white photos of poor folks in Appalachia, shot by Walker Evans during the Great Depression, began to flash in my mind.

The night ended strangely. Mariel said she felt exhausted and thought she would head back to her mother's, a short cab ride away. We hadn't danced, hadn't socialized with anyone in the bar, hadn't downed any drinks, hadn't made out on the couch, hadn't done anything we couldn't have done over the telephone. She thanked me profusely again for caring enough to listen, and then we parted. It was a little before 1:00 am, a time when many denizens of the city's club scene are just getting ready to leave the house. I rode with her in the cab to her mom's place, kissed her goodnight, then headed for the nearest subway. I had a much longer ride home. On the train I wondered what she wanted from me. Was she looking for a lover, a friend, a psychotherapist, or all three combined?

The following day I questioned whether Mariel might be bringing too much unwanted drama into my life. Last night there had been so much darkness, talk of sickness, tragedy, death. I had already had my share of that for the year, I thought, even though it was only the end of June. In late April my father, only 63, had nearly collapsed while walking back to his office after lunch. Tests revealed severe blockages in his arteries and he was scheduled for a triple bypass within the next few days.

During the operation a surgical clamp that was placed in my dad's chest either slipped or broke off, causing a rupture in the wall of his aorta -- the largest and most important artery in the body. He lost massive amounts of blood and his blood pressure dipped to life-threatening levels. The surgeons spent hours after the initial operation just trying to stabilize him, giving blood transfusion after blood transfusion. By 10 pm that night they still could not tell us that he was out of danger. Eventually the doctors were able to repair the torn artery and thankfully, by the end of the week, Dad was home with a good prognosis.

Then, already shaken after haphazardly bumping into the specter of bloody premature death, I was totally unprepared for what happened about a month or so later, when I happened to be rushing back to the office from my lunch break. I was in a pretty good mood and walked over there cheerfully, never suspecting that something dreadful lay ahead. At the time the area around Columbus Circle and the New York Coliseum was undergoing some new commercial development in an effort to revitalize a drab looking area of town far removed from the bustle of Midtown Manhattan and Wall Street.

One of the projects was a high-rise condo tower on Eighth Avenue, just near the beginning of the big traffic circle. I was in the habit of walking down Eighth Avenue from 59th towards the low-50s every day on my lunch hour. I was always attracted to the construction site, because the apartment tower looked so huge and impressive, dwarfing almost everything else in the area. I would try to imagine what kind of stupendous view the residents would have of Central Park from an apartment on one of the higher floors. And the site was always so busy and so noisy that one couldn't help but look up. Gargantuan cranes rising skyward, swaying girders dangling by ropes, hard hats moving about up there like so many animated splotches of bright orange -- quite a stage production, all to the earsplitting sound of jackhammers.

On this particular day it was exceptionally windy. I'm not talking about brisk breezes or ripples of air currents. This was the kind of strong gusty wind that blew your hat off your head, whipped bits of sand and gravel into your face, scattered sheets of discarded newspapers every which way, overturned trash bins and sent them rumbling down the street. In other words, a dangerous kind of wind. But scarcely did I know just how dangerous. As I hastily walked north on Eighth Avenue I began to approach the site of the apartment tower near 57th Street. I could see police cars and a small crowd of shaken onlookers gathered on the street, looking at an area directly across from the tower, and pointing to a certain spot on the sidewalk. It was a spot I passed every weekday at just about this time; I was headed there now. What on earth happened up there, I wondered, as I hurried toward the site.

The poor fellow's remains had just been carried away. I learned that some piece of debris from one of the upper stories of the tower had been turned into a lethal weapon, sent hurtling to the ground by the ferocious whipping wind. Tragically, it happened to land right on a young man, an aspiring actor on his way to a casting call. The chunk of steel or metal or wood -- I didn't know what exactly -- struck him with such force right against his head that he was partially decapitated. I gasped and shuddered to think that had I arrived just a few minutes earlier I might have witnessed the accident, might have seen up close the unspeakable sight. That I might have come face to face with the random collision of inanimate object with human flesh, heard the noise and the shrieks, seen the gushing blood, the crushed skull torn violently away from its body, and the eyes that moments before were sparkling with hope and eager anticipation reduced to lifeless gelatinous marbles devoid of purpose or plan. The sheer and utter horror of it! I nearly fainted just picturing the scene.

And of course, if I had been walking up that stretch of Eighth Avenue earlier still, it could easily have been *my* broken body lying on that sidewalk for passersby to gawk at. The next morning there was a picture of the unfortunate young man on the front page of the New York *Daily News*. He was a very good-looking fellow, and no doubt quite talented. He may have lost some sleep thinking about how difficult it would be to break into the acting profession in a city as tough as New York. But never in a million years could he have imagined the cruel and terrible way that his future would be stolen from him.

And now I thought of Mariel's brother Connor, and how awful it must have been for the family on that terrible day. I didn't want to dwell on these things anymore, not only because I had no answers, but because doing so posed a threat to my own mental health. I found myself hoping Mariel would not call to continue the gloomy conversation. I had had my fill of darkness for the time being and was not equipped to play the role of comforter.

But about three weeks later, when she did call me again, I was in for yet another surprise. She was all bubbly, giggly, and flirtatious, just like that first time at *The Saint*, before I even knew her name. She wanted to know if I had missed her, how many times I had thought of her since the night we'd gone out. The question blindsided me and I had to laugh. Then she began chirping about things like a great pair of shoes she had just bought on sale at Bloomingdale's, the latest antics of her cat, *Sir Galahad*, and the delicious French toast she had made from scratch that morning. There was not a trace of melancholy or angst in her voice. She said she had come to an understanding with her girlfriend, and they had been able to agree on an amicable separation. Mariel said she felt exhilarated, wanted to celebrate her newfound freedom. There would be no reflecting back on the past, no fear for the future, just a joyous reveling in the present. God, I thought, how does she just turn this stuff on and off -- like a switch on a radio or something.

She wanted to meet again as soon as possible, so we planned a rendezvous for Saturday night. We were going to check out a brand new women's bar that had opened on Hudson Street. It replaced some third-rate dive that had been there before, and so far was getting rave reviews from those in the know in the community. It was called *The Cubby Hole.* My spirit of adventure was aroused. And so, with all morbid thoughts shelved away for the moment, with the slate wiped clean and bright for Mariel, the two of us sailed forth like a couple of intrepid sixteenth century explorers in search of the New World.

The Cubby Hole lived up to its reputation. Happy noise and laughter and loud music could be heard seconds after we had turned the corner at Morton Street. Was it my imagination, or was this place packed to the gills with some unusually attractive women? It was nearly impossible to get anywhere near the bar, much less sit on a bar stool. There was a live DJ spinning some hot jams. There wasn't a whole lot of room to dance, but somehow a half-dozen gals were dancing as if possessed. We finally managed to order two drinks and find a tight corner to squeeze into. The drinks were good and strong and before long everything became hazy and the whole environment -- the noise, the music, the incessant buzz of voices and clinking glasses -- draped itself over us like a warm blanket. I thought back to the days when alcohol, rather than pot, used to be my drug of choice, days when facing the cold world with just a pair of earmuffs and a scarf seemed safer than donning a high tech helmet with built-in 3D goggles.

We had a fine and dandy time at the club and stayed almost until closing. Then we headed to *David's Pot Belly* restaurant on Christopher Street, open 24 hours, for unbelievable omelets. That night she took me home with her to her mother's apartment. Mom was already sound asleep, of course. So we pulled down the sleeper sofa in the living room and turned it into a bedroom for the night. But by then we were both pretty plastered and spent. Mariel grabbed some old baby doll pajamas from a hall closet and tossed them to me. Then she went into the bathroom quietly, careful not to disturb her mother. As for me, I fell out almost as soon as my head hit the pillow. I woke up to find Sir Galahad stretched out next to me, and Mariel standing there topless, winking at me with a devilish look, and extending a cup of coffee. "My mom's gone to work," she said. "We've got the whole place to ourselves."

I found the bathroom, quickly washed up and threw on a robe she had hung on the back of the door for me to use. We had some *Cocoa Puffs* for breakfast and she made a fresh pot of coffee. It was misty, overcast and drizzling out, a perfect day to spend indoors. Mariel was ebullient, cheerful, in high spirits. All of a sudden, I felt a bit nervous. The liquor had worn off and I suddenly realized that within an hour or so we would likely be in bed, would officially become "lovers." Mariel looked great, that golden hair of hers all in luxuriant, Rapunzel-like flowing curly waves, reminding me of some lush burgeoning growth in a jungle garden. Her body, long-limbed with smooth gracefully curving lines and well-shaped if not large breasts, was that of the fresh-faced model one might find gracing the pages of *Ingenue* magazine. In other words, this gal was "hot," but not in a strip club *Penthouse Magazine* kind of way. Her girl-next-door sexiness seemed to come with a PG rating.

Yet I still wasn't quite sure just who she was or what I actually felt towards her. Physical attraction, certainly. Fondness and affection too. She was sweet and fun to be with, fun to dance with, to paw, to squeeze, to kiss. I liked having someone to go to a movie or restaurant with, hit nightclubs and bars with, exchange lighthearted banter with. But there wasn't much of a true meeting of minds here. In fact, we really had very little in common. I had nothing against recreational sex, but it just seemed like something you did with men. With a woman I wanted more -- an emotional connection, an instant understanding, a feeling of minds in sync. What I sought most in an intimate relationship was a mutual unveiling and stripping away of all pretense and posturing, a deep recognition as of a person you already know. Roxanne always used to say, "I never meet strangers," and with her I always had the sense that my whole naked soul was exposed whenever our eyes met.

Then there was the way Mariel was acting. It seemed that the party showgirl was back on display, brimming over with confidence, slightly naughty, well aware of how sexy she looked. I started wondering with just a touch of trepidation, what being in bed with her would be like. After the breakfast dishes were washed and put away, she excused herself to go into the bathroom. I walked into the bedroom and strolled over to the window looking out on the alley. The same window through which Mariel's brother had jumped or fallen to his death less than a year before. A little shudder went through me. I sat on the edge of the bed and waited, feeling slightly awkward. Then she emerged from the bathroom wearing only a loosely fitting robe. I could smell a subtle fragrance, like orchid blossom or jasmine or some other sultry scent. She came over to the bed, pulled back the sheets, and began to remove her robe, and then mine. We embraced, her skin cool and satiny smooth against mine.

And then, chameleon-like, she metamorphosed again, this time from *Ivory Snow* Girl into porn star. With a wicked grin, she got on top of me and immediately took control. I couldn't believe how aggressive she was, how delighted to be in the dominant position. "I really know how to please a woman," she purred in a low, throaty tone. I felt peculiar. It seemed so odd to be lying under this gorgeous laughing "blonde bombshell" bent on demonstrating her sexual virtuosity. I was both startled and pleasantly amused. This was not my idea of how to romance a woman. As she skillfully demonstrated several of her well-honed techniques in an attempt to get me off, I found it difficult to concentrate due to the strangeness of it all. A funny saying I had heard in some bar: "Femme in the streets, butch in the sheets," popped into my head and made me laugh out loud. I suddenly felt like I was twelve years old again at a slumber party playing exploratory sex games with a friend, breaking out laughing every two minutes. Well, it *is* nice to laugh in bed, I thought.

Later on we sort of changed places, but I felt a bit timid after having just witnessed such a bravura performance. I could not match her expertise or her experience with women. I found myself wondering how my lovemaking compared to that of the lover she was currently breaking up with. Then I found myself wondering why I was allowing myself to be distracted by thoughts that had nothing to do with the person I was making love to, to become detached and remote, a spectator, in that sad familiar way I had of protecting myself when some part of me felt vaguely threatened. This hadn't happened with Roxanne only because the sheer depth of feeling, the sense of being soulmates or something close to it swept me along like a tsunami, knocking me senseless and making me forget myself for a spell. But now I was frightfully self-conscious and began to *think about* why I was so frightfully self-conscious, and to worry whether and to what extent it showed. Then I chastised myself for thinking about THAT, and on and on it went like the reflections in a hall of mirrors, an infinite regress that took me further and further away from where I was supposed to be.

Mariel took it all in good stride, however, chalking it up to my bashfulness in our first time getting horizontal. Actually, I think she found it rather charming. We got dressed and left the apartment, went out to a Chinese restaurant, and dined on King Pao Chicken. Then it was almost time for Mariel's mom to come home from work and for me to be heading uptown. So we took our leave, promising to meet up again next weekend.

After that we got together almost every Saturday night. We would go to *The Cubby Hole* or maybe to some other bar or club someone had told her about. We got ourselves on mailing lists and followed all the private membership parties that moved from club to club. We met other couples and made friends, got invited to house parties. But in truth our relationship was for the most part an ill-conceived, liquor-fueled roller coaster ride that left us out of breath and with a slight case of motion sickness. Whenever I went to meet her I never knew which one of her multitudinous personalities would show up. One Saturday night we would wind up dancing till 4 am, the next would be spent sitting in her room trying to comfort her while she cried over what happened to her brother.

Sometimes I would see her early in the morning holding a bottle of vodka that she'd just run out to the liquor store to buy. She would open the bottle and put it on the night table before getting back under the sheets. Then we would spend the entire day in bed, getting up only for bathroom breaks. Other times she would be distant and unreachable, would tell me horror stories about her father or former abusive lovers and bemoan the ugliness of the world. Sometimes the Earth Goddess would re-emerge, serene and wise as she moved about the apartment tending the potted plants, cooking a gourmet dinner for us, and reposing on a wing chair with Sir Galahad, running her fingers contentedly through his gray velvet fur, looking as unruffled as the Mona Lisa.

There were times when she seemed impatient, wanting more out of our relationship than an affair or just "seeing each other." After finally breaking free of an oppressive seven-year "marriage," Mariel, I thought, would surely welcome the chance to cherish and enjoy her new "singleness" before making a commitment to somebody new. But even as she complained about how possessive her ex was, I could see in her a deep-seated need to be possessed again, to belong to someone. As the months passed without the slightest hint from me of wanting a deeper commitment, she became resentful, hurt, and angry. She demanded to know exactly how I felt about her, what I wanted from her. Why was

I afraid of commitment, what was I running away from? The simple answer was that, while I felt all the tenderness and affection in the world for her, there was just no passion there. I loved going out with her, being seen with her, having other people think we were a couple. But I was not in love with her. I didn't want her to fall in love with me either. After having my own heart pummeled and tossed about like a frisbee by Roxanne, I could hardly bear the thought of doing that to someone else, especially not to one as dear to me as Mariel had become.

But I came to realize that she was really seeking a replacement for her ex, someone to fill the gaping void the messy breakup had left in its wake. The breakup had, in fact, been so traumatic for her, coming as it did so soon after her brother's death, that she had gone into therapy. Her doctor had even put her on anti-anxiety medication. I couldn't make her understand that I was not the person to fill that role, could not be the cuddly new puppy that you get to replace your dog who got run over by a garbage truck. She didn't understand or didn't want to. She became petulant, testy, irritated with me. We would spend hours on the phone with her alternately reproaching me and cajoling me, fulminating and letting off steam, then pleading and begging. I was overwhelmed by all the drama and at a loss how to respond. In bed I became increasingly distracted and unresponsive. She suggested I might be more repressed and blocked than I knew. At one point she told me I needed to consult a sex therapist.

At other times she would lighten up and we became like a couple of childhood friends, hanging out in Central Park or going to the movies. I brought her up to my place and we explored the woods and trails of Fort Tryon Park. In the summertime we would take the subway to Penn Station and then catch the Long Island Railroad out to the beach for a day of surf, sand, and sun. Those were lovely times with just the two of us, enjoying life's unremarkable ordinary pleasures away from crowds, scenes, and artificial intoxicants.

But two weeks after one of these idyllic weekends, Mariel would call me up and say something like: "Listen, you're gonna kill me, but I just have to tell you.." What would follow would be an X-rated tale of her midnight romps, of one-night stands with women she had picked up in bars, of quickies in the ladies' room, of doing it on the roof of an SUV, of secret trysts in hotel lobbies. I would just listen without comment, not knowing whether I was supposed to express shock, jealous anger, or detached amusement -- or maybe pretend disbelief. "*She gave me a little bit of coke and I just became a maniac*," she would croon, and go on to describe, in graphic detail, another escapade with some hot temptress.

I was surprised at my own gut reaction. I began to feel concerned, protective almost, like an older brother. "You know you ought to be careful, picking up strangers like that," I heard myself say, "there's a whole lot of crazy people in this city, psychos even, out there." I told her I wanted her to stop the bad girl behavior, told her that if she was doing it to punish me or make me jealous it wouldn't work because I could see right through it. I told her that ultimately whatever a person does out of spite to provoke someone else only winds up hurting them. I said I wanted her to tell her therapist about all the crazy acting out and why she was doing it. At length she admitted that I was probably right.

We continued to carry on some semblance of a relationship, and indeed I spent more time with her than ever just to keep her in check. But she was not easily tamed. One night we agreed to meet at a popular high-end women's bar that also attracted a good number of men, straight and gay. Mariel showed up wearing this sleek black Italian leather jacket that must have cost well over three hundred dollars (a gift from some admirer?) with boots to match. The jacket beautifully set off her Farrah Fawcett hair, into which she had added some shimmery new highlights, and she strutted about in time to the music, gleefully basking in the blazing heat of a dozen laser stares from guys and gals alike, as if soaking up solar rays on a Caribbean beach. I just sort of slipped unnoticed into the background, disappeared in the shadows. It felt uncomfortable, awkward. Often people would look carefully around to see who she had come in with. But I resisted any temptation to make proprietary gestures such as slipping an arm around her waist, or a hand upon her shoulder. I had no right to, not after steadfastly resisting all her attempts to make me her "official" girlfriend, her partner of record. Let her play, I thought, let her show off if she wants to, what's the harm?

But after these triumphant spells in the limelight Mariel would come home emotionally drained, exhausted. And then she would collapse, take on this wasted air and turn right into a version of Allie May Burroughs, that Depression-Era icon and emblem of rural poverty in America made famous by Walker Evans' large format camera. I could only shake my head in amazement. One day she told me that she and her therapist had stripped away the excuses and rationalizations and arrived at the true motive behind all of her provocative behavior. She simply needed to be in a satisfying, committed relationship. "I need to be attached to someone, to tie the knot," she announced with an air of resignation. And, she continued, since it was clear that I was unable or unwilling to fulfill that need it would probably be best if we just stopped seeing each other. I had to admit that given the circumstances this was probably the best solution. Mariel ought to focus her time and energy on trying to meet somebody else, somebody who could give her what she wanted and needed. It was only fair.

So we just stopped calling each other. I was left with a peculiar, empty sensation. It was as if some grainy poorly plotted B movie had finally ended and, while relieved to exit the theater, a week later I could still recall the film with a certain fondness, its very cheesiness and bad taste making for some uncanny irresistible appeal. I found myself missing her, thinking of her often and wondering how her love life was faring. But I fought the urge to call her, feeling that it was best to leave her alone. About six weeks after our official breakup, she called me. She sounded happy, wanted to tell me that she had met a wonderful woman and was almost certain she was "the one." We talked for over an hour and came to the conclusion that there was no harm in the two of us resuming our friendship. Besides, she really wanted me to meet Jordan.

Over the next several months I joined a circle of friends that included Mariel and her new girlfriend. Jordan was a few years older, slender and attractive, and as straight looking as Mariel. Everyone was glad to see her so happily coupled. But unfortunately for Mariel, the domestic bliss would be short-lived. A fairy-tale romance this was not, despite all appearances to the contrary. Little misunderstandings, spats, and bouts of jealousy began to rear their heads, minor annoyances flared into heated arguments; old patterns began to repeat themselves. I knew all of this because of the new role I had assumed in Mariel's life: I had become the dumping ground for all her bitter complaints and anguished protests, the sounding board for the biting retorts and swift rejoinders she should have used in the last argument but didn't. An hour after another heavy scene with Jordan, my phone would ring. Mariel could recognize the same tired old script playing itself out once more. She felt ill-used, taken for granted, toyed with.

After Jordan there was Natalie, and then Linda, and then Paige. Then she gave up on love, wanted no part of it. Almost two years had elapsed since we had first met, and we now began spending much more time together. And it was then that I became acquainted with the most curious and intriguing of her many personalities -- Mariel the mystic. One afternoon when I went to visit her at her mother's place, where she was now living again, the lights were turned low and I heard what sounded like Gregorian chant coming from the bedroom. She showed me the CD. It was called *CHANT* by The Benedictine Monks of Santo Domingo de Silos. She told me she had decided it was time to "get close to God again." Raised in an Irish Catholic home, and educated in a Catholic school, she said she still felt very drawn to the Church and had started going to Mass again with her mother regularly.

"Despite what a lot of people think," she told me, "I am actually a very spiritual person." She said she had recently gone to confession for the first time in a couple of years. "A couple of years?" I thought, trying to remember the last time I had gone to confession. I could not imagine ever doing such a thing again. I pictured myself kneeling in the dark confessional behind the screen murmuring: "Bless me father, it has been twenty-five years since my last confession…." How many *Hail Marys* and *Our Fathers* would be sufficient to wipe away over two and a half decades of sin?

I found something sweet and pure in Mariel's unashamed, unapologetic religiosity. I may not have been ready to return to confession or Sunday Mass, but I was receptive to anything which sought to strip away the superficial and the superfluous in life and get down to its bare essentials. She began to share unusual experiences with me, things she had not talked about in years. She said she had once undergone a "religious ecstasy" similar to that described by Christian mystics such as Saint Teresa of Avila, during which Christ had appeared to her briefly in shivering waves of white light. Another time, she told me, she had been praying fervently to the Blessed Mother Mary when all of a sudden a distinctive aroma of roses permeated the room. I listened with a certain amount of envy. I had known several people who claimed to have witnessed such supernatural or "paranormal" events. I never had. I felt cheated.

I had always been fascinated by the amazing stories of many of the saints -- some were said to have been able to levitate, have out of body experiences at will, perform miracles. I never knew what to believe, how to separate fact from fiction, legend from reality. Mariel and I began spending many hours visiting some of New York's beautiful Roman Catholic churches, most of which I had never set foot in, and talking about God. Standing in a near empty church under soaring arches, in the glow of daylight softened and filtered by rainbow-hued stained glass, surrounded by candles and crucifixes, I couldn't help but feel a sense of awe in the presence of the immense silence, the endlessly creative void, the still, grave womb from which every thought and everything that moves and breathes must have sprung. I wasn't sure just what sort of God I believed in, if any. I only felt strongly that there was much more to this life than meets the eye -- or at least my eye -- and I was captivated by the thought that Mariel just might be one of those rare individuals who possessed better than 20-20 spiritual vision.

It was curious to see the transformation in her. She had become the serene Earth Goddess once more, only stripped of all secular or pagan tones. She would have a faraway look on her face as she discussed, in a knowledgeable, almost authoritative way, passages of scripture, or the "Dark Night of the Soul" that St. John of the Cross rhapsodized about in his famous poem of despair followed by enlightenment. Before long this sexually precocious high school dropout was lecturing me on the arcane mysteries of soul purification and original sin. I was somewhat stunned but happy to engage in the philosophical and theological discussions, which often went on for hours.

And so, an improbable love affair had turned into an even more improbable friendship. It felt as if I had come to the end of a wild and wacky amusement park ride, a *Ripley's Believe It or Not* tour of the sublime and the ridiculous. I had seen her many faces, yet Mariel as a person was still an enigma to me, a rare find like some curious object you discover while browsing in a flea market. You have no idea what you will do with it or where you'll put it, but you buy it anyway. No -- I had not found a woman to replace Roxanne, and maybe never would. But no person can ever replace any other person and Mariel needed no justification for being in my life.

When I had been at my job long enough to earn a two-week vacation, I decided I would fly out to California to visit my sister in LA, and then head north to the bay area for maybe a week. San Francisco, yes. I loved the blue and gold city of clanging cable car bells, maddening hills, sourdough bread, and the most vibrant and uninhibited gay scene in the country. So I chose the dates, requested the time off and booked a flight to Los Angeles.

After spending five days with my sister, I took a bus to San Francisco and checked into a cheap motel. One day, while walking around in a newly trendy part of town known as SOMA (acronym for "South of Market Street") my eyes were drawn to a very bright and conspicuous sign hanging outside what appeared to be some sort of cafe or bar. I couldn't resist walking into *Lipps* on the corner of Howard and 9th Streets. It was a wonderful tavern full of rich dark wood, a sleek gorgeous bar, and what must have been the biggest and most beautiful gleaming brass cappuccino machine I had ever laid eyes on. The place looked utterly inviting, so I went inside and joined the handful of patrons seated at small round tables and ordered coffee. The fresh brew was served in a mug made not out of ceramic or clay but crystal-clear glass.

While tapping some cinnamon into my glass and staring at the awesome cappuccino maker, it suddenly hit me what the essence of Mariel was. She was like Rome! Rome, with its bizarre juxtaposition of the sacred and the profane, the divine and the decadent. St. Peter's Basilica where the Pope delivered homilies, and the Coliseum where gladiators and wild beasts fought to the death to the sounds of cheering bloodthirsty crowds. On the one hand you have Vestal Virgins and images of the Blessed Mother in her powder blue robes, on the other hand you have Sylvia and Marcello cavorting in the Fountain of Trevi in *La Dolce Vita*. Yes, that's Mariel. I suddenly recalled that ashtray I had found at the bustling *Porta Portese* flea market in Rome and taken home as a souvenir. The metal trinket was a rough reproduction of one of four figures in a famous renaissance fountain known as the *Quattrro Fontane.* It depicted a reclining goddess wearing swirls of drapery which manage to leave her plump round breasts fully exposed, and a blissfully sedate look on her face. The rest of the ashtray -- the part where you drop your ashes in -- resembled a seashell fanning out in a semicircle from her body. Mariel had a birthday coming up in a couple of weeks. I thought I would go home and find that old souvenir, wrap it up nicely and give it to her as a birthday present. I couldn't imagine a more appropriate gift for her.

26
Makes Me Wanna Holler

I NEVER THOUGHT I would ever cross a picket line. But when one is dangling by a thread, comfortable assumptions like that go flying out the window. I was in a situation -- a dire one. A few days after I returned home from San Francisco one of the partners at the law firm where I was working took me aside. They had noticed certain disturbing patterns regarding my work habits which were cause for concern. For one thing, I seemed reluctant to put in extra hours at night and come in on weekends when we were racing to meet deadlines and rack up as many billable hours as possible. But for the salary they were paying me, 40 hours a week Monday thru Friday seemed just about right. For another, I had a tendency to disappear at lunchtime rather than order in like everyone else did, and often came back late. And perhaps most disturbing of all, I seemed to prefer working alone and was not much of a "team player." After consulting with the other partners, they had decided that I was no longer a good fit for the firm and should be dismissed.

They gave me two weeks to wrap up any projects I'd been working on and then it was sayonara. I'd had a feeling this was coming, but not quite so soon. I had lost count of the number of times I'd been fired from a job, and I was beginning to feel like a bum. My self-esteem was fast dissolving, and this time I had little or no savings to tide me over in the event of an extended period of unemployment. In other words, I was in deep doo-doo.

About two weeks before my trip out West, workers at New York City's premiere tabloid, the *Daily News*, had gone out on strike. Surprisingly, rather than immediately caving in to the union's demands as was so often the case in a city like New York, management held firm. They continued to publish the newspaper with a skeleton staff and announced their determination to put up a good fight. And they kept right on fighting, even after most of their biggest advertisers, like *Macy's*, had pulled all their ads, even after newsstand owners, intimidated by the strikers, refused to carry the paper, and even after several delivery truck drivers were attacked by union thugs. Rather than back down, the company hardened their position and prepared for a protracted strike. An urgent call for replacement workers was issued city-wide.

At first I felt some sympathy for the strikers as I watched them doggedly marching with their picket signs in front of the *Daily News* headquarters on East 42nd Street, all bundled up in Eskimo parkas, fur hats and scarves under the frigid gray skies. Day after day there they were, chanting their slogans while clutching steaming cups of coffee with gloved hands, as bitter November winds made their placards rattle. But then I learned what kind of wages these guys were making on their union pay scale. The job classification for "Copy Passer," for example, required a person to review classified ads and correct minor misspellings -- to change "cemetary" to "cemetery" on a death notice, say. A job that any competent sixth grader could perform. Yet it paid nearly $10,000 more per year than any job I had ever held, even with my college degree and special paralegal training! Being apprised of such a fact splashed some ice water on my sympathies. What the hell were these folks complaining about?

After I had been out of work for six weeks and was beginning to panic, and with the strike showing no signs of a resolution, I made up my mind. The following Monday, as tempers flew on East 42nd Street and negotiations continued to break down, I approached the building armed with resume and references, sidestepped the pickets and made my way in through a side entrance. I went up to Human Resources and volunteered to be a replacement worker. They hired me on the spot.

But I knew the job wouldn't last. I knew the strike would be settled one way or another and those workers would soon be back at their jobs, even if a new owner had to step in to rescue the proud, nearly 75-year-old New York icon -- as closely identified with the city as the Empire State Building or the Yankees. So, odd as it sounds, even as I embraced the job with enthusiasm and was delighted at the new infusion of steady cash into my pockets, I began to slip into a depression. All I could think of was: But what happens when the strike is over and I'm back out on the street?

I had come to a sort of impasse in my life. I knew that I just could not keep on living this way, bouncing from job to job, getting fired for lateness because I couldn't control my solar addiction or because my social skills were so lacking. I could not keep eroding my self-respect by taking jobs that didn't challenge me or make any use of my talents. Could not keep haunting bars and dance clubs like a stranger in the night seeking some elusive lover to take all the pain away. Could not keep dealing with anxiety-driven obsessive-compulsive behaviors like two-hour showers and long-drawn-out grooming rituals. Could not keep swinging emotionally back and forth between acute loneliness and blind anger, between crying spells and uncontrollable rages. Could no longer accept being looked upon as an eccentric weirdo by nearly everyone I met.

One day, while cleaning at home, my eyes fell on a thick paperback book on the top shelf of my bookcase. It appeared to be brand new, with no sign of dents or creases on the spine. I pulled it out. The book was titled, *The Primal Scream: Primal Therapy, The Cure for Neurosis*. Suddenly I remembered that this book was a popular and controversial best seller back in the '70s when I was in my teens. It was reported that John Lennon and other celebrities had undergone this therapy with dramatic results. I must have purchased the book to see what all the fuss was about back then, but had never gotten around to reading it. Looking at the title I had to laugh a bit. Who would be so bold and presumptuous as to proclaim he had found a "cure" for neurosis? But that only made me more curious to find out what he was talking about. So I decided to read it.

It may seem strange to hear the cliché, *I couldn't put it down*, applied to a serious work of nonfiction, but that was exactly the way this book struck me. It was utterly compelling. It described a radical form of psychotherapy in which the patient is required to spend the first 48 hours locked up in a room. He or she must remain alone in the room for the entire time and is not allowed to watch TV, turn on the radio, make phone calls, or even read. He may eat, sleep and wash but there is no access to coffee, alcohol, cigarettes, or drugs, not even aspirin. The whole idea is to isolate the patient, remove all distractions and pacifiers, and force him or her to confront himself or herself in the raw. Naked and alone, with nowhere to hide.

The ultimate goal of the therapy was to strip away the security blankets, to totally break down the patient's every last defense, until he or she becomes a squirming terrified bundle of sheer emotional pain, lying on the floor in a fetal position, literally screaming out for Mommy and Daddy. Hence the term, "Primal Scream." Once the patient actually begins his regular therapy sessions the therapist will continue the process, chiseling away at the patient's carefully constructed protective walls until he "breaks," much like a prisoner of war subjected to torture. The process takes place over an intensive three-week period during which the patient sees his therapist every day for several hours at a time. Being forced to face his inner anxieties, fears, and miseries bereft of his usual armor, deprived of ways to release tension such as smoking -- this is supposed to rouse the patient from his neurotic waking dream at last and thereby effect a "cure." According to the book's theory, once all of that pain is truly "felt" at last, as opposed to being hidden away in layers of defenses and denial mechanisms, the patient will be freed of his crippling burden -- an invisible ball and chain he has been dragging around for years without knowing it.

After I finished reading the book I couldn't get it out of my mind. For the next several weeks I was almost in a daze trying to imagine myself going through such a harsh, unforgiving course of treatment. This was worse than "tough love"; it was more like going cold turkey to overcome heroin addiction, where you simply surrender to the terrors of withdrawal. It's awful, but it works, and takes far less time than checking oneself into a rehab program. Maybe, I thought, it takes a treatment this drastic to undo decades of psycho-emotional trauma and accumulated pain. Conventional therapy seemed like such a long haul, and usually produced only modest gains. All those hours spent lying on couches pouring out one's angst while a sympathetic shrink looks on, checking his watch every fifteen minutes, all those dollars paid to have someone hold your hand and act like he really cares while you're telling him how rotten your life is -- what do you actually get for all of that? Maybe all you get is a chance to knock a few pings in the lid of the drum where all your toxic waste is stored, but you never get to bust it open and let all the crap out. It is as if a person suffering a severe bout of food poisoning were unable to vomit.

I decided I wanted that vomit-inducer. I wanted Primal Therapy. I needed it, maybe more than I ever needed anything in my life. I made up my mind that I was going to get this therapy no matter what I had to do or how much it cost. First I had to do some searching to assure myself that the therapy was still being practiced and to find out who could do it and where I could get it. I scanned the yellow pages and sought out agencies offering referrals for psychiatrists and psychotherapists. I was willing to devote weeks of diligent research just so I could be sure I would be getting the real thing. But after many letters and phone calls it turned out that the only place where "the original" Primal Therapy could be obtained was at a locale called *The Primal Institute* in Los Angeles. Any other practitioners claiming to offer Primal Therapy, I was warned, were at best offering a watered-down version that would not give the desired results. Whoever wanted the genuine article had to be willing to relocate to Los Angeles for about six months. And had to be willing to fork over thousands of dollars up front.

Disheartened at first, I eventually told myself that I would find a way. And that it would be worth the time and expense. I knew the job at the *Daily News* would be over in a matter of months; the minute the strike was settled all the replacement workers would be told to empty their desks and get lost. Since the job paid so well, I was able to stash away every other paycheck and before long had built up a substantial fund. Also, I had my sister living out there in LA. She could probably let me crash on her couch for six months. Then, dear Granny, who had been in declining health for most of the year, at length suffered a heart attack and passed away a few days later. We learned that she had left a small amount of money -- money she had saved up from her job as a traveling beautician -- for each of her three grandchildren. The amount she left to me just about covered the cost of the therapy itself. (I took this as a sign that the gods were with me on this one).

All that remained was the issue of my apartment. How was I supposed to pay my rent for six months while unemployed and living on the other side of the country? The answer, of course, was to sublet my apartment for that stretch of time. Perhaps someone thinking of moving to New York might like to have a place to live at reasonable cost while checking things out. As long as I did not seek to profit by charging the subtenant more than the rent I was paying, I felt it should be perfectly legal. So I began to draw up a sublease -- an easy task given my familiarity with leases from years of working as a real estate paralegal. I planned to put an ad in the *Village Voice* as soon as I was ready to show the apartment.

Meanwhile, rumors were swirling about that some British baron might play the role of knight in shining armor galloping to the rescue of the beleaguered *Daily News*. Negotiations with the nine unions were deadlocked, a federal mediator had left in disgust, and the paper was on the brink of bankruptcy. Sure enough, within a week or two a rich and eccentric Brit named Robert Maxwell offered to buy the tabloid and make peace with the unions. The *Chicago Tribune*, which owned the *Daily News*, was eager to make a deal.

And shortly thereafter, we, the "scabs," were all dismissed, and the striking workers came back triumphant, having gotten most of their demands met by the affable Mr. Maxwell. Weirdly enough, before the year was out Maxwell would be found floating in the waters off the Canary Islands, naked and dead, having either fallen or jumped off his yacht (or been pushed).

I contacted *The Primal Institute* in Los Angeles and requested an application. Completing it was quite a project. They wanted a detailed autobiographical profile at least four pages in length in which, among other things, you had to explain to them why you thought you needed Primal Therapy. There was a long questionnaire to fill out which asked about childhood experiences, your relationship with your parents, your psychiatric and emotional problems, your sex life, your physical ailments and complete medical history, and more. They also wanted a recent photograph to be attached to the completed application. It took me over a week to finish it all and get it in the mail.

About three weeks later I received a letter from the Institute telling me that I had passed the initial screening; all that remained was an in-person interview. For that I had to fly out to Los Angeles. I called my sister and booked a flight. When I arrived at *The Primal Institute* I was interrogated by Vivian Janov, wife of Arthur Janov, author of *The Primal Scream* and the man who had founded the Institute. A week after the interview I received a letter telling me that I had been accepted as a patient. I was to call them to work out a schedule for when I would begin my therapy, and send them a deposit.

So -- that was that. It was actually going to happen. I was going to get Primal Therapy. I was going to take "the cure!" I could hardly believe it. I made arrangements with my sister for her to put me up for six months. All I had to do was sublet my apartment and choose a date to leave. So I went down to the *Village Voice* offices and placed a listing offering the use of my two-bedroom furnished apartment in northern Manhattan. Then I waited for the telephone to ring. I soon got a call from a young couple who had just relocated to New York from Ann Arbor, Michigan and were shopping around for a condo. They signed the sublease agreement and planned to move in on the first of the following month. That gave me about two and a half weeks to put all of my non-furniture possessions into storage, decide what I would need to bring for six months in LA, pack my bags, and buy my plane ticket.

My parents, not quite understanding what could be so urgent as to require a sudden move across the country, drove me to the airport and wished me luck. Upon arriving in LA, I took a cab straight to the cheap motel where I had reserved a room for three days. Tomorrow I would report to *The Primal Institute* for my formal "orientation." Then I would have to stay in the motel room for the next 48 hours in "isolation," before reporting for my very first session of Primal Therapy. I called my sister to let her know I had arrived and that I would be moving into her spare back room in a few days.

Unpacking my things at the motel, I took a deep breath and tried to collect my thoughts. Why had I completely disrupted my life in this way? I had pulled up stakes, moved to the West Coast, set aside thousands of dollars of my savings to embark on an adventure I knew nothing about -- all because I had read some twenty-year-old book. But that book had promised a real cure for what was destroying me and I desperately wanted that cure, excruciating though it promised to be. I truly wanted to have my defenses dismantled, wanted to see all those layers of polystyrene which had insulated me from my "real feelings" and kept me from experiencing "my pain," mercilessly stripped away.

Recalling the moving case histories described in the book -- of tormented souls painstakingly restored to emotional health like stroke victims slowly learning how to walk or talk again -- I realized I had come here on a mission of mercy, a sense that if I could just stop hating myself long enough, it might not be too late to save myself. And so, like the successful Primal patients before me, perhaps I too could liberate the hurting child cowering within my depths who had buried her feelings and denied her real needs. Yes! I would gladly submit to this brutal regimen. I would be a voluntary prisoner of war. A prisoner not brave enough, not tough enough to hold out till the end. A prisoner who offers no resistance, who lets herself be broken and willingly gives up her secrets. Wasn't it all worth it if, after a mere six months, I could emerge a cleansed, healthy, loving individual, open to life and strong enough to no longer need defenses against a cruel uncaring world? Wouldn't that be more than worth the ordeal?

But, what the hell, I thought as I placed my toothbrush and hairbrush in the bathroom, it was too late to turn back now anyway. I decided to get a good night's sleep. In the morning I would be meeting my fellow patients, a small group of people who were scheduled to begin their therapy at the same time as I was.

Three and a Half Weeks Later

Place: Ye Olde King's Head (A British-style pub in Santa Monica)

Characters:
Me, 38, from New York City
Charley, 23, from Knoxville, TN
Sandy, 44, from Sacramento, CA
Dennis, 31, from Dublin, Ireland

(All four of us had started as patients at The Primal Institute the same week)

Scene: We are all sitting around a table, lifting heavy pewter tankards of *Guinness Stout* to our lips, waiting for the waitress to deliver our orders of fish & chips, bangers & mash, and such like fare.

Charley: "Well, how's it goin' guys? How're you likin' your therapy?"

Dennis: "Don't know, man. It all went so fast, and, I mean. . .our three-week intensive is almost over. Can you believe it? I really thought by now I'd feel like a totally different person."

Sandy: "I honestly can't say I feel any different or even better, that's for sure. I mean yeah, I dealt with some deep shit, got some issues resolved maybe. But I can't say I really feel any happier than the day I walked in here."

Charley: "Okay, full disclosure everybody, tell the truth. Has anyone actually had a primal? Actually experienced the Big Scream?"

Me: "Well, I've been doing lots of screaming at my mother, banging on walls, punching pillows, asking her why she had to criticize me so much. Why she made me feel like some defective widget rolling down the assembly line and destined for the scrap heap. But no sudden outburst of primal terror, no so-called catastrophic realizations, nothing like that."

Sandy: "Well, I think I did have a primal. It happened the day I was talking about the time they had to put me away in the hospital for eight weeks. I was four years old and had contracted some rare infection. I was vividly recalling the scene, the way I just sat up in the bed after my parents left and cried out for my mommy till I couldn't cry any more. Man, I have to say, that was deep..."

Charley: "So, you were actually able to relive that memory?"

Sandy: "Yeah, after a whole lot of probing and pushing by Danny, my therapist. At first I just didn't want to go back there. I'd catch a flash of the memory and then just flinch away. But Danny insisted I stay with it, not let it go. So I finally stopped resisting and just let it wash over me. And when I did I just screamed out in pure horror at the realization -- as a four-year-old -- that I had just been abandoned by my mommy and daddy."

Dennis: "Wow -- that's heavy, man!"

Charley: "Well, I had a pretty intense session reminiscing about my Uncle Seymour. I mean -- like writhing on the floor, really sobbing. I was telling her about the day I came home from school to find out he'd blown his brains out, right in our guest room. I mean, I was gasping for air, practically having convulsions."

Dennis: "Looks like you're making real progress, then."

Charley: " Well I don't know. All of that happened on my third day of therapy. There's been nothing like that since. No screams, no cries. Nothing."

Me: "Nope -- nothing remotely like that has happened to me. In fact, I've barely been able to cough up a few tears since starting therapy."

Dennis: "Well maybe your childhood just wasn't that traumatic."

Me: "No? Then how did I turn out so fucked-up?"

Dennis: "I feel like I've just vented a lot of anger and rage, cursed out my dad, got a lot out of my system. But did I really have to travel 7000 miles just to do that?"

Sandy: "Did you hear about that therapist who was supposed to have just up and quit right before we started? I heard some people in the lounge talking about it."

Charley: "Yeah, I heard he wrote a really scathing article, published it in some psych journal -- trashing the whole clinic, the slipshod way they're doing the therapy. He claimed the wife and son are just in it for the money."

Dennis: "The truth is, for all the hours I've spent in therapy here, I've gotten nothing that I couldn't have gotten from any dime-a-dozen head doctor back home in Dublin."

Me: "I don't know what we all got out of this so far. But I know what they got. Twenty thousand dollars from the four of us. Can you believe that?"

Sandy: "Hell no."

Charley: "Now that is something to scream about, ain't it?"

Dennis: "All I know is it took me three years working sixty hours a week just to save up the money to be able to come here. And now I've blown it all in three weeks".

We all looked down at our plates, shaking our heads. Even two more rounds of *Guinness Stout* could not drown out that "catastrophic realization."

27
Born to Lose

A HUSH HAD settled over the semi-darkened hall; no one made a sound. All eyes were glued to the screen in front of us. All staring at the image of a grown man lying on his back on the floor in an otherwise empty room. He is flailing his arms and legs and making weird noises with his mouth. A sound that seems a cross between a shriek and a grunt is coming out of him. Every three seconds he contracts his body, drawing his arms and legs in close. Three seconds later the limbs are flailing wildly again. He is fairly gasping for air and appears to be in great distress. We watch him for several minutes in disbelief, perplexed, waiting. Then it all becomes clear. This man, we are solemnly told, is in the process of reliving his birth. A process which, we are also told, is a crucial step for anyone who wishes to be rid of the common psychological maladies to which the human race is so susceptible -- anxiety, insomnia, depression, sexual dysfunction, fears and phobias, drug and alcohol abuse, addictions like overeating and compulsive gambling. Such conditions cannot be eradicated by talking, by psychoanalyzing, by insights or intellectual exercises, nor by medications. The only way they can be removed is by force. Like any stubborn and oppressive regime, they must be violently overthrown. And it all begins by reliving and thereby resolving the very first trauma -- being born.

We were seated on metal folding chairs in what appeared to be a renovated parking garage in Venice, California. We had all come here to see the man in the flesh, the man who had single-handedly invented the "cure for neurosis." And there he was, standing next to the screen -- Dr. Arthur Janov. And with him his hot French wife, blonde, wearing a black leather miniskirt and low-cut blouse. Dr. Janov had gained a great deal of notoriety as well as raked in a great deal of money over the past twenty years. Author of the blockbuster best seller, *The Primal Scream* and founder of *The Primal Institute* in Los Angeles, he had become something of a celebrity. The Institute boasted a sterling record of success, claiming to have transformed hundreds, if not thousands, of nail-biting neurotic malcontents from all over the world into healthy, fully feeling, life-embracing individuals.

Janov's book and his Institute, of course, were the reason I was now living in Los Angeles. I had moved 3000 miles across the country for the magical cure his book had promised. I had flung the dice, not quite sure what to expect, knowing it would be a foray into spooky and unchartered territory. But radical psychotherapy was not like a dress in a department store that you could "try on" before buying. So I went for it with blindfolds on. Now, seven weeks later, I could only wish that I had had the opportunity to see Janov in person, to attend one of his seminars, before I ever got on that plane.

Almost from day one my sneaking suspicions that Primal Therapy might not live up to its billing began to be confirmed. Sitting somewhat nervously in a circle together with my three co-patients for our initial orientation, I listened to Vivian Janov and her son describe what we could look forward to in the coming weeks. She explained how we would each be assigned a therapist to whom we would report every morning for the first three weeks during the "intensive" portion of the therapy. This would be followed by a series of group therapy sessions. Each of us was asked to give a brief bio of ourselves while being videotaped. At the conclusion of our therapy, we would each be videotaped again, to show off our healthy new selves as contrasted with the screwed-up miserable selves we had left behind.

But there had been a curious absence. Where was the Institute's founder, the creator of the therapy and author of *The Primal Scream*, Dr. Arthur Janov? Evidently, much had changed since the book first appeared. I would learn that Dr. Janov no longer had anything to do with *The Primal Institute*. During the preceding two decades he had refined and perfected the therapy, written several more books, divorced his wife and remarried, and taken off to set up his own clinic in Marina del Rey. The original Institute was simply abandoned, left in the hands of his ex-wife and son. Now, Janov claimed, *The Primal Institute* in

Los Angeles was no longer offering genuine Primal Therapy, but only a streamlined, truncated version that unsuspecting patients had no way of distinguishing from the real thing. As the weeks passed since my first day alone in that motel room, I would experience firsthand the truth of this. Much of what I had been anticipating from reading *The Primal Scream* simply failed to materialize.

It soon became apparent that much of the nuts and bolts of the therapy so graphically portrayed in the book had been discarded, left by the wayside. The techniques and approaches that sounded so revolutionary and groundbreaking when discussed in the book were nowhere to be seen. *An aggressive, full-frontal assault on the patient's defense system?* Not exactly. That must have proved too intimidating for many already traumatized patients. If anything, we were coddled more than we were challenged. *Long, open-ended sessions in which the therapist never glanced at a watch and the patient was given "all the time he needs"?* Nope – nearly every therapy session ended abruptly after about 40 minutes, and in no case lasted more than two hours. *A strict ban on all "artificial" remedies that "only treat the symptoms" i.e., medications?* Far from it. The Institute had a medical doctor on staff whose sole function was to prescribe anti-anxiety pills, tranquilizers, muscle relaxants, sleeping pills, antidepressants, and anything else which could help the patient make it through the rigors of the therapy. *Adamant refusal to indulge the patient's need to turn the therapist into his Mean Mommy or Cold Daddy -- a phenomenon known as transference – because that would merely re-enact rather than eliminate the neurotic struggle?* Not on your life. Not only did the therapists at the Institute tolerate this behavior, they actively encouraged it. *Significant breakthroughs made in the first three weeks of the "intensive phase" as the patient's defenses start to crumble?* No way. Many patients, I soon learned, had not so much as shed a tear by the end of the intensive phase. And finally -- *Primal Therapy as a direct, no-nonsense treatment in which most patients were substantially "cured" of all symptoms in less than a year?* That was probably the biggest lie of all. Many of the patients, I found, had been coming to the Institute for two years, three years, some as long as six.

After the screening, the lights came back on and Janov took some questions from the audience. He explained that he had learned much since *The Primal Scream* was first published and that an understanding of the original birth trauma was essential to rooting out every last bit of neurosis. Just lying on the floor and screaming out for Mommy and Daddy -- powerful and emotionally liberating as that was -- could not effect a permanent cure. Janov did not say whether he had called up the patients who had undergone the old version of the therapy and offered them refunds. Then Janov's new wife Francois came up to the podium to speak. In a thick French accent, she spoke about their hopes and ambitions for the new clinic -- that it would attract a whole new generation of suffering patients and would eventually be known as the only place in the world where the authentic "new and improved" Primal Therapy could be obtained.

Before leaving the podium Janov's wife assured us that the Institute in Los Angeles would soon be exposed as a fraud, and that anyone unfortunate enough to have signed on with them was welcome to apply to the clinic in Marina del Rey. Applications could be picked up from the table near the exit. After Francois stepped down, a few of Janov's "trainees" came up to address the audience. Former patients, most talked about their lives, both before and after treatment. All claimed to have relived their birth at least once. One claimed to have relived his birth four times. Apparently, the more times the better. None of them looked or sounded professional. Nor did anyone look or sound remotely happy. I couldn't imagine wanting to be treated by any of them.

Besides, I just wasn't buying it. No one, I thought, can have any conscious memory of being born. The brain of the newborn is simply not sufficiently developed to be capable of encoding such memories in the neuronal circuits. Therefore, there is no way they can ever be retrieved later, and thus no way to resolve the original "trauma" of one's violent forced expulsion from the womb. I mean, what was all this bullshit anyway? If just being born makes you neurotic then the whole human race must be sick. If so, then how can we ever define what is "healthy" or "normal"? If sickness is universal then wouldn't sickness be "normal"? The whole thing made no sense.

No -- it was all too plain now. This was not a legitimate psychotherapeutic practice, nor even a highly unorthodox school of therapy. This was a cult. I turned away in disgust, getting up from my chair and heading for the door while Janov, seated at a table in the back, was attempting to hawk both his latest book, and videotapes of "birth primals" such as the one we had all just witnessed. I walked out into the brilliant sunshine on Abbot Kinney Boulevard and just started walking in no particular direction.

One Month After the Dinner at Ye Olde Pub

After the so-called intensive phase of Primal Therapy ended, we were entitled to four "Group Sessions." In these 3 to 4-hour communal meetings we were encouraged to do our primal thing in the presence of our fellow patients. Today was Wednesday and I was scheduled for my second group.

I walked into the large, poorly lit room. There were maybe twenty people already there, all of them on the floor, either sitting or lying down. In the center of the room was a gigantic stuffed brown and white teddy bear -- the largest one I had ever seen. Everyone seemed to be undergoing his or her own private therapeutic ordeal. Some people were crying softly; sniffles and nose-blowing could be heard from various parts of the room. I heard some low moaning and groaning, as if someone were in physical pain. A man with his head in his hands was sobbing loudly. Some folks had paired up, were in small groups, whispering to one another. There were no therapists to be seen.

I found a spot on the floor, lay on my back and closed my eyes. I tried to transport myself back to earliest childhood. I pictured my mother as a young woman of 24, nervously holding her firstborn, feeling out of sorts and confused, finding that "motherhood" did not feel quite like she had imagined it would. I had once been told by Granny that her labor had been horrendous and made her quite ill, that she had tried to breastfeed but her milk was dried up due to her nervous condition, and that she actually dropped me once! These unfortunate circumstances, I was sure, had put me on the fast track to lifelong neurosis, with faulty and unsatisfactory "bonding" with mother right from the get-go. What could be a more ominous portent of psycho-emotional disaster to come? Even if I were able to relive such a birth, what good would it do me now, I thought as I lay flat on the floor.

It was no use. I couldn't remember anything, no matter how hard I tried. Terry, my therapist, had continually hammered into me the importance of actually RELIVING the early traumas. It was not enough to recollect, to recount, to describe in words -- however vividly. You had to actually go back there, recapture the FEELING you felt then but immediately tried to shut out of consciousness. But without some kind of truth serum or deep hypnosis there was just no way I could get back there. Terry, I had once believed, would apply just the right techniques, would be my well-equipped tour guide back into the murky forests of ancient sunken memories. She would know how to help me dredge them up and confront them head-on without flinching. But all she ever did as I lay on the floor struggling was to sit in a corner behind me where I couldn't even see her, ask me a few questions, and repeat the constant refrain: "But how did that make you FEEL when it happened?"

At length the private, quiet portion of the Group Session came to an end. The "confrontation" portion was about to begin. Here, individual patients stood up facing a roster of therapists and proceeded to voice any current grievances, issues, or demands. Slowly, the therapists began filing into the room, taking seats behind a large table in the front. A woman named Carrie had gotten up and was addressing herself to a therapist named Mark.

"Why didn't you return my call? I called you three times. It was bad enough you had to cancel our last session. God -- you make me feel like shit. . ."

Mark said nothing. Carrie, on the verge of tears, sat down. Another woman, Daryl, stood up and began talking to my therapist, Terry.

"You didn't even read that piece from my journal that I sent you, did you? I bet you never so much as glanced at it. I'm starting to think you just don't like me, so why the hell don't you just say it!"

Terry replied that she had read the journal piece, and wanted to know what, exactly, made Daryl think she hadn't. Daryl mumbled some reply that I couldn't make out.

Next up was Troy from Toronto, a well-built military guy with a fresh crew cut. He seemed to be addressing all the therapists at once.

"Look, I'm fed up with all the bullshit. You guys are just fucking with our heads. I've spent thousands of dollars at this place and I think you're all just milking us for everything we've got. Look around you, does anyone look "cured" here? Anyone look happy and healthy?"

Hisses and murmurs of disapproval could be heard. Voices were raised in protest. One guy shouted out: *"Man, you're still struggling with your neurotic hope, still wanting miracles. You need to give it up and get real!"*

I myself had no complaints to register publicly, no angry tirades to launch into. It all seemed beside the point now. I slipped quietly out of the room and wandered into the hallway. A couple of other stray patients were standing around, smoking cigarettes, sipping from styrofoam cups of coffee. Funny. I recalled reading Janov's boast in *The Primal Scream* that nearly all patients, after several months of therapy, having been freed from the terrible body tension that had kept them taut as a drum or running like rats on a treadmill for most of their lives -- virtually all of them, he bragged, had happily given up their tobacco and coffee habits. No longer needing to siphon off that tension with caffeine and nicotine they simply no longer had any desire to smoke or drink coffee. Yeah right, I thought, watching everyone sipping and puffing away. I just shook my head and frowned, thinking what a sick joke it all was.

I left the building and walked out into the bright blue sparkle of a cloudless LA afternoon. My mood kept shifting back and forth between rage and despair. Part of me wanted to take action -- do something. But what? Demand my money back? File a lawsuit? Call other defrauded patients and try to mount some kind of mass protest? All of these scenarios paraded boldly through my mind in vivid technicolor, horns blaring, bells ringing. But I knew I would do none of them. There was nothing to do but face the sorry truth. That I had been taken for a ride, had plunged impulsively into a risky venture that had turned out badly. Very badly. That was all.

I walked all the way up Westwood Boulevard to the vast green expanse that was the UCLA campus and found my favorite spot under a tree in front of the Dance Building. Basking in the remnants of a slowly sinking sun, I pondered over my predicament. I decided it was pointless to attend the last two group sessions. Why go back there at all? It was over. And yet, only weeks ago I had signed a lease on a small studio apartment in Hollywood, mere blocks from the original *Paramount Pictures* studios. Staying with my sister had become trying, and when Congress extended unemployment benefits an additional 26 weeks on account of the recession, I knew I would have a steady stream of income until I could find some kind of job.

Indeed, I had been living on unemployment checks ever since getting laid off from my newspaper job back in New York. Now I would have another six months of checks, which would allow me to eat and pay my rent if not much else. But the future that now stretched out before me looked desolate and unknown -- like a Martian landscape. Here I was, stuck in La-La land, half-broke, without any friends, and as neurotic as ever. Now what?

28
Lost in the City of Fallen Angels

I'M WALKING DOWN Western Avenue and it almost looks like Beirut after the civil wars. There are piles of rocks and debris and broken glass in the street, huge hunks of twisted metal looking like weird avant-garde sculptures sitting on the sidewalks of deserted blocks. I am stunned to see what has become of one block that only last week was alive and buzzing with human activity. A block where there were bustling Mexican bakeries and crowded laundromats, sounds of music, hollering, and children's laughter, fresh produce stands thronged with customers, clothing racks on the street hung with bright colored discount apparel eagerly being picked over by savvy bargain shoppers. Now it looks like a tornado ripped through it and there's not a soul to be seen. Looking all around, I see a large furniture warehouse reduced to blackened shards of wood and steel. And over there, an off-price jeans outlet still standing but totally emptied of merchandise, and a few yards down I spot a *7-Eleven* store shorn of its plate glass windows which lay in thousands of glinting bits on the street.

It was the aftermath of the infamous "Rodney King Riots" -- that fury of social unrest and violence that erupted following the shocking acquittal of four white LAPD cops who -- as captured for all time in a video aired repeatedly around the world -- had mercilessly kicked and beaten a black motorist, Rodney King, whom they had pulled over for a routine traffic violation. I had just returned to LA after a few harrowing days spent in a New York City courthouse trying to hold on to my upper Manhattan apartment. For the past several evenings millions of Americans had sat riveted to their TV sets, gasping in disbelief at nonstop coverage of raging fires, billowing clouds of black smoke, overturned cars and rampaging mobs of angry, mostly black and Hispanic youths. They had been treated to images of teenage boys laughing as they brazenly hauled big-screen TV's out of busted up stores, roving bands of thugs avenging their grievances by yanking terrified white drivers out of cars and trucks, fat, sweating Latinas carrying jumbo packs of *Pampers* and *Charmin* toilet tissue out of burnt-out supermarkets, and defiant Korean shop owners standing in front of their storefronts brandishing loaded semiautomatic pistols.

All told, 55 people were killed and over 2000 injured. Luckily, I had missed the actual event but now had to contend with the fallout of rubble and ash as well as fear, mistrust, and outrage that settled over much of Los Angeles. Somehow, it all fitted in perfectly with my mood. Having just squandered thousands of dollars on a radical therapy that turned out to be bogus, in serious jeopardy of losing my New York City apartment after the landlord discovered I had sublet it, and having not a clue as to what to do or where to turn next, I was probably as full of rage and frustration as the Rodney King rioters. I seemed headed for a colossal meltdown.

A couple of weeks after the deadly riots, partly as a distraction from the toxic mood that still permeated the air and exacerbated my own worries, and partly out of hope that I might be helped, I enrolled in a clinical study sponsored by a psychiatric research institute. It was a trial of a new medication for Obsessive Compulsive Disorder. Although that, perhaps, was not really my problem except in the mildest sense, I had nevertheless filled out their detailed questionnaire and discussed my symptoms with the doctor administering the study. Participants would be paid but had to commit to a 16-week trial. I was almost surprised when I got accepted into the program. In this double-blind study both the experimental group and the "control group" would receive medication, but the control group would begin with and stay on a relatively low dose while the other group would gradually receive increased doses up to a maximum potency four times the strength of the starting dose.

Five weeks into the study I was struggling to cope with side effects which were turning me into more of a basket case than I already was. Profuse sweating, especially from, of all places, the backs of my ears. Thin streams of liquid would trickle down my neck as I walked around outdoors, and I always had to carry a dishcloth with me to act as a blotter. Strangely falling asleep standing up, in the middle of the day -- just instantly dozing off with no warning while waiting at the bus stop or checkout aisle, only to snap out of it 40 seconds to a minute later. Severe constipation which could mean not having a bowel movement for days. Excessively vivid, active dreams which seemed to spill over into waking consciousness and linger for several minutes after awakening.

But the pills also seemed to help me in some important ways. They seemed to quiet the "noise" in my head. Whenever I was depressed or feeling anxiety, there would always be this constant din in the back of my mind, not so much a literal sound as a feeling, a continual low scraping sensation as if the moving parts of some large machine or contraption were trying to function but someone had forgotten to oil them. At times of severe depression I was often reminded of a scene in Ralph Ellison's wonderful novel *Invisible Man* in which the residents of a Harlem tenement building, facing yet another brutal winter night with no heat, begin simultaneously banging on their pipes, as Ellison's protagonist wonders what in God's name that crazy sound is. The OCD medication, whatever else its effects, seemed to at least markedly mask or muffle the sound of those clanging pipes.

By the end of eight weeks, I just couldn't handle the side effects of the OCD meds anymore. I worried that I was in the group that would keep getting higher and higher doses and that things would only get worse. So I quit taking the pills, more or less cold turkey. After only a few days off the meds, the "noises" in my head began to return. I was starting to hear those banging pipes again.

One day I was waiting for the bus back home from Santa Monica beach. The No. 4 bus was a long and nasty ride. It rumbled down Santa Monica Boulevard from the eastern-most portions of LA all the way to the coast. The beautiful thing about it was that I could pack a small bag with a blanket and a book, board the bus at my street -- North Van Ness Avenue -- and, in less than an hour, be lying on the sands of Santa Monica beach listening to the Pacific Ocean crashing against the shore. But the odd collection of humanity the bus picked up along the way was not exactly what one would call "beautiful": shriveled-up old ladies trying to manage three or four bulging bags of groceries from *Ralph's* supermarket, chubby Mexican women holding screaming babies who badly needed a diaper change, loud teens carrying skateboards they planned to ride along the promenade near the beach, grungy junkies on their way to the methadone clinic, foulmouthed forty-something banshees stinking of tobacco, loudly airing their personal business for all to hear, unkempt unshaven unemployed men who hadn't bathed in days. Indeed, for most Los Angelenos, who wouldn't be caught dead on a bus, the No. 4 bus ride across Santa Monica Boulevard would have felt like and smelled like a zoo on wheels.

This particular afternoon had been unusually hot for the beach, and I was starting to sweat heavily. Even absent the OCD pills which stimulated the sweat glands, the back of my shirt was soaked and I couldn't wait to get home and take a cool shower. The bus was at least ten minutes late, then twenty, then twenty-five. Thinking it must have broken down, I began walking. After about ten or so blocks, I spotted the No. 4 bus approaching far behind me and ran to the nearest bus stop. When it finally arrived, the driver appeared to be in a rotten mood and the bus was packed. One man, standing up front, clinging to an overhead rail because there was no place to sit, kept asking the driver for directions. He spoke very broken English and looked utterly lost. The bus driver, rather than assisting, kept telling the poor guy to go and find a seat.

"You can't stand here sir -- there are seats in the back. Move to the rear, please."

The man, frustrated, tried to explain that he just wanted to know what stop he should get off that would be closest to a certain street address. The driver would have none of it.

I was sitting a little ways down, having parked my butt uncomfortably on the edge of a seat next to two bulky shopping bags belonging to the passenger next to me. Getting impatient with the scene in front of me and shocked that the driver would be so rude, I at last stood up and yelled out something to the effect of:

"Hey listen, fellah. You're a public servant. So why don't you serve the public! The guy's just asking a simple question. Don't forget who pays your salary, you asshole."

At that, the driver stopped the bus and asked that I get off. I said I paid my fare and would do no such thing. He repeated his demand that I get off the bus immediately. I remained defiant. Blocking traffic, he was forced to resume driving, but I heard him get on his radio and call for a police unit to meet him at a certain bus stop.

Sure enough, about five minutes later, when we arrived at the designated stop, I saw the familiar black and white LAPD car parked across the street, and an officer approached the bus. After the driver identified me, I was forced to exit the bus and got slapped with a summons to appear in court. I walked the rest of the way home in disbelief, vowing to find some way to buy a beat-up used car, like the jalopies the Mexicans careened around with.

After a while I went back to Dr. Fogelson, the doctor I had been reporting to regularly before dropping out of the OCD study. I asked if he could put me back on a low dose of the drug I now knew was called Anafranil. I told him I felt it had helped me in certain key respects and if he could just write me a prescription, I could start getting the drug on my own. So he gave me a script for a two-week supply and suggested I find a regular psychiatrist to administer the meds thereafter. He told me about a low-cost clinic I could check out.

Beginning to feel somewhat calmer on the meds, and with greatly diminished side effects, I began looking for a job. I had no idea what I should look for. My paralegal skills were quite rusty after almost three years of being away from that field. So I would have to rely on my experience in copyediting and proofreading, the kind of work I had done for the *Daily News* in New York. But Los Angeles was not a terribly literary place as compared to New York. There were few major book, magazine, or newspaper publishers, and my lack of wheels meant I had to restrict myself to within a small radius of the downtown LA area -- not where most of the good jobs were located.

Nevertheless, I had a couple dozen resumes printed up and mailed them out to anyone I thought might have a need for such services. After a few weeks of totally striking out, I got a brief letter from a company that said they were currently looking for a copyeditor and would be very interested in seeing me. They requested that I call to set up an interview. The outfit was called *Bridge Publications*, a company I had never heard of.

A few days later, having scheduled the job interview for that afternoon, I found my way to the address they had given me. Almost immediately I noticed something strange. As I approached the location, walking up Fountain Avenue, I seemed to be heading towards a particularly striking building I had noticed many times while strolling along tacky, tourist-thronged Hollywood Boulevard. Walking past the legendary *Grauman's Chinese Theater* with its famous sidewalk of stars and footprints, *Frederick's of Hollywood* lingerie, and all the rest, the towering edifice had often attracted my attention. It was a huge, shiny, sky-blue building with the word "SCIENTOLOGY" prominently emblazoned across the top.

"Oh no!" I thought, not the Church of Scientology! How did they get my resume? And why on earth would they ask to interview me for an editing job? But a job was a job, after all, so I continued on to the office. A woman wearing a painted-on smile greeted me and asked me to sit down across from her. She explained that *Bridge Publications* was indeed the Church of Scientology's publishing arm, and that they were seeking someone with a good eye for detail and strong editing skills who could help to assure "quality control" for the massive amounts of books, brochures, course manuals and similar publications the Church was continually putting out. First, however, I would need to become fully acquainted with the Church, its history, and its mission. She led me to another room.

I sat down in front of a large TV monitor. There was a table with pens and legal pads in case I wished to take notes. I was then treated to a series of informational videos which presented, among other things, the story of sea captain turned science fiction writer L. Ron Hubbard, the charismatic larger-than-life individual who had founded the Church. I learned about the core beliefs and principles of Scientology, and the important projects the Church was currently involved in all over the world. I was handed a book titled *Dianetics and* told to read it thoroughly before our next meeting the following week.

I got home and took a good look at the hefty paperback with its red and yellow cover and immediately recalled that I had seen this very book numerous times on the sidewalks of New York. A dozen or more copies would be laid out on a long table on which stood a large sign that read: "Free Stress Test." If you stopped by, they would take your pulse or something and suggest somehow that you needed to purchase and read this book.

But after I began actually reading *Dianetics*, I found that it contained nothing of what I had expected. It was neither science nor fiction nor was it some New Age self-help program. This was -- surprise, surprise -- a form of *psychotherapy.* Here were laid out the very same themes and concepts I had learned about from reading Arthur Janov's book, *The Primal Scream.* Yes -- the identical ideas, just expressed with different words! We all possess a primitive, subconscious part of our brain called the "reactive mind," where memories of past pain and childhood trauma are encapsulated and stored away in the nervous system in the form of "engrams." These engrams, though we are not aware of their presence, affect our every waking moment and are the source of all so-called "neurotic" behavior. The only way to become healthy and neurosis-free is to return to these buried memories, unblock and re-live them, and thereby neutralize them by discharging their force. This is accomplished via a process called "auditing."

So -- Art Janov ripped off his "groundbreaking" insights and ideas from none other than L. Ron Hubbard! *Was that it?* But if he did, that meant a great opportunity for me. If I was not able to get the "real" Primal Therapy because it had somehow turned into a sinister moneymaking scam, then maybe I could get this "auditing" and achieve the same results. Perhaps it was a kind and gentle twist of fate that had led me to this place, or God had taken pity on me and was showing me another way. All of this set my mind to humming and, overwhelmed by a sense of new possibilities, I eagerly awaited my next interview.

The second interview was much longer than the first. I arrived at the building around 1 pm. The day consisted of a complete tour of the facilities, more videos about L. Ron Hubbard and his great works, a battery of "psychological diagnostic tests" which took hours to complete, interrogation about whether my dad had ever been in the CIA or worked for the Justice Department, what illegal drugs I had ever taken, and what sort of medical and/or psychiatric treatments I had ever undergone. There was a visit to the special L. Ron Hubbard exhibit on Hollywood Boulevard, and my first sampling of an actual auditing session. That was a weird procedure in which you answer questions while hooked up to some kind of meter with a very sensitive dial -- something akin to a lie detector. I left dazed and confused and armed with about ten pounds of course material that I was to read and study. Incredible as it sounds, I did not arrive home till well past midnight!

But, hey -- when do I begin the actual job? -- I couldn't help but think. The copyediting job I had applied for, that is? And what about the salary? No one had mentioned either. I was supposed to return in a few days for a third and final interview.

Interview No. 3 was even more bizarre than the second one. Upon arriving, I was introduced to a group of people all wearing sailor's uniforms. They explained to me that every rookie Scientologist is required to live with a crew of experienced members for an unspecified time period. I would have to temporarily give up my apartment and move into a dormitory-like residence with them. All meals would be provided, laundry and shopping would be taken care of, and I would be given my own custom-made sailor's uniform. I was then handed a contract at the bottom of which was a statement affirming that I pledged myself from here on to the Church of Scientology "*for a billion years.*"

I was stunned. Yet not knowing what else to do at the moment, and desperately in need of a job, I signed the damn thing. I was then told to return home, make whatever arrangements had to be made for the care of my apartment, possessions, etc., gather up at least three weeks' worth of clothes and personal items, and show up the following Thursday to begin my "basic training" program.

I walked back home almost in a trance. Of course, it took only a few hours before reality set in with a loud wallop. There had never been any intent to interview me for a job, nor any actual job in the offing, for that matter. My resume had simply afforded them an opportunity to recruit me into their way of life, just as they attempted to recruit thousands of other naive and curious individuals through various means, like phony "stress tests." The Church of Scientology was obviously a wacky, warped, and scandal-ridden cult, appealing, perhaps, to troubled youth or alienated adults who craved a sense of identity or belonging -- lost orphans in need of a family.

Looks like I had struck out again. There would be neither gainful employment nor a second chance at therapy. Damn!! How does this happen to me?

Two weeks later there were two letters in my mailbox. One, from *Bridge Publications,* announced that they still wanted to hire me and urged me to come back whenever I was ready to get on board, literally, with the crew. The other envelope contained a notice informing me there was now a warrant out for my arrest, since I'd neither shown up in court nor paid the fine in connection with last summer's bus driver incident. I was looking at up to six months in jail, the notice sternly warned, if they ever caught up with me.

As the summer got underway and my next birthday approached (one of the last that would begin with the number "3") I attempted to return to my job search in earnest, but I just couldn't concentrate.

As the holidays approached that year, I began to feel anxious, angry and dark again. I considered increasing my medication, but the side effects would be too intolerable. I thought about flying home for Christmas, sleeping at Mom's a few days, just as I had done when I went back east for the court case. But I doubted I could afford it, with my funds fast disappearing. Helping raise the level of panic was the letter I had just received from the New York State Unemployment Office informing me that my claim was nearly exhausted. At best I could expect maybe three more checks to trickle in before the faucet ran dry. My sister was going to Hawaii for the Christmas break, so, short of my dad loaning me the airfare, I would be spending the holidays alone.

I called my parents and found that they were more than willing to pay for my plane tickets, knowing the dire straits I was in. So I felt that the least I could do was to show up with some thoughtful, carefully chosen gifts for everyone, since I certainly had plenty of time on my hands. Of course, anything really nice -- a sweater for Dad, a pretty scarf or necklace for Mom -- was out of the question. So was anything too heavy or bulky to pack in a suitcase. I thought I ought to look for a few novelty or offbeat items, "stocking stuffers" if you will, to serve as tokens of my love and appreciation. After all, it's the thought that counts, right?

Where to shop? Where else -- *Melrose Avenue*. That famous strip of chic shops, trendy bars, and hip eateries that stretched from LaBrea to Fairfax was known for its brazen in-your-face attitude and its outrageous, nowhere else to be found merchandise. An oddball mixture of kitsch and art, the stylish and the tawdry, the refined and the vulgar, Melrose Avenue was at once a tribute to all that was bold, daring, and quirky in pop culture, and a campy celebration of bad taste. On any Friday or Saturday night the street was crawling with upper middle-class teens from "the Valley," decked out in the latest punk fashions and hairstyles, as well as legions of wide-eyed onlookers seeking diversion and spectacle.

So one afternoon I walked all the way over from my apartment and thought I would have a look in each store, just to see what I could find. There were plenty of hot fashion items -- black leather biker jackets, trashy looking Madonna-inspired club clothes, "authentic" cowboy boots and hats, Prohibition-era gangster garb, and broken-in used *Levis,* every rip or tear adding to their appeal. *Marvel* comic books were a popular item and Madonna's coffee-table volume of racy photos, simply called *Sex*, was on display everywhere. How many folks would be getting that for Christmas? Then there was all the retro stuff -- Wurlitzer jukeboxes, Coca-Cola memorabilia, pink flamingo garden decor, even half-century old gas pumps.

For those with expensive tastes and pocketbooks to match there was exquisite Florentine pottery, vases, and dinnerware to be found at a shop called *Cottura*. But I saw mostly tourists and older folk in there. The teens and twenty-somethings, especially the girls, were rummaging through the racks at such cutting edge fashion meccas as *Wacko* and *Retail Slut*. For those into bongs, hookahs, and other pot paraphernalia there was plenty to choose from. Purveyors of skulls, crossbones and black nail polish were doing a brisk business, and gear designed to evoke your wildest S & M fantasies -- chains, studded dog collars, leather whips -- were provocatively displayed in one store window. And, if you were really bent on something utterly unique or bizarre you could head for a shop called *Black Market* and walk out with, among other things, a glass jar containing a dog fetus preserved in formaldehyde. It was only $19.00.

Needless to say, I came away from Melrose Avenue with nothing to wrap up and tie a ribbon around for my mom, dad, or brother back home. Sigh. I finally decided I'd better pick up some chocolates and a bottle of wine at the duty-free shop in the airport instead.

29
Midnight Desperado

IT'S EARLY IN the afternoon and I really ought to be pounding the pavement looking for work. Or maybe cleaning my apartment or doing a laundry. Instead, I'm at the *Los Angeles Gun Club* on East 6th Street off Alameda. It's an indoor shooting range about a twenty-minute walk from my apartment and I am here trying out different firearms -- everything from antique looking pearl-handled Smith & Wesson pistols to .38 caliber snub-nosed revolvers to 357 Magnums. For the fifth day in a row I'm running on about three hours of sleep, after yet another long midnight ramble around the neighborhood. My nerves are frayed and I am venting my fury and anger by shooting guns at paper targets. Even with my ear protectors on, the loud cracks of gunfire all around me are deafening. My aim is off -- it was much better the other day. The sleep deprivation is starting to get to me.

Back in my little efficiency apartment -- a five-minute walk from the iconic double-arched gates of the old *Paramount Studios* -- I open the refrigerator to see if there's any food left. What the hell was I still doing in Los Angeles? The year before I had sublet my New York City apartment to a couple from Michigan and prepared myself for an adventure that was supposed to change my life. I had become burnt-out from chronic depression, twisted into butterfly knots with anxiety and vexation. I'd grown excruciatingly bored with my own psycho-emotional maladies. This was the pre-Prozac era, before anyone was talking about neurotransmitters or serotonin deficiencies or "chemical imbalances" in the brain that could be corrected with the right pill. One had to search far and wide for radical, unorthodox treatments because, given what the psychiatric profession was offering at the time, anything less amounted to putting a dab of cold cream on an infected, festering sore. And so I had sought out something intense, something life-transforming, something that would "fix" once and for all whatever was ailing me.

But the solution I had put my faith in – Primal Therapy -- turned out to be anything but a fix. Just about everything I had read and believed about Primal Therapy -- its core philosophy, its approach, its therapeutic techniques -- bore about as much resemblance to what was actually going on at *The Primal Institute* in Los Angeles as a chamber music recital at Lincoln Center might bear to a traveling carnival. This groundbreaking one-of-a-kind therapy (even John Lennon had praised it to the skies) that was supposed to smash all of my neurotic defenses to smithereens and liberate my "authentic feeling self" consisted of, what? Chiefly it was my therapist urging me to bang on a padded wall while yelling hateful things at my mother. It had been almost laughable.

And, still in shock from the realization that I had just blown thousands of dollars with nothing to show for it, fate threw me another curve. I learned that my landlord back in New York had challenged what he called the "illegal" subletting of my apartment. I was taken by surprise, not even sure how he had found out. I had simply needed someone to occupy my place and cover the rent for about six months while I was living on the West Coast. There had been no intent to profit from the sublet or disregard the terms of my lease.

Nevertheless, in my rush to get a paying tenant into the apartment before I had to be in Los Angeles to begin my therapy, I had neglected to obtain the landlord's express written consent. This gave him a neat excuse to take me to court and possibly evict me from the rent-stabilized apartment I had lived in for nearly ten years. He could then renovate and lease out the unit to a new tenant for a considerably higher rent. If I failed to appear in court to plead my case, my landlord would win by default and could throw both me and my subtenants out at once. So I had to fly back to New York on short notice and stand before a judge in New York City's Housing Court.

Déjà vu. For the second time in less than five years, there, across the table from me in front of a judge's bench were my landlord and his lawyer huddled together whispering. Waiting for my turn to speak in the antiquated courtroom, I was well aware that my prospects were dim. Technically, the landlord was right. I should not have gone ahead with the sublet without getting his permission. As such, I was in violation of my lease and unless I was prepared to "cure" the offense within 15 days he could get a court order to evict me immediately. The man in the black robes wasted no time making that crystal clear to me.

So, it was either I pack up all my stuff, bid adieu to Los Angeles and move back into my apartment within two weeks, or else lose it forever. But, with a place of my own in LA to worry about, I didn't see how I could possibly wrap everything up and accomplish a cross-country move in such a short amount of time. Besides, what about Ira and Grace, my subtenants? They had signed a contract with me to use my apartment for six months until they could find a condo to buy. They still had a month and a half left under the sublease and had not yet found a suitable home. The couple had nowhere else to go. How could I just throw them out on the street in two weeks! What a rotten thing to do.

It was quite hopeless. My landlord had even offered Grace and Ira a one-year lease if they chose to remain in the apartment, that is, unless I moved back in to reclaim it. I could see no way out of the situation. Thoroughly exhausted, drained from the ordeal I had just been through, still suffering jet lag from the long flight, and practically broke, I had no energy left to fight or to protest. So with barely a whimper, I told the judge I could not comply and gave up my Manhattan apartment. Just like that.

When I returned to Los Angeles it took a while for the new reality to sink in. The reality that I now had no place to go back to, having just given up my home. That I was stuck in this vacuous land of endless freeways and smog-shrouded hills with no money and no job. And one fine golden California morning as I gazed out my window at swaying palm trees, the ugly state of affairs at last registered in my mind with the finality of a crocodile's jaw snapping shut on the leg of a hapless wildebeest.

Facing this stark truth head on with no fuzz or filters, I became incandescent with rage. How could it all have come to this? What had I done to deserve it? Were the gods toying with me again, using me for target practice? I did not react well to that kind of bullying from above. It seemed so arbitrary and so unfair. And I knew that, in my precarious emotional state, it might not be long before I would begin acting out in unhealthy ways. Almost all of my savings were gone by now and the unemployment checks had stopped coming. I was practically destitute. And bad things began to happen.

Partly out of desperation and partly out of anger, I began to shoplift at the local *Von's* supermarket, stealthily slipping cans of *Bumblebee* tuna or *Old El Paso* refried beans into my backpack, sometimes even packages of chicken legs from the butcher's counter when I could get away with it. I almost got caught by a security guard while trying to slip two boxes of tampons underneath my oversized sweatshirt. If I'd owned a car, I would have considered living in it. One evening in a soaking rain I arrived home half drenched, only to find that I had locked myself out of my apartment. I had to go around the back and use the butt of my wrecked umbrella to break the glass storm door, sparking painful memories of a similar rainy night featuring busted umbrella and shattering glass, many many years before.

Folks in the neighborhood began to eye me strangely. Unable to sleep at night, I took to aimlessly roaming the streets of Hollywood in nervous fits, straining to make sense of the grotesque film noir my life had become. I became fixated on my slinking shadow cast from the streetlamps as I silently prowled the sidewalks, moving in no particular direction, occasionally locking eyes with a crouching feline out for some nocturnal hunting. Often, at two or three in the morning, I would turn onto a quiet residential street and suddenly one or two large, vicious dogs would run up to the gate or fence, bare their teeth and bark riotously. Once or twice I feared one of them would leap over the fence and attack me. I tried to imagine what it would be like to be mauled to death by a Rottweiler.

A dark thought reared its head. Maybe I ought to get a gun. In the immediate aftermath of the Rodney King fiasco, hundreds of perfectly respectable citizens were rushing out to buy firearms. Local gun and tackle shops were doing a brisk business. It was really no big deal. Out of sheer boredom, I had gone to the shooting range a few times, had selected and sampled a variety of handguns. Because I happened to have fairly small hands most of the pistols had too much recoil for me. But there was this one that I tried -- a black semiautomatic that looked like it was made of industrial grade plastic. It had almost looked to me like a toy gun. It felt very comfortable in my hand and had hardly any kick when fired. I thought it was kind of neat.

There was a gun shop I had passed many times -- it was off LaBrea, right next to the *Thrifty Drugs* store. One day I just strolled casually into the shop and looked around for the same pistol I had used at the gun range on East 6th Street. I spotted it in the display case. It was a high tech Glock 19, a nine-millimeter semiautomatic with a clip that held about 14 rounds. "Cool!" I said to myself, "Let's get it." But, oops -- look at the price tag, $545.00. Ah, I thought, but why should that be any deterrent? Hadn't I already flushed thousands of dollars down the toilet for some worthless therapy? *Swoosh. Gurgle. Gurgle.* All gone. At least in this case I would be getting something of real value.

It happened I had just sold some furniture and lamps I didn't need and had some extra cash. And so, I went back to the gun store, approached the dealer with a bit of embarrassment and asked whether or not I needed to produce a "permit" in order to purchase a firearm, as was commonly the case in the Northeast. No permit needed, just a two-week waiting period to allow them to conduct a criminal background check. I put down a deposit. After the two weeks passed I returned, paid the remaining balance, picked up some ammo and put my slick new piece into my backpack. Now I would be ready for the next riot, or anything else. I had been defrauded, cheated, robbed, and kicked out of my home. But I didn't feel that way now. I no longer felt like a "victim."

On my next midnight stroll past all those fancy upscale homes I was the picture of insouciance: inhaling the cool night air with its hint of dewy dampness, humming a punk rock tune, kicking stones down the road, heedless of outdoor security lights tracking my every move. And no growling guard dog could scare me now. I was packing heat. If one of them so much as barked at me too nastily with that killer look in his eyes, a quick shot to the face would cure him of his bad attitude. At one point on a moonlit night, I seriously considered shooting one of the more ferocious canines just for the hell of it -- that's how deranged I was from lack of sleep. But luckily I thought better of it and started to walk away and head home. By the time I got there, still sullen and cross, it was well past four in the morning and it was starting to get light out. A bunch of loudly squawking birds were perched on a skinny tree right outside my bedroom window, just as they had been the night before and the night before that and the night before that.

Whenever I went to bed in the wee hours, their incessant chirping always kept me from sleeping -- no matter how physically spent I was. Not this time, I thought. Not again. I approached the tree, pointed the gun upward and fired two shots. At once all the birds fled. I immediately felt like a complete idiot and wondered if any of my neighbors had heard the gunshots. As soon as I walked in and quietly shut the door it occurred to me that the best possible use of my new toy would be to provide the "final solution" to all of my miseries. Why not just check out now, I thought, and avoid entirely the impossible task of trying to stitch back together the threads and patches of a shredded life? A challenge every bit as impossible as trying to unscramble an egg and put it back in its shell. Failure was a given, and what then? Instead, in less than a second, using the tip of one finger I could make it all go away.

For a fleeting moment I was tempted, and put the barrel of the gun against my temple just to see how it felt. But then I recoiled at the thought, picturing my landlady or sister or someone else discovering the lifeless body with bits of brain matter splattered on a nearby wall, my poor dad having to fly out and identify me in the morgue. Ugh. I walked towards my bed, turned on the light, and opened the door of a high narrow closet. Hmm, I thought, a couple of belts or maybe even nylon stockings slung from a bar up there would make a pretty good noose, in case I preferred a less bloody way to exit. I shook my head in sadness, exasperation, and a tinge of fear. Using a stool and a broomstick I shoved the pistol to the far back of the highest shelf. I did not touch it, or even think about it again for months.

30
Death Begins at Forty

THIS IS HARD to believe. I mean, how could I be shivering -- actually *shivering* -- when it's nearly ninety degrees? It's August and I have come to a popular beach on Long Island. I'm sitting on a blue bath towel spread across the sand, with my legs bent, knees pressed up against my chest and my arms wrapped tightly around them. I feel like there's a hundred-pound dumbbell pressing down on my head, and it has nothing to do with migraines. Earlier there were tears, copious amounts in what seemed a never-ending flow, making me thank God no one was close enough to notice. But the tears finally stopped. For once the sun beating down on my scalp is not soothing, but only oppressive. Watching and listening to each wave crashing on the shore I feel as if those tons of water are thundering down on my very last defense -- that flimsy crumbling seawall that yet shields me from the real, stark and ugly truth. And that truth is that I cannot go on living much longer.

I fix my gaze on the ocean, study each mighty rushing, gracefully curling peak of turquoise sea as it rises and then dissolves into white foam and it's as if I can hear a foreboding drum roll, a clock ticking, reminding me that my time will soon run out. I can feel the battering ram pushing against that weak wall and know it's just a matter of days, weeks perhaps, but not much longer, before it all comes tumbling down. There is just no way this pain-drenched, angst-ridden, misbegotten life can or should continue. I feel nauseous, not just in my stomach but in my head, in my mind, in fact. If only my mind could retch out all the poisonous bile that has accumulated over forty years of flagrant failure. If only there was a window I could open to let out the fumes, rather than be stuck in a dark cellar with the putrid rot of dead dreams, shattered plans, squashed ambitions, torpedoed hopes -- the stench of which now pervades my entire consciousness. But there is no window, no release! I don't know how to purge the decay, how to unload the toxic mess. And

I just can't bear it any longer. I think about the recent past and another shiver ripples through my body.

Three months ago I moved into my parents' house, having left Los Angeles for good after the Primal Therapy disaster and the loss of my New York apartment. I came back crushed, broke, and broken. It was the opposite of the happy scene I had once envisioned: my triumphant return home as a transformed, healthy and mature individual ready to strut out on stage for her Second Act. Instead, here I am back living with my mother, my old tormentor, in an apartment on Webster Avenue in the Bronx that has no room for me. After Granny died, my brother, dealing with his own drug woes and shipwrecked life, moved into her bedroom. So I am reduced to sleeping on the couch out in the living room. And my parents are none too thrilled about having two of their grown-up loser children moving back in with them. Who can blame them? I can't fathom what kind of work I can get after almost three years out of the job market. Most office jobs now require some computer literacy, which I lack.

Trading on my experience as a copyeditor for the *NY Daily News*, I was able to obtain a number of freelance editing assignments from various New York book publishers. But such jobs, though well-paying, are few and far between, and not sufficient to provide me the financial independence I need to get a place of my own. The lack of privacy here is getting unbearable. Mom is actually making an effort to be sympathetic, which just goes to show what a sorry wretch I must have looked like when I walked in that door with my battered suitcase, humiliation and defeat written all over my face. Making matters worse, I just received a letter from my landlady in LA informing me that she will not be returning my security deposit because of a mold and mildew condition she detected in the bathroom, apparently the result of my excessive water use. There is no point protesting because I am probably guilty.

I don't suppose anyone is overjoyed about turning 40, but for someone like me, as might be imagined, it was a uniquely miserable occasion. I had absolutely nothing to show for forty years of taking up space on this planet. My education had availed me little, confirming my mother's belief, often expressed when we were growing up as kids, that a college degree ain't worth the paper it's printed on if the person lacks common sense and "character." Here I was about to enter "the autumn of my life," but instead of the mellow amber and copper tones of fall foliage and the fragrance of apple orchards, all I could see ahead was a desiccated colorless landscape inspiring only dread. An unshakable feeling that life was coming to a grinding halt, a sensation of being slowly sucked into a vortex like a leftover scrap of hamburger being pulled swirling down the drain of the kitchen sink. On the night of my 40th birthday, my parents and brother had offered to take me out to dinner. I refused to go, preferring to sit and sulk on the sofa, wishing I had never been born. There should have never been a "birth day" to begin with.

But now it's gone way beyond sulking, way beyond sadness and regret. I can feel a strange kind of terror beginning to envelop me. There is a soundtrack to it; I hear ominous jarring chords slowly but inexorably rising to a crescendo, just like the sounds one hears in a horror flick moments before something truly bloodcurdling happens. I can see a dark curtain, like a shroud, descending. A dull throbbing pain reverberates throughout my body. I feel trapped; on all sides of me, in every possible direction, I see traffic signs reading "Wrong Way," "Do Not Enter," "Not a Thru Road," and "No Exit," and they're getting bigger and bigger, closer and closer. There is nothing I can do, nowhere I can go. I simply can't go on like this, sleeping on the sofa in my parents' living room, as emotionally shredded and deranged as ever, with not a dime to spare, no job prospects, and scarcely a friend to talk to -- a friend, that is, for whom having to listen to me in this dreadful condition would not be a severe imposition. Everything around me has suddenly become meaningless.

I get up in the morning and begin brushing my teeth. Then I stop and think, *why am I doing this?* What's the point? Looking in the closet to select an outfit to wear that day suddenly seems an absurd exercise. What the hell does it matter what I wear!! Why get dressed at all? I pick up a book and try to read but I can't focus, can't concentrate. I read the first sentence over and over and yet again, trying to make sense of the words, trying to discern the meaning, but I cannot. There seems to be a roaring in my head, a little jet engine creating a deafening noise that grows in intensity until everything else is blotted out. From time to time I feel dazzled by unspeakable phantom sights, startled by grisly sounds that no one else seems to hear. I've lost my bearings and am sinking bit by bit into a bubbling quicksand. I'm losing myself. I'm going down. It's all over. The torture needs to end soon, needs to end now.

And at this very moment, as I clutch handfuls of warm sand and watch it trickle through my fingers while the sun momentarily gets lost behind a cloud, I know what I have to do. It's the only thing that makes sense. This is a life that should never have happened, that should have been snuffed out in the womb (which would have spared my mother the pain and sickness my unusually difficult birth caused her). But better late than never. Some of my belongings that I brought home or arranged to have sent home from LA are still in boxes that haven't been opened yet. Somewhere among those boxes is the Glock 9mm handgun I bought the year before. There are also two packs of *Fiocchi* brand ammo -- full metal jackets and hollow point bullets (hah, what was I thinking with that last one?) This would be the easiest and quickest way to do it. Would take less than a second. Imagine that? A fraction of a second, then, deliverance. Of course it would have to be done somewhere away from home. Perhaps outdoors in the woods, or in some cheap motel room. As a matter of fact, a new motel called *The River Road Inn* just opened next door to our apartment building, despite noisy protests from neighborhood residents who feared the kind of traffic a motel offering "hourly rates" would generate. But then again, I think I would want to be a bit farther away from Mom and Dad's house than right next door.

Should I write a note? I would probably need to leave something behind, mostly something assuring anyone who cares that it was all for the best. That they should feel relieved, even happy for me knowing I was now out of my pain. Surely that wouldn't be so hard to understand, would it? Looking again towards the sea, at the collapsing waves, I get an almost peaceful feeling. A welcome bit of clarity washes over me. My little sojourn here on earth, this "life" of mine, much like that of everyone else in the cosmic scheme of things, really amounts to not much more than a stray bit of flotsam getting tossed about by the waves for a spell before settling finally to the eternal darkness of the ocean floor. That is all our lives are, really, are they not, all religious propaganda to the contrary notwithstanding?

Later that week I begin to actualize my plan in earnest. Waiting until no one was around, I started searching among my boxes, located and opened the right one, retrieved the pistol and taped the box shut again. I found a secret and secure hiding place for the gun. I decided to go through all the rest of my junk and throw out useless things. I particularly wanted to destroy any diaries or journals I had kept over the years -- the thought of my mother or brother leafing through them after I was gone was sickening. I wanted to make everything as easy as I could for my parents, and also to extinguish as many traces of my existence as possible. I tried to plan the best time to do the deed. With summer ending, pretty soon we would be moving into the holiday season. I decided I ought to plan for the second week of January, in order not to totally ruin my parents' Christmas. But I debated with myself whether I could or should hold out that long.

I had recently seen the movie, *Scent of a Woman,* starring Al Pacino. It was a great film, I thought, particularly Pacino's crusty but sensitive portrayal of a blind, single, former military man who's grown bored and restless, and finally decides that his uneventful and loveless life is no longer worth living. He resolves to end it, but to spend one final weekend doing the things he had always dreamed of doing but could never afford. So, with no future retirement to worry about, he liquidates his assets, empties his bank account and goes all out. He reserves a plush hotel suite in the city, rents a Ferrari for a day, enjoys lavish feasts, expensive wine, ladies of the evening and all the rest. First thing Monday morning he plans to blow his brains out with his trusty sidearm. Of course, in the film we get the typical Hollywood ending we expect -- the distraught man is rescued from the brink of self-destruction by a lovely woman who happens by, just in the nick of time.

I knew there would be no such happy ending for me, but I liked his plan, or part of it, anyway. A four-star private hotel room in the city -- that would be a nice setting. I could put it on my credit card. When the moment came, I would put the TV on at full blast to disguise the sound of the gunshot and avoid scaring other guests. I would pull the blankets over my head first and try to position myself in such a way that most of the blood would spill into a corner on the carpet rather than splash all over the bed and the sheets, making a less gruesome scene for the maid the next morning. The fancy cars and escorts I could do without, and I thought I would likely prefer to do it on an empty stomach. But wine, or better, hard liquor, would probably be a necessity. I wasn't completely sure I would have the nerve to pull the trigger stone cold sober. It was only the fact that it required just a split second and caused instantaneous obliteration that made this the only possible method. I seriously doubted that I could ever get up the nerve to jump off a bridge, lay down on railroad tracks, or put my neck in a sling and then kick the chair out from under me. Too scary, too much time to experience last gasps and dying throes. But even shooting took some guts, and I thought a few hard drinks would help me to relax, to not care about a thing, and make the whole experience kind of fuzzy and surreal. I pictured myself completely wasted, smiling goofily into the mirror. Bye Bye, Boom!!!

The weeks and months passed, and a curious calm began to come over me as I contemplated a certain and not too far-off ending to all of my misery. Now, happily, nothing mattered, nothing at all. I would find myself listening with amusement to my parents' and brother's conversations. They would say something like: "Next summer we ought to take a trip out West. I'd love to visit the Grand Canyon," or, "I think I'm gonna finally get my Bachelor's Degree. I applied to Bronx Community College," or "Right after the holidays we have to get this carpet cleaned" -- and I would just sit back and think, *Well folks, good luck with college, the Grand Canyon, and the carpet. Too bad I won't be around to see any of it. Hee hee.* I could picture my absence from all kinds of places and events where I would otherwise be -- the hair salon, sitting on a lawn chair in Van Cortlandt Park, my favorite table at the library, Thanksgiving dinner. Just an empty, untroubled space where my body would have been. It was refreshing. I could even enjoy things again, like TV shows, music, meals. I could leaf through a newspaper calmly. I could actually smile. I could exhale peacefully. Not to worry -- soon it will all be over. Having made my final decision, there were no others I had to make.

When my mom mentioned that some store was having a sale on winter apparel and asked me if I wanted to take a drive with her to pick out a coat, I had to keep myself from blurting out, "No that's okay, Mom, I won't be needing any more coats, thank you." Calendars, schedules, appointments, all dissolved into meaninglessness. I got a letter asking if I wanted to renew my subscription to some magazine. The dentist sent a postcard reminding me that I was due for a cleaning in February. All anxieties over getting a job or finding some studio apartment I could afford or desperately seeking out some shrink or therapist who could help me at last, just flew out the window like cigarette smoke. It occurred to me that if I could just keep this relaxed, easy feeling going indefinitely I wouldn't even have to kill myself.

Occasionally I would think about how friends like Maxine, or my closest friend, Peyton in North Carolina, would feel when they learned of my demise. Of course they would be shocked, hurt. But I would hope they would empathize with my need to be delivered from my pain. I had heard that suicide was in many cases really a form of defiance, an attempt to punish those who had failed you, to shout at them in indignant fury: "**See -- look what you made me do! *Now* are you satisfied!?"** But I didn't think this applied in my case. My anger towards my mother had long ago turned into resignation and acceptance of the plain fact that, through no fault of her own, she simply did not understand me. It was just a mismatch, a personality clash. If anything, I was far more angry at myself for making such a mess of my life, and maybe at the whole world in general for making it so hard for me to find my place in it. No, this would be a simple mercy killing, nothing more.

But then I thought of my brother. Jimmy, 38, was close to me in age, temperament, ideas, and tastes in everything from music to clothes. He had a number of mental and emotional issues of his own, including substance abuse, severe attention-deficit disorder, and a covert form of manic-depression. He had written me a ton of letters when I first went away to college, often shared his deepest concerns, feeling that I could relate and understand. And indeed, I recognized something in him that mirrored something in me. But we had drawn apart over the past several years because I was quite intolerant of his drug use.

There had been a time, after his girlfriend chased him out of their Brooklyn home and I was living in that two-bedroom apartment in upper Manhattan, when Jim asked if he could stay with me for a while. Since I had the spare room I could hardly refuse. But things became very ugly when I found that he had graduated from "snow" (powdered cocaine) to rock or "crack," which I considered to be much more dangerously addictive and self-destructive. One night when I caught him talking on the phone to a friend, explaining in graphic detail how to prepare and use a crack pipe, I lost my temper and threw him out. But lately Jimmy had been trying to improve himself, had checked into a rehab and emerged clean, and had even decided to continue his education by pursuing a college degree (something he had never shown interest in at age 18, even though he had the brains for it). I thought about the many midnight heart-to-heart talks we had had over the years.

What would Jimmy think when he found out what I had done? What would he feel? He would surely be devastated, having lost one of the few people who truly understood him. He would also probably resent, maybe even hate me, for taking the easy way out and leaving him stranded and alone. Should I try to explain it to him first? No, he didn't even know I had a gun and after hearing my morbid intentions would no doubt insist that I hand it over to him. If I refused, he would search every corner of the house until he found it. The thought of all of this gave me pause. We had been raised Catholic, and according to the Church suicide is a grave sin, a "mortal" sin. Only God gives life and only God has the right to take it away.

I had of course, long ago rejected religion, and Catholicism in particular. I considered Catholicism something of a voodoo religion, what with the soaring church vaults with their florid, excessive ornamentation, the long flowing purple and red robes, mysterious chants and mumblings uttered in Latin, wafting aromas of incense, candles glowing in the dark, statues and figurines everywhere, the idolizing of saints, the collecting of relics from their dead bodies, the Virgin Mary cult, the obsession with blood, pain, and sacrifice. And not to even mention the subculture of pedophilia which had plagued the Church for centuries, or the ridiculous pronouncements that issued from the Vatican, such as the prohibition against birth control. But I had to admit that their view of suicide had a certain merit, at least if one still believed there just might be a God.

One night when everyone was asleep, I snuck over to where I'd hidden the pistol and took it out. I examined it closely. It was loaded, but the safety lock was on. It looked exactly like the pistol I had seen guys whip out and hold with two hands, arms extended, on a hundred cop shows.

I pointed it at my temple for a moment to see how it would feel. Then I tried placing the barrel up against the back of my head in "execution style" fashion. Would I feel the bullet break through my skull, even for a fleeting instant? Would little squishy bits of my brain get spattered on the wall? I removed the clip. It contained maybe 12 or 13 rounds. Of course, I'd need only one -- or would I? The gun could jam. Worse, I had actually heard stories of people who had been shot in the head, even at close range, and somehow survived. Like Mary Buttafuoco, for instance. She had been the victim in last year's celebrated case of Joey Buttafuoco and Amy Fisher, the latter a disturbed 17-yr-old girl with whom Joey -- Mary's husband -- was having an affair. Amy shot Mary in the head at point blank range with a .25 caliber pistol. But Mary walked away with only partial hearing loss.

My God! Just imagine if the first bullet failed to do the job. I began to get a queasy feeling. I wondered if I would have the guts to do it after all, even if I fortified myself with liquor. I tried to imagine every possible scenario. Ah, damn it, I thought -- here I go again, getting myself ensnared in a trap of my own making, the trap of doubt with a capital "D." It was something to which I was peculiarly susceptible. In my lifelong quest for whatever was true, beautiful, and good, I questioned everything, and lately had despaired of ever getting the right answers. Confused and upset, I hurriedly shoved the clip back in and put the firearm, which had suddenly become repugnant to me, back in its hiding place.

One afternoon I was browsing in a bookstore and came across the recently published book, *Listening to Prozac* by Peter Kramer. Prozac had been introduced a mere five years before but had quickly become one of the most popular and widely prescribed drugs in the nation. It represented a major breakthrough in antidepressant medicine because it had an entirely different formulation which targeted serotonin, a neurotransmitter believed to play a major role in mood.

But, without any kind of health insurance, trying to begin sessions with a psychiatrist who could legally prescribe such a medication would be prohibitively expensive. Besides, no medication, however amazing, could change the circumstances of my life, could land me a job, or get me an apartment, or push back the hands of time that had already left what should have been "the best years of my life" far behind. It would be too little, too late. No, I decided, Prozac was out of the question. I had already chosen the remedy for my woes; it was similarly shaped, wrapped in metal rather than gelatin, a bit larger than a pill, and a lot less expensive too. Plus I only needed to take one, thank you very much.

Once again I became overwhelmed with suicidal feelings, along with a sense of urgency that told me I could not afford to wait a few more months. I had to do it now. Now, or never. But there was another pleading voice in my mind, not much more than a loud whisper, that was trying desperately to get my attention, to register a frail but urgent protest. The resulting emotional tug of war left me weak and drained and I was quickly coming to the brink of a nervous breakdown.

One day, after returning from a trip into the city and while walking away from the train platform, my eyes chanced to fall on the building across the street, and in particular on the words *Our Lady of Mercy.* It was a well-regarded Catholic hospital, the same hospital where Granny had spent her final days. I could fondly recall standing in the ICU with my mother, on either side of Granny's bed, both of us watching her as she drifted peacefully away with that sweet, ever present smile on her face. It was a soft gentle curve revealing no teeth, but always accompanied by a playful childlike twinkle in her eyes -- a smile that always reminded me of one of those friendly bottlenose dolphins that delight the folks at *Sea World.*

Maybe it was Granny's spirit that was calling me, but before I realized what I was doing I crossed the street and walked right into the emergency room of the hospital. I told them I was struggling with strong suicidal impulses, suffered from severe clinical depression, and had latent violent tendencies that could possibly be triggered if I continued to spiral out of control. They wanted to admit me immediately, but they asked whether I would mind being put in a cot out in the hallway, as all of the beds in the psychiatric ward were filled at the moment. I asked them when they expected a bed to become available and was told not more than two weeks. I told them I felt I could hang on until then, and would be back in two weeks to take the next empty bed. There was some processing and paperwork to complete first, so they politely requested I take a seat in the outside waiting area while they put together some forms. Relieved, disarmed by their kindness, I headed for the waiting room and sat down.

31

Tall, Dark, and Stark Raving Mad

"...because the only people for me are the mad ones, the ones who are mad to live, mad to talk, mad to be saved, desirous of everything at the same time, the ones who never yawn or say a commonplace thing, but burn, burn, burn like fabulous yellow roman candles, exploding like spiders across the stars and in the middle you see the blue centerlight pop and everybody goes 'Awww!'"

Jack Kerouac from *On the Road*

THE CLOSEST I ever came to real certifiable madness -- that soaring effervescent kind that Kerouac speaks of -- was meeting St. George. My first two years of knowing him were like a dizzy trek through the twilight zone landscape of a sci-fi adventure novel complete with heroes and villains, intergalactic warfare and cosmic conspiracies. Before I could catch my breath or get my bearings he took me on a rollicking romp through the looking glass of his own fevered imagination, a world as bizarre as anything Alice ever dreamed of. A place where ancient wisdom merged with ultramodern science and a child's sense of wonder to create a whole new kind of theme park. A theme park which included such line-around-the-block attractions as a special mind-manifest chamber in which thoughts are magically transformed into things in the blink of an eye, "shitless" bodies that stayed forever young and never had to use the toilet, and a hipper version of the Second Coming in which Jesus returns to the world in a spaceship from a planet called Arcturus. Entering St. George's strange and precious world was like stumbling into the ultimate escapist fantasy, where you checked your sanity at the door, took off your shoes, donned wings and set off for the wild blue yonder, guided by signposts painted in skywriting pointing the way to MAGIC, MOONBEAMS and MIRACLES. A circus fun house where everything moved at the speed of light, a crazy thought-experiment, a vivid waking dream, an unforgettable chapter in my life.

But none of that chapter would have been written were it not for that god-awful day on a Long Island beach a couple of months before.

I sat there in the reception area outside the emergency room of *Our Lady of Mercy* hospital, staring blankly ahead of me, trying to convince myself that I'd made the right decision in coming here. At one point I turned to look around a corner and noticed a tall well-dressed black man nervously pacing back and forth behind the glass, in what appeared to be a separate small room. He wore glasses, looked distinguished, quite intelligent, and radiated authority, even though he appeared to be only in his twenties. I assumed he must be a young doctor, and started to wonder what he seemed so agitated about. Maybe something bad had happened with a patient and he was blaming himself. I noticed his walk. It was straight, deliberate, dignified, having absolutely nothing of that arms-swaying, side-to-side swagger that so often characterized the younger generation of urban males.

I found myself curiously drawn to him, as if he were someone I had known before, in some long-ago time in some faraway place. At several points while pacing across the room he put his hand under his chin and seemed to be deep in thought, deliberating about very important things. He was well over six feet tall, had a slender but powerful build, broad well-shaped shoulders and just a shadow of a beard on his face. I thought him handsome in a Sidney Poitier sort of way. I couldn't shake the feeling of magnetic attraction I felt, as if I already knew this guy and he already knew me. No -- this was no stranger; even though I had no idea who he was I couldn't take my eyes off him. At one point I think he caught a glimpse of me staring at him and I turned my head away in embarrassment. I looked down at my hands, waited a few seconds, and then began staring again. I couldn't resist. But then the nurse called me over to sign some papers and give me directions on who to see and what to say when I came back in two weeks. When I left the nurse's station the tall black man was no longer there.

I went home and explained to my mother what I had done. That in two weeks I would be a self-admitted patient in the psychiatric ward at *Our Lady of Mercy* hospital. She seemed to understand and think it a good idea. My father, who had declared me a dependent on his tax return seemed to think he could get his employer's health insurance to cover the cost, and as the hospital was just a few blocks from their apartment building, it would be quite easy for them to visit me. I then began to make a list and set aside a few things I thought I might need while there. I fetched a small suitcase from the closet. I reminded myself that the last time I had been hospitalized, after that disastrous first semester of college in upstate New York, it hadn't been all that bad. I had met some weird but cool people, did arts and crafts, made friends, talked, played. By the time I was discharged after a month-long stay I felt genuinely better. It had worked once, maybe it could work again. For the time being, I put all suicidal thoughts on hold. I truly resolved to do whatever I could to make sure this second chance at life didn't slip away, to trust the doctors and hospital staff and pin my hopes on their experience and expertise. Much new knowledge and a host of new treatment options had arisen in the past decade to deal with the problem of depression; the odds were good that somewhere in that grab bag of possible remedies would be something tailor-made for me.

The two weeks of waiting and psyching myself up went by fast and I began to have some apprehensions about what situations I might encounter once I arrived on the ward. What would my fellow patients be like, who would I room with, how was the nursing staff? Just how sick or disturbed might some of the worst residents be? After all, I had been appalled when Ben, that Japanese guy I met in LA, took me to a state psychiatric hospital and tried to have me committed. Now I was committing myself. Who knew what sort of untoward and unpredictable scenes lay ahead. So I tried to brace myself emotionally and summon up the courage to deal with the dreadful, the repugnant, the scary, and every other Hollywood horror flick trope associated with mental hospitals.

Arriving early the morning of my admittance I was taken up to 7 South, the wing of the hospital reserved for mental patients. I was shown my room and met my roommate, an older Polish woman who spoke with a thick accent and was tenderly clutching a small wooden crucifix when we were introduced. I didn't think she would be a problem. After putting away my few articles of clothing and toiletries in the narrow closet and chest of drawers provided, I said a few words to her – her name was Basia. Then I headed for the hallway to check out the rest of the premises. At the end of the corridor was a large lounge with sofas, coffee tables and a TV. Several patients were sitting around.

Just as I was about to enter the lounge, HE walked out. Oh no! I couldn't believe my eyes. I had nearly forgotten all about the intriguing black man I had seen the day I first went to the emergency room. I had been so caught up with my preparations for being in the hospital that his image soon faded from my mind. Now here he was, in the flesh. And he was dressed in a T-shirt and jeans, not doctor scrubs. So that meant he was, what. . . a patient? A mental patient on the ward? Could it be? He walked by quickly and I doubted he remembered me -- that older white lady he'd caught glaring a hole into him two weeks ago. I wanted to know who he was and why he was here. I needed to know.

The following day I went into the lounge and found him sitting at one of the small tables writing something furiously on a yellow legal pad. He looked up when I walked in and seemed slightly perplexed. Finally he said, "Excuse me, but did I see you sitting in the waiting area outside the emergency room a couple of weeks ago?" I said yes and told him I had recalled seeing him there. He said, "Oh yeah, now I remember. You were that bedraggled housewife who was staring at me."

"Bedraggled housewife"? I thought. What on earth. . . "Well, welcome to Seven South," he continued, "It's nice to see a fresh new face, especially an attractive one." I felt the slightest blush coming on. To change the subject, I asked him what he was so busy writing. He paused for a second, then said:

"Well, it would take a few hours to explain it all but this right here (pointing to the yellow sheet of paper in front of him -- half covered with black scribbles) is my Corporate Mission Statement for Capstone Diversified Universal, or CDU, the greatest corporation slash government slash institution slash ministry slash multinational conglomerate there ever was or ever will be."

The words poured out of his mouth in a fluid even stream, each word crisply pronounced in a commanding voice which bore a slight trace of a Jamaican or West Indian accent. "*What!?!?*" was all I could think to say. I noticed that there were maybe six or seven loose yellow sheets of paper alongside the one he was writing on, all similarly covered with black handwriting. He was using one of those old-fashioned fountain pens where you have to insert a cartridge full of ink, which then flows out through the tip of the pen in precise wet dabs almost as if one were painting with an extremely fine brush. From where I was standing, his productions reminded me of pages of medieval illuminated manuscripts I had seen in museums, their flowery serpentine lettering an art form in itself. I was fascinated. He asked me my name and I told him. He told me his, Calvin St. George Bentley, but said he preferred to go by his middle name, given to him by his father in honor of the Christian martyr saint who slew a dragon. Well that's pretty cool, I thought.

Just then I heard my name called. The doctor who would be treating me during my hospitalization had arrived, so I went to meet him for the first time. Dr. Hennessey was a British-born psychiatrist who was also a certified psychoanalyst of the Freudian stamp -- attainments which required years of training. He was eager to hear the story of my experiences at *The Primal Institute* in Los Angeles and told me that there had been a considerable shift in thinking over the past several years about the best way to treat sufferers of depressive illness and other mood disorders. Often, Dr Hennessey said, it was far more likely such disorders resulted from simple chemical imbalances in the brain than from improper toilet training or repressed sexual desires for one's daddy.

The doctor said he was very encouraged by the results he had achieved with many of his patients through the use of the new class of antidepressants which targeted specific neurotransmitters, and whose most famous exemplar was Prozac. He told me he would be treating me with another medication -- Zoloft -- a member of the same family of so-called "SSRI" drugs. Dr. Hennessey would be starting me on a small dose, to be gradually increased during my stay.

I returned to my room to find Basia sleeping. Relieved not to have to engage in polite meaningless small talk, I sat on my bed to think and write in a little diary I had decided to keep while in the hospital. I was glad that I would get to try, at last, the new wonder drugs that had attracted so much publicity of late. I was also feeling quite positive about my new friend. I decided I would seek him out in the cafeteria at dinner time and learn more about him. Soon the bell would sound for "meds", and everyone would queue up to receive their daily dose. I would get my first sample of Zoloft, along with a mild anti-anxiety pill often prescribed to patients to ease them through their first few days in the hospital. I called home from one of two pay phones out in the hallway to tell my mother how everything was going. Then I went back to write until dinnertime.

At dinner I spotted "St. George" sitting at a table and approached him. He seemed delighted to see me again and welcomed me with a big smile as I took a seat across from him. The original feeling I had gotten when I first saw him -- the sense that I already knew him -- persisted intact, which made it unusually easy to talk to him. I wanted his life story and he was happy to oblige. I learned that he was 25 years old, the son of a Baptist minister and church founder who had emigrated to the United States from a seaside rural village in Jamaica. The only son among three children, St. George had been carefully groomed by his father to follow that path and to one day pastor his own church. However, the young man had plans of his own which involved telecommunications and broadcasting. Precocious and unusually bright, he had been accepted into one of New York's most prestigious high schools where he racked up an impressive academic record, was elected president of the student council, and distinguished himself in other ways. By the time of his graduation, he was Harvard-bound and the pride of his Bronx neighborhood.

But then, without warning, everything fell apart. One day during a church service he felt a mysterious invisible hand descend gently upon his head and a distinct inner whisper that seemed to come from his heart. This "heart voice" as he called it, told him in no uncertain terms that he had an extraordinary destiny which set him apart from other earthly mortals. The traditional time-honored path to success and privilege -- Ivy League education, great corporate job, hobnobbing with the social elite -- would not be his. He had been sent to earth with a special mission: to gather around him a select group of highly evolved and enlightened souls who had already played key roles in helping mankind advance to higher moral and spiritual plateaus.

These higher souls returned to earth periodically, in cycles, according to when and where they were most needed. They had been around, for example, during the signing of the Magna Carta, that famous charter of 1215 which curtailed the powers of despotic kings and laid down the concept of "the rule of law" by which all modern democracies are governed. They were around at the time of Christ, reappeared during the Renaissance, helped ensure the Allied victory in World War II, launched the Civil Rights era, and were now needed more than ever as a brand new millennium approached.

At several points during his revelations, St. George would stop, look at me with an ironic expression, and say something along the lines of, "Are you really interested in hearing all of this, or are you just pretending? You're just humoring me, aren't you?" "Oh no, not at all!" I protested. "No -- I mean, I'm really into this kind of thing. I love history, I love the "heavy" subjects, spiritual stuff, all of that," and I wasn't kidding. Those were the kinds of topics that got my mental juices flowing, as that astrologer, Charles House, had correctly divined after examining my nativity chart, not that I ever needed anyone to tell me.

"Well then," he continued, "you are the first woman I've ever met who was willing to listen to me expound on all of this without laughing. I take that as a high compliment. But then again, I'm not really surprised. You see, from the moment I noticed you looking at me in the waiting room, I suspected you might be one of my people. Now I'm sure of it."

"One of your people? You mean..."

"One of that special group of evolved souls I was just telling you about -- I call them the People of the One."

So, I thought to myself, maybe there really was something to that strange flicker of recognition I had felt when I first laid eyes on Mr. Calvin St. George Bentley. I was not averse to believing in reincarnation. What better way to explain the strange phenomenon of feeling you already know someone you've never even met?

Not long after his "heart voice" began speaking to him, St. George started acting odd. He forgot all about college and took to a room in the basement of his parents' house and began his "monk life." Wearing a pair of thick professorial-looking glasses, he would spend hours on end just writing, writing, writing, as the thoughts came to him, as the great plans unfolded, as his true destiny became increasingly clear to him. There were goals short-term and long to shoot for, instructions to follow, special directives to guide him along the road to greatness. It all had to be inscribed on paper in painstaking detail. St. George was penning the entire blueprint for his life, a blueprint as exquisitely precise and intricate as God's instructions in the Old Testament for how to build the Tabernacle.

After several months living the secluded life of a scribe, St. George's room was filled almost from floor to ceiling with numerous stacks of paper, which in short order began to crowd out everything else. He began to neglect his personal hygiene, rarely changed his clothes, forgot to eat, and cut off almost all communication with the outside world. Eventually his parents became alarmed and confronted him. The result was a violent outburst which ended with St. George being committed to the Bronx State Psychiatric Hospital with a diagnosis of delusional paranoid schizophrenia.

He was treated with various anti-psychotic medications over the course of a year, many of which had frightening side effects, and at length was finally released into a group home for the mentally ill. Such homes served as a kind of halfway house for patients attempting to gradually readjust to society with the help of effective outpatient treatment. Recently St. George had found his medications wearing off, had stopped taking them, and quickly began to "decompensate" and display symptoms of illness. Hence his arrival here at *Our Lady of Mercy* hospital. He had been admitted two weeks before I came, on the very day I had seen him in the emergency room. His doctors had started him on another medication for schizophrenia, along with a second pill designed just to counter the unpleasant side effects of the first.

We got into a routine of meeting every day in the cafeteria, taking our meals together, sometimes accompanied by one or two other of his friends. I would talk about myself and my life, but mostly would listen to St. George spin his fantastic tales and ambitious schemes, which I found more entertaining than any TV show. While the others would finish their meals and walk away, I would stay glued to my seat, in rapt attention. I sat there taking it all in as if I were breathing some rarefied air too heady for ordinary folk, or being entrusted with esoteric secrets normally kept under lock and key. St. George said he planned to found a special organization of black scientists -- astrophysicists, chemical engineers, cosmologists, cyber experts, astronauts -- a super elite squad of brilliant beautiful brown men who would plot strategies for benevolent world domination and the ushering in of a new golden era for humankind in the 21st Century and beyond. White men, unfortunately, would have to be excluded because they had racked up too much collective "bad karma." Women of all colors, however, were more than welcome. They would be needed to provide beauty, grace, and charm, as well as to bear and educate the children of their heroic male protectors.

I began looking at everything through St. George's daft prism. That was remarkably easy to do in such a setting -- a psychiatric ward isolated from the workaday world, full of eccentric outsiders who simply perceived things differently. An awesome new age for humanity was on the horizon. It would be a world created and ruled by the formerly oppressed, a world that would wonderfully fulfill Biblical prophecy and realize Jesus's promise that "the last shall be first and the first shall be last" in a hitherto unimagined way. St. George envisioned the new world as a high tech Garden of Eden with lush tropical foliage bursting with fragrant fruit, sparkling waterfalls, eternal youth, and all the other trappings of Babylonian splendor minus the decadence. But there would also be time travel, interstellar communication, visits to faraway galaxies, and recreational pleasure rides in custom-designed spacecraft. At long last, man would have mastered the trick of creation via *The Word* alone and become full-fledged partners and co-creators with God, just the way He had originally intended.

When I asked St. George where he had gotten all these wild ideas, he asked me if I had ever read about the American prophet and mystic, Edgar Cayce. I was familiar with the name, knew that he was some sort of clairvoyant who had gained notoriety in the 1930s, but otherwise knew nothing of his work. St. George gave me a book to read, a biography called *There Is a River*, which, he told me, had been for him a "life-changing" book. I began reading, and what I learned shocked and amazed me. This was a man with less than an eighth-grade education, the son of a tobacco farmer, who had the uncanny ability to put himself into a trance and make accurate medical diagnoses of people suffering from mysterious ailments, all without even seeing them! People from all over the country who had gotten wind of Cayce's extraordinary gifts would write to him describing baffling, sometimes life-threatening medical conditions that no doctor had been able to cure.

These letters would be read aloud to him while he lay on a couch in a self-induced hypnotic trance. After a few minutes, a detailed explanation, replete with technical medical jargon and terminology the young man could not possibly have understood in his waking state, would pour out of his mouth in a strange sounding voice unlike his own. After identifying the patient's condition Cayce would then prescribe specific remedies, usually calling for natural, holistic ingredients like potato poultices and castor oil packs. Of those patients who followed his instructions to the letter, a very high percentage reported the complete disappearance of their symptoms.

News of Edgar Cayce's achievements spread worldwide, letters poured in by the thousands, teams of doctors came to his home to observe his work firsthand, and even some professional skeptics and debunkers showed up at his door intending to expose him as a fraud. But the man continued on with his work undeterred and refused to accept any money or other compensation for his services. According to *There Is a River*, almost all of the medical cases, some 14,000 in total, were fully documented in writing and now reside in a facility Cayce's descendants founded in Virginia Beach, VA, available to anyone who wants to take a closer look.

After about two and a half weeks in the hospital, having increased my dosage of Zoloft twice, I thought I was beginning to notice tangible effects. At the worst moments of my black depressions, such as that terrible day at the beach, I would be aware of a subtle, low-grade kind of physical discomfort. It was as if I could actually feel, in a very visceral way, the gears moving and grinding within my body's workings, and inside my brain. As if I could actually feel them scraping up against each other, could hear the little screeching noises, especially towards the back of my head. It was one of the most debilitating features of the depressive episode, because it would render me unwilling to move, nor even think, lest I set those gears in motion and give rise to that excruciating friction. It made me just want to jump in a bed and cover myself with blankets.

But now I was noticing this painful sensation diminishing considerably, as if someone had poured some motor oil into my bruised and battered engine. The Zoloft, apparently, was flooding my brain and body with some kind of protective balm which had formerly been lacking, a kind of insulation which was just as necessary to healthy functioning as the black rubber coating is to the electrical wires in your house. I was surprised at how much of a difference it seemed to make.

I also noticed the gradual fading away of that constant "background noise" that seemed to hover around me continually. A steady irritating hum or buzz that made up the soundtrack to my every waking thought. It reminded me of the incessant whirring of leaf blowers you might hear for hours at a stretch in your neighborhood on an otherwise lovely October afternoon. After just twenty days on the new medicine, the noise had been silenced and I could actually appreciate simple sights, sounds, and smells again. I suddenly became aware of things -- birds in flight, a basket of fresh fruit on the kitchen counter, snatches of children's laughter, the scent of the air after a soaking rain, the gleam of polished silverware -- that would have gone unnoticed before. I could finally relax without artificial aids like alcohol or tranquilizers. My breathing became deeper, calmer. It was a subtle but amazing turnaround.

By the time I had been in the hospital three weeks, I was actually feeling good, really good, for the first time in years. More and more I looked forward to my conversations with St. George. We always ate our meals together, met during some of the planned activities like art class or bingo, spent our spare time in the lounge playing cards or just joking around. He too was doing much better on his medication, although he confessed that he feared completely losing touch with those inner voices that had revealed such a glorious future. I assured him that I would not let that happen. Having bought into much of the madcap fantasy myself, to the point even of convincing myself it was by no means impossible -- not if all that stuff about Edgar Cayce was true -- I encouraged St. George not to think of it as a "delusion" but rather as a project.

After a while it was obvious that our friendship was taking on flirtatious and romantic overtones, despite the age difference. St. George often told me how attractive he thought I was. He liked to tease me gently, and asked me numerous times if I had ever been married and if

I had a boyfriend, now or in the recent past. He refused to believe me when I answered no. I felt comfortable enough with him and all his craziness to consider telling him about my ambivalent sexuality, but he beat me to it. One day he blurted out with a knowing look, "You're gay aren't you, or at least bisexual?" I pleaded guilty to the latter. He then said he was delighted to hear this, because his plans for the women of the hip new civilization soon to rise up out of the smoldering ashes of the pale and dying West required that all females be bisexual. That way the women would not lack for pleasant diversionary activity while the men were off on critical missions. He said he believed bisexuality was the natural state of women and that society repressed it mainly to keep women subordinate to and dependent on men.

I could not help but be flattered that a handsome guy of 25, albeit "mentally ill," would be physically attracted to a 40-yr-old cheerless sexually confused loser like me. Of course, the attraction was much more than physical, but still St. George was overflowing with compliments about my facial features, my suntan, my hazel eyes, my walk, and more. I could feel my libido slowly waking up from the coma it had been in for at least the last four or five years.

Two days into my fourth week on the ward St. George announced that he was being discharged the following day. He was doing well on his medication regimen and would be able to continue his treatment at the outpatient clinic. I was really happy for him, but wondered what I would do without him for the rest of my stay. He asked me to write down the number of the pay phone out in the hall and give it to him before he left; he promised he would call me at least every other day, at about 9pm. And he kept his promise. As long as no one else was waiting to use the phone (which was most of the time since there was a second phone more conveniently located down the hall) we could have hours-long crazy conversations about our future fantastic plans. Such as establishing a new world religion, an eclectic faith which would take the best from the three major Western religions as well as Eastern traditions like Buddhism and Hinduism.

Dr. Hennessey was quite pleased with my progress on the Zoloft. I was now up to my maximum dose, the highest safe dose recommended by the manufacturer, and I no longer needed any of the anti-anxiety meds, such as Klonipin, that I had been put on when I first arrived. After 30 days in the hospital, it was no exaggeration to say that compared to the pathetic trembling wretch who sat rocking on a beach last August contemplating self-extermination, I was now a different person entirely. Dr. Hennessey felt I was ready to be discharged, and so did I.

I realized, of course, that I still had a long way to go in terms of putting my life back together. At 40, after several years of being for the most part unemployed, it would be a monumental task to establish financial independence again. I still had considerable fears -- I didn't know how much my obsessive-compulsive quirks, such as the bizarre sun addiction, would be mitigated by the medication once I was out of the hospital setting. Only time would tell. So, as additional insurance, I asked Dr. Hennessey if he would assist me in applying for social security disability benefits, on the basis that my illness might prevent me from getting the type of job for which I was qualified. He agreed and signed all the required papers. The benefits provided would be meager, but at least I would have a steady source of income.

I was discharged from *Our Lady of Mercy* the day before Thanksgiving and for the first time in decades, I felt I truly had something to be thankful for -- namely the second crack at a future I had just been given. I couldn't wait to see St. George.

32
The Magic Fades

ONCE OUT OF the hospital and back in the real world I knew my perspective would shift and the universe would look slightly different. I also knew that the thing I had going on with St. George would take on different contours. A relationship hatched in a psych ward between two mental patients is bound to change once the clinical setting is left behind and the demands of the straight sane world begin to impinge. At the same time, I did not want too much "reality" to tame the wild and crazy dreams the two of us had been riding on like a magic carpet for the past four weeks. I wasn't ready to leave Disneyland just yet, and didn't think it would be good for St. George either. For, truth be told, many of his so-called delusions were not all that preposterous or out of reach after all. With a bit of unleashed imagination and creative thinking, I could picture the two of us boldly stepping out as the architects of a new millennial faith, co-founders of a New Age cult that would captivate and inspire the hip hop generation. Kind of like celebrity evangelists Jim and Tammy Faye Bakker, only *we* would be honest, immune to the lures of fame and fortune, and truly dedicated to the spiritual elevation of mankind, as opposed to a couple of slick profiteers packaging religion as if it were a *McDonald's* Happy Meal.

I also realized that when St. George and I got together it would probably have to be on his own turf -- I wasn't sure how my dad would react to a certified schizophrenic six-foot-four black dude fifteen years my junior showing up at our house. So I asked St. George to give me the address of the new group home he had recently moved into. The thought of viewing St. George as my "boyfriend" seemed a tad ridiculous at first, all things considered. But then again, why not? The attraction was mutual, it was nice to have a percolating libido again after such a long drought, and besides, I was never one to conform to anyone's idea of what was normal or appropriate. So I decided just to allow things to take their natural course. St. George introduced me to his two roommates: Richie, a paranoid schizophrenic, and Antonio, who was bipolar, both of them former psych in-patients making the transition to independent living. He invited me into his sparsely furnished room, and there we sat for hours talking about his plans to launch a new "televangelist" ministry along the lines of Pat Robertson's *700 Club*.

St. George told me that one of his sister's friends worked at a low-budget local public access station. St. George, eyes glowing with enthusiasm, hands gesticulating wildly, spelled out his vision in detail. He would create an original TV show, a show that would pull out all the stops. Using some of his father's connections, he would bring on board fabulous gospel choirs, preachers who could bring the house down, as well as dynamic lay speakers. It would provide a unique and intoxicating blend of cutting edge science and Bible based old-time religion.

He would call his program *Greater Works Than These* -- from a saying of Jesus to his disciples wherein he tells them that one day they will not only perform all the miracles he did, but even "greater works than these." All who tuned in would be taught not to fear their own greatness, nor shrink from their destiny as co-creators with the Almighty. As for me, being kept aloft on the whirling air currents of my own "high," thanks to the deluge of serotonin my pills kept pumping into my brain, I failed to see anything impractical or "crazy" about any of these ideas. Far from trying to dissuade or bring him "down to earth," I became St. George's greatest cheerleader, for which he was profoundly grateful.

By year's end St. George and I had achieved such a meeting of minds, a mingling of spirits, a harmony of hearts, that when we finally became physically intimate it was almost beside the point. It happened, oddly enough, at his mother's house. He had excitedly reported to his mother about the great new friend he had found and the whole family was eager to meet me (imagine that). On New Year's Eve, while his pastor dad was out presiding over a special church service, he brought me home with him. I met his mom, who invited us both to partake of some curried goat soup and jerk chicken, signature dishes of her native Jamaica. Then she showed us into an upstairs apartment where St. George's older sister used to live before moving out a year ago.

After a full day out on the town, we were both a little tired and just lay down on the bed and dimmed the lights. There was a small TV in the room, so we turned on *Dick Clark's Rocking New Year's Eve* to watch the ball drop amid the crowds in Times Square. At the stroke of midnight we shared a long wet Happy New Year's kiss and then St. George, as sweetly and shyly as a 13-yr-old boy, began to slowly coax my clothes off, while he undressed himself. I would have preferred a glass or two of champagne first, but, alas, all forms of alcohol were verboten as his parents were strict teetotalers. But even without a champagne buzz, it was refreshing to feel like a sexual being again. It had been at least four long years since I 'd had sex with anyone, man or woman.

And so we just fell into our romance with abandon and the delusional roller-coaster ride continued. St. George was making me believe that life was intended to be beautiful, glorious, and full of adventure. What made it drab and boring and unremarkable was only humanity's ignorance of its own destiny and true nature. It was a powerful thought and it put wind under my wings.

About three weeks into the new year, I got a phone call. St. George was in the hospital. He told me that for the past several weeks he had, without informing me, been cutting down on his medications hoping to avert some of the troubling side effects, which included sporadic sexual dysfunction. Since we had been together he had understandably become more concerned about that aspect. But in recent days he had started to "decompensate" badly and that morning he had experienced a full-blown episode of the rapidly escalating disordered thought patterns and tiny fissures in the fabric of reality that accompany a schizophrenic breakdown. He felt that voices coming from the TV and radio were speaking directly to him. He thought he could detect secret messages in popular songs that were intended to reach him in particular. And they were all coming at him at once -- no longer was he able to screen out superfluous stimuli the way normal people do to avoid sensory or information overload.

St. George's "voices" were not and never had been frightening or mean; they never told him that anyone was "out to get him" nor to do anything violent. But they still put him far enough out of touch with the real as to severely impede normal day-to-day functioning. The news came as a blow to me, as if I had just plain forgotten that St. George was certifiably insane. When I asked him how long he thought he would be in the hospital he said he couldn't tell, that it all depended on what the doctors thought after examining him.

The hospital he was taken to was not *Our Lady of Mercy*, where we had met. He had been placed in a much larger, all-psychiatric facility up in White Plains, NY—*The New York-Presbyterian/Cornell Medical Center*. Situated on beautiful landscaped grounds, it was a throwback to the days of isolated "lunatic asylums" which were placed in quiet sedate settings full of trees, chirping birds, and lush foliage. Here, it was believed, a confused disordered soul could enjoy winding stone-paved paths, serene glistening ponds, tennis courts, an outdoor swimming pool, and Victorian style gazebos nestled in delicately manicured English formal gardens. It would all serve to help the mentally afflicted cope with their screeching angry demons. There was even a nine-hole golf course on the premises! If I took the railroad up to White Plains, a short cab ride would conduct me from the train station to the hospital. I told St. George to let me know when visiting hours were, and if he would like me to bring anything when I came.

For three long months, I managed to visit St. George at least once a week and spend a couple of hours with him. After several weeks he was given ground privileges -- he could walk about the grounds unsupervised for a few hours. He was under the care of a well-respected psychiatrist who wanted him to try a controversial anti-psychotic medication which had once been withdrawn from the market, because it triggered a dangerous illness in a handful of patients. The drug, called Clozapine, had been reformulated and was now approved by the FDA, but only for patients who had not been successful with any other kind of treatment. It required weekly blood tests because of a potentially lethal side effect involving one's white blood cell count. I was concerned, but St. George said he trusted the doctor and was willing to give it a try. He was very moved that I came to visit him in the hospital, rather than being frightened away by his relapse. He began to talk, vaguely at first, about bringing our relationship to a "new level," as he was now convinced that I was "the only woman for him."

I myself had started reporting regularly to an outpatient clinic near my home. At Dr. Hennessey's insistence, I agreed to undergo at least six months of traditional "talk therapy" with a licensed psychotherapist. My therapist, Bernadette, was a warm, attractive woman in her early fifties who encouraged me to simply pour out all of my accumulated anger, resentment, fear and frustration without holding back, without feeling embarrassed or foolish or ashamed, and without giving a thought to how it all might sound to her. I spent the first few sessions talking about my mother, the next few about my sexual ambivalence and confusion, the next few about the "sun problem" and my other OCD-type symptoms. I got choked up, shed hot tears some days, blanked out on others, shouted, fumed, and swore on still others, and even had a few good laughs now and again. Bernadette listened intently, then provided critical insights and perspective, different ways of interpreting events that I had not considered. I felt I was making decent progress.

Eventually I got around to talking about St. George and our unusual relationship. I told her I did not think of myself as "serious" or "in love with" St. George -- I would say that I was madly infatuated. We were friends, the friendship had blossomed into sexual intimacy, and neither of us saw anything wrong with that. But Bernadette cautioned me that it could be foolhardy to plunge into a relationship like this, before I was finished with my own therapy and on a more stable footing regarding my own mental and emotional health. Schizophrenia, she warned, is a potentially devastating illness which has no cure. And schizophrenics, however intelligent, even brilliant they might be in some respects, however talented or gifted, very often suffered from peculiar emotional deficiencies and immature behaviors.

I thought about some of the less attractive things I had noticed about St. George. At times he did seem emotionally stunted -- his reactions to things I might say or do, his offhand remarks, some of his comments in bed, were what might be expected of a fifth grader. At first I had found it charming, cute even, but then it began to get annoying. He was also extremely sloppy, sometimes forgot to change his sheets or take out his garbage; his room was often cluttered with pizza boxes and empty ice cream cartons, dirty laundry piled in a corner, dust everywhere. And in public places such as restaurants he would often embarrass me by coming out with inappropriate remarks or ridiculous questions. He seemed strangely indifferent to disturbing things like a leaky faucet in the bathroom sink, cockroaches darting out of cabinets in the kitchen, a wobbly table one of whose legs was held up with an old Gideon bible -- taking no steps to remedy any of them. Now he was in the hospital again experimenting with a new medication whose effects no one could predict.

And lately, there had been a new wrinkle. St. George had started writing me long saccharine letters saying how lucky he felt himself to be, having met someone like me. Yes -- I was truly one of the "Capstone Generation," the name referring to the multinational, multi-planetary super conglomerate combo corporation and government that he had christened *Capstone Diversified Universal* (or "CDU," as he preferred to call it). St. George had once shown me the actual documents -- the legal articles of incorporation for the company. He had gone to the trouble and expense of preparing the necessary paperwork and dutifully filing it in the NY State County Clerk's office. He wrote that he now thought of me as a true forever friend, a soulmate. He began to talk about getting married.

In late February I received a letter from the Social Security Administration informing me that my application for disability benefits had been approved. They made a calculation based on the number of years I had worked, my salary, and the amount withheld from my paychecks, in order to arrive at my monthly benefit. Unless I was willing to keep living with my parents or move into a subsidized housing project, it was just about enough money to live on, no more. Nevertheless it was a security blanket of sorts since it guaranteed an uninterrupted flow of cash.

I continued my weekly trips to White Plains to visit St. George and was pleased to see the progress he was making. He seemed to be getting excellent results with the Clozapine. He didn't think the radio or the TV was talking to him anymore, nor was he spending hours scribbling his thoughts onto yellow legal pads like someone possessed. His doctors felt he would be ready to be discharged in a matter of weeks. Meanwhile, a social worker assigned to his case was trying to enroll him in a housing program that would enable him to get his own apartment at a substantially reduced rent -- a step up from the group home he was living in. It would be another important milestone on the road to eventual independence.

Once he jokingly asked me if I would still find him as interesting were he to become just another sane and sober everyman. I laughed, but secretly wondered if he would lose something special and sweet if the new meds stripped him of all of his "delusions of grandeur." Yet I could not help but be happy for him, to see doors that were once shut begin to swing open, raising hopes that one day St. George might be able to put his considerable intelligence and creative talents to profitable use. If ever there was a person who should not have to "hide his lamp under a bushel basket" it was St. George.

One day in early spring he called to tell me he was being discharged from *New York-Presbyterian* and would be moving into a spacious apartment in a section of the Bronx only blocks away from the hospital where I was born. Delighted, I told him we would have to go out on the town to celebrate. I was more than happy to help him fix up the new place and put my own personal touches on what I cheerfully told him would be our personal hideaway -- the first time we would have a completely private place all to ourselves. Wasn't it romantic?

For the first several weeks St. George and I reveled in our newfound freedom and luxury. I stayed over most weekends, cooked spaghetti dinners in the big eat-in kitchen and helped St. George keep the place spotless. In the evenings we would sit together in the living room and mull over our latest plans to rescue humanity from spiritual darkness, while St. George would eat strawberry ice cream out of a huge soup bowl.

But, in fact, real life was catching up with us, and the breezy fantasy playland we'd been romping around in since that autumn day we first met on the corridors of Seven-South was about to shut down for the winter. At the suggestion of his social worker, St. George had registered with VESID, a state agency dedicated to helping individuals with various disabilities find employment in their communities. And I was beginning to take a long hard look at the future. I now deeply regretted having lost my rent-controlled Manhattan apartment. New York City was a frightfully expensive place to live. I knew I could never return to the confining fluorescent-lit gray cubicle existence of an office worker in a law firm or insurance company. Indeed, being over 40 and having been absent from the job market for three years, made landing any kind of good-paying job highly unlikely. My dear friend Peyton, who by then had been living in Charlotte, North Carolina for almost fifteen years, suggested I might have better luck down there, as rents were much cheaper, and the local economy was booming. I began to think about moving again.

My sessions with Bernadette were going well. I had signed up for six months and had about a month left to go. She had helped me grapple with my mother issues until I was able at last to forgive my mom for all the ways in which she had hurt me or failed to support me. Bernadette also helped me accept my sexuality for the odd patchwork-quilt of emotions and propensities that it was, without feeling the need to put a specific label on it or force it into a tidy box.

She continued to caution me about my relationship with St. George. The age difference alone made it impractical and unwise, and now that St. George was showing such promise it could be a distraction and hindrance to his further progress and self-improvement. I had to admit that the initial red-hot glow of attraction, fueled no doubt by serotonin coursing through my brain tissues, was beginning to pale. The novelty was wearing off, the dizzying hayride finally coming to a dusty halt. It had all been a blast, a colorful chapter in an otherwise monochrome life, but now it seemed time to get serious and move on.

Within six weeks St. George found a job at a retail clothing store in Brooklyn. He started as a salesclerk and quickly graduated to floor manager. He was earning real money and had real responsibilities. Indeed, he was doing better than I was! I began to give serious consideration to Peyton's proposal that I relocate to Charlotte. She had told me I could stay in her guest room for as long as it took me to get settled and find an apartment. I spoke to my parents about it; they said it might be worthwhile to check it out, live there for six months or a year. Bernadette was not quite so enthusiastic, warning me to make sure I didn't latch on to Peyton's offer as a convenient way of putting off dealing with the thorny issues of establishing permanent independence from my parents and finding a solid means of making a living. I suspected I might be doing just that, but assured her I wasn't.

I was so happy for St. George a month later when he told me he was being considered for a far better job than floor manager at a discount clothing store. The agency which had secured an affordable apartment for him had decided to go completely over to a "consumer-driven" model. By "consumer" was meant anyone who themselves had used the services the agency provided -- in other words, the mentally ill. By hiring only those who had already benefited from the help offered, the agency would represent an encouraging model for the future -- the mentally ill community helping and advancing its own -- and would make more efficient use of the taxpayer dollars that supported it by focusing funds more narrowly where they were most needed. From now on St. George would have to wear a suit and tie to work and sit at a big desk. He would be working as a housing advisor, helping other former mental patients find homes of their own, just as he had done.

A great apartment, a great job. How far St. George had come since that day I first saw him pacing anxiously up and down the hall, face twisted in deep thought, in the emergency room at *Our Lady of Mercy* hospital. Later, after he had been on the new job two weeks, he wrote me a beautiful letter telling me that none of his recent accomplishments would have been possible without my loving friendship and unstinting faith in him. Though I suspected that Clozapine had far more to do with St. George's success than I did, it was one of the most sincere compliments I have ever received and it touched me deeply.

I had reached a kind of stable plateau with my medication. I was no longer aware of feeling better or different in any way. I was not depressed, but there was none of that palpable sensation of what I can only call "extreme well-being" that I had experienced my first few months on the drug. Side effects were minimal, but there were some. Dry mouth in the morning, occasional short-lived bouts of insomnia, and every now and then an emotional bluntness in which normal feelings or reactions to things seemed muted, as if my heart were wearing a thick coat of fleece.

I assumed I would have to be on the Zoloft, or something very similar, for the rest of my life in order to keep the black dogs of depression permanently at bay, and no one could say for sure how decades on these medications could affect the body, the liver especially. But it was a price I was willing to pay. It is no exaggeration to say that Zoloft saved my life. Now there was only the rest of it to worry about. My sessions with Bernadette would soon come to an end and I would be essentially on my own. After mulling it over carefully for a good week or two, I picked up the phone and called my friend Peyton. I told her to get the guest room ready, I was moving down South.

33
Carolina Blues

AS USUAL, I'M sitting in the back of the city bus staring out the window as it continues its long bumpy and unpleasant ride to the CMC-Randolph Center. The clumsy vehicle makes all kinds of jarring turns and swerves around blind corners and narrow winding streets as it takes me on a tour of some of the poorest parts of Charlotte, past ramshackle huts and crooked leaning hovels posing as houses, where most of the city's black underclass lives. This is the only affordable way for me to get across town to Billingsley Road where the "Behavioral Health Center" (read mental hospital) is situated on a large institutional campus. There's a clinic which accepts low-income and uninsured patients on a sliding scale and this is the place where I have to go to get my medication.

I've been living in Charlotte, North Carolina a little over a year now and have slipped into a kind of blue funk. Less than two years ago I stepped out of the psych ward at *Our Lady of Mercy Hospital* in the Bronx, where, thanks to one of the new SSRI-type antidepressant drugs, I was miraculously lifted out of a suicidal pit. Shortly after cooling down my wild and improbable affair with a fellow patient, I, somewhat impulsively, accepted my friend Peyton's invitation to move down south. At the time, it seemed imperative to get out from under my mother's constant scrutiny. And the move would be a chance, everyone agreed, for me to get a fresh healthy start in cleaner, sunnier, more peaceful surroundings.

For the first six weeks I lived in the guest room of Peyton and her husband's pleasant suburban home, where I spent many a day sunning myself on their backyard deck and scribbling in my journal, trying to figure out what to do next. Peyton drove me all around town to help me find an apartment I could afford to rent on a disability check. Eventually I settled on a bright one-bedroom on the unfashionable side of town. It was in one of those prefab-looking complexes that kind of resemble budget roadside motels minus the neon signs -- a two-tiered longitudinal structure where the apartments are a series of numbered doors that run from left to right on an upper and a lower level, featuring vertical blinds, fenced-in balconies that look out over the parking lot and cheap vinyl siding. The place called itself *Glen Hollow*. It was popular with transients, recent immigrants to the U.S. and community college students. The apartment unit itself was perfectly adequate for my needs, even desirable, with central AC and a real walk-in closet. I could not have hoped to find anything like it in New York, not even for three times the rent I would be paying here.

So I moved in, bought a bed, a few sticks of furniture, lamps, kitchenware, a garbage pail. Peyton gave me some decorative knickknacks -- a picture to hang on the wall, artificial flowers in pretty vases, wicker baskets and the like, to make it look like home. Later on I sent for some of my stuff that I still had in storage back in New York. I settled into my new digs comfortably. Standing out on the balcony surveying the nicely landscaped grounds, the nearby laundry center with its brand new washers and dryers, the bus stop conveniently located right outside the apartment complex, I felt I had no right to complain.

Yet it wasn't long before, despite all my attempts to maintain a positive outlook, I began feeling ill at ease, confused, and lonely. Perhaps in my eagerness to escape the oppressive shadow of my mother's constant presence I had acted too rashly. I just didn't seem to belong here. After about six months, much of the novelty and initial elation of starting over in a brand new place had worn off.

For one thing, I seemed particularly ill-suited to thrive in a place like Charlotte. Here was a city whose "downtown" consisted of a handful of sleek shiny skyscrapers erected by national banks, and where everybody seemed to walk around with clip-on smiles, and which counted more churches than libraries, theaters, and museums combined. The city core was ringed by a vast network of highways and expressways which served as a major hub for tractor-trailers and big rigs crisscrossing the country from coast to coast. To get anywhere, whether for work or play or the smallest of errands, one had to drive for long miles, sometimes on the Interstate. The ever present tinge of diesel exhaust in the air was at times so pungent you could taste it. And once you got beyond the web of freeways and frenetic traffic it was suburban subdivision and shopping mall hell as far as the eye could see.

Transportation instantly became an issue, my lack of wheels making it virtually impossible for me to commute to any job that didn't just happen to be located near one of the few bus lines. And if I were hoping to land any freelance copyediting or proofreading jobs like the ones I had occasionally gotten in New York, then I had surely come to the wrong place. There was simply no one in this town publishing books (except maybe bibles). Worse, as soon as I set foot beyond the verdant, well-maintained grounds of my apartment complex there was no place to walk, no paved sidewalks or pathways, nothing to do but walk gingerly along the edge of the road as car after car whizzed by kicking up dust. Luckily for me, there was a fully stocked supermarket in a shopping center right across the street. This meant that buying and carrying home groceries did not have to be the all-day project it had been in LA. Other than the mall, though, the only places to go to were the main library, easily reachable on the No. 9 bus, and the local cemetery -- the closest thing to a park that I could walk to in less than an hour.

On this particular day I was determined to ask the doctor to start me on a new medication, because the Zoloft I had been taking ever since leaving the hospital appeared to have gone stale on me, its mood-elevating effects mysteriously beginning to wane. Or did it just seem that way because I felt so out of my element in my new surroundings?

Upon arriving at the clinic I learned that my doctor had been called out on some emergency but was expected back within the hour. So I found myself a seat in the outer reception area. Across from me sat a fellow patient, a man in his thirties, who kept rocking his leg and whose hand visibly trembled as he held and read a newspaper. Ahh...side effects from his meds no doubt, I thought with a frown.

From where I was sitting I could see a small photograph of a toddler, maybe two or three years old, under a headline which read: **Child Dies, Crushed by Falling TV**. "What!" I thought. This seemed so bizarre to me, almost like a joke. I could not make out the text well enough to read any of the story, but I instantly imagined a possible scenario. A portable TV sits precariously perched upon a dresser in Mommy and Daddy's bedroom. Mommy's in the kitchen preparing dinner; Daddy should be home from work any minute. Little Johnny is playing with the cat, chasing it around the room, then into the bedroom. The cat dives under the bed, Johnny in hot pursuit bangs hard into the dresser, TV wobbles, tips over, falls ...

With nothing to do but sit silently and wait, I gave myself over to morbid thoughts about a news item I would likely have known nothing about had I not happened to glance at that guy's newspaper. I shook my head as I pictured the horror of it. It amazed and astonished me to think that such vibrant, raucous, kicking screaming life could be utterly stilled in a moment of time, snuffed out like a candle in the wind. How could LIFE be, on the one hand, so tough, resilient, and hell-bent as to force its way up through tiny cracks in the sidewalk the way weeds do, yet on the other hand be as fragile and delicate as a snowflake or a footprint in the sand, disappearing in a poof like magic? What did it all mean? It must mean something significant, something profound. Questions like that nagged at me and demanded answers. That no one could provide them offended me.

I took these and other dismal thoughts into my session with Dr. Hendra. She wrote me out a prescription for a new medication, Luvox, and advised me to find something constructive with which to occupy my time and my thoughts. If I couldn't find a job, she said, then volunteer or join some club. Anything -- just to be engaged in positive and productive activity. Okay, I said, as I pocketed the prescription, paid my fee at the desk and walked out.

Outside it had turned into a beautiful spring day with an expansive deep azure sky that the locals proudly liked to call "Carolina Blue." There was a fluttering breeze, glowing sunshine, and the sound of birdsong in the air, so I decided that, rather than take the bus all the way home I would exit at Tryon and Trade Streets, right in the heart of downtown Charlotte. It was lunch time, so I strolled around the bustling streets of the business district, watching well-dressed people darting in and out of office buildings, cafes, shops. I entered the soaring atrium of the *Bank of America* tower, the largest and most impressive skyscraper in Charlotte, and stood scanning the scene. Dozens of lively folks sitting at little round tables scattered all about, sipping beverages, biting into sandwiches, absorbed in conversation. A palpable hum reverberated all throughout the huge cavernous space, seeming to grow louder the longer one listened until it became a velvet roar.

Back on the street, I walked all the way over to the new football stadium, lately the pride and joy of the town, home to a new NFL expansion team, the Carolina Panthers. I stopped by the ultramodern cream-colored concrete and glass Convention Center, watching small armies of businessmen with swinging briefcases and folders under their arms swarming out of the doors in a steady stream, as others swarmed in. Smiling wide-eyed tourists could be seen prowling the streets toting chic looking shopping bags or emerging from the lobbies of fancy hotels. Women in tailored business suits and wearing expensive pieces of jewelry stood on corners talking seriously into cell phones. Walking around, feeling the buzz in the air, hearing the sounds and the voices, I began to get that distinct feeling of being invisible again. Here I was in the midst of all these animated, purpose-driven people, people with things to do and places to go. I seemed to be watching it all from some other plane of existence. There I was in the middle of it all, but somehow not really there.

Turning away from the noise and glitter, I began walking down Church Street. At the corner of 5th I came to the Old Settler's Cemetery. According to the informative black and gold plaque mounted on a tombstone near the entrance, this was the town's oldest burial ground, dating back to Revolutionary War times. It was a serene place with lovely old trees and brick laid walkways and gravestones so ancient all of the lettering had been polished away by the ravages of weather and time. Many were knocked over and cracked. I looked around. I spotted a couple quietly talking as they walked a small dog. The quiet and stillness here was as deafening as the *Bank of America* lobby I had just stepped into and walked out of minutes before. Okay -- admit it, "positive and productive activity" this was not. I headed for the transit center across from the Bobcats Arena to wait for my bus home.

After I got home I took a hike over to the *Brugghers* bagel shop to sit and ruminate over a mug of fresh brewed coffee. Then, apparently still in a funereal mood, I wandered farther down Central Avenue to the Evergreen Cemetery, about fifteen minutes walking distance from *Glen Hollow*. These peaceful hallowed grounds were a favorite haunt of mine. On this day I found myself meandering about the tombstones, noting the dates of the deceased's birth and death. One man born in 1872 died in 1969. Hmm, pretty impressive, I thought. But another, born in 1896, died in 1940. Then I stumbled across one somber gray stone, looked down, and got a little chill. A small rectangular plate on the ground seemed to take on a golden cast as the sunlight spilled over it. The inscription read:

INFANT SON OF
Sharon G. and Travis R.
Meredith

The year of death -- 1971 – stood out starkly in large figures beneath a small engraving of a pair of baby shoes. That image was flanked on either side by the date of birth, December 3rd, and the date of death, December 5th. Only two days old and he was gone. Compared to him, the unfortunate toddler I'd read about in the newspaper that morning was elderly. I gazed down at the lonely little image for a few moments, then walked on. A few yards away I was confronted by a large and imposing charcoal gray headstone with the single word SORROW staring out in finely chiseled block letters. Lying on the ground was a flat stone with more details. Jamie Reese Sorrow had met his demise three years ago. Lucky Mr. Sorrow. Unlike Baby Meredith and the kid in the newspaper, Jamie Reese had made it to the ripe old age of 92.

Three Months Later

Summer has arrived and I'm feeling slightly better on the new medicine. I've even managed to find a respectable part-time job as sales associate in the women's casual/sportswear department at *Dillard's Department Store.* It's located in the Eastland shopping mall which happens to be right across the street from where I live, literally a stone's throw from my apartment. The fall merchandise had just arrived and the store was busy enough to keep me from getting bored. As I walked around my department straightening clothes, folding sweaters, and removing stray articles from the try-on rooms, I could smell the aroma of fresh baked cinnamon buns that emanated from the *Cinnabon* kiosk just beyond the doors which led out into the mall. A fairly steady influx of shoppers and teens coming to the ice-skating rink on the upper level made for a pulsating atmosphere and the time seemed to go by quickly.

Eventually, with the money I was earning starting to burn a hole in my pocket, I thought I ought to be having something resembling fun. So I pestered Peyton to meet for dinner at some trendy restaurant or take in a film at the local art cinema. The problem was she lived all the way over on the "nicer" side of town. We could manage an occasional outing, but the 50 minutes or so that it took her through heavy traffic to get to my place and then back home again was time she could ill afford. At the time, Peyton was working on a career-related book as well as raising an 11-yr-old daughter.

What the hell. So I decided to venture out on my own and check out the gay scene in Charlotte. I quickly discovered there was almost none to speak of. A clamor had erupted over the proposed staging in a downtown theater of an award-winning show called *Angels in America.* This was a play by Tony Kushner which dealt candidly with the subject of homosexuality and AIDS. Angry crowds of evangelicals carrying picket signs held regular protest rallies in front of the theater, loudly decrying what they viewed as an invasion by the forces of cultural decadence into their fair and genteel town. The ensuing controversy not only sparked fierce arguments around kitchen tables but became a national spectacle as folks back in the Northeast, where the play had drawn sellout crowds and lavish praise as well as won a Pulitzer Prize, looked on in eye-rolling amusement. Clearly, Charlotte wasn't quite ready for Gay Pride.

So no surprise, then, that the "scene" amounted to little more than a handful of what were known as "alternative" bars and clubs in a certain section of town. Poorly lit, hidden cubbyholes in buildings with no signage – as you approached you could detect the reverb of dance music spilling out of a cheap sound system and the lingering odors of stale tobacco and bourbon. Customers would slip in and out one at a time like phantoms in the night. All of these clubs were mixed, that is, the clientele included both men and women, and you usually had to come equipped with your own booze. The boys usually outnumbered the girls and there could always be found the usual contingent of straights who showed up chiefly to be startled or creeped-out by the sight of two men dancing together. I couldn't fathom how or where I would fit into such a setting and saw no prospects of striking up either friendships or romances with people who seemed to be living secret lives.

One particularly torrid day I decided to take advantage of one of the three small built-in swimming pools that were among the amenities offered at *Glen Hollow*. As I lay on my back perfectly still, eyes closed, floating on the cool bed of water, I could hear words being exchanged by a middle-aged couple sitting around the pool in lounge chairs. Something that one of them said jolted me out of my pleasant oblivion. Since late June there had been a rash of burglaries at the complex. Apparently the crimes were being committed by opportunistic teenagers with too much time on their hands, who took full advantage of sliding back doors and windows carelessly left unlocked on summer nights. The complex was a particularly good target for such activity since a good many of its residents were recent immigrants from places like Cambodia and South Vietnam, many of them undocumented and thus reluctant to report crimes to the police. Luckily my own place had been left untouched, not that there was anything worth stealing there anyway. My ears perked up as I heard the woman telling her husband that a neighbor of theirs got robbed the other day; an expensive camera and some jewelry had been taken. "The same thing happened last summer," piped up some young guy in the pool when he heard them talking. "The cops don't do nothin."

Later that same night at work, I happened to notice Mr. Latimer, who lived in our complex, trying on leather jackets in the men's department. He was a nice-looking, unassuming man who worked at the reference desk in the main public library. I asked him if he had heard about the recent burglaries and whether he or anyone he knew had been victimized. He uttered a sharp laugh and said that he was not at all surprised by the recent spate of criminal goings-on. "Didn't you know," he said, "that *Glen Hollow* has quite a rep?" He told me there had been break-ins every year of the six he had lived there and, in fact, just the year before, a shooting and assault had taken place three doors down from him.

He turned, looked right at me, and said, almost in a whisper:

"The place has always been plagued with crime. Some people even think it's cursed, especially since they found out that serial killer Henry Louis Wallace had met one of his victims in an apartment there. He strangled her to death right on the premises."

Shocked, I jumped back and exclaimed, "You're kidding! When? What apartment was it?" Mr. Latimer said it had happened maybe two years ago and he'd forgotten which apartment, but it was all over the newspapers back then. "Get back issues of the *Charlotte Observer*," he said, "if you want to know more about it. We have them on microfilm at the library."

Even though I was supposed to be working in the women's department, I helped Mr. Latimer find a beautiful chocolate brown jacket to go with the worn but handsome leather attaché case he always carried around. It was a bit pricey, but a perfect match. I was happy to do it because management closely tracked the sales of all the associates on the floor. Whenever your volume fell below a respectable level you were given subtle warnings. After ringing up the purchase and handing it back to him I sighed and said, "God, I sure hope they catch those burglars before they strike again." "So do I," he said. "Keep your rear door and windows locked at all times, no matter how hot or stuffy it gets."

I felt vaguely disturbed by his revelations and wondered if I should make a point of always leaving my TV and lights on whenever I left for work to discourage any would-be intruders. And – that serial killer! What was that all about? Was the guy safely behind bars? I was due for another appointment with Dr. Keller at the clinic. I told her I feared I was slowly sliding back into depression. I bemoaned my inability to make new friends and my total lack of a social life. I fretted about my job – how they were actually threatening to cut my salary if I didn't keep my sales totals up. That was just unheard of, I told her indignantly. Why on earth couldn't I find a job that more closely matched my skills and education? I complained about the place where I lived and anguished over the fact that I could not afford to live in a more attractive, safer part of town. The doctor suggested that perhaps I needed to rethink my decision to move down south. At least up north I had family and friends nearby, she pointed out. In contrast, here in Charlotte I had no family and my only friend lived an hour away, had a full-time job, and could barely find the time to visit. We agreed to try raising my dosage of Luvox and Dr. Keller wrote me a new prescription. I left the office feeling anxious and dissatisfied.

When I reported for work that night, before beginning my shift the supervisor asked to see me. "Oh, no" I thought, "here comes another warning." Sure enough, I was told I had exactly three weeks to get my sales figures up to par. After that I would have to accept a 20% slash in salary. All during my shift I did my best to put on a pleasant face for the customers, but below the surface I could feel my simmering resentment starting to snap and crackle. On my way home I picked up my meds at the drug store and ordered some fried chicken and gravy biscuits from the *Bojangles* fast food outlet on my block. Their biscuits are made from scratch and baked fresh throughout the day. They were plump, buttery and uncommonly delicious. Well at least there are some truly great things about this place, I thought, as I sunk my teeth into a fried chicken leg.

About two weeks later my mom called. She told me that their landlord had sent them a new lease to be signed within 60 days if they intended to stay another year. The rent would be raised, of course, and my parents were not sure they wanted to stay. There had been some maintenance issues with the building, and problems with the upstairs neighbors. A slightly sleazy motel had opened on the corner of the block and there was more noise and traffic as a result. Plus, my mom was tired of hauling a basket full of laundry and a heavy bottle of *Tide* up and down the elevator to the basement every time she had to do a wash. Likewise, my dad was sick of always having to circle the block in search of a parking space. This was the first time my parents had ever lived in a large multi-unit apartment building. After selling their house in Florida and returning to the Northeast, they had always lived in two or three-family homes, where they had the use of washing machines and a driveway or garage. Mom told me they were seriously considering looking for something like that again, in a quieter, greener neighborhood.

By the end of three weeks my sales volume had failed to reach the required level and I had the humiliating experience of getting a paycheck with a twenty percent markdown. I was on the higher dose of Luvox, but I couldn't tell if it was helping me or not. A trio of community college kids moved into the apartment directly across from mine, replacing an older single man with a green thumb who had filled his balcony with potted plants and flowers. Now in place of the flowers there was a bicycle with a flat tire, cheap plastic lawn chairs and a small table dotted with empty beer bottles and overflowing ashtrays. Every weeknight I was treated to several hours of nonstop rap music that made my walls vibrate, and on Saturday nights the music was accompanied by sounds of drunken high-pitched laughter, usually female. And occasionally, breaking glass.

That November the town was hit with a severe ice storm. Two days of hail and sleet had turned the roadways into slick and treacherous death zones and tree branches swooning under the weight of huge clumps of ice had snapped and fallen into power lines. Our apartment complex, and hundreds of homes in the area, were without electricity for five days. I was caught totally unprepared, without candles or flashlights, and could do little but sit in the dark and grope around in the kitchen cabinet in search of a manual can opener so I could crank open a can of tuna. Having a fully electric rather than a gas stove, I was not able to cook or heat up anything.

It felt like "reality" was starting to cave in on me. It soon became as crystal clear as the icicles outside my window -- Dr Keller was right; I needed to be back up north where I belonged. Thanksgiving Day approached and I found out I would be spending it all alone. Last year I had been invited to Peyton's house to spend the holiday with her family. But this year they were taking a trip to colonial Williamsburg, Virginia to enjoy a special Thanksgiving weekend in the town where Peyton's husband had attended college.

On Thanksgiving Day I feasted on a frozen *Swanson's Hungry Man* turkey dinner and an *Entemann's* pumpkin pie from the supermarket. Then I picked up the phone to call my parents. I wished them a happy Thanksgiving and then, with an air of inevitability and desperation I told them not to sign that apartment lease. Instead they ought to start looking for another place to live and make sure it had an extra bedroom. I was coming home.

34
Mania Meets Music

IT'S A FIRE-BREATHING-DRAGON kind of night in July, with a bright half-moon peeking out of a clear blue-black sky speckled with silvery dots. The heat makes me dart quickly back inside to the large round table in a corner of the cafe at *Border's Books*, where I had been trying to study. The AC doesn't seem to be working all that great. I slip back into my chair and every few seconds take a grateful sip from my 16 oz. cup of Mocha Freeze, a frozen coffee/cocoa concoction the clerk at the counter noisily whipped up in the blender a few minutes ago. It really hits the spot on this parched summer night. A loose-leaf notebook and several computer textbooks are laid out in front of me on the table. One is on Java 2 programming, another on Java Script, a third is titled *HTML for the Worldwide Web*. But I can't seem to concentrate. I had less than three months to go before I would officially complete the program at *The Chubb Institute*, a highly regarded technical school specializing in computer training. My enrollment there, nearly two years earlier, had been something of an act of desperation. After moving back to New York from North Carolina, finding myself once more without a job and forced to move in with my parents, I racked my brains trying to figure out what I could possibly do in the way of work.

By that time I had pretty much forgotten most of what I had known and practiced as a real estate paralegal. Whatever had not faded over time had been knocked out by the dozen or more electroshock treatments I'd undergone during my last hospitalization. Before relocating to Charlotte, I had done some freelance copyediting work from home. I would ride the subway down to the offices of small publishers of school textbooks, romance novels or young adult fiction and pick up several manuscripts. At home I would carefully proofread and edit them, spreading marked-up pages all over my parents' dining room table. I took my time and charged clients by the hour; it was challenging and satisfying work. But I could never count on getting enough of it on a regular basis to be able to make a decent living. There had to be another way, I thought.

It was the late '90s, the personal computer had become ubiquitous, and the world was being revolutionized by the Internet. All the hottest jobs seemed to be in the field of Info Tech and one couldn't open a newspaper without seeing ads placed by training and technical schools promising to equip you with marketable skills and point you toward a lucrative new career in IT. I was certainly no techie, for sure. I didn't even own a computer. But I was genuinely fascinated by the Information Revolution and the dizzying array of possibilities it seemed to offer. Could I possibly learn something as dry and oppressively logical as computer programming? I didn't think so, but having reached my mid-forties with nothing to bring to the marketplace except a dodgy work record full of gaps, I was at a dead end. If I was ever going to make a major career shift, to learn something entirely new and at odds with all my prior training, it would have to be now or never.

So, when browsing the newspaper one day and coming across an enticing advertisement placed by *The Chubb Institute*, my mind instantly flashed back to a certain Thanksgiving dinner at which a relative with a great job as a Systems Analyst mentioned that she had received her training there. I read through the ad and decided I would attend the free introductory seminar at their center in White Plains, NY. I was quite impressed by the presentation, especially when they told us that upwards of 90% of their graduates were placed in good computer jobs within six months of graduation. So I signed up to take the qualifying exam. The exam contained quite a bit of math and tested skills that were not exactly my strong suits, like pattern recognition and spatial reasoning. I wasn't even sure I had passed, but a week later I received a letter welcoming me to their next class. Relieved, I used my Visa card to make a down payment.

It was an evening class that met Mondays through Thursdays, from 6pm to 9pm. Initially it had been fascinating, delving into the mysteries of computers. They appeared to be such amazing near miraculous machines, yet all they could do, in fact, was receive data, juggle it around, and spit it back out. It was just that they could do it at blazing speed. In the computer's inner workings, everything was reduced to a code consisting of two symbols, 1 and 0, or more precisely, *on* and *off.* When current flows, read "On," when a switch momentarily breaks the circuit, read "Off." There was nothing to it but miles and miles of electronic circuitry compressed onto silicon chips so tiny that the actual etching of the circuits had to be done under high-powered electron microscopes.

To try to fathom it, I pictured a detailed map of a major metropolis like Chicago, shrunk down to the size of a grain of sand. All information or "data," whether presented as arrays of numbers, letters, symbols, or combinations thereof had to be converted into strings of 1's and 0's in order for the computer's processor to be able to crunch it. Like secret signals sent across the river via the precise beating of tom-tom drums, the meaning depended on the pattern of repetition. A string of eight *on* or *off* signals represented a single "byte" of data. The letter "A" for example, was represented by *on-off-off-off-off-off-on-off.*

Bits, bytes, binary arithmetic -- it was all so different from anything I'd ever studied before. With all earnestness, I jumped in with both feet, determined to grasp the concepts no matter how many times I had to read over my lessons. But as the course progressed the material became increasingly difficult and alien to me. So many strange words and symbols. I'd get home from class and look at my notes the next day and just shake my head:

```
EXEC PGM=IEWL,PERFORM=&PERF
REGION=&LKDREG,COND=(5,LT,COB),
PARM=(LIST,LET,X)
```

Next to that piece of programming code I had scrawled, "This procedure is used to create the source module." What the hell did it all mean and what was it going to lead to?

Right now, I was in the White Plains *Border's* bookshop, attempting to supplement and enhance my studies with some of the newer books from the store's large and impressive IT section. At times I suspected I was only kidding myself, because it now seemed clear that if studying this stuff was so arduous, then actually having to do it eight hours a day would probably be migraine inducing. What if I was just not cut out for it? There was a silver lining, though. I had learned all I could ever want to know about computers and was now thoroughly computer literate. Before taking the course I barely knew how to turn one on, and thought a "hard drive" was some kind of golf club.

I closed the books and sighed, thinking I'd better call it a day. Just as I started slurping up the last drops of my melted drink, hoping no one would mind the obnoxious sound, my ears picked up on another one. It was a loud voice – masculine, urgent, excited, alto in range. Out of the corner of my eye I spied a small group gathered around a table across the room. The man whose voice I heard was standing while the others were seated. There was a steady din in the cafe, which was fairly crowded now, and I couldn't quite make out what he was saying. But every now and then snatches of speech drifted my way. My curiosity was soon aroused. He was saying something about *The Five Spot*, which I knew to be a legendary but long-gone New York City jazz club that once stood near St. Mark's Place in the East Village. A bit of a jazz buff myself, I fondly recalled the romantic tales I had heard about the place, about all those artists and beatniks venturing out of their seedy flats and walk-ups to make that club a favorite hangout in the late 1950s. Thelonious Monk and Charles Mingus used to play there.

As he continued speaking, images flooded my mind. How often had I wished I'd been born about twenty years earlier so that I could have taken part in that hipster scene, that incredibly cool world of swirling reefer smoke and snarling saxophone riffs in the dead of night. Of unshaven poets wearing tilted French berets nodding and bopping to syncopated beats and bent notes, a clandestine world of half shadow and gauzy light. In my mind I could hear the soundtrack, a horn bellowing out a tune accompanied by incessant plucking on the fat strings of a bass fiddle, creating a galloping sound that made your backbone buzz and your feet move and carried you away in rapture. And, at last, those shivering cymbals sounding *ssshhhhhhhhhhhhhh...h....h...h* when the ride was over. To me it all seemed magical and irresistibly sexy. But it was so rare to find anyone in my generation who seemed to appreciate, care, or even know anything about that era.

Instead of leaving, I got up to order another Mocha Freeze. While standing in line I could hear the voice, still talking nonstop, saying something about the City Lights Bookstore in San Francisco, famous haunt of the so-called Beat Poets: Lawrence Ferlinghetti, Gregory Corso, Jack Kerouac, Allen Ginsberg. I had visited the place, which I believe still stands on the same corner in North Beach, on my last visit to San Francisco. From what I could make out, the guy appeared to be talking about the scandal that erupted in the America of *Father Knows Best* and *The Donna Reed Show* when City Lights, on their own avant-garde press, published Allen Ginsberg's epic poem *Howl*. The poem's graphic freewheeling depictions of sex and drugs led to charges of obscenity being brought against the store owners. The ensuing court trial drew national attention and became a cause celebre for artists, beatniks, and free speech fanatics everywhere. A few minutes later, I heard the same voice refer to Miles Davis and the song *Freddy the Freeloader*, which I happened to consider one of the coolest songs ever recorded.

Who the hell is this guy! I thought, as I paid for my coffee shake and walked back to my seat. I glanced over to their table to take a good look. The voice was emanating from a guy who resembled the iconic "Mr. Clean," with his shiny bald head, well-muscled arms, and gold hoop earring in the left ear. He was holding court before a group of rapt listeners; I counted five sitting around the table. He was about 5'9", trim and compact in build, appeared to be in his late fifties, and was wearing a short sleeve black sport shirt emblazoned with pictures of imported beer bottles. He was extremely animated, gesticulating wildly with his hands as he talked. I was intrigued, and tried not to stare.

I settled into my chair again and turned away from them, but kept my ears tuned, eager to hear what he'd say next. Who was he? Some eccentric college professor taking a few select students out for coffee and an impromptu lecture on the counterculture? I'd known a few of those. I tried flipping through my Java 2 book to the section on *Appletes* -- those brilliant new mini-programs that gave interactivity to web pages. Not to be found in the outdated textbooks used at *Chubb*, they were barely mentioned in my programming course. Now, Java was the hottest programming language out there.

But it was no use. The words -- crazy stuff like:

```
public void update (Graphics g)
```

just swam before my eyes and the page became a blur. I was captivated by Mr. Clean's words. Now he was talking about a place called *Small's* in the West Village. It was a jazz club I had visited several times, a wonderful unassuming place housed in a basement where you brought your own liquor and got up close to the musicians who jammed into the wee hours. For a modest cover charge you could listen to sizzling live jazz all night long. Was this guy a musician? I wondered.

I looked over a few more times and noticed that his audience was dwindling. The bookstore would be closing in an hour and a few of the others had left. Soon Mr. Clean was all by himself. I watched him go up to the counter and order a small cafe latte. When he turned to walk back to his table he noticed me staring at him. Within mere seconds he was sitting at my table. I think he quipped one of those tired old lines like, "Haven't we met before?" but did so in an ironic winking way that made me feel strangely relaxed. Then he said something about being able to pick up on my "spiritual vibes," tune in to my "frequency," and similar new-agey nonsense. But instead of being turned off, I found myself smiling. Who knew? Maybe we *had met before*, many lifetimes ago. I told him I couldn't help overhearing his conversation and asked him how often he went to *Small's*.

It turned out that he happened to be at *Border's Books* tonight because this was the night, Tuesday, that he led a weekly poetry group at the nearby *NY Cornell Presbyterian Hospital*. That was the psych hospital, the loony bin on the hill as the locals called it, the place I used to trek to regularly to visit St. George five years ago. I learned that Mr. Clean was a published poet, keyboard musician, certified Reiki master (an ancient Japanese healing art), a would-be jazz singer, and former mental patient. Hmm, interesting, I thought. We started talking about music, poetry, and politics and stayed there until closing. We walked out into the balmy air, and he said he'd be back with his poetry group the same time next week. He told me his name was Noah.

All during the rest of that week his image danced blithely through my mind to an imaginary soundtrack featuring Charlie Parker's slithery sax and some whispered bits of incendiary poetry punctuated by the beats of bongo drums. I knew I couldn't and wouldn't resist showing up at *Borders Books* in White Plains next Tuesday night.

The next time I saw him there, he was reading aloud a poem he had written which had been published in a journal. It was called *Waiting for Madonna at the Croton Diner*. Later that evening Noah and I were having dinner at that very diner. He told me he had always been a jazz enthusiast. He had three kids from a prior marriage and one of them, a son, was a professional bass player who worked gigs at local jazz clubs with his trio. Noah said he had recently been taking lessons with a voice coach, trying to realize at last a fondly held dream of being a jazz singer. Like his cousin, he said. She had started singing in local clubs, then moved to England where she met and married a jazz saxophonist and perfected her craft. Eventually she made something of a name for herself and recorded several albums. Noah told me he had recording equipment at home and was currently working on the Cole Porter classic, *Night and Day*. Would I care to take a visit and hear what he's done so far? Well of course!

I marveled at his little yellow house in a nearby village northwest of White Plains. The living room looked like a recording studio with big reel-to-reel tapes, amplifiers, karaoke machines, and a professional looking microphone. Along one wall was a high-end *Yamaha* electronic keyboard. He sat down and played bits and pieces of popular jazz standards. I was delighted. Outside of my mom, I knew no one among my friends or relatives (with the possible exception of dear Alejandro, with whom I had sadly lost touch years ago), who understood the beauty of a well-crafted song. As much as I was a child of the sixties and grew up listening to the Beatles, Stevie Wonder, the Supremes, Janis Joplin, and Bob Dylan, still, whenever I was in a sing-in-the-shower mood I always found myself warbling tunes like *Where or When*, *Our Love is Here to Stay*, or *Stardust*.

Then, to give me a live demonstration, Noah put on some Jamie Ebersol tracks. Especially designed for singers who need to prepare audition tapes, the Ebersol tracks featured a host of standard tunes, containing only the background arrangement and rhythm section minus the vocals. He took the mic in hand and began crooning:

Day and night, why is it so,
that this longing for you follows wherever I go?

In the roaring traffic's boom,
in the silence of my lonely room, I think of you.

His voice was smooth and silky, with a few rough edges which could be polished away with practice. His phrasing and breathing needed a little work, but basically it sounded pretty good to me. Afterwards, satisfied with his performance, Noah walked over to a closet and, smiling broadly, took out a large festive looking bottle of Italian Chianti wine. Sitting snugly in its straw basket wrapper the fat bottle looked like some stage prop to be trotted out for a romantic scene in an Italian restaurant, strategically placed between the bunch of grapes and the loaf of bread. But it had real wine in it, and, peeking into the closet, I spotted another just like it along with various other bottles.

After downing a few glasses of the ruby red libation, I felt loose enough to try out the microphone myself. Noah talked about his latest project. There was a new art form on the scene, he said, that they were calling "Po' Jazz." Supposedly a fusion of jazz and spoken word poetry, it was becoming popular at clubs and cafes around town. A jazz combo would perform in the background while a self-styled poet would come up to the mic and proceed to recite in sync to the music. Noah was working on some poems which he hoped to perform with his son Jackson's trio. He brought me over to his computer and showed me a sample of his creations, some already published and some works-in-progress.

He asked me if I would like to see Jackson perform at a nearby club. Noah knew all the jazz clubs in the lower Hudson River Valley, places I had never heard of -- like *Dudley's* in Ossining where the famous prison was, or *DeFemio's* in Yonkers where my parents used to live. Famous jazz emporiums like the *Village Vanguard* and the *Blue Note* were great, of course, but Manhattan crowds, steep cover charges, exorbitant parking fees, and other hassles tended to make him avoid those too familiar places. Instead, there were venues right in the local area that were fresh, inexpensive holes-in-the-wall where one could hear fantastic music from brilliant upcoming artists who could never hope to get booked at the more famous establishments. "If you love jazz, " he told me, "just hang with me awhile and I'll show you things that will blow you away."

I was hooked. Noah, I thought, was possibly the coolest guy I'd ever dated. I had just gotten through nearly two years of stressing out my brain trying to twist it around cryptic computer code that might as well have been Egyptian hieroglyphics, for all that I was able to penetrate it, even after diligent studying. After several more bouts of mild depression, after feeling impossibly trapped still living under my parents' roof, after the long and futile job searches, I desperately needed someone to *take me away from all this,* please! And who better to do it than this bald-headed hipster who could belt out the American songbook and spout verse like a wandering troubadour. I felt like a teenager again, speeding around in his fire engine red 2-door *Dodge Avenger.*

We began going to a club called *Ernaccio's*, where life-sized statues of Louis Armstrong bracketed the bar, and you could hear live jazz right in the main dining room while feasting on stuffed loin of pork or seven-bean chili. Then there was *Isabel's Cafe* in my old college town of Tarrytown, NY. We'd head over there for the Wednesday night open jazz jam. Comfortably propped up on wrought iron saddle bar stools, enjoying a bowl of the club's famous French Onion Soup, we could listen to some of the finest new young jazz players in Westchester play swing and bebop alongside the old-timers.

To me the music always sounded like a joyful celebration of being alive, of pure existence itself. A celebration of breathing, of moving, of a beating heart and a pulsing brain. A way of temporarily dissolving the boundaries that separated us as individuals from everything else in the universe. It was music that expressed the intoxicating joy of just getting to BE for the few moments we are here on this earth. In contrast, much of today's modern music, particularly the popular hip hop and rap genres, sounded less like celebrations than angry rants and defiant assertions of self. Whereas the joy in jazz consists always and only in letting go of self.

But our favorite spot by far was a no-frills joint that didn't even serve food or alcohol called *One Station Plaza. One Station* was strictly about the music. We all sat on wooden folding chairs in a room that resembled a kindergarten classroom, its walls decked with paintings created by local artists. We would get there early and spend hours listening to a cadre of up-and-coming jazz musicians playing Mingus and Miles as well as their own compositions. Most nights the room was packed and all conversation ceased as the sounds flowed. Noah's son played some nights with his trio and sometimes Noah himself got a chance to perform. In front of a friendly, fully supportive crowd he would stroll up to the microphone clad in one of his colorful print shirts and practice his latest version of *Night and Day* or some other standard.

Afterwards we would go to his place, sip wine and talk. Noah told me about the horrible motorcycle accident seven years ago that did a number on his brain and nearly cost him his life. He had slammed his bike into a tree on a moonless night when the roads were still slick from a torrential downpour that morning. He was in a coma for ten days with severe head injuries. After he regained consciousness he underwent delicate surgery and then faced months of recovery. Due to the accident, he was able to apply for Social Security Disability, which was now his chief source of income, supplemented by his extracurricular activities, like teaching poetry and occasionally doing Reiki.

Noah told me he would have never made it without the help of some guardian angel type character that he swears made several visitations to his bedside while he was in a semi-conscious state and convinced him the world could not afford to lose him. He said that this mysterious personage often came in the form of a bird of prey, and so Noah chose to call him "Papa Hawk." Long after he was fully recovered from the accident, he said he would often experience bouts of mania -- hyperactive mental states in which his mind would race, his energy level would soar, and he would find it impossible to sleep. Once, after not being able to sleep for eight straight days, he checked himself into a hospital, where he was treated with various medications. Now, he told me, he was able to keep the manic episodes under control with his pills and weekly visits to his psychiatrist in the city. I shared with him a bit of my own psychiatric history, my own memorable tours through the cuckoo's nest.

Noah had mentioned that he was a certified Reiki master and I asked him about that. Reiki, an ancient Eastern form of therapy, was based on the idea that within each of us there lies an unseen "life force," a hidden current of energy that flows through us and causes us to be alive. This energy can become depleted, or its movement hindered by stress and overwork. The Reiki master heals by "laying on of hands" and by gently coaxing and guiding the life force until it regains its vigor and proper flow. Administered by a skilled practitioner, the technique is supposed to promote deep relaxation and facilitate the release of toxins and waste products from the bloodstream. Noah said that Reiki had helped him heal after his motorcycle accident. He pointed to a poster on the wall of his living room which displayed what appeared to be five large delicately inked Japanese letters. He told me they were the five Reiki symbols denoting the different stages attained during the "attunement process."

I invited him to perform some of his techniques on me. He put on a loose-fitting robe and assumed a certain pose. I had to resist the temptation to roll my eyes a bit -- part of me was a tad skeptical of the ease and flippancy with which Western hipsters often glom on to these Eastern spiritual practices without having undertaken the years of rigorous training required to fully master and appreciate them. But watching Noah gracefully and confidently demonstrate the various hand positions he would use on a client, it was obvious that if he wasn't the real thing, he could play the part very well. Looking every bit the professional, he laid his hands on me and asked me to breathe deeply and relax. With his exotic King of Siam look and his satin robe he appeared like a genie released from a bottle. His every manner signaled: *Your wish is my command;* yet there wasn't a trace of subservience or servility in his posture. There was no doubt who was in charge.

Noah was always full of projects. He told me he was currently working on a poem about me, and then he showed me the rough draft on his computer. He was planning to have his son Jackson's trio record a jazz track that he would use as accompaniment when he gave a live recitation of the poem at a local writer's center. And he was working on a tape he wanted to send to some woman named Golda who he said ran a "Po' Jazz" series at a well-known locale in the West Village.

All the things he talked about intrigued or excited me. I could sense a growing, deepening bond between us, based on shared experiences of music, madness, and mystical aspirations. At first, I was somewhat turned off by the idea of Noah as a lover. Only once before, with Mike, had I been with a man more than ten years older than me. But those considerations gradually evaporated in a haze of cheap Chilean wine and shimmery August moonlight filtering through the back porch door of his clapboard house.

He had a surprising, clumsy way of trying to seduce me which had its own kind of goofy charm. One night he gestured me towards the bedroom, then lay flat on his back on the bed and patted the space right next to him.

"Ever been in an heirloom bed?"

"A what?"

"It's an experience not to be missed. This mattress I am laying on is a priceless hand-me-down. It's been in my family for generations. It was handcrafted in Scandinavia and is one of the finest mattresses money can buy."

"What's so great about it?"

"They put in four times the number of springs as any other mattress --*four times* -- and use only pure 100% natural foam rubber," he said as he began to roll back the bedspread and pat the space next to him again. Come over here, slip under the covers and try it." He then turned the lights way down, reached for the remote and said, "Let's watch a movie."

But the music was the ticket, no other seduction was needed. Friday and Saturday evenings were spent listening to Noah practicing his scales and doing the exercises his voice coach had suggested, working on his phrasing. Then he would pick up the microphone, put on some Jamie Ebersol track and serenade away. All this as I busied myself preparing a platter of cheese and crackers and placed it on a snack table in the bedroom, then fetched a couple of wine glasses and coasters to set on the night table. Later, feeling quite pleased with himself, Noah would come join me. With the alcohol, the moonlight, the music, and the mattress -- which did indeed feel like sleeping on a cloud -- it was all, well, heavenly. And Noah, eager and passionate, could perform like a man half his age and last twice as long. Soon, to my parents' great surprise, I began spending more and more nights away from home, sometimes even weeknights when I had computer classes the next day.

Noah did not believe in old age. Convinced the process of going senile could be put in reverse, he had embarked on a serious health and exercise kick. He had a collection of small-scale exercise equipment, like an abs trainer and a gravity bar and ankle weights. The most conspicuous thing in his kitchen was his big white *Jack LaLanne Power Juicer.* Each morning he would take out a plastic bin full of fresh vegetables and fruits -- cucumbers, carrots, beets, kiwis, celery, bananas, whatever was available -- and one by one, force them into the demolition machine where they were pulverized into a viscous, dark purplish liquid that spilled out from a spout at the bottom. He insisted that I drink a full 12 oz. glass of fresh-squeezed juice almost immediately upon awakening. Noah swore it was the quickest, most effective way to get vital nutrients into the bloodstream. Vitamin pills and mineral supplements were a waste of time, he said, because they isolated one or two factors out of an array of natural substances that were designed to work together interactively and could be found only in fresh whole plant foods -- rendering the pills and tablets essentially useless.

One morning the particular combination of smashed vegetables didn't seem to agree with me. We were driving down to Manhattan to see Noah's shrink, who had an office on the Upper East Side just off Fifth Avenue. As usual, Noah was driving faster than he ought to and my stomach began to feel queasy. Within a few minutes waves of nausea came over me, increasing in intensity. I had no choice but to thrust my head out the window while we were racing down the FDR Drive to make the appointment on time. Liquefied beets and spinach splattered all over the gleaming red door panels of the *Dodge Avenger*, as I tried to blurt out my apologies. After we parked, the first order of business was to get hold of some discarded rags or napkins and wipe the crap off. Noah wound up being late after all.

He was now working on a new song and was determined to grasp its peculiar harmonic structure. The tune, called "You Go to My Head," made its debut in 1938 and was later recorded by Billie Holiday. It's a wistful tune with barely perceptible shifts between major and minor keys, and a real challenge to sing well. Played solo on a saxophone or trumpet, the song is lush and dreamy. But what I especially loved was the lyric:

You go to my head
And you linger like a haunting refrain
And I find you spinning round in my brain
Like the bubbles in a glass of champagne

Noah put on the background tracks and practiced in front of me, asking me to point out anything that I thought could be improved. After a while, he was able to make his voice sound like hot melted butter, knew just how much to stretch out each note and got the phrasing down pat. We decided that, as soon as he really nailed it, it would be a blast to go down to one of those laid-back jazz clubs that held an "open mic" night. On such nights rank amateurs were welcomed to the stage in an atmosphere of appreciation and respect for the music. Unlike in a karaoke bar where everyone is drinking and laughing and waiting for you to make a fool of yourself, in the intimate cabaret setting of a serious jazz club everyone was rooting for you to breathe new life into an old standard. A friend had told him about a relatively new venue in Manhattan that welcomed would-be singers with open arms. It was way up on Broadway in the 90s and was called *Cleopatra's Needle*. So we made a plan to go.

We went for their Sunday brunch which was always followed by live entertainment. The place had a relaxed funky feel with its no cover charge policy, back wall of exposed brownish-red brick, and gigantic wooden clock. Noah put his name on the sign-up list. We ordered from the Mediterranean menu and waited. People began to file in from the street and the place was soon crawling with enthused jazz aficionados. Several singers came up before Noah, but he finally got his turn and was very well received. It was so much fun, we went back several times.

Back at the house the stereo was always tuned to WBGO, the all-jazz station out of Newark, NJ, or sometimes to WKCR, the radio station of Columbia University, which had birthday tributes to major jazz giants that were essentially all-day marathons. With no nearby neighbors to worry about we could turn up the volume as loud as we wanted. It was all about the music for us, and after a drink or two I felt transported to a different time and place.

The fluid sensuous sound of Coleman Hawkins's sax on *Body and Soul* seemed to hearken back to a purer, sweeter sort of romance, one all but forgotten in an age of coarse reality TV and celebrity sex tapes. Listening to the *Hot Club of France* with Django Reinhardt strumming his guitar at a feverish swing tempo felt to me something like taking a thrilling ride through the countryside in the back of a hay wagon. The way Lester Young could float above and below the bare skeleton of a tune, embroidering in all the notes and flourishes that the original merely suggested demonstrated artistry as refined as Monet's or Picasso's. The suave bossa nova-tinged sounds of Stan Getz seemed impossibly sexy. The silky, mother-of-pearl perfection of the voices of Sarah Vaughn and Ella Fitzgerald might not be heard again for a century or more. The gorgeous wail of Clifford Brown blowing out the haunting theme from the film noir *Laura* took your breath away. Ben Webster playing his version of *Prisoner of Love* -- my God, how many babies were conceived to that! And John Coltrane's accompaniment to Johnny Hartman on *My One and Only Love* sounded like something sacred. No one else out there at the dawn of the new millennium seemed to care about this music anymore. But we did, and for long delirious stretches of time we just tuned the rest of the world out.

But Noah was every bit as dedicated to his poetry as to his music. He told me he often read aloud at the *Hudson Valley Writer's Center*, a non-profit arts venue located in the quaint little village of Sleepy Hollow, NY. He took me there so I could experience the readings firsthand. They had set themselves up in a restored railroad station overlooking the riverbank. I sat in a bright airy space with wood beam ceilings and a massive brick fireplace and listened as writers and poets of all ages came up to the podium to read samples of their work. When Noah went up he almost embarrassed me by telling the crowd he was going to read a poem he had written for "my lady," and then glancing pointedly at me. He then proceeded to read out loud the poem he had written especially for me, which I had not yet seen or heard. I thought the piece quite good, and the audience seemed to agree.

But Noah's real dream was to fuse his love of jazz and his love of poetry into the new art form called "Po' Jazz." Noah told me more about Golda Solomon, a woman who had started her own record label specifically to promote the new genre, beginning with her own creations. Noah wanted her to listen to the tapes he had made with his son in the hope that she would add a couple of his pieces to one of her CD compilations.

One day Noah told me there was going to be a big party for his mother who would soon be celebrating her 80th Birthday. The party would take place at some posh hotel room or restaurant the family had rented out. Noah wanted me to come and meet his mother, as well as his ex-wife, his other son, and his daughter. I felt a bit strange at the notion of meeting his family, but was too curious to pass up the opportunity. And oh, I would get to meet his cousin Stacey, who was in town briefly. She was the jazz singer who had moved to London and married a jazz musician.

On the day of the party Noah pulled into my parents' driveway looking quite respectable in a casual sweater and blazer. My mom and dad even caught a glimpse of him. At least a hundred people thronged the hall where the affair was being held. Noah's mother looked remarkably well-preserved and was in great spirits. We walked around to meet and greet; Noah ran into his ex-wife Olympia, an attractive woman and the mother of Jackson. Evidently, he was not entirely delighted to see her; he introduced me briefly and we moved on. I wondered what had gone wrong in their marriage.

Then I met his daughter, Emily. She looked and sounded just like him. With her was her boyfriend, Martin, engaged in lively conversation with those around him, and their five-month-old baby girl. This was the first time Noah had ever met Martin, and he looked at him searchingly. Martin was a New York City firefighter stationed in lower Manhattan. He was a nice-looking guy in his mid-thirties who was obviously thrilled to be a father; the baby was their first child together. He was talking about how he planned to retire from the department in about seven years, collect a very generous pension, and spend his free time golfing and tinkering with his 1963 Mustang. He and Emily were planning to marry soon. They made a handsome couple.

We were later joined by a stylishly dressed woman whom Noah introduced to me as Stacey, his jazz crooning cousin. I could tell how impressed Noah was by her and, I suspected, not a little bit envious of her success in the very field he dreamed of breaking into. He talked to her about the songs he was working on and asked if she'd be willing to take a listen. Things finally started to wind down and we began the long drive home.

Noah got right back to his pet projects. At first, he was enthusiastic about the collaboration with son Jackson and spent hours trying to come up with just the right lyrics to set against the music. We worked together, him at his computer and me sitting on a wicker chair on the back porch with pen and notebook. However, as time went on, Noah began to get increasingly obsessive about it. Indeed, he seemed to be getting obsessive about a lot of things, including our relationship. Although I was spending virtually every weekend at his place, sometimes tacking on a Friday or a Monday, he said he thought I should move in with him. He told me that I had become his muse, and that he now found it difficult to write either poetry or music without me by his side. But I simply was not in the market for a live-in situation, probably because I secretly sensed that our affair would be short-lived. There seemed no doubt that we were on a wild and breathless roller-coaster ride that would soon be approaching its final exhilarating dip before coming to a quiet halt. But Noah became more and more insistent, even mentioning marriage on one occasion.

Whenever Jackson would send him tapes of the jazz tracks his trio had come up with to accompany the poems, Noah seemed to find fault with all of them. At one point he told me he was cutting back on his medication because he felt it was dulling his perceptions, slowly filing away his creative edge. His psychiatrist did not agree, and they argued about it. I felt I could see the signs of mania returning. He would stay up later and later, practicing his singing or writing poetry until 3:30 am, and then he still wouldn't come to bed. I'd wake up at four in the morning to find him sweeping the kitchen floor, cleaning out the refrigerator, or frantically pecking away at the computer keyboard. While driving to the city he became increasingly reckless, bragging about his radar detector and how he knew exactly on what stretches of parkway the state troopers liked to lurk. He would routinely do 90 or 95 in a 60-mph zone and would even do childish pranks like gripping the steering wheel with his knees, releasing his hands and shouting, "Look -- no hands!" Soon I was almost afraid to get in the car with him. He began to spend money like crazy, coming home with dozens of CDs and hundreds of dollars' worth of audio equipment from the *Sam Ash* music store in White Plains. He bought a 1K diamond stud earring to replace the 24K gold ring in his ear.

He became unreliable. One time he called to tell me that Stacey, who was still in town, would be doing a gig at the Oak Room -- the renowned supper club housed in the storied *Algonquin Hotel*. She had sent Noah two tickets. I had read quite a bit about the hundred-year-old Hotel Algonquin, how it had once been home to the so-called Round Table, a gathering place for some of the most scintillating wits of the 1920s, like Dorothy Parker, Ring Lardner, and Tallulah Bankhead. One legend has it that Dorothy Parker, attending a Halloween party, was asked if she would like to try "ducking for apples." She is alleged to have replied: "Change one letter in that phrase and you have the story of my life." Considering that the cover charge to get into the cabaret was probably more than I used to earn in a day, I was elated at the prospect of getting to go there as a guest. I actually went out and bought myself a new dress -- a garment I hadn't worn in years -- and a pair of high-heeled shoes. But two hours before Noah was supposed to meet me in my parents' driveway, he called me up with some cockamamie excuse about misplacing the tickets or forgetting the date or some such nonsense. I was shocked and angry, as I had thought he was as eager to go as I was.

I began to avoid him somewhat, telling him I thought he needed to have his medication adjusted, that he no longer seemed happy the way he did when we first met. That life-embracing, overflowing joy that had once captivated me was gone. Now he just seemed unnaturally high-strung, all lit up and blinking like an over-decorated Christmas tree, nerves about to snap. One day he called me up in a hysterical fit. He said he had made some Po' Jazz tapes and sent them to Golda Solomon, the woman who had started up a record label to promote the genre and who arranged gigs at local clubs to showcase new talent. Apparently, she was not exactly bowled over by Noah's creation and sent him a cold response. He was furious. He wanted me to go with him to confront her at her office. I told him he needed to cool off and calm down first. He began pleading with me about how hard he had worked to perfect the tapes, spending hours practicing his recitations and making Jackson record the background tracks over and over again until they were just right. He was practically in tears.

We had planned an excursion to the Caramoor Jazz Festival, an annual three-day celebratory event featuring some of the finest contemporary jazz artists, held on the grounds of an opulent old estate in Katonah, New York. It was about an hour's drive from the city, and I recalled having seen posters announcing this year's festival. I had always hoped I would get to experience Caramoor one day. So when Noah told me that he had bought tickets as a birthday present for me and had reserved a room in a small hotel, I was touched and excited. I just hoped and prayed that he would be emotionally stable and in a good frame of mind.

He seemed fine when we left Friday afternoon. The festival grounds were lovely -- ninety acres of wooded trails, landscaped gardens and secluded walkways surrounding a Mediterranean style villa. The first performance took place in an open-air Spanish courtyard. A series of talented musicians took the stage, playing new compositions and old standards before a jazz-literate audience. In between sets we picnicked on the grounds and explored some of the treasures stored in the main house, where the estate founder's stunning assortment of medieval, Renaissance, and Eastern art was on display: hand-painted Chinese wallpaper, Florentine paintings, an exquisite jade collection, Venetian furniture.

But Noah appeared to be getting bored looking at art objects; instead, he seemed intent on critiquing some of the performers we had just listened to. Evidently some of them did not meet with his approval for reasons I could not decipher. Also, the unpleasant scene regarding Golda Solomon and the Po' Jazz tapes was still fresh in his mind and chafed at him. As we walked about the lush gardens he became increasingly distracted, agitated, and upset. I asked him if he was taking his medication and was shocked to hear that he hadn't taken it in two weeks, despite the urging of his doctor. I began to worry.

At the evening performance, as we sat under a huge pink pavilion with Greco-Roman columns, I glanced over at him. He was squirming in his seat, glaring at the stage. He then began complaining about one particular tenor sax player who was performing a solo. At one point Noah actually stood up, cupped his hands around his mouth and shouted something like, "You can't play, man – give it up!" while I cringed in embarrassment. Pretty soon the whole evening was a wreck and I couldn't wait to leave. I told him to cancel the hotel reservation; I wanted him to drive me straight home. On the way back he drove so recklessly I feared we might be killed.

After the disaster at Caramoor, I resolved not to call him again until he got himself stabilized. I felt confused, deeply disappointed, angry, and sorry for Noah. It seemed a shame that all of his genuine talent and creative vitality should go to waste just because of a mood disorder, an illness over which he had no control. But I faulted him for going off his medication, because it was his responsibility to consider the effect his behavior had on others and to do something about it. I couldn't imagine going off my meds. For almost seven years those little pills had kept me from slipping and falling into the tar pit of suicidal depression. Having once been rescued, I had no intention of letting myself tumble back down. I considered calling his shrink, but decided that might be too intrusive. After all, I wasn't his wife or his daughter. Should I call Jackson? No, he was no doubt well aware of his father's condition, having himself been subjected to Noah's bullying and impatience throughout their collaboration on the Po' Jazz project. In the end, I decided to do nothing for the time being and just wait things out.

Then the strange phone messages began. I would arrive home and my mother would tell me that someone had left a message for me on the answering machine. Sometimes the voice sounded pleading and pathetic, sometimes terse and sarcastic, sometimes loony or drunken with hysterical laughter, and sometimes even threatening. He didn't understand why I was "leaving him." At first I refused to call him back. Then his rants started sounding more and more crazy. He would ramble on about how I'd "stabbed him in the heart," how he could not believe that I *("You,* of all people!!!") would wind up betraying him. My father began to ask me if there was something wrong with the guy -- what was he doing, stalking me? Since I did not want to argue over the phone or risk getting him still more agitated, I figured the best thing to do was to write Noah a letter.

So I wrote a letter explaining that I felt we needed to spend some time apart, that he seemed to be getting too dependent on me and I was starting to feel suffocated. I told him he was wrong to flout the advice of his psychiatrist, that mania was a serious illness and he needed to trust his doctor, that he was playing with dynamite, that "Papa Hawk" probably would not want to see him like this. My tone was patient and sympathetic. It was also very appreciative. I told him how much I had enjoyed everything we'd shared -- the wonderful music, the venues, the people, his poetry, his singing -- it had all been awesome. But all good things had to end, and maybe now he needed to set aside some time to just get quiet, turn off the radio and the keyboard and the karaoke machine and just take care of himself. I sincerely meant every word.

I mailed the letter, and the phone calls stopped for a while. About three weeks later I received a letter from him. It was written in a childish scrawl, using block letters penned with some kind of heavy marker. He said that he had suffered a "breakdown" shortly after I had stopped calling and had required an "intervention." That led to a ten-day hospital stay. His tone was accusing, as if he held me responsible. There was no mention of seeing me again or resuming our relationship. It made me feel quite sad. I hoped he was under a doctor's care and being properly treated. Mental illness was such a sorry affair, I reflected. The lack of any surefire "cure" for it, the way it often sneaks up on you, the way it tears you asunder, pitting one part of you against another, the social stigma attached. I just wished Noah well and tried to put him and the high-octane whirlwind of a romance we had enjoyed out of my mind. The time had come, at last, to file those cherished once-in-a-lifetime memories away in some hidden drawer in the back of my mind, not to be reopened until my wretched nostalgia-craving old age.

It must have been about six weeks later when I received a package in the mail. There was no return address, but the postmark suggested it likely came from Noah. In it I found two items -- a local poetry journal put out by the Hudson Valley Writers Center, and a tape cassette. A bookmark had been placed in the journal. I opened to the page and there was the poem Noah had written about me and had read aloud that night at the Writer's Center. The tape cassette was a recording of *You Go to My Head* that he had made in the house while I was there, the best one of several "takes." There was no letter. There was only a brown slip of paper with the words, written in red: "Thanks, Papa Hawk."

35
The Day the Towers Fell

A STEAMY, SWEATY day in late August -- one of your classic "dog days of summer." The last thing I felt like doing was hiking to the train station, riding the rails down to Grand Central Terminal and then schlepping all the way to Fulton Street on the No.4 subway. All to attend *The Chubb Institute's* 30th Anniversary celebration party. It seemed like a pointless exercise to me. All recent graduates were invited, and I had received my gilt-edged *Diploma in Computer Programming* the year before. That piece of parchment now lay under glass in a wooden frame shoved somewhere in the back of my bedroom closet. It had hung proudly on the wall for several weeks after graduation, while I met hopefully with my counselors at the job placement office. Surely, I thought, these pros, utilizing their experience, contacts and connections would certainly help me land an entry-level job somewhere. That's what they had promised us. But apparently there was no market for the skills I had damn near killed myself to obtain. The school, despite its stellar reputation, had somehow failed to anticipate the rapid new developments in Web-based programming. As it turned out, the material it had taken me so long to master was, by the time I graduated, hopelessly outdated.

For two years I had devoted hours, armed with pencil and ruler, to methodically drawing flowcharts, had learned to read and write ancient computer languages like COBOL and FORTRAN, had struggled to wrap my mind around stuff that went by a host of confusing acronyms: JCL, DBM, SQL, CICS. It took forever to get the hang of it, and I even had to drop out and repeat a semester or two. I had started out taking evening classes in White Plains, NY -- a half hour bus ride from home. Later on, I switched over to daytime classes at the school's main branch in lower Manhattan, so that I could spend more time working in the computer labs and have more access to the instructors for advice and support. After each class ended I would spend hours in the labs practicing what I had learned.

Every so often I 'd take a break and walk two blocks over to the World Trade Center. There I would stretch my legs walking around the maze-like concourse beneath the North Tower. It was full of high-end shops and restaurants, but I usually wound up at the *Borders Books* store. I would pick up a book or magazine, grab a table, order coffee, and sit down, trying to get my mind off hexadecimal math, partitioned data sets, and storage dumps. If the weather was nice I would stroll about the plaza in the sunshine, or I might take the elevator up to the 106th floor and watch people going into the famous *Windows on the World* restaurant. I had always longed to go there and dine while taking in a view of the Manhattan skyline from a quarter mile up. After my break I would head back to the Chubb building for another hour or two of intensive practice and study.

But developments in the field of information technology were moving at such breakneck speed that by the time I attained proficiency in a skill, it was already on its way to becoming obsolete. The school, top-heavy with bureaucracy like every large organization, had been caught off guard, unable to revamp its curriculum fast enough. They were still using the same textbooks they had been using for the past five years. Worse, at the time I was enrolled, the whole business community was obsessed with the "Y2K" problem. Dire predictions of massive power outages, airplanes falling from the sky, clocks stopping, elevators getting stuck between floors, and Vegas slot machines spitting out untimely jackpots dominated the news for months.

That the crisis could have been caused by something as mundane as the space-saving convention of representing a year with two digits instead of four -- '75 for 1975, '62 for 1962 -- made it seem almost comical. It was widely believed that computers would not be able to tell the difference between the year 2000 and the year 1900 (both abbreviated '00) and hence all kinds of havoc would be wreaked. Half of my time at Chubb, it seemed, was devoted to how to write programs that would rectify the problem. But by the time I graduated in late January, New Year's Day 2000 had come and gone with nary a mishap or a ruffled feather. A few teams of well-trained and well-paid consultants armed with a couple of easy-to-apply software patches had done the trick handily.

So, long story short, the school's promise of rapid job placement turned out to be as broken and hollow as an empty beer can rolling in the gutter. Virtually none of what I had been trained in, none of the competencies I had acquired was any longer in demand. All I was left with was a huge credit card debt. No surprise that now, more than six months after graduation and with no job in sight I was scarcely in the mood for a celebration. It had been several long weeks since I'd last checked in with the job placement office, and I expected nothing more from the school.

Nevertheless, I ultimately decided to go to the party for the hell of it. At least it would be air-conditioned, no small consideration in this sweltering heat. When I got there, I saw the balloons and the banners along with a tempting spread of cold cuts, cheese and crackers, chips and dips, soda and doughnuts. There were maybe a few dozen recent and older graduates milling about, grabbing paper plates, trying to appear cheerful. We were treated to a few unconvincing speeches about how *The Chubb Institute* was gearing up for the new millennium and looking forward to an exciting future. I met a handful of former classmates who, like me, had failed to find jobs in the IT industry. Some were resigned, others were bitter. One talked about filing a class action lawsuit on behalf of all of us. Another said it would probably take too long and get us nowhere.

Our little group of disgruntled graduates made an early exit from the festivities and headed over to Two World Trade Center. The day had started off hazy with veiled sunshine, but now, late in the afternoon, had turned crystal clear and a cooling breeze had picked up. We decided to give ourselves a treat – you might call it a booby prize -- by going up to the WTC observatory. I had twice been to the top of the Empire State Building, once in the daytime, once at night, but had never been to the observatory deck atop the South Tower of the World Trade Center. After waiting in line for nearly an hour, we boarded the elevator. My ears popped as we raced upwards.

We stepped out onto the 107th floor only to enter another elevator which led to the 110th floor outdoor observatory. We walked out to the edge of the deck. The view was incredible. From that vantage point high above the island of Manhattan, the Statue of Liberty standing proudly in New York Harbor looked like an action figure you might find on a ten-year-old's night table. From another direction, I could see the silhouettes of both towers falling over the beautiful Woolworth Building. We left the towers feeling buoyant and renewed. Not in a million years could we have imagined what would take place on a similarly crystal clear gloriously blue day, just two weeks after our visit.

No words can adequately capture the surreal horror of September 11, 2001. On that morning I woke up unusually early for me, about 6:40 am, and for some peculiar reason was unable to get back to sleep, even though there was no noise or excessive heat from the radiator or anything else that might have caused me to waken. Instead, I felt vaguely uncomfortable, a feeling which seemed totally out of place when I looked out the window and saw the vast stretch of sheer brilliant blue that was the morning sky. Two hours later the TV was on and I was watching a crazy apocalyptic movie, some sci-fi thriller or something like the film *Independence Day*, in which aliens obliterate New York and Los Angeles. The Hollywood special effects were stunning, unbelievable. The awesome sight of two magnificent towers, the tallest structures on the planet when built, simply collapsing down one after the other like accordions amid colossal plumes of billowing black smoke! How did they do it? Why, they must have used miniature models of the buildings, demolished them, and then blown up the images for the screen, right?

Early on I had assumed, as did so many others, that it was some kind of weird and dreadful freak accident, a drunken or ill pilot somehow veering madly off course, the air traffic controllers not able to alert the copilot or crew in time. But the moment I watched that second plane crash into the other tower less than twenty minutes after the first, I could feel my stomach shrivel up and fall to the floor. It was the mind and body shock of knowing that someone had deliberately done this. An act of war!!! A planned attack on America by twisted evil individuals willing to sacrifice their own young lives just to make some kind of sick political statement.

With my eyes glued to the ghastly spectacle unfolding on the television screen I recalled the countless times I had been to the WTC site, had strolled all around the sunny five-acre Venetian style plaza, had circled the fountain with its statue of Atlas holding a huge golden globe on his back. The times I had taken in an outdoor concert or performance there, and the times I had actually stopped to gaze up just like a typical tourist, dumbfounded by the buildings' immense, impossible height. And now, to stand and watch those two massive white towers simply implode into dust and rubble within the space of a half hour was the most unreal belief-defying sight I had ever witnessed. And the people! How many had been killed?!?! I thought with a shudder of the folks who worked in the area, who were out on the street and had actually witnessed the stomach-turning sight "in person." I could have been one of them. I had to get away from the TV, fast.

It was startling to see how beautiful it was outdoors, as if no one had told Mother Nature of the disaster that had just befallen us. I walked up to the campus of Sarah Lawrence College. I enjoyed spreading out a towel and sitting on the expansive lawn in front of the music hall. Away from the dorms and main academic buildings, it was probably the quietest part of the campus, except for the occasional sounds of pianos and violins as music students practiced their scales. Usually I brought a book to read, but today I just sat there feeling strange, upset, uncertain, and lost. God -- what would happen now? To our country? To New York City? Who did it and how did they pull it off? How many unsuspecting innocents had their lives cruelly wrenched away from them? People whose only crime was showing up for work this morning. I knew the death toll must be in the thousands. What was the president gonna do? It was too much to take in, too much to process. After a while I just lay down and dozed off, making up for some of the sleep I'd missed in the morning. When I awoke it had gotten cooler and the sun was low in the sky. I folded up my towel and headed back home. For the next two weeks people spoke of little else but the September 11th attacks.

It wasn't until the beginning of October that Noah got around to telling me the news. I hadn't seen Noah since the day of the Caramoor

Jazz Festival, when he'd embarrassed and disturbed me with his erratic behavior and refusal to take his medication. I had written to him urging that he get the help he needed. He sent me two little "thank you" gifts, but neither of us phoned or wrote to the other after that. Then one evening he called. His voice sounded uncharacteristically somber. He asked me how I was doing. And then:

"Do you remember Martin, Emily's boyfriend -- my daughter Emily? You know, the guy she's living with, we met him at my mother's 80th birthday party?"

"Yeah, Martin, the fireman. Sure, I remember Martin."

"Well...he was in Ladder Company 22. They were one of the first units to respond to the emergency at the World Trade Center...."

"Oh, no... not. . ."

Martin turned out to be one of the 343 brave New York City firefighters who gave their lives to help save others on that awful day. In December, when *The New York Times* did a special series titled *Portraits in Grief*, they published photos and capsule profiles of as many of the World Trade Center victims as they could gather information about. I saw Martin's picture there, looking as bright and optimistic as he had looked and sounded that day at the party. I can only hope and pray that his soul, as well as those of all the other victims, is truly resting in peace on the other side.

By that time I had decided that I, too, needed to make some kind of transition. New York had sunk into a financial, emotional, and psychological quagmire in the wake of the worst attack on the homeland since America's founding. All of that death and destruction had taken an ugly bite out of the Big Apple and people were still, figuratively speaking, walking around in a daze. My chances of finding a decent job using my half-baked programming skills were now next to nil. My parents could not understand why several thousand dollars and two years of hard work and study had failed to translate into a new career for me, as I'd promised them it surely would.

Perhaps I needed to be in a smaller, quieter, less conspicuous place. Maybe there was some small town somewhere where people with advanced computer skills were few and far between, where I could find at least an entry-level or assistant position. In any event it seemed it was that time again -- time for a move. Time to get away from Mom and Dad again, hopefully this time for good, once and for all.

So where could I go now? I had tried California, tried North Carolina. Hmm, I thought. How about New England? Bucolic scenes of black and white Holstein cows grazing in green pastures, lovely white church steeples pointing towards heaven, began to drift across my mental canvas. Canoes gliding peacefully along the silvery surface of pristine lakes. Brilliant flame-colored bursts of fall foliage as far as the eye could see. Quaint village squares sleeping under plush carpets of freshly fallen snow. Well, let's see. Maine was too far north and too cold, Massachusetts too expensive, Rhode Island too tiny, and Connecticut, well, it wasn't *really* New England was it, what with all those hedge fund managers living there? That left Vermont and New Hampshire. When I pictured New Hampshire what came to mind was the New Hampshire Primary, Dartmouth College, and granite quarries. When I pictured Vermont I saw maple syrup, ski slopes, green mountains, and *Ben and Jerry's* Ice Cream. I chose Vermont. Almost immediately I began making plans for an exploratory bus trip to Burlington the following spring.

36
Moonlight in Vermont

IT WAS LIKE walking into a blazing fire without the heat or the smoke. I was leisurely padding down Lake Street past the dairy farm whose placid marbled bovines came right up to the fence and eyed me curiously, when I looked skyward and was mesmerized by the sight. The brilliant vibrating golden yellows, crimson reds and tangerine oranges flooded my vision on all sides, with nuances of rust, brick, and saffron. A glorious pageant of trees I could not name, of all shapes and sizes, all aflame in their fall splendor. Millions of autumn leaves broadcasting their intense colors and vividness in one last defiant death throe before falling down and crumbling into dust. I had heard about those "leaf peeper" tours -- about the folks who booked special vacation trips to New England at this time of year solely to experience the magnificence of the fall foliage. Now I understood why. This was early October in St. Albans, Vermont, a small town about 15 miles from the Canadian border.

The brief time I spent living in Vermont wound up being a fuzzy, somewhat surreal, hard to recall interlude between the September 11th terrorist attacks in New York and the sickness and death of my mother. A strange dream in which the thrill of new discovery and the keen ache of mourning were mingled together in a bittersweet ballad. Years later there remain only echoes and shadows, small recollections, fleeting glimpses of incidents and scenes, people and places, voices and faces.

Like the cheap rooming house I stayed in when I first arrived in Vermont, overlooking the busy bustling atmosphere on Church Street in downtown Burlington. An endless parade of humanity haunting the coffee parlors, organic food markets, art galleries, and independent bookstores, all housed in spartan early 1900s buildings. Street performers in costume, impromptu outdoor jam sessions, funky kiosks peddling handmade jewelry and stenciled t-shirts, hordes of college kids from the nearby University of Vermont, saloons serving up foamy craft beer. And not a sleek office tower, modern high-rise apartment building, or proud skyscraper casting its shadow anywhere.

There I am at the local community college offering my services as an assistant instructor in computer basics. I had prepared a resume in which I detailed all of my extensive training courtesy of *The Chubb Institute*. After receiving the resume along with my cover letter, the school had asked me in for an interview. I walked over there with eager anticipation, dressed in a sharp blazer and skirt with stylish black pumps. But after a forty-minute interview with two administrators which I thought had gone rather well, I heard nothing from them for the next several weeks. Finally I presented myself to the *St. Albans Free Library* and offered to teach an intro course as a volunteer, no pay. That went nowhere either.

And there was that dusty used books store around the corner from the *Food Lion,* where the books were piled haphazardly about the floor, sometimes in stacks five feet high, creating a dizzying maze and the sense of a treasure hunt as one prowled around picking up a curious volume here and there. The owner's green-eyed calico cat snoozing on a lumpy velvet couch while he brewed herbal tea for his customers, no charge. A special table devoted to the works of local writers and poets. Soft piped-in Brahms occasionally interrupted by a whistling tea kettle. That place, though I can't even remember what it was called, became one of my favorite hangouts.

And who can forget that brash teenager in the apartment next to mine who aspired to be a white rap artist. A skinny lower middle-class kid enthralled with the hip hop sound and culture. I never did learn his name. Having discovered that rents in Burlington were out of my reach I had come up north, towards Canada, and landed in the town of St. Albans, a stone's throw from Montreal. I had found an affordable two-bedroom apartment, a duplex with kitchen and living room on the lower level, bedrooms and bath on the upper.

It feels kind of neat going up and down the stairs in my own apartment. But I am in a so-called "town house" that contains four such units and the walls separating them are plasterboard thin. Before long I'm being routinely shocked out of a quiet dinner or reading session by the *BOOM! BOOM! BOOM!* of my wanna-be-Eminem neighbor blasting his synthesizer and rapping along to the beat. At first all I can do is kick the walls in frustration, but that goes unnoticed by him and his delirious friends. One night, at my wits' end, I run out to the trash bins and grab a jagged slab from a cracked bathroom sink that I had noticed earlier, drag it into my apartment, hoist it up and begin slamming it against the wall with wild abandon. At last the kid is roused and is angrily knocking on my front door demanding to know why I had just broken his mother's mirror, a family heirloom.

Then, there I was getting fired from my part-time job as a telephone interviewer at *Macro International,* a market research firm with a branch office on Kingman Street. My offense? Failing to read a survey questionnaire verbatim while recording responses from my interviewee. The survey, commissioned by a public health agency, is a lengthy probe into healthcare practices and includes such questions as "When did you last have an eye examination" and "Are you planning to get a flu shot this year?" The person I am talking to has identified himself as a 69-yr-old man. When I come to a section in the survey about pregnancy, prenatal care and menstrual cycles I just skip over it. A supervisor with headphones listening in from the main office catches the unpardonable breach of protocol and I get canned on the spot.

Delightful sights and smells on North Main Street as I watch four-horse open carriages bearing large buckets of sap proudly parading down the avenue during the annual *Vermont Maple Festival.* Lively crowds pouring into the streets, lavish pancake breakfasts at the local elementary school, clever amber-colored maple-themed displays in every store window on the main drag bar none, guided sugarhouse tours in the woods.

Other weird scenes and incidents unfold in my mind, random and disconnected:

Having decided it might be a good idea to take up driving again if I was going to be living in such an out of the way place, I remember taking a refresher course at the local high school. Next thing you know I'm driving a rented *Nissan Maxima* all around the shoreline of Lake Champlain until dusk falls, and then I manage to get lost in some remote farm country where there are no paved roads. I don't find my way home until well past midnight.

Store manikins dripping with blood, strategically placed on front lawns, pirate skulls hoisted on broomsticks -- dagger protruding from the back, red bandanna still wrapped around the forehead. Kids dressed up as scarecrows wielding scythes and pitchforks, loudspeakers blasting *Monster Mash* and screams from the *Psycho* movie soundtrack. Hideous gargoyle faces peeping out amidst cobwebs and blood-soaked rags, bats hovering about cracked tombstones. It was Halloween night, and I was to learn that in St. Albans, Vermont this holiday is taken seriously -- *very* seriously. It was also the night I saw my first shooting star.

There I am hunched over the kitchen table trying to pen a two-page autobiographical profile and filling out endless forms in order to apply for a job with the *Department of Immigration and Naturalization*. That federal agency, as a result of the 9-1-1 terror attacks, was now subsumed under President Bush's all-purpose **Department of Homeland Security**. The regional office was located in a vast federal complex mere blocks from my apartment. I had responded to a notice posted on the bulletin board at the center announcing that DHS was looking to hire college graduates.

I remember the time I invited Maxine up for a visit and we spent a fun afternoon riding an open-air wagon through nearby *Shelburne Farms*, a working, sustainable 1,400 acre farm which boasted a rustic historic inn and an old breeding barn on the premises. We took pictures of each other posing with friendly goats and sheep. Then we were treated to a fascinating live demonstration of how to make artisanal cheddar cheese from scratch, starting with a tank of warm raw milk just collected from the resident herd of Swiss brown cows. For the first time in my life I learned what the phrase "curds and whey" from the nursery rhyme *Little Miss Muffet* actually meant.

Fretting about whether or not I might have killed "Waldo," my next-door neighbor's charcoal-gray cat. I had made a practice of inviting the slender feline in on bitter cold nights to sleep on my couch because my neighbor refused to allow the cat inside of his house. I bought some discount cans of cat food from the local supermarket to feed him, and they came in several flavors. Waldo seemed to prefer the stinkiest one, the chicken liver. Then one day I looked out my window and to my great shock saw my neighbor hovering over the creature as he lay prone on the grass, white caked spittle around his mouth. Later that same day Waldo died. Had he been allergic to the foul-smelling entree, or gotten a contaminated can?

Spending Christmas all alone the year my mom died, having dinner at *Lucky Wok*, the All-You-Can-Eat Chinese buffet up the block. They had the dining room all decked out in red and green garlands for the occasion and there was one elderly couple and a young family across the room from me. We were the only customers in the restaurant that evening. The Captain Tso Chicken and Kung Pao Shrimp were okay, but the egg rolls were way too greasy.

Taking a midnight stroll in the midst of a heavy snowstorm with no wind at all and the large fluffy flakes not so much falling as floating gently. An uncanny and lovely silence all around and feeling strangely warm and wonderfully wrapped up in a gentle white blanket and knowing exactly how Robert Frost felt when he was moved to write his famous poem, **Stopping by Woods on a Snowy Evening.** You know, the one that ends, *"and miles to go before I sleep, and miles to go before I sleep."*

One day my father called to give me the news that they had finally figured out the cause of my mother's unusual pain in her left arm. It had all begun with a mysterious achy feeling and had progressed to the point where she could barely use her arm. She had been to orthopedists, neurologists and other specialists and had undergone half a dozen tests, all with no fruitful results. Even the possibility of a "mini-stroke" was suggested and then rejected as unlikely. Seven years earlier my mom had gone for a colonoscopy during which doctors had detected a polyp. A biopsy revealed it to be malignant and it was removed, the doctor assuring her they had "gotten it all out." But it was now apparent that some stray cells had escaped that earlier procedure and had slowly metastasized over the years, spreading to other parts of her body. Now, as X-rays revealed, they were invading her spine, the tumors pressing on nerves that ran out to her arm. That's what was causing the inexplicable pain.

Ah shit, I thought. Like the rapist who assaulted you seven years ago who you thought was behind bars suddenly showing up one day at the corner *7-Eleven*, the Cancer, vicious little smirk on its face, was back and scarier than ever. My mom was started on an immediate program of intensive chemo and radiation therapy. Two back surgeries followed which resulted in her having to wear a neck brace. But with the cancer so far advanced, her prognosis was not good, and my father was quite distressed and worn-out. I scheduled an extended visit to New York to see what I could do to help.

Over the next several months I made a number of such trips. My poor dad grew increasingly helpless as my mother was put through an excruciating regimen of PET and MRI scans, rehabilitation therapy, powerful anticancer drugs, and supposedly state-of-the-art radiation treatments. But it was all for naught. All of those expensive interventions, we eventually came to realize, served only to prolong her dying.

Rumors were circulating around the apartment complex that the property was being sold to a new owner who planned to perform extensive renovations and hike up the rents substantially. Tenants who could not afford to pay the higher prices would not be offered a new lease when their present one expired. I was already paying almost half my income on rent and without a much better job than the telephone gig I had just lost, I would have no choice but to move out. I still had not heard anything from the **Department of Homeland Security** to whom I had forwarded my completed job application weeks before. And my lease was due to expire the following spring – just a few months away.

Almost as soon as it had begun, it seemed, my New England sojourn was drawing to a sad close. A pall had come over everything and once again I found myself in a place that no longer felt like home, if it ever had. To make matters worse, a grim milestone was approaching. I could not quite believe it, but I was about to turn 50. I had hit the mid-century mark – halfway along on my journey to nowhere.

37
Goodbye, Mom

I WAS SITTING in the salon waiting for my hair color to take, casually flipping through the pages of a magazine when my gaze was arrested by a small black and white photograph accompanying an article. It was a vintage New York City street scene. I studied the photo closely, focusing on the fresh excited faces of teen girls all huddled together in a crowd, eagerly awaiting their chance to get into the *Paramount Theater* near Times Square. Many were wearing black and white saddle shoes, "poodle skirts," and white socks pulled down to the ankles. And many had those carefully contoured, swept-back hairdos that were so typical of the 1940s. Across the street from the girls were several cops, billy clubs at the ready, just in case the overexcited crowd got unruly. These "bobbysoxers," as they were affectionately called, were waiting to see their latest heartthrob -- a skinny, scrappy Italian kid from Hoboken, New Jersey named Frank Sinatra. Gracing the front of the marquee was an immense sign featuring the singer's smiling face.

I looked up from the picture and instantly recalled how my mother, who grew up on Belmont Avenue in the Bronx -- just minutes via subway from the *Paramount Theater* -- had laughingly described how thrilled she and her girlfriends were to get to go to that show. Now I scanned the photo looking for her face amid the mob of giddy girls, trying to imagine the sound effects that went with the scene. Screeches, shouts, the pulse of hearts beating faster, bodies trembling in anticipation, stepped-up breathing. I zeroed in on one girl who somewhat resembled my mom but I couldn't be sure.

I wonder if memories of that Sinatra concert ever made their way into Mom's consciousness at any time during those last few months, as her mind became increasingly fogged over with fatigue, time distortion and morphine drips. One time, shortly after taking her regular dose of Hydrocodone, she exclaimed, smiling, "*I feel like dancing!*"

It was almost impossible to reconcile the image of my mother in the last eighteen months of her life with the image I'd always had of her while growing up. All through my childhood and teenage years she had been a force to be reckoned with, a turbocharged paragon of cool competence and efficiency, the ultimate homemaker. I can still see her whirling about the house, dishrag or dust mop in hand, waging war on dirt, disorderliness, and clutter with the ardor of a medieval crusader. A bundle of nervous, restless energy, she would bounce out of bed before anyone else each morning and by 10 am, while other moms were still lingering over their second cup of coffee, would have gotten us kids off to school, washed and dried the breakfast dishes, made all the beds, vacuumed, and put in a laundry. A double Virgo, my mother had all the obsessive perfectionism and craving for order associated with that astrological sign. She could no more tolerate a crooked picture on the wall or a telltale ring on the coffee table from a carelessly placed glass than she could a roomful of screaming, fighting children.

But to a kid like me, given to lazy reverie and creative sloth and dedicated to the proposition that life's highest aim was to have fun, she was a holy fright. Her constant lectures to my siblings and me, full of words and phrases like "responsibilities," "first things first," and "know your place" left me cold. Often she would nag me, even while I was hunched over my desk studiously doing homework, about some unfinished or forgotten household chore. At such times Dad would often take my side, pointing out that doing well in school was a bit more important than washing dishes. Mom would have none of it. *"All the straight A's and honor rolls in the world don't mean a thing if she has no character,"* she would pronounce indignantly.

Her perfectionist bent made her an excellent critic, wonderfully adept at uncovering the hidden flaws, defects, and downsides of everything we encountered, whether a new dining room set we were thinking of buying, a prospective new house, my dad's choice of wardrobe, or our vacation plans. But when she trained that critical eye on me, her own daughter, I felt something like what an 18th century African slave must have felt standing naked on the auction block, having his teeth inspected and biceps squeezed by some avaricious Southern planter. Mom would calmly reel off a litany of my faults, foibles, and foolish ways, and -- lest

I think I was a hopeless case -- throw in some helpful hints as to how they might be corrected. Restless and annoyed, I stood still and listened patiently. Then, feeling misunderstood and resentful, I would vow to do better and slink away to my room.

At times I would make genuine efforts to be more helpful around the house, to not act so selfishly, not be so "rambunctious," to tidy up my room better and the like. But, since the slightest offenses could set off the alarm (from the far side of the house I'd suddenly hear the siren sound of her voice calling me to task) -- offenses such as leaving tissues in the pockets of my pajamas when I tossed them into the laundry hamper or failing to securely cap a canister of grated cheese before putting it back in the refrigerator, or letting the fork hit against my teeth noisily while eating -- I soon gave up. It seemed a lost cause.

Six months after the doctors informed my mother that -- a) the small malignant growth in her colon which had been removed seven years earlier had not, in fact, been wholly eradicated, and b) a tiny remnant of it had grown over the years and was now invading her lungs and her spine -- all had changed. Mom was no longer the mother I remembered or had grown up with. Weeks of intense chemo and radiation therapy had resulted in her losing about 25 pounds and much of her hair. She had to wear a back brace and neck collar to bolster her spine, the vertebrae of which were slowly being strangled by the expanding tumor. She had nearly lost the use of one arm and was prone to lose her balance when she walked. Mom was afraid to fall asleep at night because of frightening dreams and would sit up in a chair, refusing to lie down on the hospital bed the nurses had set up in my parents' bedroom. She seldom raised her voice and did little around the house except sit in the big recliner in our living room and watch TV.

Now she was meek and uncomplaining and polite towards me, this despite the fact that during those several weeks I stayed in their house to help my dad with her care, I still did the kinds of things that had always infuriated her. Things like leaving my books and papers all over the dining room table and running the water too long in the bathroom.

Indeed, she was grateful, even delighted, when I would do little favors for her like helping her file her nails or cooking up a bowl of "pasta va zul," one of her most beloved dishes from the time she was a child. Mom was also, strangely, afraid to be alone in the house and whenever Dad and I would jump in the car to go out for groceries it wouldn't be long before his cell phone began ringing -- every 15 minutes.

She was not old -- only 73. In fact, just before that fateful diagnosis wherein a routine physical revealed the lesion on her left lung, she had returned with my dad from a two-week vacation in Orlando, Florida. The two of them had stayed in a lovely time-share resort and had toured Disney World and Universal Studios. They enjoyed those attractions every bit as much as a pair of 14-yr-olds would have.

The contrast between Mom now and the Mom of long ago was so stark that it almost made me question my own memories. All during my childhood she had been to me like a mini tornado whose devastating path I dreaded getting caught in. A force of nature that thoroughly intimidated me even when I was able to avoid or hide from it, and inflicted lasting damage when I could not. But now that force had been conquered by a far more awesome and terrible force of nature -- terminal illness. And so, it turned out, Mom was only human after all.

When it became clear that all the aggressive and cutting edge treatments had failed to stop the cancer's relentless advance and that my mom's poor body had taken all the poison it could handle, we reluctantly agreed it was time to put her in hospice. When the truth finally hit, it came as quite a shock to me. I had never thought I would lose my mother so soon. Unlike my father, who at the age of 63 had to undergo an emergency triple bypass, she had been reasonably healthy and active most of her adult life. Mom was the one who quit smoking the minute the Surgeon General's damning report came out in the mid-1960s, who had severely cut down on fat and sugar saturated foods in her diet, who spent 40 minutes each morning on an exercise bicycle, and who ordered regularly from a vitamin catalog. What did all of that mean now? As it is so wont to do, LIFE once again played one of its cruelest jokes.

As I watched my mother slip into a semi-dreamlike state under the influence of morphine, Hydrocodone, OxyContin, and similar painkillers, it brought to mind the handful of occasions when I had seen her actually slow down, unwind and enjoy herself. Those few and far between times when she had been both willing and able to step off the treadmill and take a deep breath. Back when both me and my brother were still in grammar school, there was a year or two when we would wait on a certain corner every Wednesday afternoon after school let out. Soon Mom would arrive, always on time, and shepherd us off to the local bowling alley. It was an exciting novelty for us kids. And it was also a rare kind of relief to watch Mom heave that heavy bowling ball and send it rumbling down the lane, cracking a little smile when she'd managed to knock down several pins, as if the earsplitting din and clamor of those falling bowling pins brought some satisfying release of a load of nervous tension.

Sometimes she would sit on the carpet with me in the living room and spread out a deck of cards so she could show me how to play Solitaire. She could be enormously patient when helping one of us kids with a school project. I can still see her carefully stirring kernels of white rice into simmering pots of dye on the stove, just so I could have a variety of multicolored grains of rice to paste onto my collage piece for the annual sixth grade Art Fair.

But by far and away, the times when my mom was most able to relax were when she was immersed in music -- whether playing it or listening to it. She had learned to play piano as a child and had once entertained the fantasy of a career as a songwriter. While her earliest piano lessons focused, as most piano lessons do, on simple well-known classical pieces like *Claire de Lune* and *Fur Elise* my mother soon found her musical tastes shifting towards the popular swing music of the forties, taking as her model artists like Teddy Wilson and Fats Waller. Every once in a blue moon I'd come home on a Sunday afternoon and find her sitting in front of our slightly out of tune piano tapping out some mean boogie-woogie.

Mom was the first person on our block to buy a stereo console in the early sixties, at the time the latest fad in both furniture and audio equipment -- a stylish and massive wooden cabinet that stood on the floor, equipped with a record player in the middle, flanked on either side by large built-in speakers. Each speaker broadcast the sound from a different direction so as to create a more realistic "high fidelity" experience that simulated a live performance. She joined a record club and ordered albums by the month -- everything from Judy Garland to Benny Goodman to Xavier Cugat and the Baja Marimba Band. By the time I started paying attention to the wondrous sounds that would fill our house in the evenings and on weekends she had hundreds of record albums. Glossy black vinyl platters that she would stack six at a time on the spindle of her turntable, where they would drop and slowly spin at 33 revolutions per minute, each one in turn, creating hours of continuous music much of which I came to love.

Then there were all of those ancient 78 rpm records made of shellac that she had collected before she got married. Sometimes when she wasn't around, just out of curiosity I would take an old portfolio out of the closet, carefully pull one of the heavy brittle discs out of its sleeve, set the record player to the 78-rpm setting and let it rip. To hear, for the very first time, amidst all the scratching, hissing and popping in the background, the splendid sounds of Billie Holiday belting out "*Oooh ooh ooh, what a little moonlight can do to you*" with the Teddy Wilson band was a revelation and opened the door to a whole new world for me.

There were those odd moments when some fanciful notion would take hold of her, and my mother would announce that she was going to learn to play the guitar or the ukulele. Next thing you know she's got a brand new guitar and someone is coming over the house to give her lessons. These escapist detours from drudgery never lasted long, because it soon enough became apparent that she would never be able to fit practice time into her rigid schedule. But that didn't stop these curious urges from popping up every now and again. The most curious was the time she decided she wanted to learn the accordion. I don't remember if she rented it or where she got it from, but the sight of her holding that funny boxy instrument that one had to squeeze back and forth like bellows to get any sound out of conjured up weird images in my mind. Like wandering mariachis approaching your table at a fancy Mexican restaurant, or the old Italian organ-grinder on the street, monkey in tow.

Oh well, so at least it wasn't all work and no play after all, I realized with some satisfaction, even as I watched her slipping away from us. By this time Mom was fully resigned to her fate. She no longer had any inclination to bravely "do battle" against an illness that had its own unstoppable agenda. "I've lived a pretty good life" she would say. "It's okay -- I'm ready to leave it all in God's hands." The concept of death was and still is an impenetrable mystery to me. I still cannot fathom how a human personality -- vibrant, unique, transcendent -- can really be "here today, gone tomorrow." Poof! It seems to violate some universal law of physics or something. During those final weeks in her hospital bed Mom was intubated and unable to speak to us although she was fully conscious and could hear everything we were saying.

Our in-home hospice care, in which all treatment is strictly palliative and keeping the patient comfortable is the sole objective, had, unfortunately, to be discontinued when one afternoon, Mom began suddenly gasping for breath. It was caused by extreme fluid buildup around her heart and we had no choice but to call an ambulance and rush her to the ICU. Now she lay on the bed helpless, hooked up to various monitors. The nurses had placed clumsy mittens on her hands to prevent her from trying to pull out her tubes in sheer frustration. At this stage, death seemed more like sweet deliverance than anything else. But would she really be going to "a better place," as everyone always said? I didn't know.

At one point, when she began suffering from congestive heart failure and we all knew it was only a matter of days, I sat at the side of her bed and gently stroked her forehead, telling her that very soon she would be seeing her mother (my dear Granny who'd left us 13 years earlier), her father, and a host of other friends and relatives who had passed on. But did I really believe that? I had read with deep interest the accounts of people who had so-called "near death experiences." People the world over who had been rescued from the brink of death had reported such experiences, and when interviewed they described remarkably similar scenarios. There was always a sense of going through a dark tunnel, an unimaginably bright light at the end accompanied by a warm loving presence, a feeling of suddenly knowing and understanding everything, and, very often, encounters with long dead relatives.

Neuroscientists had dismissed these accounts, claiming that this response was simply the result of a dying brain being quickly deprived of oxygen -- the bright light caused by the sudden rapid firing of millions of neurons in a kind of desperate last gasp attempt to go out in a blaze of glory. But whether or not this was the case (and if it was, it seemed odd that none of these survivors having just undergone such severe oxygen loss showed any signs of brain damage afterwards) I just hoped that my mother would experience that light and that love, whether real or fake. It seemed a pretty cool and appropriate way to check out. I mean really, it was the least life could do after having inflicted so much pain and misery.

So, Mom, I don't know where you are now but I want to thank you. Thank you for being a responsible hardworking mom who tried to instill values and character into her children. Thank you for being the kind of excellent and conscientious homemaker that put others to shame. And, yes, thanks even for the "constructive criticism" that I know you truly believed was for my benefit, even though it was sometimes tough to swallow. Thanks for the little things -- like those great scrambled egg and ketchup sandwiches you packed in my lunch box and for letting me keep that one-eyed stray cat I found cowering under a car. And above all, thanks for the music. It has stayed with me all my life and is a source of joy and endless wonder. I know it will be playing in the back of my brain, drowning out any noisy erupting neurons, when I check out of here.

38

You Can't Go Home Again (Until You Have To)

I WAS ABOUT to hang up the phone when Dad suddenly blurted out, "Oh -- I almost forgot, Phil and Tina told me some strange men came over their house, said they were from the government, FBI, CIA or something. They wanted to ask them questions about you."

"No way -- you're kidding," I said, genuinely surprised. Somehow I never believed real government agents would actually show up at my neighbor's house to vet me. But there it was.

After Mom died I went back to New York and spent about a month with my grieving father, trying to help him navigate the strange new world he was now entering after fifty years of, if not domestic bliss, certainly a contented married life. His world was forever changed, and I had to convince him that someday, with the passage of time, he would be able to feel comfortable and safe in it again. Plus, there were the practical matters of disposing of my mother's clothing and belongings, and choosing an urn to house her ashes.

But then I had to return to Vermont, to my own home. And it just so happened that the unassuming town of St. Albans, the lakeside hamlet I had wound up in, was regional headquarters for the U.S. Department of Immigration and Naturalization. After the September 11th World Trade Center attacks the Department was reorganized, expanded, and rechristened the *Department of Homeland Security*. Word was out that they planned to greatly increase their staffing and were particularly in search of college graduates willing to take entry-level positions.

I flashed back to the day, three months earlier, when I had walked from my apartment over to the vast office park where the impressive glass and steel edifice that housed the Department – probably the largest building in all of St. Albans – was located. I picked up the lengthy federal application, took it home, and spent several tedious hours at my kitchen table filling out the forms and providing detailed information including what elementary school I attended and every address I had ever lived at since the day I was born. There was even an essay to write explaining why I wanted to work for the Department and what skills and personal assets I thought I could bring to the job. The position would involve evaluating immigration claims and it required a security clearance. I had to provide numerous references with addresses and phone numbers, all with the understanding that any or all of the references I gave could be personally contacted by the Feds.

After returning home from New York, I was immediately confronted with a challenge. It was not clear how much longer I would be able to remain in Vermont. Aside from the gloomy pall cast over everything by my mother's death, several other bad omens had recently presented themselves. Despite diligent searching, I had failed to find any kind of job where I could apply my computer training and had finally settled for a part-time gig working the phones at a market research firm. Then I had somehow managed to lose even that job.

And then there were those unpleasant new neighbors who had moved into the East End of our apartment complex. Due to some state law or city ordinance a certain portion of the apartments in the development had to be designated "Section 8" affordable housing. This was federally subsidized low-income housing for which eligible candidates waited, sometimes as long as seven years, and finally received vouchers which could be used in place of a substantial portion of their rent. Needless to say, the program attracted plenty of genuinely needy folks on fixed incomes as well as single women raising children, but also some unsavory characters, "system-gamers," and other undesirables.

Like the Gallagher family, which consisted of a hard-drinking late fifty-ish mother and her sour-faced adult daughter. Mother and daughter didn't get along; within days of their moving in, loud profanity-laced screaming matches could be heard almost nightly, issuing from the open windows of their ground floor apartment. Strange folks could be seen coming and going from their place at all hours of the day and night. Some people suspected they were dealing drugs. It wasn't long before the new arrivals and their gamy guests began to leave unmistakable marks of their presence throughout the complex. The outside courtyard area through which I had to walk to get to my building unit was usually kept clean save for some stray toys. But now it was decorated with cigarette butts and broken beer bottles. Sometimes bags of garbage would be left out on the walkway because the new residents apparently were too lazy to walk all the way across the yard to the West End where the trash dumpsters were located. Graffiti began to appear on the sides of buildings and some tenants had their car radios stolen or their tires slashed.

Almost overnight, it seemed, my once idyllic leafy haven where the air was cool and fresh and the clarion peals of church bells rang out every evening at five and old-fashioned coaster bicycles with baskets were as commonplace as cars -- had been turned into a raucous trailer park.

As if all that were not bad enough, in mid-January came word to all the tenants that we would soon have a new landlord. When I received the letter containing the updated rent schedules for the different types of apartment units, I was startled. The rent on my apartment, a two-bedroom duplex and one of the premium units in the development, would be nearly doubled. Spoiled from all my years in New York City where stringent rent control laws limited landlords to only paltry rent increases, even when costly improvements were made, I was totally blindsided. Clearly, if I was going to stay in Vermont I would have to find another place to live.

But the only way that would be possible was if I were able to land that good-paying job with the *Department of Homeland Security*. Three weeks before Mom died I had received a letter from the Feds informing me that I had passed the initial screening and there remained only the comprehensive background check to determine whether or not I could be granted a security clearance. I started to get my hopes up. I could think of no reason why I would not pass the background check.

But I was quite mistaken. Much of the tuition for my computer training program at *The Chubb Institute* had been paid via credit card, for I had assumed, of course, that as soon as I started the excellent job the school promised I would get, there would be no problem paying it off. But when no such job materialized, I could not keep up with even the minimum payments and defaulted. That raised a red flag for the feds because the notion of unpaid debts suggests an individual who may be susceptible to taking bribes. And so, a few weeks after that phone call with my dad, a second letter arrived from the Department of Homeland Security stating simply that my application could no longer be considered due to my poor credit history. That meant one thing: I would have to leave Vermont.

When March of the new year arrived, I informed my new landlord that I would not be renewing my lease. Once again it seemed, someone "upstairs" had stepped in to sabotage my intentions and put me back on that Montreal to New York Amtrak special with a one-way ticket, my scanty possessions following on a moving truck. Soon I was knocking on the door of the house I thought I had left for good just two years before.

Once back there, I struggled to adjust to the eeriness of that apartment absent the constant sight of my mother in action. The memories abounded. There she was laying clumps of fresh parsley out on paper towels to dry on the dining room table, or carrying a basket full of laundry up the stairs from the basement, or loading a handful of CDs into her cherished *Sony* multi-CD-player, or meticulously wrapping Christmas presents at a cheap card table set up in her bedroom, or sitting comfortably in the *Lay-Z-Boy* recliner excitedly watching an episode of *Star Search*, hoping her favorite ingénue singing talent would walk away with the grand prize, or sitting in the kitchen reading a Danielle Steel romance novel while waiting for the macaroni water to boil, or doing all the other things that made her the energy center, the sun around which all else revolved, of that home. Now there was only dead air and dust where she used to move and breathe.

My father clearly had not gotten used to life without her and just couldn't think what to do with himself. I tried to keep him sane and healthy by cooking nutritious meals and seeing to it that we both got outside and took some exercise, and by inviting friends and relatives to the house so he wouldn't feel so isolated. But I was sinking into a depression myself. The place was just too big to clean and keep after, and all of the old minor annoyances – the shower that routinely ran out of hot water in five minutes, the deafening sound of multiple leaf blowers going constantly on spring and fall afternoons, the worn-out windows that let in drafts and rattled horribly in the wintertime, the flimsy cardboard-thin ceiling that allowed me to hear the guy in the apartment above snoring, the blindingly bright super sensitive motion detector those same neighbors had installed on the outside porch, directly in front of my bedroom window – all of these irritations now seemed magnified tenfold. It simply didn't make sense for either me or my father to stay here, continuing to pay rent on a three-bedroom, two-bath apartment that was unwieldy, filled with sadness and haunted by memories.

It so happened that at about that time, my friend Peyton had decided to take a real estate course and study for a broker's license. The housing market was booming and my ambitious friend wanted to get a piece of the action. Northerners were still flocking to North Carolina in droves and new homes were sprouting up like mushrooms after a heavy rain. One could scarcely drive five miles in any direction without seeing a construction site. Eventually Peyton got her license and took a job with a housing developer. Taking note of our sorry situation, she suggested we consider purchasing one of the smaller home models that her company was building. Even with home prices soaring, these decent but no-frills houses were surprisingly affordable. Peyton extended an invitation to both me and my father to spend a couple of weeks at her home in Charlotte so that she could take us around and show us what was available.

Dad was intrigued by Peyton's generous offer and was inclined to take her up on it. As for me, the thought of actually moving to North Carolina again struck a sour note -- it bounced around uncomfortably in my mind like a water bottle rolling on the floor of the car threatening at every second to get wedged under the brake pedal and cause a crash. My gut reaction was protest: *North Carolina again? Hell, no....never gonna happen.* But my mind was seriously weighing the options. Staying right where we were seemed like surrendering to despair. Trying to find another decent apartment in Westchester County, given the rent inflation of the past several years would prove challenging to say the least.

We felt like weary wanderers standing bewildered at the fork of a road, every possible path looking equally unappealing. But my dad was willing to at least check things out in North Carolina; surely it couldn't hurt to have a look at whatever there was to see, trying to keep an open mind. Besides, it had been almost ten years since I'd lived there. Things may have changed for the better in any number of ways. Maybe now you could actually get a decent bagel or slice of pizza somewhere in town.

So, out came the suitcases again and in late June we made the trip to that town of NASCAR, gleaming bank towers, and a church on every corner. Peyton put us up very nicely, my dad in the guest room, myself in the abandoned room of her daughter, now living on a college campus -- the fat and fuzzy monkey doll I'd given her as a gift when she was two years old still lying on the bed. For two weeks Peyton took us on a whirlwind tour of all the new residential developments in town, walked us through every model home being offered by the company she worked for, showed us other houses of varying shapes and sizes. She drove us through different neighborhoods pointing out the amenities as well as the drawbacks. There were developments geared for seniors, with lovely landscaping, tennis courts, and planned activities. Many of the fancier places had clubhouses and built-in swimming pools. There was so much to see that I was beginning to feel overloaded. By the middle of the second week it all seemed a blur.

After our two-week stay I was thoroughly exhausted and could scarcely remember anything I had seen, despite having taken copious notes. Yet my father seemed pleasantly surprised, even delighted, at the quality of some of the houses, the attractive designs, the generous-sized rooms, the ample garages and lush front lawns. He seemed taken with the Southern hospitality everywhere on display, from the cheerful morning greetings of perfect strangers on the street to the honey-toned voices of pretty blonde waitresses bringing trays of grits and country-fried ham to our table at any of several eateries where we stopped for lunch. Dad noted with approval the beautiful supermarkets, the clean and tidy streets, the well-tended gardens, the flowers in bloom, the powder-blue skies. A far cry from what we had just come from. He was also happy to hear Northeastern accents frequently, testament to the large number of Northerners who had already relocated there.

I was less than impressed, finding myself focusing on things like the traffic congestion and the smell of diesel fumes, the lack of sidewalks and the boring and sterile strip malls that seemed to appear regularly, on cue, every five miles or so. All the things I had disliked when I lived there a decade ago and which had only gotten worse. But I had to think of my father. What would his future be? He had recently turned 80 and deserved some peace and comfort in his winter years, especially now that

Mom was gone. If there was any possibility that he could be happy down here, perhaps make some new friends or take up bridge or golf, then who was I to let my little pet peeves get in the way.

Dad had seen one house that struck his fancy. It was about five years old and when we went to see it, all of the owner's furniture and fixtures were still in place. There was a beautiful bath in the master bedroom, over twice the size of the one back home, and the whole house seemed filled with air and light. I don't know if it was the fine furniture, the artfully placed pillows and throws, the faux fireplace, or maybe all those family photos plastered over the front and sides of the refrigerator, that gave it such a cozy homespun feel, but the look in my father's eyes said, "Yes, this will do!" The house had been on the market a while and the owners were anxious to close the sale, so anxious they had not only lowered their asking price but were throwing in some of the furniture and carpeting. The Realtor representing the seller was a good friend of Peyton's, someone she had studied with to get her real estate license.

Still, to sign a contract of sale and put down a deposit right then and there seemed a bit too rash. Relocating down south would be a major move, and at my father's age likely a permanent one. There would be no going back. Shouldn't we at least return home and discuss the matter with my brother and sister first? And to buy a house meant things like mowing lawns and fixing leaks in the roof and cleaning out the garage and replacing a broken washing machine. Did it really make sense at this time in Dad's life, even if he could hire others to do some of those chores? But Peyton was pushing me to act quickly. Another couple who had looked at the house seemed interested. A few more days and it could be gone. All of the doubts and questions pummeled me and nagged at me and I simply didn't have an instant answer. A slow torment ensued, akin to the sound of a dripping faucet in the middle of the night. Ahhhgrrr!!!! After a while I just couldn't think straight.

So -- Dad signed the contract. We then returned home to make the financial arrangements. And there was hell to pay. When my sister in California found out what had happened she was furious and demanded to know why she had not been consulted. Months earlier she and I had discussed the possibility of our father getting a modest condominium in Florida, perhaps near Melbourne, where his nephew lived with his wife and son. But that was when I was still living in Vermont and Dad would be on his own. My sister regarded the notion of a man in his eighties, recently widowed and still in mourning, pulling up stakes to go buy a house in a town he knew nothing about and where he had no friends or family -- all on the basis of a breezy two-week visit -- to be insane. She could not believe I had let him do it.

What's more, my sister, who had worked in both real estate and financial management, suspected it was only a matter of time before the overheated housing bubble burst, meaning that if our dad's experiment in home ownership should go awry he might be forced to sell at a substantial loss. How could I have sat back and allowed him to do something so stupid? I couldn't give her a reason.

Within a week a rash of phone calls were made and the contract was rescinded. My father, feeling dismayed and guilty that he had not discussed it with my sister first, decided she was probably right after all, and resigned himself to being overruled. And my brother Jim, who it turned out might be moving in soon, having recently lost his job, pointed out that Dad would probably wind up hating North Carolina anyway, whatever his first impressions may have been. "You won't be able to watch Yankee baseball on TV or even get the *Daily News* there, Dad!"

To me it was all a bad dream. I almost wished I could be back in St. Albans, kicking discarded *Colt 45* cans aside, walking across the courtyard, hearing Mrs. Gallagher screaming and cursing at her daughter. At least there would have been some local color and I would have retained my independence and a smidgen of self-respect. Now I was caught in a spider web of family melodrama and emotional friction that I could feel tightening around me by the minute. A welter of feelings – anger, remorse, helplessness, confusion – began to assault me from all sides. It was meltdown time again.

Two Weeks Later

I am sitting on a couch in front of a bridge table helping a schizophrenic nun put together a 1000-piece jigsaw puzzle. The puzzle depicts a detailed, vividly colored illustration of the Grand Canal in Venice. We had gathered all of the straight-edged pieces first to carefully assemble the border – that was the easy part. The rest might take days. We were in the main lounge in the psych ward at St. Vincent's Hospital in Harrison, New York. It was the very same hospital I had been sent to after getting expelled from school halfway into my freshman year of college.

I was here because I knew what I needed. Like how sometimes you have to kick the vending machine when that *Kit Kat* bar you selected gets stuck against the glass on the way down to the chute -- in that exact same way my brain needed a swift angry jolt. It was not giving me the answers I needed or any constructive or helpful thoughts. It made feeble tentative attempts at best, and then just keeled over into apathy. It required a reboot.

And the best way to do that was through good old-fashioned One-Flew-Over-the-Cuckoo's-Nest electroshock therapy. It was a therapy that seemed to have the ability, like no other, to give the brain a loud wake-up call, to sweep out years of accumulated debris and reset the defaults, so to speak. It might cause some short-term memory loss, but that was a small price to pay for a complete mental makeover. I had been diagnosed at various times with major depression and "schizo-affective disorder," the latter an umbrella term that encompassed a range of symptoms from obsessive-compulsive behavior to social anxiety to hearing voices. I was slated to receive about a dozen ECT treatment sessions over a 21-day period.

It was certainly a change of scenery. My fellow patients were an endless source of entertainment. My roommate was a young woman from New Delhi who had once won a racquetball tournament and twice attempted suicide. An ancient snow-white-haired lady named Gerty wore a different hat every day and told stories about her life as a torch singer in the 1930s, occasionally belting out snippets of a tune as if to demonstrate: *Trouble in paradise, how did it start? We were in paradise, now we're apart...* "Glen Gray and the Casa Loma Orchestra," she'd announce afterwards. Then there was the red-headed guy with the pink eye patch who was constantly asking other patients to play a game of Gin Rummy. It seemed to be his passion and he always won.

After the series of shock treatments, all the dust and cobwebs seemed to have been blown out of my mind and I could see clearly again. My doctor at the hospital suggested I change my medication -- it looked like I might have developed a tolerance to the one I had been on. After those twenty-one days I left the ward and returned home, but continued to go to the hospital for weekly visits as an outpatient. Eventually I stabilized on the new medicine and felt ready to grapple with life once more. And, as so often happens, fate stepped in -- this time taking some pity on me -- and freed me from having to make some difficult decisions.

My brother had indeed managed to lose yet another good job as a field technician with *Verizon*, the result of his never-ending issues with drugs, attention-deficit disorder, and bipolar illness. He would have to give up his apartment and move back in with my father and me. He told us that since he would never consider living in North Carolina or Florida, perhaps our best option was to look for another, smaller apartment in the immediate area. He said he would drive a cab six days a week, and between the three of us we could swing the rent on a new place. That way we as a family could get off to a fresh start, gently wrapping up all the sad memories connected with Mom's final illness and storing them safely away and out of sight.

After several weeks of careful searching, we managed to find an apartment in another two-family house on a quiet dead-end street. It just happened to be located in the town where my father grew up, Mount Vernon, New York. So at least it would feel like home to him. I tried not to think about what was suggested by the spectacle of two over-50 adult children moving back in with their father. I just told myself that I was helping him get over the difficult hump of my mother's death and that eventually, all in good time, I would find a job and get a place of my own. I had no other choice but to tell myself this. To think or imagine anything else would have been to invite the snarling hyenas of clinical depression back in again. And that had to be avoided at all costs.

39
Blood and Treasure

JIMMY WAS ALWAYS saying he wanted to write a book someday. He kept on saying it long after his life had turned into a grotesque helter-skelter safari through a wilderness of drugs and psychosis in a runaway jeep that finally ran out of gas and left him stranded miles from civilization. My brother had come to believe that if he made an honest attempt to create something out of the sordid details of his life, to translate them into plain black words on clean white paper he could rise above his situation. That the act of "writing it all down" could be cathartic, therapeutic even -- at the very least a healthy exercise. He felt doing such a thing might kick-start a cascade of new insights and revelations that would point the way forward, steer him toward some bright new path hitherto unsuspected. Maybe even lead to some kind of redemption. I encouraged his efforts. After he had written out a few chapters, he showed me his rough draft. It begins with a hint of promise -- his vivid account of undergoing an unorthodox treatment for heroin addiction at a clinic in Florida -- a unique and unforgettable experience to which he had been led by a friend and fellow drug addict. Here's how he starts:

You're Just Another EYE on the GODHEAD

Like a brilliant mirror of awe-inspiring majesty the Gainesville morning sky's reflection so peacefully sat, at once regal and unassuming periodically cut clean by the sharp easy glide of semi-exposed prehistoric heads that would appear as suddenly as disappear in the natural beauty of Gainesville's Gator Lake. Surrounded by the earth's flowing top growth a deep green with a paradoxical innocent wisdom within which dancing fuchsia smiles completed the picture with song. Yet none of this fine morning's splendor and radiance had been allowed to enter my hotel room. The drapes were covered tightly with the bedspread in an attempt to keep the room as dark as possible. The clock radio unplugged to prevent the beams of pretty blue-violet light generated by the cool Liquid Crystal

Display. Somehow Blue Violet is a perfect color for LCD's. Telephone disconnected to prevent its simulated electronic bells from ringing. Lying there I became acutely aware of my heartbeat. I thought I could actually feel the blood coursing through my veins, but something seemed a bit off. As if the blood was taking a different route, perhaps through the veins of another body. The body of an innocent seven year old boy, who was lying in his bed on the top floor of an attached house on Brinsmade Avenue in the Bruckner Blvd section of the Northeast Bronx. I kept getting this funny sensation of something similar to a smell but not quite, like something was burning but it wasn't anything physical. The feeling was getting quite eerie. Something at once visceral and emotional which emanated from a reluctance to confront the impurity of my childhood, into which I became completely engulfed. I was overtaken by a subtle rancidness of being that seemed to accompany me along my journey through the streets of the Northeast Bronx as I re-lived my grade school years.

It was my first Ibogaine trip. Ibogaine was a powerful hallucinogen from Gabon in Central Africa which for hundreds of years had been used by the BWITI people in passage rites. The Bwiti are a pygmy tribe who practice this sacrament once or twice per year, using the root bark of the Iboga plant for the initiation of young boys. It is supposed to be a religious experience whereby you can achieve a transport through a portal of time and "meet your ancestors." Which may explain why it had such a powerful effect on the subconscious mind. During the 1960s a young junkie, from the Bronx no less, discovered its properties by pure accident and those properties were such that they not only produced a beautiful hallucinogenic experience which lasted nearly a day and a half, but they also seemed to miraculously break his heroin addiction free of any withdrawal symptoms. Seeing how this was so marvelous and unexpected he couldn't wait to try it on some friends who had addictions as well. It helped nearly all of them who tried it to successfully quit drugs. So he spent the next several years trying to get ibogaine officially approved by the FDA for use in the treatment of drug addiction. Unfortunately he failed in those efforts for various reasons.

A few chapters later, while fondly recounting some drug-related episodes from his early teen years, he writes this:

Me and Bob and Stevie and the others would all meet at "The Bin." The Bin was this makeshift little club house we had set up out of an unused laundry room in the basement of the apartment building where Bob's dad was the superintendent. It was our little private hang-out. There was a double sink that we put a sheet of plywood over and on top of the plywood put a mattress which we covered with something that gave it the look of a sofa and we even found some old painting in the garbage room that we hung up over it. Some simple realist "still-life" painting probably by some unknown artist, the kind that usually bored me. You know, a fruit basket or a vase full of flowers. I mean those kind of paintings were so GENERIC that they served the purpose perfectly, which was to make the place look more homey.

The TRIPPY thing I was about to mention here is (or WAS, I should say, since they pulled the magic formula off the shelves about 30 years ago, give or take) Romilar. It was a cough medicine that my friend Al Spicer told me gave a buzz a bit like an ACID high. It wasn't codeine nor dextromethorphan that created the effect. It was the combination of chloroform and alcohol that they used to put in Romilar in the 60's. Mostly the chloroform -- man that stuff just made the whole world turn into a BRIGHT CARTOON with VIVID COLOR and all the time you felt like you were a NEON SIGN with this COOL light. I LOVED it. But I never had a compulsion to do it. I only did it when someone offered it or bought it for me. Then me and Stevie, we would sit in the playground and drink a bottle each and just talk. And in, like, 22 minutes we would be GLOWING in the DARK and this lasted pretty much the rest of the evening. It was FUN and that was that.

But I eventually quit hanging out at The Bin by the time I was 17 and stopped getting HIGH. I recall one time going down to the Village with Al to panhandle. He had broken his leg from being a bit too high on sleeping pills so he probably thought it would be a great idea to solicit money with his big leg cast and the crutches and I just looked so young and innocent by his side he figured I would help inspire sympathy too. So we set out one day and got on the subway and got off somewhere around Bleecker Street or something and he took one end and I took the other end both of us at the top of the stairs where the people were coming up from the subway with a BIG CAN saying "Madam/Sir, can you spare any change?"and I remember this nice elderly black woman pulling a dollar out of her leather handbag saying: "What's a NICE BOY like you doing PANHANDLING?" with such a lovely face that I almost wanted to tell her not to even bother. For all I was really doing was helping a friend raise some money so he could buy something he really didn't NEED. Some PILL form of magic mushrooms or something. Blue pills. I remember seeing them being put into his hand by a really weird looking kid who claimed to have had a metal plate in his head.

Too bad Jimmy never got to finish his book.

Almost ever since Mom died I had been living with him and my father. It was odd, unfortunate, and a bit creepy, since my brother and I were both in our fifties and my dad in his mid-eighties. But still, we were the only semblance of "family" any of us had left. I was officially a "spinster," having never married nor had children. Jim did have two daughters from a failed relationship that had ended decades earlier, but they were all grown up and living in London. There was not much contact and the only time he ever saw his daughters was when one or the other of them would come to the States to visit other relatives. There was my younger sister in California, but she now had her own family with her husband and two young boys. So my dad, Jimmy and I were all that remained of the original family unit. It was a peculiar arrangement, but at least we had each other.

Living with two men I tended to naturally fall into the homemaker role. I did much of the cooking, all of the cleaning, and all of the laundry. Dad spent most days poring over the *Daily News* and running errands in his always well-polished Buick Century sedan. Most of his evenings were spent plopped in front of the TV watching baseball or the Fox News channel. Jimmy, having recently lost a high-paying job as a field technician with *Verizon* -- an outcome anyone could have predicted who knew his history of untreated bipolar disorder and substance abuse -- had resigned himself to driving a cab off the books.

It could be an uneasy, fraught relationship, suffused with tension, shame and simmering resentments. We wondered, for instance, what the Landlord thought when my dad was the only one to put his signature to the lease on our three-bedroom apartment. Whenever old friends of my parents would call to see how my father was coping since the recent death of my mother, they were often shocked to hear that his son and daughter -- both of us old enough to be grandparents -- were living under the same roof with him. And I don't think anything made me cringe more than the sight of the three of us heading out for dinner on Father's Day. In *his* car, with *him* at the wheel, since he did not trust my brother driving his car and because I, though I had a driver's license, did not own a car and hadn't driven one in years. Even worse, it was usually Dad who picked up the check -- yes, even on Father's Day!! That's because Jim and I were chronically broke.

But somehow we managed to swallow our embarrassment and get on with the business of living our lives of "quiet desperation." There were still holidays and food and good TV shows to watch together at night and birthdays to celebrate and old picture albums to leaf through. Recollections of Mom, of happier times, funny stories to retell, history remembered. And a nice warm glow after I'd cooked a big dinner and we were all sitting around the dining room table sipping wine or just relaxing on the couch in our oversized living room. We were family, after all.

But all of that began to change drastically after an event both inevitable and long anticipated. That fateful event was, intriguingly enough, none other than the death of my 104-yr-old grandmother.

My father's mother had never been sick a day in her life. Born in Panama, she had met my grandfather in the early 1920s when he was a civil engineer who had been assigned to the Panama Canal project. A smart and ambitious teenager, she had no intention of remaining forever in a mosquito-infested poverty-stricken backwater town. My grandfather, though at least two decades her senior, would become her ticket out. Benilda became a frequent visitor to "The Zone," where all the Americans congregated, and she quickly turned her attention to the serious, reserved guy who didn't say much. That was Arthur, my dad's father. Old black and white photographs that I have seen of my grandmother in her teens show a slender, dark-haired charmer who bore a striking resemblance to the actress Hedy Lamarr. Benilda, having zeroed in on what she wanted, knew how to play her cards. She struck up an acquaintance, nurtured it into a friendship, and let it blossom naturally into something more. Then she waited patiently until Arthur's assignment ended and then, marriage papers in hand, she and he boarded a boat heading north, never to look back.

As soon as she arrived in the U.S. she learned English, went to beauty school, and found a way to open a small hair salon. She soon grew tired of her middle-aged husband and shortly after giving birth to her second child -- my father-- she and my grandfather divorced. Benilda then met an enterprising German immigrant whose ambitions and determination to squeeze every drop of milk and honey out of this promised land of purple mountains and fruited plains matched her own. He married her, opened a butcher shop in Manhattan's Yorkville section, and bought a small house in the country on a couple of acres of land for the two of them. Bold dreams, hard work and thrift paid off handsomely and his shop eventually became a thriving, well-regarded business. When he died he left my grandmother a tidy sum of money.

But Grandma could never get over the way that he died. Werner had always been physically fit, spry, and agile. And his energy didn't slacken as he aged. Well into his seventies, brimming with German industriousness, he spent his free time not relaxing in front of the TV or snoozing in a rocking chair but engaged in outdoor hobbies like raising hens, vegetable gardening, and even, for a time, beekeeping. In the wintertime there were indoor projects, such as building a full gleaming bar in the basement, stocked with the finest Bavarian beers and spirits, where he and Grandma often entertained guests. By age 77 he still had the stamina and vigor of a 40-year-old. He always delighted us as kids with his infectious enthusiasm and playfulness; there did not seem to be a grumpy, slow, or sleepy bone in his body.

All of which only made our shock that much more jolting when we found out what happened to him. One evening he was going down the stairs to the basement, something he had done hundreds of times. Somehow a paint can or tool or something had been carelessly left on the second or third stair from the top. Werner tripped over it and went plunging down the rest of the staircase to the concrete basement floor. He hit the floor head first and cracked his skull wide open. By the time the ambulance pulled up to the hospital emergency room he was already gone.

After that Grandma was never the same again. She lapsed into bitterness and became something of a recluse. Whereas before, she and Werner had liked nothing better than to invite friends over and serve up prodigious helpings of braised brisket and garden-picked vegetables in an atmosphere of laughter and lively conversation at their big dining room table, now she shunned guests, drew the shades, and the house fell silent. She began to drink more. She got rid of the chicken coops and the beehives and let the small frame cottage out back go to ruin after the last tenants moved away. She still arose early each morning and had her glass of fresh squeezed lemon juice in warm water (it cleanses the liver, she always told me). But she became morose and unsocial, seeming to find fault with everyone, particularly her two sons who visited often to help her manage her financial affairs. And then, just a few years later the eldest son - her favorite - suffered a hemorrhagic stroke and died suddenly, at the age of 68.

With such a burden of grief we fully expected that Grandma would shortly follow Uncle to the grave. Instead, we were quite surprised when she made it to the ripe old age of 90, having somehow evaded all the typical ailments of aging in America. Indeed, up until just two years earlier the woman was still driving. That only ended when she had a fender bender one day and the family decided it was time for her to surrender her driver's license.

By the time she reached 95 she began complaining about being alive. "I lived long enough," she would moan, "I'm getting tired, it's time for me to go. Please, God, let me go." And yet even then, the only visible physical infirmity she suffered from was slight loss of hearing. Incredibly enough, she went on to live nearly another ten years, even after a few bad falls in which she had cracked some ribs. And even though she had become so unpleasant to be around that the family rarely visited anymore, once Grandma reached her 100th birthday we just had to throw her a party. She actually managed to be in good spirits for it, enjoying the attention, having a drink or two, grinning for the camera. I still have the snapshots of her smiling and cutting into her birthday cake. By that time my mother was often heard to exclaim, "Believe you me -- she's gonna outlive us all!" She was right on one count. By the time Grandma reached her 102nd birthday Mom was dead and buried.

At length Grandma was no longer steady enough on her feet to be trusted living all alone on that property. Indoors and out, there were just too many opportunities for her to lose her balance and fall. We tried hiring a day nurse or two and then a sleepover home health aide. But it did no good since Grandma was cold and unfriendly to all of them. She simply disliked having strangers in her house and would accuse them of stealing things. Finally there was no choice but to put her in a nursing home. We found a lovely assisted-living facility in upper Westchester County.

But still her body refused to give out. At one point the nursing home called to tell us that Grandma had blacked out and suffered a seizure. We began making funeral plans, but alas, her number wasn't up just yet. Two more years dragged on, with Grandma constantly proclaiming her wish to die. Finally, in desperation, she simply refused to eat. No family members were present when she breathed her last, with the exception of a cousin a few years younger than I -- Grandma's favorite of her seven grandchildren. By this time the news was quite welcome, and we all planned a big bash to send her off in style. At her funeral we were all smiles as heartfelt eulogies were delivered, fond memories recounted, laugh-filled stories told, and copious amounts of food and liquor consumed.

It turned out that much of what Werner had left Grandma had remained in the bank all those years, earning interest. By the time the property, including the house, cottage, and two acres of land were appraised and sold, and the bank accounts liquidated it became apparent that my father, as the lone surviving son, would be coming into a pretty decent piece of change. Certainly nothing extravagant by today's standards, but for someone accustomed to a low maintenance lifestyle, simple creature comforts, and no cravings for luxury or expensive toys, it was a nice little windfall. Yet Dad was already in his eighties; what would he do with the money?

My brother had some ideas. His life by then had become a dreary and withered affair. Twelve-hour overnight shifts six days a week driving a taxi, usually picking up drunks from local bars too wasted to drive themselves home. Returning the taxi to the garage at six in the morning, then heading for an all-night diner or 24-hour *McDonald's* to await the opening of the methadone clinic. And then, after getting his fix for the day, walking all the way home and crashing in his bed, waking up just in time to throw on some clothes and start the cycle all over again. A friend of his, also a recovering heroin addict, had cobbled together enough cash to buy a used pickup truck with which he scoured vacant lots and dump sites for bits of scrap metal to sell. The guy was actually making a halfway decent living at it. Another friend had purchased a van and some equipment and set himself up as an independent contractor, steam cleaning carpets.

Jim became convinced that if only he could afford a vehicle of his own and some start-up capital to invest in inventory and equipment, so that he could set up a business -- even a franchise like *Roto-Rooter*, unclogging drains, whatever -- he could break free of the miserable grind of cruising around hustling for fares every night. He would be doing something positive, something constructive, something that didn't scream "LOSER" to anyone who cared to take notice. His own business, even a very modest one, would give him a reason to wake up in the morning, would go a long way toward helping him gain some measure of self-respect. Now that Dad had come into some money, surely, Jimmy felt, he would be able to help his desperate son.

So a few weeks after Grandma's estate had been settled, Jim approached my father and asked him for "an advance on my inheritance." He requested a sum that would cover the costs of investing in some sort of franchise or independent business, buying a van or a truck, outfitting it with whatever equipment would be required, and the expenses involved in getting the enterprise off the ground and building up a clientele. *Look, you're in your eighties now, I'm going to get this money when you die, so why not just give it to me now when I really need it* -- was the gist of his argument. Dad was sympathetic to the idea at first, thinking that such a project, demanding focus, sustained effort and discipline, might be just the thing to help my brother turn his life around.

But once my sister in California got wind of the idea, she determined to talk my father out of it. Advancing such a large sum of money to a manic-depressive with a history of drug addiction, she pointed out, was an even more rash and foolish idea than buying a house in North Carolina had been. She reminded Dad, correctly, that Jimmy had within a matter of months, blown the substantial pension he had received when he lost his job as a U.S. postal worker fifteen years earlier. That he had not managed to accumulate any savings despite earning an excellent salary for three years working for *Verizon*, while at the same time living in a very cheap illegal basement apartment. She felt certain that Jimmy simply did not possess the self-control, the work ethic, or the organizational skills to be able to successfully launch an independent business. Therefore, the money would be wasted, the inheritance squandered, and he would wind up worse off than he was before.

I stayed above the fray while my brother and sister battled it out with my dad. I knew my sister was right, yet at the same time I thought there must be some way my father could help my brother, some way that wouldn't involve simply handing over a large chunk of cash. It filled me with sadness to see my dad caught in the middle of the feud. My sister ultimately prevailed. My brother excoriated my father for caving in, accused him of betrayal and vowed revenge. That bit of melodrama was but the opening act in an ugly, long-drawn-out chain of events that eventually left me the only one standing.

40
'Tis the Season...Sigh...

IT'S A BLUSTERY day in mid-November and I'm climbing out of a subway station near Wall Street, on my way to a second job interview at the *Century 21* department store. The store, which specialized in discount designer merchandise, was equally popular with tourists and native New Yorkers alike. I applied for a job there because I knew they were hiring dozens of people for the busy holiday season and hoped that a seasonal position might possibly lead to a permanent job in the new year. Since they called me to come in for a second interview, I felt pretty sure I had landed the job.

Oops -- not so fast. That second interview turned out to be more of a quick training exercise. After a cursory once-over demonstration of the cash register and the protocols for ringing up sales, processing returns and the like, we were each given a ten-minute hands-on test. The emphasis was on speed, since the store always drew mobs of ravenous shoppers for the Christmas season. The situation around checkout could get quite chaotic. And getting those paying customers through the long lines as swiftly as possible was crucial. ("cha-ching...*Next*, cha-ching... *Nex*t, cha-ching...) I wasn't fast enough.

Fast forward to Christmas Eve. If I had gotten that job at *Century 21* I'd probably be crashing on my couch right now, after working like a demon all morning and early afternoon. Instead, I've just arrived at St. Ursula's church on Lincoln Avenue. I've come to attend Midnight Mass. It happens to be a beautiful winter night. Snow is falling silently, soft as silk, and a thin carpet of white already blankets the ground. The winds have died down, all the trees are frosted and perfectly still as if posing for a picture and there is nary a car to be seen. It will be the first time I've gone to a Mass in years. I wanted to go to St. Ursula's because that was the same church I used to go to with my grandmother when our family lived in the neighborhood.

I follow a family of five through the red doors of the humble gray stone church. As soon as I gaze upon the statues of St. Peter and St. Paul on either side of the recessed altar and hear the thundering strains of the organ pipes, the images and sensations come rushing back: me singing out loud as the sacred hymns play, the aromas of incense and burning candle wax, the red velvet curtain of the confessional that I timidly part as I enter to recite my sins of the week.

There is a lively hum in the room. The long benches are packed with people, many holding prayer books -- both the regular churchgoers and those who only attended church on Easter and Christmas Eve. There are potted poinsettia plants all around, their crimson leaves adding a blast of vibrant color that makes the whole place come alive. There's a real Douglas fir Christmas tree in one corner and a beautiful Nativity scene made of carved wooden figurines in another. People are smiling, whispering to each other, waiting for the special Mass which will feature lots of music and a choir. The atmosphere is warm, glowing, festive, with an air of happy, hopeful anticipation. It seemed the perfect place to be on such a night. I took my seat and tried to take it all in.

But now I'm all alone again, sighing to myself as I pour more of the creamy yellow concoction into a 12-ounce plastic party cup. I am sitting at my dining room table, trying to get half a buzz from the do-it-yourself eggnog I just mixed up in the blender. I used heavy cream, raw eggs, brown sugar, and half a bottle of that *Bacardi Dark Rum* I picked up a few days ago. Maybe I was supposed to use brandy -- I'm not sure. I've thrown in a smattering of cinnamon and nutmeg. I take another sip -- ah yeah, the stuff does have a pretty nice kick to it. As I drink, I begin to ponder. What's to look forward to in the coming new year?

Filing for bankruptcy, possibly. I managed to max out two credit cards and now owe thousands of dollars despite having sworn it would never happen again. After being denied that federal job in Vermont a few years ago due to my poor credit history, I really tried to get my credit back in shape and adhere to a strict budget. I did okay for a few years until just recently, when Dad finally got fed up with digging his car out of snowbanks and ducking the flying shrapnel of my brother's frequent manic outbursts. He at long last accepted my sister's invitation to move to California to be closer to her and her family.

Dad has been living there now for almost a year and a half. He is okay I suppose, even though he is but a shadow of his former self. When my sister took his driver's license away it was the beginning of a long slow decline. For a man who had driven his own car virtually every single day for the past 70 years, the shock of suddenly losing that freedom and independence was profoundly jarring. He slipped into a blue funk and began to exhibit signs of senility. But at least he had gotten himself away from blizzards, bone-chilling cold, and my toxic brother.

I had not been so lucky. At first, I had actually thought I might move to California with my father, so that I could be of help to him and he wouldn't feel so alone in whatever humble dwelling my sister managed to find for him. My father had never lived alone in his life. He had gone from his cozy childhood home to his father's house after his parents divorced, to army barracks, to my mother's family's home when he got married. But I didn't really want to live in Los Angeles again (my sister was now living in one of the coastal beach towns, a far cry from downtown LA, but the vibes were still the same). I wasn't quite ready to uproot myself all over again, not at this stage of my life. But what to do? Lacking other feasible options, I wound up taking a two-bedroom apartment around the corner from my old junior high school with my brother. I did this even though I knew Jimmy could not always be counted on to pay his share of the expenses. And sure enough, six months after we settled into the new place he got himself into a serious car accident while driving his cab, shattered his hip and pelvis, and was not able to work for almost a year.

I myself have not been able to find any kind of decent job although I have meticulously filled out dozens and dozens of applications over the past two years. Even low wage retail and call center jobs, once so easy to come by, seem in short supply. And age becomes a factor when I have to compete against folks in their twenties and thirties for the few positions that are available.

I glance over at the twinkling lights on the miniature Christmas tree I picked up at the *Value Drugs* store and sigh again. Okay, yeah -- I probably could have sprung for a full-size, even if artificial, tree. But I just didn't feel the "spirit" this season. I have propped the mini-tree up on a windowsill (that's how small it is) and it seems to add a nice touch to the dining room, along with those pine-scented candles I picked up the same day I bought the rum. I suddenly notice the clock on the wall. It's already six minutes past 3 am. I quaff another cup full of eggnog -- it's actually pretty good if I do say so myself -- and wonder how I've managed to arrive intact into the second decade of the 21st century.

Just then I hear keys in the door lock and Jimmy walks in. He's a bit early. He usually works till 5am, drives the cab back to the garage and walks the two miles home. I ask him if he had a good night. He says some Irish drunk he picked up at a bar near Woodlawn gave him a hundred-dollar tip for Christmas and so he decided to call it a night. I offer him some eggnog; he declines and heads for his bedroom down the hall. Poor Jim. He looks exhausted and I feel sorry for him, seeing what his life has finally come to -- living with his middle-aged spinster sister and driving drunks home to make a buck. He still walks with a slight limp, despite having gotten a full hip replacement three months ago. I let a sigh escape wondering if things will ever improve for him.

Later today -- Christmas Day -- we will have to decide how to celebrate. My brother and I won't be exchanging gifts this year but if he gets out of bed at a reasonable hour, I suppose we could pretend to be Jewish and go down to Chinatown. The one place in the city where all the stores, restaurants, barber shops, banks, and dry cleaners are open and crawling with hordes of happy tourists and folks with no family gatherings to go to. We'll walk along the narrow winding streets past dead ducks, heads still attached, hanging from racks in butcher shops, specialty medicinal stores where every kind of ginseng and Chinese herb can be found, massage and acupuncture parlors, Buddhist temples, teeming fish markets with varieties you've never seen before, gift shops full of jade trinkets, rice paper paintings, lanterns, teapots, swords and sabers, hanging scrolls, and a dozen different kinds of Buddha statuettes made of wood, stone, ceramic or bronze. When we tire of sightseeing and window shopping, we'll choose from among an array of inviting eateries where a savory meal, complete with tea and fortune cookie, can be had for under $15.00.

Sure -- it will be a pleasant distraction from my brooding thoughts and fears for the future. After will come the long, lonely stretches of time waiting for the next distraction. I finish off the eggnog, get up from the table, lift the empty pitcher from the seat of the blender and put it in the kitchen sink. I'll wash it out tomorrow morning. I pull the plug on the little Christmas tree and the twinkling lights go out. Sigh.

41
It's a Family Affair

One of the Last "Poems" My Brother Ever Wrote:

St Mary's Germe

A bright red dotted FROG whose lips have been hermetically sealed and drained with every ounce of ingratitude...... dipped his TEETH in body carbon liquid to ram street against the game.................DESI CLAIBORNE.................. let him sit on a fork.........brings brides along the sahara......shakin~ snakes around the fire listening for lovers who cast spells of darkness on wide toed geese and flutters with the swans......Not so much to take food away from the mom..........but to loosen the fabric of a society once drenched in the bile of its own reward stenched in sin and laced with shame this godly creature raises its ugly head thus declaring war on the SAINT and I for one break bread in a foreign gia and rake the blackened into piles of unspoken dust..........to feed upon the rare and nest against the blossom of SAINT MARY

MENTAL ILLNESS IS said to run in families. Depression is officially classified as a mental illness. But if you compare me to my brother, I unquestionably appear the sane and normal one. The two of us were very close as children, not only in age (he was two years younger) but in disposition. We had similar tastes in toys, television, humor, music, and pop culture. I resemble my brother physically, more than I do my sister. And we were both on the same page in our reactions to our parents, finding both of them hopelessly clueless about who we were and what drove our passions, motivated our actions, made our hearts sing.

But Jimmy's mental, behavioral, and nervous "issues" were far more acute and visible than mine, and they started very early. Before the age of two his extreme restlessness and anxiety led him to do things like climb up on furniture, play with his toys so roughly that he broke them, and constantly lose his balance and fall. One time he was jumping up and down on my parents' bed so hard and so wildly that he flew into the nearby dresser, banging his head smack against the sharp corner and suffering a severe concussion. He lost consciousness and had to be rushed to the hospital; Mom and Dad were frantic thinking they might lose him.

Another time when he was about eight or nine a bunch of kids on the block were all gathered at a neighbor's house. It was a hot summer Sunday and Mr. Tedeski -- my best friend Michael's father -- had just set up his gigantic new metal frame swimming pool in the backyard. All of us kids were in our bathing suits, waiting in the kitchen by the back door, until Michael's Dad shouted out: "Okay -- everybody in the pool!!" One by one we dashed out the back door and jumped into the water. When it was Jimmy's turn he was in such a mad rush he failed to push aside the storm door before exiting. Instead, he jumped right through the clear plate glass! Our fun day at the pool turned surreal as Michael's parents screamed and rushed toward the bloody little boy writhing on the ground in a pile of broken glass. An ambulance was called as we all looked on in horror and disbelief. Thank God his cuts turned out to be superficial.

Before he was out of grade school Jim had been diagnosed as hyperactive and put on whatever medication was in vogue in the early 1960s. By the time he was in high school, truancy was a constant problem, as were fainting spells (possibly the result of bad reactions to the meds). He fell in with kids from the wrong side of the tracks, including kids who were doing drugs or had been in reform school. Before long he began to romanticize the "outlaw" life and actively seek out the bad boys. He was good-looking with his dark locks, broad shoulders, and little mustache. He looked great in tight blue jeans and was a magnet for teenage girls.

At 17 Jimmy became a bit full of himself. He got an earring in his left ear and a pint-sized tattoo on his upper right shoulder. He wore these really cool t-shirts and wrapped bandannas around his head. He rented an alto saxophone and started taking lessons. He was good at drawing and covered his bedroom walls with sketches and cartoons. He was thoroughly girl crazy. He became obsessed with the idea of traveling the world to meet all kinds of women. At 19 he made his first trip abroad -- to Central America. It was just one of many such trips he would take.

Jim was a smart kid, yet he almost became a high school dropout. When he was on the verge of failing algebra his teacher gave him an impossible ultimatum. Take the final exam in two weeks and get a perfect score. That was the only way his grades would average out to passing. Otherwise, he would fail the required course and would not be allowed to graduate with the rest of his classmates. So he asked me for a quick algebra tutorial. I worked with him every night for the next two weeks. Jimmy took the final and scored 100 percent.

My brother wanted to do so many things. Be a musician. Be a filmmaker. Be an illustrator or graphic designer. Maybe open some kind of small business, like a pizza shop. One time he and his best friend bought a Kodak 8mm movie camera. They wrote up an entire script for a murder mystery, enlisted some friends to play the various roles, and actually filmed most of it. But his energies were scattered all over the place. His attention span was about ten minutes, no matter what the subject. Projects got started, but never got finished.

He had already begun experimenting with drugs by the age of 15 and often stayed out all night. Somehow he always came home in one piece, but my mother was constantly worried all during his teen years. By age 18 he'd already decided he wanted to live on his own. He had landed a job right out of high school as a long-distance telephone operator for AT&T. The job paid well enough so that he could afford the rent on a modest apartment in the Fordham section of the Bronx.

A year or two later he showed up at our door with a sweet young gal from Guatemala whom he introduced to us as his "wife." This turned out to be the beginning of an obsession with foreign-born "exotic" women. He made most of his contacts through his job. As a long-distance operator he frequently had to touch base with phone operators overseas in order to place the calls. Virtually all of the overseas operators were young women. Jim would strike up conversations with the girls, they would eagerly respond. Soon phone numbers and addresses were being exchanged, invitations to visit were extended, and another name would be added to Jim's little black book. This sort of extracurricular activity made the job fun and exciting, but soon became enough of a distraction that he received warnings from his supervisor to keep it in check, or else. The warnings did not deter him. He was on a roll.

And so, within less than two years of starting his good-paying job at AT&T Jimmy got fired. He then took a summer job driving a *Good Humor* truck, delivering fresh ice cream to grateful kids all over lower Westchester County. That was how he met a pretty girl from the Philippines who was working as a domestic for a wealthy family. The two of them had a casual fling which lasted until the fall. It seemed to whet his appetite for more foreign travel. Taking them up on their invitations to visit, he flew down to South America to see a couple of his international phone friends. By the time he returned he was speaking reasonably good conversational Spanish.

But now he needed a real job again. The U.S. Postal Service, which provided a fairly cushy job with decent salary, health benefits, and early retirement, was hiring. My brother took the four-hour civil service exam and scored in the highest percentile, which put him at the top of the waiting list. Within six weeks he was offered a job and a mailman's uniform. Jim loved the idea that he would be on the move all day long and not confined to some desk in an office. He dug the fact that he wouldn't have to dress up in a suit and tie every morning. It was on one of his regular postman routes that he met Jean, the woman who would become his live-in partner and the mother of his two daughters. But drug abuse and the hidden bipolar illness that was just beginning to surface were to wreak havoc on both his relationship and his job. He would lose both within a few years.

Jimmy was well into his late thirties before he received his official diagnosis of bipolar disorder. By then he was a chronic substance abuser, which only complicated matters. Among other things, it made it difficult to determine which of the many medications his doctors treated him with were truly effective in combating his bipolar illness. He was in and out of drug rehab facilities over a span of some fifteen years. He always got clean and stayed that way until some adverse life event caused him to relapse.

There are other things I could tell you about him. He had a marvelous sense of humor. During the times we lived together I would often walk by his room and hear him howling and guffawing at the antics taking place on some popular sitcom, or the jokes of some upstart stand-up guy he had just discovered on a comedy channel. "Vicki, come in here...you gotta see this!" he would shout in between gasps of laughter. He also, like me, had a certain bent for philosophy. We would have long rambling discussions touching on subjects like quantum physics, the world views of Taoism and Buddhism, the big bang theory and evolution, all the arguments offered to prove the existence of God and all the arguments offered to prove there is no God. He got off on that kind of stuff as much as I did.

In his early forties he decided he wanted to earn the baccalaureate degree he had never achieved when he had the chance. So he enrolled in a community college. He majored in Health Administration and hoped to start a new career as a substance abuse counselor. He wrote to me when I was living in Vermont, gleefully describing his courses in American literature and chemistry, telling me how much he loved school. He even made the Dean's List. But the new career never materialized. Nor did any of his other dreams, schemes, or fondest desires. His life was always a work-in-progress. Always sowing seeds but never reaping the harvest.

Jim and I took our own separate, one-of-a-kind journeys into the unchartered wasteland of mental and emotional illness, each with our own unique coping strategies, strengths and weaknesses, resources and skills, phobias and fears, beliefs and delusions. We had our own ways of confronting our demons, our dark sides. Along the way we encountered different obstacles, took different adventures, underwent different experiences. His involved hard drugs and crippling psychological disorder. Mine were absent the drugs and involved a milder, easier-to-tame disorder. His pathway eventually led to a cliff and a steep, precipitous decline. Mine stayed relatively level, less exciting, less dangerous. That's why I'm still here and he isn't.

42
Minus Two

MY BROTHER WAS about 37 before he was properly diagnosed as manic-depressive (the older and more descriptive term for what is now called "bipolar disorder.") That was because Jimmy presented such a confusing array of symptoms. From his earliest childhood he suffered from high-strung nerves, phobias and crying jags, a tendency to lose his balance, extreme restlessness, crippling anxiety, fainting spells. His adolescence was marked by truancy, minor brushes with the law, and the label "hyperactive" being stamped on him by the family doctor, who was quick to supply the appropriate remedial medications. Before the age of 25 Jim had tried just about every street drug, from pot to speed to crack cocaine to ecstasy to quaaludes to heroin, and was forever either in the grip of addiction or undergoing rehab.

By the time he received his bipolar diagnosis it was almost beside the point, because unlike with most patients who can be successfully treated with drugs such as lithium, no one could ever seem to find the right formula for my brother. Some of the meds did nothing for him at all, some would fix the mania but not the depression, others did the opposite. One pill in particular was especially problematic. Jim found a doctor who prescribed a powerful medication called Nardil, a controversial drug which had initially run into some roadblocks with the FDA and had to be reformulated. It worked beautifully, like nothing he had ever tried before, to wash away all traces of depression and quell every quiver of anxiety. But it kicked the mania into overdrive, creating a supremely self-confident state of bulletproof euphoria that transformed my brother from a fretting child cowering beneath blankets afraid to look under the bed, to a brazen swaggering megalomaniac. Needless to say, Jimmy was delighted with the effects, despite the obvious dangers. But after a few disastrous episodes in which friendships were destroyed, jobs lost, girlfriends frightened away, or police called to the scene, he finally took the advice of his doctors and flushed the Nardil pills down the toilet.

But a couple of years ago, in the wake of our mother's death and after having lost the best job he'd ever been lucky enough to get, he slipped into a state of inky black despair, found himself a new shrink, and began taking the stuff again. This time, with the three of us -- myself, my brother, and my dad -- all living under the same roof in a simmering hotbed of tension and resentments, it turned Jimmy into a monster. He began terrorizing my father and me, demanding money, threatening to trash the house if anyone got in his way. He went for days without sleeping, stayed out all night partying or cruising in his cab, barged in and out of the house at all hours. His bedroom, never a model of tidiness, began to resemble a colorful junkyard, a real eyebrow-raising spectacle. A quick peak inside revealed a peculiar assortment of objects juxtaposed together in a crazy collage: open textbooks on eastern philosophy and mathematics, sketch pads with pen and ink drawings of mandalas, serpents, and unfinished self-portraits, empty pints of *Ben & Jerry's* ice cream, shopping bags overflowing with just purchased clothes, tags still attached, a dozen mobile phones, multiple decks of playing cards, wooden chess pieces, tottering stacks of DVDs, reams of lined composition paper covered with writing, much of it gibberish, two brand new flat screen TV's.

With his grip on reality ever loosening, he wrapped a bandanna around his head pirate style, sported hoop earrings, adopted a new name and created a fantasy persona online. He began frequenting music sharing and international dating websites, cultivating virtual relationships with half a dozen women from around the globe. At three or four o'clock in the morning you could hear him on the phone talking a blue streak to someone in a far-off time zone. When my father got the phone bill there would be calls to Bogota, or Jakarta, or Nairobi. When the cable TV bill came there would be a host of mysterious charges for pay-per-view programs and triple X-rated adult films. When Dad confronted Jimmy over these charges he offered denials, excuses, and promises to pay, but never an actual red cent. At length he wore out my father's patience and exhausted every last ounce of sympathy.

After that, profanity-laced outbursts, temper tantrums and loud shouting matches in the wee hours of the morning became routine, creating a rude disturbance on our normally quiet cul-de-sac and alarming the neighbors. Sometimes my sister would call from Los Angeles in the middle of an argument; hearing the screaming in the background she would demand to know what was going on and why I was letting it happen. But I had no power to either force my brother to leave, or to make him get off the devilish medication that was causing all the grief. In desperation I wrote a letter to my brother's psychiatrist, begging him to stop prescribing it. But I knew that even if the doctor agreed it would be only a temporary solution. Jimmy would just find himself a more cooperative shrink.

After several months of on and off chaos I decided that the only remedy was for me and my father to move out. I engaged a real estate agent and began a search for a two-bedroom apartment. But my sister had a better idea. She insisted that Dad move out to California to stay with her and her family. She considered it something approaching criminality to continue to subject our 85-yr-old father to the predations of a severely ill and wayward son. The risk to his health and well-being ought to be obvious. It was a cruel enough twist of fate that Dad had lost his wife of fifty years, and to now force him to spend the final chapter of his life being tormented by a deranged and manipulative child was, well, unforgivable. There was no escaping the essential rightness of her argument, and for me to protest meekly that my father, a lifelong New Yorker, would probably not like living in California, seemed lame and irrelevant.

Caught somewhat off guard by my sister's sudden resolve, I was loath and unprepared to handle another major disruption in our lives. My support for the notion of Dad moving out west was lukewarm at best. I couldn't picture it, and felt that secretly my father almost dreaded the thought of living in southern California. It just seemed wrong. Nevertheless, like it or not, less than a year after Jimmy began his campaign of terror and rabid dog madness my dad was on a jet plane en route to Manhattan Beach, California, the tony little beach town where my sister and her husband lived, just south of Los Angeles. His natural resistance to such a jarring change, his reluctance to so abruptly pull up his roots, simply crumbled in the face of an undeniable truth: for my father to remain in such a poisonous environment was a genuine threat to his health, sanity and peace of mind.

In the end I had no choice but to remain behind with my brother. Relying on a disability check as my chief source of income, I could not afford a place of my own. And I had no real desire to live in LA again. Eventually Jim and I found a smaller apartment in the neighborhood, and I hoped that perhaps being away from our father for a while -- the focus of so much of his rage and resentment -- might give Jimmy a chance to cool off and reassess his situation. He was not able to manipulate me nearly so easily as he had our dad and it soon became clear to him that he could not come to me for money or special favors, that the days of free overseas phone calls and pay-per-views were over, and that I expected him to share in all the expenses of the apartment. It was a pretty sobering reality that I felt certain would knock him off cloud nine.

But I didn't know he would come down with such a crash -- literally, that is. One night in early January, less than six months after Dad had moved to California, I got a phone call. My brother had been in a horrific car accident. Out on his overnight shift, he had been taking three teenagers to an after-hours bar in White Plains, NY, speeding along the Bronx River Parkway, an old winding road full of blind curves and pockmarked pavement. The road's surface was still slick after a light slushy snowfall earlier in the day and my brother and his black Lincoln Town Car careened wildly into the guardrail, did a back flip, and plunged 70 feet into a ravine. Miraculously all survived and none of the teens suffered more than minor cuts and bruises. But Jimmy shattered his hip and pelvic bones and faced a long painful recovery and rehabilitation.

Meanwhile, the news from the West Coast was not much better. My father had begun to suffer from a variety of ailments. He developed a heart arrhythmia and required a special invasive procedure. They also discovered he had an abdominal aneurysm that needed to be closely monitored. For at least a year before he left for California, I had been noticing signs of approaching senility. Dad had become quite forgetful, constantly misplaced things, showed poor judgment while driving, sometimes had difficulty writing, forgetting words. None of it seemed particularly alarming at his age, just a preview of what was to come.

But after less than a year in California, all of these symptoms seemed to accelerate dramatically. My sister had taken him in for a cognitive test and he had failed miserably. The doctors diagnosed him with early dementia.

From there things went downhill rapidly, for both my father and my brother. After six weeks in the hospital, some sort of metal plate contraption was placed into my brother's hip so that he could be discharged pending a possible hip replacement later in the year. He was given a wheelchair, a pair of crutches, and told to take extra care not to exert too much pressure on the hip while moving around. Restless and desperate to get out and about again, Jim disregarded the doctor's advice, threw all caution to the wind, and began attempting to walk, albeit haltingly, without using the crutches. One day, while he was hobbling to the local pizza shop a screw suddenly sprung loose and the plates fell apart, causing him excruciating pain and sending him back to the ER.

Another surgery had to be performed, followed by transfer to a rehab facility. While he was there a fiendish irony played itself out. Since the accident, Jimmy had been off his troublesome bipolar medication, Nardil. Years before he had similarly quit illegal drugs, such as crack cocaine and heroin, and had even managed to wean himself off methadone. Now, with nothing to alter his consciousness except the searing pain of his injuries, he had to be treated with large doses of Vicodin, Percocet, and similar potent narcotic-based painkillers. He had come full circle and was back on the yellow brick road to addiction.

I flew out to California to visit my father and was sad to see the state he was in. My sister had taken his car away, fearing that his judgment and depth perception had become too impaired to trust him trying to navigate LA traffic. For a person who had been driving almost daily since the age of 15 this seemed a cruel deprivation and left Dad feeling helpless. My sister had found him a rather pleasant apartment in an attractive senior living complex surrounded by swaying palm trees and a soccer field. The place was just a five-minute drive from her home. There were several group activities available for the residents -- Sunday brunches, movies, card games and bingo in a big recreation lounge, hired entertainment, scenic bus trips. Dad could even sit out on the balcony and watch a soccer game or read a newspaper. It seemed like an ideal situation.

But my father felt disoriented and out of place in his new setting. He simply was not used to “old folks’ home” activities. On the weekends my sister would pick him up and bring him to her house where he spent many fun afternoons playing ball with his grandsons or strolling along the picturesque promenade down by the beach, sitting on the pier and gazing out at the blue Pacific. But during the week he scarcely knew what to do with himself.

On a later visit a few months later I found Dad even further deteriorated. He could no longer write out a check properly, not being able to recall what went where. He would sometimes put a quart of milk back into the microwave rather than the refrigerator. He had trouble trying to put on a pullover sweater, and sometimes forgot how to use his cell phone. He would put a tea kettle on the stove to heat water for coffee but forget to put the water in it first. He forgot how to get his keys into the lock to open his apartment door and would be left stranded in the hallway. He would call my sister in a panic, and she would have to rush over there to unlock his door.

Meanwhile, after nearly eight months of being laid up, Jimmy was finally scheduled for his hip replacement. All of his hospital bills were being covered by Medicaid; in the meanwhile, I was maintaining our apartment all by myself, with some financial assistance from my dad and sister. A social worker in the nursing rehab center met with my brother and walked him through the process of applying for temporary disability. When he was finally discharged from the facility and came home, artificial hip in place, he was able to walk again, but with a noticeable limp. The picture he presented was a far cry from the bragging nonstop-talking narcissist, pockets full of cash and women’s phone numbers, who the year before had commanded center stage. Now he was a pathetic creature, a man in his late fifties without a dime in his pocket and with a new drug habit.

A few miserable weeks of stewing in his room convinced Jimmy he needed to get back to work driving a cab. Amazingly, even after the dreadful car accident, the little Pakistani-owned taxi company where he had worked was willing to hire him back. He got his doctor to write him a prescription for an opioid antagonist designed to help him get off the painkillers. He also got a fresh prescription for Nardil, but promised me emphatically that he would take a much lower dose -- just enough to ward off the blues but not enough to get him roaring like a jet engine.

He resumed his presence on social media, reconnecting with some of the women he had been corresponding with before the auto accident. He got more involved with a fellow cabdriver who ran a lucrative side business selling weed. The guy got the stuff from a cousin in California, where medical marijuana had been legalized. Before long I would pass by Jim's room and see him at his desk carefully measuring out a gram or two of bud on a small silver scale and stuffing it into a little glassine bag. As long as he paid his share of the rent and expenses, I decided to leave him be.

The news from California regarding our father began to get grimmer. His symptoms had grown worse. He couldn't sleep, had taken to walking around the hallways at all hours of the night, was no longer steady on his feet and had experienced several falls. He had let the toilet overflow in the apartment and had left gas jets burning on the stove. Jimmy, who had been so wrapped up in himself that he had paid scant attention to what was going on with Dad, was genuinely shocked when I told him Dad had been diagnosed with dementia and that the illness was progressing rapidly. "I knew he should NEVER have gone to California!" my brother shouted in anguish. Overcome with guilt and the realization that it was his own behavior that had driven our father to the other side of the country, Jim made up his mind to go out there and spend some time with him, trying to make whatever amends he could.

My brother spent three weeks with my dad and was horrified at what he saw. A man who had been there for him all of his life, always ready to lend a sympathetic ear, take his side in family arguments, bail him out of trouble, forgive and forget, was now barely recognizable. Jimmy came back in a state of near hysteria, blaming my sister for everything. After that last visit, my father declined rapidly. When he began walking into mirrors, or into other tenant's apartments, the management of the complex told my sister that they could no longer accommodate someone who needed to be in a nursing home. So she had to put him into an assisted living facility. When he became agitated and began to act out with the staff, they put him on powerful anti-psychotic drugs which wreaked havoc on his system.

Along with his heart and blood pressure medications my father was now taking Alzheimer's drugs, anti-anxiety meds, antidepressants, and who knew what else. A witch's brew of chemicals which created the illusion of effective treatment but was in reality a smokescreen to hide the fact that they did not have a clue how to help him. He began to have seizures, no doubt brought on by the meds, resulting in an anti-seizure medication being added to his daily cocktail. When I called him on the phone he could no longer speak in coherent sentences, often lapsing into senseless babble, although he did manage to get out the words: *I think they're trying to kill me.*

I felt helpless and just wished it would all be over. And soon enough it was. While I was contemplating a trip to LA to see my father for the last time, my sister told me he had been moved to a hospital because he was having trouble swallowing. If I was going to fly out there I had better do it that week. But two days later, after I had all but booked my flight, the phone rang early in the morning. Dad had suffered one last major seizure, accompanied by a loud shout. By the time the nurse ran in to see what had happened, he had no pulse. He had made his final exit, three days shy of his 89th birthday. When my brother heard the news he was completely devastated. From the vantage point of the warped prism through which he viewed the world, it had all happened shockingly fast and so unexpectedly. But that was only because he hadn't been paying attention. It had in fact been two and a half years since our dad moved to California.

Jimmy responded to the emotional jolt the only way he knew how, by self-medicating. He purchased a fancy, very expensive weed "vaping" device that looked like a big balloon, and began inhaling marijuana mist every night. He also stepped up his dosage of Nardil, breaking the promise he had made to me earlier. But even that wasn't enough. He had become close cyber friends with some young woman in West Africa, a woman he had met through a popular music sharing website.

The two of us flew out to California for our father's cremation and funeral. About six months later my brother and I received the proceeds of two life insurance policies our dad had carried. Jimmy promptly announced that he was going to Senegal to meet his new friend. I warned him that it was more than likely he'd gotten himself entrapped in an all-too-common internet scam. Such fraudulent schemes had become rampant on dating sites all over the web. Several men find an attractive young woman whose pictures they post online, hoping to lure some middle-aged American loser with a taste for the exotic. A down on his luck schlub desperately seeking a chance to leave his baggage behind and reinvent himself in some romantic foreign locale. In most cases, all of the correspondence from the gal to her American friend is actually penned by the scamsters -- the woman herself, usually uneducated and from some backwater village, does not even speak English. Once the hapless American is hooked, every manner of deception is employed to gradually relieve him of his cash. I had read articles about the victims of such scams and showed them to my brother.

But he would have none of it. Ever since he had been introduced to the magical African cure whose praises he had sung in his book -- *Ibogaine* -- he had dreamed of going to Africa, which he called "the original Eden." And so he took thousands of dollars of cold cash he had been socking away, cash he had earned from dealing high-grade weed and driving a cab 12 hours a day, six days a week. He combined that with the proceeds from the insurance policies and booked a flight to Dakar, Senegal. He planned a three-week stay and was clearly in the stratosphere again, his Nardil having catapulted him into an extended manic episode. His African trip was preceded by a week of sleepless nights marked by feverish activity: nonstop ranting about his plans, frantic shopping for gifts and clothes, greedy inhaling of pungent clouds of cannabis vapor, furious scribbling in notebooks, frenzied packing. Since there was no stopping him, all I could do was stand in awe in the driveway as he placed his big red suitcase in the trunk of the limo that would whisk him to JFK airport, and wish him good luck.

It was the last time I ever saw him. What followed were five insane months of crazed phone calls and bizarre emails. Apparently, the part of town he had landed in was something of an unofficial open-air drug emporium -- his new "friends," well aware of his predilections, were all too happy to give him the grand tour. His first phone calls to me were about how fantastic the hashish was and how incredible the high when you mixed it up with codeine. His first emails bragged about the beauty of the beaches, how hip and laid-back the people were, his joy upon meeting in person the lovely woman he'd only known online and how delighted she was to have met such a cool American. And even though she couldn't speak a word of English, she sounded oh-so-charming speaking French.

After that came calls and emails telling me how his friends had shown him some "business opportunities," how for a small amount of capital one could open a modest storefront on the beach. All kinds of money could be made, he assured me, by hawking handcrafted, hand-carved native souvenirs -- wooden animals, baskets, beads, colorful cloth, and the like -- to affluent European tourists willing to shell out big bucks for an authentic taste of the dark continent.

But after Jimmy had been gone about six weeks -- three weeks longer than originally planned -- the emails and phone calls began to take on a hysterical tone. There was no talk of coming home, despite his having already doubled his intended stay. Instead, he gave me his secret P.I.N. number and directed me to use a credit card he'd left in his drawer at home to take out cash advances and then wire the money to him by *Western Union*. Evidently all of that cold cash he arrived with had already been sucked down the drain, squandered on drugs, his new girlfriend, and business "investments." After he maxed out all his credit cards he would call me demanding I lend him more money via Western Union. When I refused he went ballistic.

Sometimes one of his "friends" would call, tell me in broken English that Jimmy had been taken ill and desperately needed cash to buy medicine. By now his emails to me had turned into hallucinogenic ravings about who really built the Great Pyramids, parallel universes, "Zeno's Paradox," the power of the number "9", and how sublime it was to lie on the roof and look up at the stars while passing around the hash pipe. "This is Paradise!" he exclaimed. "Please come here, Vick -- you've got to see this to believe it." A few days after receiving such a euphoric email I would get an angry phone call cursing me out and demanding to know why I hadn't wired any money.

A month passed like this, then another. My brother did not seem to be staying in any particular place, but was moving all around. I could not contact him on his cell phone -- he had either lost it or else his account had been suspended. He would call me from public places using a phone card which only allowed him a couple of minutes of talk time. Invariably the phone would cut out before I got any substantial information from him. His emails became increasingly incoherent and whacked out. He told me he was sleeping on the beach at night. That he and his girlfriend had been tossed out of a number of resorts or hotel rooms for lack of payment, for breaking things, or for otherwise causing a scene. I soon came to realize that Jimmy was becoming psychotic -- a genuine danger for a bipolar sufferer who not only abuses his medications but combines them with powerful recreational drugs.

One day I got a phone call from the American Embassy in Dakar telling me that Jim had come to the embassy dressed in rags, appearing ill and completely destitute. He had begged them to telephone me and plead for money. I immediately wired cash and informed the embassy official that I wanted it to be used only to buy a return plane ticket and that my brother was to come home at once. I hung up the phone shocked, worried, trying to figure out how I should respond, or what on earth I would say to Jimmy when I saw him, in what I felt sure would be a matter of hours, a day or two at the most. But Jimmy never arrived and to this day I do not know whatever became of that money.

Several weeks later, after a number of unsuccessful attempts to get in touch with my brother via phone or email, I got another call from the U.S. Embassy. Jim had been rushed to the hospital with a severe case of malaria. Of course, my brother had been reckless and irresponsible enough not to have bothered taking any precautions or anti-malarial drugs before embarking on his trip. Still, I had always assumed that malaria was quite treatable if the patient was brought to the hospital promptly and the proper medicines administered. But as I was sadly to learn, this is not the case if the malaria is of the most extreme form -- the kind that attacks the brain. When that happens the patient slips into a coma and his prognosis is bleak no matter how aggressive the treatment.

Jimmy had contracted the most severe form of the disease, after having had a brush with the milder version, I learned. He was no stranger to that hospital. Within one year of that early morning phone call from my sister informing me of Dad's deadly last seizure, I got another call from the U.S. embassy official in Dakar, Senegal. In somber tones, he offered his heartfelt condolences on the untimely passing of my brother. A death certificate would be issued shortly, he informed me, as soon as I made arrangements to pay my brother's outstanding hospital bills.

And so there it was. These two men whom I had grown up with, known and loved my entire life, fought with, played with, screamed at, spent dozens of merry Christmases, Thanksgiving dinners, Fourth of July barbecues with, and who in many ways knew me better than anyone else did, had been ripped away. The two men I had lived with and kept house for long after I should have been happily settled in my own home with my own family -- these two men were now gone. Within the space of a year both of them had been crudely, clumsily torn out of my life picture. Replaced by jagged holes. And so now it was just me. I alone constituted all the "family" I had left -- at least on this side of the country. A family of one.

43
Totally Unedited

Selected Excerpts from My Brother's Never Finished, Never Published Book

One of the things I recalled during my first ibogaine trip was a particular incident when I stole a classmate's money but I also remembered how the whole thing turned out and felt somewhat redeemed. Something that would become a common theme in my very uncommon life. I could see little Joeys face in tears, but O yes, how compassionate I was that, when I heard the crying and saw the panic take over his face, through the tiny square window in our little orange school bus, and how he was appealing to his grandpa for solace and comfort over losing his bank book, I slid the glass open and yelled out "Hey I found it!" and felt a genuine sense of relief, that I had ended his painful ordeal and with a self-satisfied gaze watched as his short dumpy grandpa with outstretched hand protruding from his tired old looking (he wore it every day no matter what) dirt-black rain coat, impatiently waddle toward the school bus window like a wounded penguin, his chubby unsteady paw snatching the little manila envelope from my gently awaiting 7-year old hand, and in broken English he muttered "Teefe!" while his squinty little eyes full of contempt stayed on me long enough to be satisfied that I was well aware of the fact that I had NOT fooled him for a minute with that "hey I found it bull shit". But it really felt good because although his grandpa may have been right about my being a thief I also took pride in knowing that I had a heart a big heart and although I knew that the 37cents was all mine, I just couldn't bear to see the poor kid crying like that. Besides he was my next door neighbor and that should at least count for something.

Throggs Neck was an almost 100% Italian American section of the North East Bronx where the houses were an attached style one Extra Wide house that really was two houses in one which of course was done for economic reasons seemed kind of tacky for people who never seen anything like that before. We lived in the LEFT half of the house and Joey's family (the nice kid who's bank book I stole) lived in the RIGHT. I remember when I would walk down the block in the late afternoons and about 3 houses down from mine it seemed that she would always be standing there. A retarded girl about 13 years old who was shaped like a big stuffed animal perhaps a bear a bear wearing thick black rimmed glasses and short black hair over a round olive skinned face. She would stand there right in the middle of the porch so still and she would say in a low haunting yet innocent voice........"meet ya at midnight" in exactly the same way every time I passed her house in the afternoon and usually with my sister. That is the only thing I EVER heard her say. And other than her saying that I have absolutely no other memories of her at all. Nor do I have any other memories of BIG LOUIE a kid who probably was only in his early teens but stocky build like a football player who would love to see the terror on my face and watch me panic and run for my life, in what I now believe was actually in more of a sadistic and not a playful, way, every time he would come baring down at me with wide open arms and say in the bogyman's voice "I'm goanna Throw you up in the SKY! Yes he was amusing himself at my expense with no concern at all that he was actually scaring the all mighty fuckin crap outta me but I didn't realize it then of course. I wonder if my DAD knew it because a few times he was with me when the kid did it. Perhaps he didn't realize since he was so young but it just seems kind of sadistic. Of course I did the same thing with my sisters cat once who was part of a pair she had in Mt Vernon when I was about the same age early in my teens I would chase him around the house making him run like a wild chicken without a head all around the house and later on when people came to visit there was always one cat that would hide and it was Buffy, the other was Bootsie who acted quite normal. And once when I thought about it I really felt guilty because it may have been ME that gave him his fear of people which of course would make some Karmic sense since I have had this nervous condition that I blame for ruining my entire life in which case I would transfer the blame to myself for my sadistic act with the cat.........but what about all those rotten boys who do all those depraved things like put them in the microwave or tie their tales together and throw them over a telephone wire like a pair of sneakers? No I wasn't that evil or was it that I just couldn't deal with all that phsychical pain because of my weak stomach? And I preferred a more cowardly method of torture? Yeah but I loved animals I mean I was playing with the cat and got a kick out of the Fear he had of me and I was only a kid right? Oh who knows, but questions like this would swim around in my mind for the rest of my life. I don't know if that in and of itself is any kind of indication of my decent nature or just an active guilty conscience.

There is a Saying among those who advocate the use of Ibogaine for the psychological treatment of the drug addicted by allowing the addict to go back into his memory and relive some of his childhood issues and possibly gain some insight into where the pain or the need to medicate comes from... And also what Eric told me when I asked him why I never saw certain things during my trip that were so much a part of my past, "Ibogaine doesn't give you what you want it gives you what you NEED!

There was that time in the 2nd grade when the teacher just got through showing the class FIRE BALLS that she confiscated from some other student and how she better not ever see us with anything like this again. And the way she was standing there at her front desk with that serious look on her face the look that she used to put us 7 year olds in our place. And with her stern voice and keen eye she made sure that she had the attention of the entire class and when satisfied that she had, she simply separated her fingers letting the plastic bag full of the multi colored balls that looked like GUM BALLS fall into the desk draw and with the same hand slammed it shut and then paused for effect just long enough to let the BANG echo a SERIOUS WARNING to anyone who might even be THINKING about thinking of bringing that kind of nonsense with them to school. And how as soon as the opportunity presented itself, and the cost was clear, I snuck back in the room and SWIPED them from the draw. And when we went back into the room that day and she noticed it missing, she asked who took it, and I just sat there without saying a word until the kid behind me, (don't recall what his name was, but he was one of those "outspoken" types) stuck his hand into the open bottom of my little wooden desk and slid it back out causing the gum balls to come careening down like too many hail stones that one by one echoed the same sentiment to the entire class......Jim's a thief -jimmy's a thief- jimmy's a thief until that last one finally hit the wall and rolled back just an inch or so, leaving with it the lingering condemnation of my chosen craft.........THIEF and what kind of a boy chooses such a craft except a ROTTEN one like Jimmy the thief, and on and on. But what about the fact that I loved ANIMALS and even if the owner of the biggest dog would say HEY he bites when I would reach out a hand to pet it, I would just smile and say "He won't bite me" as I rubbed the top of the boxer/shepherd mix's head and KNEW he wouldn't bite me and of course he never did. Or that I loved to talk to strangers because I had a very big heart that had room for everybody. No I didn't see that kind of a little boy. Instead I saw a mischievous little wayward trouble maker. . .

But my mom always wanted to go to Florida so one day when I was nine she pulled me out of SCHOOL and we moved to Hollywood Fl. We had taken many trips there in the past for vacation so that my mom can check the place out and we usually would stay in some hotel along the beach in Miami or Ft Lauderdale and I remember how me and my older sister would walk along the beach and I would look into the hotels and how I remember how much I loved it even then when they would be playing some Cuban music and people would be dancing and drinking it just seemed so cool to be along the OCEAN with the sandy beaches and the music and hotel balconies it was the greatest.

But of course the worst thing about Florida was getting used to the Palmetto bugs they were these big ugly flying cockroaches that would end up everywhere you would least expect. When I went to put on my sneaker i found one crawling inside and it just grossed me out. When I grabbed the toothpaste one morning one started down my arm it was awful i couldn't stand it they made me palpitate with paralyzing fear! They were so repulsive looking like creatures from HELL that would just POP out of nowhere to creep me out with their presence the way they would give you that paradoxical frozen black yet white hot laser beam stare with their eyes that weren't really eyes and the way their antenna that seemed to exist on their own and as if it kept on growing out from the oval shaped decay colored insect shell. The way they would move with a certain predatory diligence filling the room with a sinister cloud of taunting terror that would linger so hideously as if it were about to become frozen in time the way it would just stand there so still with dark menacing deliberateness that cut through you with an immaculate sharp evil, leaving no room to doubt its finality not unlike the sound of a head falling into a basket that has just been severed by a guillotine. That is exactly what they did they creeped me out and made me palpitate they were the inverted embodiment of all the romance and beauty and tropical sensuality that Florida had to offer they were its creepy crawling antithesis as ugly and grotesque and unnerving as the sensuality of the tropics was seductive. Or I guess in a way the necessary flip side, but It was certainly worth it. That was probably the only thing that I really remember hating about Florida although now that I think about it Florida is really just a tacky place mostly created by real estate developers devoid of all the history, character and soul you find in New York City but when it comes to Key West or Miami Beach there is that Caribbean feeling that is unlike anything else in America.

There were other things that I remember about Florida like the fact that I blacked out for the first time when we got paddled by the 6 foot four teacher Mr. Watts for throwing a crumbled up piece of paper on the bus with Rusty a real Tom Sawyer Huck Finn looking Bad kid who started crying and rubbing his HINEY like he had just sat on hot coals or something. But not me no I was darting around nervously exclaiming "I can't see!" "I CANT SEE!" as I began to black out and the next thing I knew they were picking me up from the floor...

I fainted for the first time; that was significant and it really should have been looked into why I reacted so abnormally. I mean since they have this paddle in the office and they obviously have used it before. They had no better excuse but that I must have a cold tells me that this hasn't ever happened before which means that I must be wired a bit differently than your average kid. But what is it that makes me Black Out when others cry? What is it that made me say I can't see I can't see when others just screamed in pain like normal bad boys getting a whopping from big daddy? No not me I simply blacked out, all the time thinking I was going BLIND! As if my body was simply reacting without any thoughts of my own. Like my nervous system just shut down.

Well whatever that nervous condition WAS or IS I don't know but I do know it EXISTS and there is some reason why I would get these dizzy spells all the time in class. My teacher said it was because i didn't eat breakfast but i think it went a bit deeper than that. I had the A D D and the over anxiousness all the time, meaning I was over-excited and over-egar. In fact it got so bad that once I fainted when I was rehearsing for a school play from the top bleacher on stage and was instantaneously knocked out when my head hit the floor the next thing I knew after things started to go BLACK was my MOTHERS FACE watching as my eyes opened just in time for her to see that I was OK as the paramedics were pushing the stretcher into the ambulance. It was just a continuation of my nervous condition that was manifest as hyperactivity or ADD but later in life turned into ANXIETY when I lost my childlike wonder that keeps all children in a constant state of LOVE of course anxiety is all about THINKING and it is all FEAR based, and there is nothing that sits further opposite love than fear...

I spent two weeks in MT VERNON hospital. I remember the kid in the bed next to me would lie flat on his stomach and would just shake his head inside his folded arms back and forth and back and forth in an attempt to ROCK HIMSELF to SLEEP and i thought HEY I'm not the only one. It was all part of my OVER ANXIOUS hyper active nervous condition I would lay flat and rock my head just like this little black kid in the bed next to me and I felt a little more normal for a few seconds. The guy 2 beds down had blown off his finger while messing around with some chemicals trying to make a bomb later turned out to be a friend of my future best friend's brother Cliffy who I sort of admired.

The next friend I began to hang out with was some BIG FAT italian kid named Paul who ended up making me one of his little PUNKS in that even though I didn't see it coming a few months down the road we were trading lunches My mom was Italian like his mom but instead of making the meatball sandwiches for him like my mom did. She would make him these boring cheese and mustard sandwiches because she didn't want him to gain any more WEIGHT i guess. But what I never could seem to understand is whenever I would eat over his house, she would INSIST that I have a second bowl of spaghetti and sausages and I recall looking for ways to hide the food without her knowing it like spitting it into a napkin and emptying the contents into the GARBAGE while she wasn't looking. All because I was too much of a punk to just say NO I'm not hungry, which I did say but it wasn't that she thought I was just being bashful I actually think she wanted to fatten me up not because she wanted my mother to have a fat son too. But she just piled the food on the plate despite protest because FOOD was somehow one of the most important things a growing boy could have, and FOOD was LOVE and family meant FOOD and Mange Mange Mange . I remember how it was nearly torture to eat over their house when I had to stuff myself that way but I just don't know why I wasn't able to refuse and why I would endure such physical pain. But whatever that weakness was, it was the same PUNKness that allowed myself to be bullied by her son. What a pussy! Not only was I letting her son trade delicious meatball sandwiches with me for boring ass American cheese and yellow mustard (not even the BROWN SPICY KIND) but here I was letting his MOTHER bully me into eating an entire overflowing plate of spaghetti and sausage that I didn't even WANT.

And it didn't end there it progressed to trading bikes. I just got a cool new motorcycle bar BANANA SEAT bike for my 12th Birthday and here I was trading it for a 3 or 5 year old out of style piece of crap. TRADING BIKES how could I have let myself be bullied like that. But for some reason I had gotten myself in too deep in the role of being his bullied punk friend. I remember when things got so bad that the next summer I was so afraid of Paul that I not only fantasized killing him in the stupidest of ways like hidden on an apt building roof top and Throwing a boulder at him when he walked by Or poising him somehow...

It was probably close to my 13th birthday and I was at a graduation for a cousin who was graduating junior high or something I'm not even sure but I wanted to get fireworks and knowing that the ladie's pocketbooks would be upstairs in the master bed room I waited until I saw somebody go into the bathroom and then I asked my mom where the bathroom was while squirming around a bit for effect as if I really HAD to go bad! And knowing she would point to the bathroom down the hall I went over by the door and tried to open it knowing it would be locked since I saw a GIRL just go in. So I shouted out AHHHHHH there is someone in there and knowing this would be the invitation to the upstairs that I needed and sure enough she said "Go upstairs" and that was when I went right into the Master BR and there were about half a dozen Pocket books of which i pilfered a grand total of $7.00 *well by today's standards adjusting for inflation let's say that seven bucks in 1968 was like $50 today.*

Well talk about KARMA now that I had enough money to get at least a half of a brick of fire crackers from China Town........Brick is 40 packs of fire crackers a pack has about 20 fire crackers so a half a brick would be about 400 fire crackers something like that and it cost about 4 bucks which comes to a penny a fire cracker if I am right about the amount in a brick and a pack which i think i probably am or at least close. So the very next day I get on the Sub way and head down to Canal St. China Town, looking for somebody anybody who may know somebody anybody. And I was standing in front of some store on canal somewhere when a guy came over he was probably in his late teens wearing a sleeveless denim vest and he stood next to me and just began coming his hair as he said very discreetly hey you need fireworks....and I couldn't believe it but I never did this before and he was reading my mind ....I said yeah and he asked how much and I said well how much is a brick he said 7 so being I had a little less since I needed car fair to get there I said what about half and he said 4 so I said OK and he said OK give me the money He came back with the half a brick as promised. So I proceeded to St. Marks place where I bought some HOT PINK day glow paint the kind of paint that glows in ultra violet light very popular during the 60s and the peter max era. and I also got a copy of the paper the RAT which I just bought to look at the pictures since I was just a punk kid with ADD I wasn't intellectual enough to actually READ this stuff like my sister or my Jewish friend IVAN so here I am in china town and I decided to cross over to little Italy and there I was walking down either Mulberry St. or some side street when 3 kids approached one said "hey Mike" or NICK or some other name and the other threw his jacket over my head and they pretty much demanded i give them all my money which I did all 20 cents and they went through my pockets and found the day glow paint and the WISE GUY of the 3 the short one said " you got the wrong color" after opening it and smelling it, then he began to slowly and carefully thrust the pink liquid from the plastic jar all over my jacket and all I could think of was these MORONS aren't even going to check to see what I have in the bag because there is a NEWS PAPER folded in my arm where I was carrying the bag and of course anything with print just turned these idiots off so as he emptied that last drop I made the saddest face I was able to muster in order to satisfy and they obviously were cause they left me holding the bag! full with a half a brick of firecrackers and seeing their stupidity nearly made the whole ordeal worth it............ Next thing I did was walk over to a local police station with the same half brick of firecrackers concealed in the bag and ask for 20 cents to get home telling them i needed to get home and had no money I have no idea of what they thought about all the hot pink paint all over my jacket.

Bobby was the first and only person who I have ever called a Best Friend and the only person with whom I felt a genuine kinship. He had this kind of practical cool rhythm of intelligence that you just couldn't help admire and feel that he somehow possessed a superior wisdom. Like me he had a love for music and art and shared a deep appreciation for creative genius. We made a few Armature Films together with Super 8 Kodak film and Reel to Reel tape recorder. I really idolized Bobs older by 1 and ½ years, brother Cliffy! I just thought he was the coolest guy i ever met. He was this kind of RANDY QUAID looking Character who would speak a very unique language all his own and would express himself in ways that had such off handed kind of rhythm that would cause me to burst out with uncontrollable laughter. He would use his own words like, BROWN for NICE or COOL or anything GOOD and when every other teenage youth would get someone's attention with expressions like HEY YO!!!!!!!! He would Holler ................SAAAYYYYYYYYYY have you got the TIME? With the sense of timing that would have everyone laughing in agreement that his CHOICE of expression so unexpected somehow perfectly FIT and made any other expression seem quite lame in comparison

Cliffy was 16 and a heroin addict at a time when heroin was HEROIN the late 60s. He had a bunch of Junkie friends that would come in and out of the BIN and I always found them to be a unique array of some very cool characters Mostly Italian guys who had that old time junkie swagger and a few of them would Dress like old school gangsters with the SHARK SKIN PANTS the ALIGATOR shoes, alpaca sweaters and sometimes DARK SHADES like jazz musicians giving them a sort of a cool inner city look that I always kind of admired, the way young impressionable, don't know any better curious teen age boys with developing egos usually do. I thought they epitomized cool and wanted secretly to emulate them. And the fact that they would stick needles into their veins injecting some powder that they would cook up inside a wine bottle cap seemed kind of heavy and commanded my respect. At that time I was much too young and naïve to appreciate their anxiety and pain. I recall one day when me and bob were down in the Bin which was a make shift little club house we had set up out of an unused laundry room in the basement of the apt building where bobs dad was the superintendent. Joe Algerie was getting OFF and me and Margaret , Bobs cute little long wavy brown hair big brown eyed girl friend were watching him trying to hit the vein he must have noticed the awe and wonder on our faces and thought it appropriate to say "IM SICK, you don't want to be like me IM REALLY SICK,,,,,,,and with that I just thought YEAH man this guy is REALLY COOL while looking at how his shiny black hair which complemented his handsome face was neatly combed back but allowed just enough of a piece left to hang in style over the right side rim of his dark glasses and I really dug the way he would accent every few words with a simultaneous sniffle and a quick unnecessary adjustment of his shades with his index finger and thumb his nose, almost as if to check if it was still there. Me and Margaret just sat and stared as he twirled the syringe between his thumb and index finger until the blood from his vein at last spurted up into the barrel while his entire body simultaneously seemed to sigh with relief at the realization that he finally was HOME FREE and the heroin was now on its merry way to his brain where it would change the chemical rhythm of his entire central nervous system rendering him in a state of a much needed much anticipated BLISS that would slowly turn into its opposite over the next 12 to 24 hours depending on how lucky he was going to be that DAY starting the cycle all over again.........but I DIDN'T realize all this NOT YET! I was 13 bob was 14 and his brother Cliffy was 16

One thing I must mention is that I was DEATHLY afraid of experimenting with LSD 25 since I heard too many HORROR STORIES first there was Eugene's brother Nick who STABBED HIMSELF and died from the wound when having a bad trip. Then there was the friend of cliffy whose body was found on the grounds of my junior HS dead of a GUN SHOT wound to the Armpit. But they never said for SURE if he was on ACID. Anyway I just heard all of these horror stories that would just scare me. Besides the fact that it was formulated in some LAB really turned me off to it as well. I doubt if my Fragile EGO could have handled LSD. To not freak out when the ILLUSION of the EGO dies you either must be a VERY cool person Which is why I think Cliffy always considered ACID a very mellow HEAD and this was coming from someone who actually INJECTED it , But you have to be the type of person who is not too self-obsessed or self-absorbed or even self-centered in anyway but if you identify too much with your ego , which most people in western culture DO then you must be very well defended which means you really have to have many defenses built up so that your EGO is not easily shattered. Of course that means that either you don't freak out on ACID because you are THICK or you don't because you are TOO COOL .

Mount Vernon had a lot of interesting characters it was actually a small town only 4 sq miles and it seemed that it drew out the different kinds of odd characters you would find in the weirdest of plays. But i have always believed in the old adage that truth was stranger than fiction and if one looks one will find something that is more freakish and amazing and fascinating than anything that anyone can Create out of the infinite imagination no matter how genius. so I will say NON FICTION is Stranger than and a lot more wonderful than fiction no matter who the author no one can touch "god" not even Shakespeare or Joyce, not Michel Angelo or Da Vinci can rival Nature. Some of the characters that I have met have been so much more fascinating than any I've read about and Mt. Vernon really did have its share.

There was one guy in particular that comes to mind but he was somewhat of a CREEPY TYPE and I must say that he was a predator type that used to follow pretty little boys around and try to get their attention in order to engage them in conversation and whilst doing that he would suddenly develop an intense allergic type of itch that usually attacks that inside corner of the eye that sits right by the bridge of the nose that is really hard to satisfy and calls for a small PINKY to get right at the heart of the ITCH which of course was the perfect way to sneak a peek at whose ever crotch happened to catch his eye at the time. He had a small round bald head and beaty little innocent baby blue eyes a funny mole like nose that was too big for his face and he stood only about 5ft 4 or so and he had this kind of high pitched ratty little voice and spoke with a nervous sense of urgency with an underlying rodent squeal, and must have resembled a SQURILL because that was his name on the street SQURILL the first man I ever thought of KILLING.

One summer while deciding to make some money I and BOB had an idea to sell Ice cream for Colonial maid Ice cream company in Mt. Vernon a company where a couple of Greek Brothers owned a fleet of trucks that they would rent out and let you buy the ice cream whole sale and take the truck out to sell on a specific route. Well we got Scarsdale and for some reason this was NOT a very good route it's a rich little village where most of these kids go AWAY for the summer they don't hang out in the street waiting for the ICE CREAM MAN to come like they do in the Bronx The first thing I noticed was the red white and blue hot pants. She was standing on the lawn in front of a typical Scarsdale House weaning the American flag hot pants stars stripes red white and blue that accentuated her healthy thighs. The sight of this young pretty Asian girl enticed me to call her over and ask for her phone number which I did after she bought her ice cream. Anyway her name was JOSI and she seemed to like me and gave me her number and that was it. Before long it became a routine for me to visit her during her dog walking break every night at 8-10pm she would walk the family German Sheppard and that is how we would see each other. I drove there and waited in my 69 Plymouth Valiant and waited until I saw her figure thorough the distance of a dark tree lined street walking the dog and the dog went in the back seat and we spent the next couple of hours in the front doing whatever guys do with girls in parked cars. Josi was the first girl I had sex with and it was on New Year's Eve when it happened but it wasn't midnight or even close I think it probably was more like 10 o clock. Well the funny thing is by this time we were sexually comfortable with one another so it was as if I had been doing it all along I wasn't nervous at all and I don't even recall being especially excited about it. But it still WAS my first time and i still had sex with a woman who I actually believed i loved. If the very idea that this person is your partner gives you a blissful feeling of security if the mere sight of them in your mind's eye makes you feel transported to a place where space and time cease to exist, if after making love you feel like you could lie there for ever and ever, if just knowing they will always be there, gives you an ebullient rush of pure joy accompanied with an all-encompassing feeling of inner warmth, serenity, and excitement, then that is all you need and it is good enough to call love. That is how I felt about Josi Yet our entire relationship consisted of a yearlong 2 hour per night meeting in a 69 Plymouth Valliant......

The best job in the world and my DREAM JOB was...a sky cap......curb side baggage guy at a MAJOR airport........raking in about 20% more than the average weekly salary for a minimum wage earner in one DAY, CASH, tax free!!!!!!!! That's right ...in Those days I guess the average tip was about .50 cents per bag and it was quite Easy for someone to get about 15 -20 tips in an hour which would mean that you can get up to 10 an hour or 80 bucks a day cash...

Now wouldn't that scenario be IDEAL for my SELF IMAGE....or my EGO IDEAL.........yeah ....the international playboy who landed this great sky cap position for "PAN AM" out of JFK or even better yet ----- Yes, of course,,,,,,, MIAMI international Yes, THAT would be divine! I've always loved that place, Miami Beach.........~`````Palm trees sensually align the streets. Through which a vividly radiant azure sky burst in a panoramic procession over my field of vision. I watch in awe, my entire spirit moved.; dancing to a soothing yet enthralling rhythm beating and growing stronger by the intoxicating sent of the Atlantic and its' aquamarine glory seen in every crashing wave, like the eyes of an intense Brazilian folk singer who is gracefully accepting the loss of her lover as she clings to a haze not unlike the color of sunglasses some choose to wear or to acquire through a daily dosage of shots of something either in 1/½ oz. giblets or 1/½ cc in blue tip or diabetic otc syringe....and before you know a thing you can feel the warmth of its seductive embrace while the debris of dead skin begin to shed and scatter like flakes of forbidden snow on a dark lonely street. Dissolving into the wet ground leaving no trace, as if it never was. How it was so shamefully pushed ahead in cowardly haste and greed, the kind that hides behind both, ignorance and fear and lives comfortably in uncertainty and apathy. As another wave washes away while a new one is being formed in the eternal dance of creation/destruction so pure and simple draw out the chapters of my life.

The ocean which is the overwhelming majority of the planet..... UNDERWATER there exists a world that is so beautiful; a world without a sun. A world without a human being a world that memorizes all of human kind. Most of the planet belongs to the ocean. The overwhelming majority of the earth is the SEA and the world under water and beneath land. Seagulls gracefully gliding throughout the air, hovering just above the excitement of the crowds of tourists and natives below. Among them, the many, beautiful women, who stand half naked on terraces of swanky pastel colored high rise luxury condos and five star hotels, overlooking the sunbathers, many of whom are just other half naked women laying out on blankets, tan bodies smooth and shiny wet with oils and lotions glistening in the blinding sun while waves crash upon the shore in a never ending verse. The sun, sky, women, birds, skin, oil, sand, laughter, and the final crash of the wave coming to shore. Birds flying over like the steady hum of something ignored but always being noticed like the silence one hears when an ongoing but forgotten sound finally ceases. Sort of like a HOLE marking a piece of matter. Just being what they are over and over again. Just dancing to the same beat. Nothing changes and life goes on being and doing what it does and is. This is why it really DOES matter to me when I love a place the way I loved Miami Beach.

What to say about the boy who is so insecure and immature that he is actually delighted by the news that he won't be allowed to attend his own graduation ceremonies, due to his unsatisfactory conduct during the academic year. Delighted, because he is too much of a wimp NOT to be embarrassed about putting on a cap and gown. Too much of a punk that he is actually worried that it will make him look somewhat "uncool". Well! Can you imagine what kind of insecurity this boy must have, to be afraid to wear exactly the same outfit that the entire student body will be wearing that day? A picture of the ceremony in which he will be but a pixel a speck of color, a stone among the mosaic that is not seen as an individual but is a vital factor in the creation of the ultimate product the collective whole. Yet his self-absorption and hyper-self-consciousness have given him the deluded notion that HE is the one who will be noticed for being uncool. As if only HE is too cool for this outfit. When the truth of the matter is that it is he who is so uncool that he cannot afford to take off his mask and be stripped down to his bare self. Because it is this "real" unaltered, untouched, unadjusted, unmodified, self that he is so ashamed of. Is it any wonder that a boy like this turned out to be such a lonely loser? Why, of course not!

I met her over the phone at work, she was from COLUMBIA, and her name was Maria, Simple enough right? Perhaps a little too simple. I made a date with her, to see her in person. Having no picture of her or her of me. I booked a RT. ticket to Lawrence Mass. Here I was on the bus I went into the bath room with a bottle of soda or something I got out of my carry-on bag, and I took out the Quaalude........why are there two 'a's -- it just makes it so much cooler. Methaqualone a Sedative/Hypnotic that comes up like an alcoholic buzz without any of the fullness or heaviness in head or stomach. Like a clean alcoholic high. I loved it! I felt so warm and inviting and receptive and sociable I wanted to talk to everyone and love everyone. Wow a Quaalude a RORER 714 which = 21 exactly how many minutes it takes to come up on you. Have a glass of white wine with it and you are off to the clouds. ... It was something that would take that horrible edge off without making me drowsy or dopey or depressed. This is something that I almost NEVER feel at all. Usually there is some edge some kind of grindiness that lingers in the pit of my stomach and middle of my throat and goes on and off but is always there waiting to be ignited by something or someone. That was my DEMON my awful secret boogie man that plagued my entire life. Over anxiousness that first began as over excitement and eagerness than very slowly like changing the pebbles on a billboard size mosaic one pebble at a time, morphed itself into ANXIETY, At best I was just hyper; at worst I was a sick kid with a serious nervous condition that caused me to black out and made me different from the rest.

So there I was in the bus station in Lawrence or wherever feeling high as a kite from the synergistic effects of the second can of malt liquor mixing with the Quaalude and I called Maria's number. A woman answered, so I asked, "may I please speak to Maria" holding my breath while anxiously anticipating a thick heavy Spanish accent saying "Ahlo?". So when I heard an American voice say "she isn't home" instead, I said "WHAT DO YOU MEAN THIS is JIMMY—I AM SUPPOSed to meet HER TODAY! WHERE IS SHE?? "She went out with friends".....WHAT!!!!!!.......DOSENT SHE KNOW--.....................(deep breath) again Deep BrEATH)....... SHe (another breath) ahhhhh......I told her I was coming to see her today, and I came all the way from NY because she told me to come and......"Well, she didn't mention anything......who are you?" "Jimmy" I met her over the phone......I am an overseas operator and I met her over the phone and she told me that she wanted to meet me in person so I said OK and told her I would come out this week end.....Didn't she tell you!.....Who is THIS anyway? "I am the woman she lives with and she didn't tell me ANYthing about you or any JIMMY coming to meet her........" "WHAT!!!!!!!!!......She told me to come she KNEW I was commig. I came all the way out by BUS! All the way from NEW YORK and Now you're TELLING ME she ISNT FUCKINHOME what the FUCK kind of SHIT IS THAT!!!!!! ??????? "Hey WATCH your language guy! ">>>>>Sorry but I am really MAD I came all the way from......"Well that is why you shouldn't meet people on the phone" >>>>>>>WHAT!!!!!! What do you MEAN! Are you blaming ME FOR THIS!!!!!! She SAID SHE WOULD BE THERE!!!!! It cost me MONEY and TIME and NOW HERE I AM........" "OK Calm Down, I will call her friend and get in touch with them so she can come out to meet you, where exactly are you!"....."I am in a phone booth right in front of the BUS STATION on the Corner of Avery and South Broadway"........"OK I will tell her to go out there." In what seemed like no time at all a Car pulls up and slows down and I see a girls face, Indian looking straight coarse jet black hair high cheek bones dark tan skin and an expression on her face as she leered over in my direction, like one who is watching an old bag lady taking a shit in public. And I felt so disgusted at the rejecting look but before I could speak I heard the girl in the driver's side say are you JIMMY? I said YEAH! Who are YOU and why are you ALL HERE I just wanted to see MARIA.........and she said WELL she is right there, can you see her? I said "HEY LOOK; I didn't come all the way from New YORK just to get a tiny little peek at Maria through some MOTHERFUCKIN CAR WINDOW!" and they drove away!......

Still high I began to hitch hike, trying to get to the main city of Boston..........I finally got a ride Two young adults picked me up. Two nice intelligent college type people who were more than happy to listen to my story of how I got stood up by some Columbian girl I never even met , except for over the phone while on the job as an overseas operator for AT&T....and how I felt the whole thing was so unfair. Usually I am not this talkative but the Quaalude was doing its thing and the alcohol gave it a huge boost! They seemed to be genuinely enjoying my whole rant. I got off in Boston and checked into an inexpensive hotel. Alone I looked around at this dive of a room very modestly appointed with an apple colored Greenish /Reddish bed spread and matching draperies and cheap looking pine furniture with a portable TV with rabbit ear antennas and an ugly looking black rotary dial phone, and started to cry, while writing a long letter to Maria saying how that evening I had realized that I was in LOVE..........

The fact that the memory ceases when a part of the brain is cut out no more proves that the source of consciousness exists in, or is created by, the human brain, any more than the music stopping after cutting a piece of an MP3 player out proves that the MP3 player created the music or that the music is STORED there. Point is, just like an MP3 player, or more precisely an FM receiver, all it does is act as a TRANSMITTER for the Radio Waves, as a brain acts as a transmitter for that which it is connected to ever since the big bang. Think about it, this so-called "singularity" which is actually a "thing" is said to be responsible for the creation of EVERYthing, with the convenient exception of itself. Now where have I heard this logic before, albeit in a lot more meaningful context. The point IS no physicist on earth can give an answer to this question of, how can some THING be said to create time/ space continuum when, in order to exist as a THING implies the existence of the time/space continuum...........

Marijuana is a lot more enjoyable once you come to terms with your unflattering characteristics, those characteristics that you fear if seen in another would be a complete turn off. But one of the coolest things and a great step in the right direction toward growth and acceptance is the ability to face what a creep you really are...

But sometimes I like to think in numbers! Numbers seem to be amazing things because, so much can be figured out with mathematics. In fact some of the Jewish people I know have said that the TORA can be reduced to a mathematical formula. Physicists often talk about the beauty of equations and the underlying story they tell. The concept of infinity and what can be seen in higher mathematics such as fractals and topology etc. really begin to get quite mysterious. When thinking about such things as Pi or Phi, (the golden ratio) it seems quite spiritual, as any mathematical genius from INDIA such as the famous Rhamanaajan will say! I have always had a fascination for numbers. Perhaps I should have tried to study higher math when I was younger, and realized that numbers came very easy to me.

Alas....it was as if I was an undiscovered flaw in an exquisitely beautiful equation that brought us the Indonesian sunset, and the great Alaskan Alps. Ironically, the most fantastic work of art the shocking incredible beauty of a coral reef and intensely rich, echoing color bouncing off the most graceful creatures dancing about blissfully encircled by a school of blood thirsty hammer head sharks. Their overwhelmingly beautiful world hidden deep beneath a terrain inhabited by an incredibly unique species endowed with the capability of dominating all the other species due to a much larger and more complex brain and the only species who had among many other things, the concept of religion, in which the entire species were considered "born sinners" or inherently "evil"....

I'm at the Dairy Queen in Guatemala City. I notice 4 young girls sharing one soda, among them, sitting a breast at a booth diagonally across and about 3 rows up from me, I took a sip of my Pepsi when I heard one of them say......"don't stare at him"........Man I felt like Scott Baio or some teen heart throb, and I got to admit it felt better than great. It was what I lived for. To be wanted by teenage girls. That they would stage something like this, just made me feel so good. So fine! Yet I knew my secret UGLINESS! Something that everyone has, or perhaps, nearly everyone. Secret ugliness is that which you know is a really ugly feature that you try to hide as best you can. Something so bad that if someone were to mention it, it would really hurt!

But I also remember a black sand beach from the Volcano or something. Yes Lake Atitlan and there was Lake Amatitlan as well but the "most beautiful in the world" was Atitlan! Yes and there were volcanoes in the background so I guess the sand was black, which is a really beautiful sight. The sand was actually a charcoal grey which if you think about it, is really a cool color for sand. Purple Turquoise iridescent looking water with Volcanoes as the back drop, would attract the peace loving hippies who wanted to live off the land like the native Indians who make hand crafts and sold them to tourists. I am sure the Native Guatemalan Indians made a lot more money, and rightly so. I mean who were these privileged Americans from their rich Brentwood California homes where their dad was a big time bank executive and their mom stayed home drinking vodka martinis and shopping for bargains on Rodeo Drive. While their daughters were tripping on acid and screwing members of the Black Panthers. Oh how dare they come here to trample upon the livelihoods of these hard working people who were direct decendents of others like them who fell victim to the white man's pillage and bad hygiene who infected them with small pox while trying to find the passage to India and steering miles and miles off course calling these people INDIANS by mistake. .

Now here I was in this paradise dubbed Land of Eternal Spring because of the low humidity and comfortable temperature which almost always stayed at exactly 75 degrees Fahrenheit and it would rain for exactly ONE HOUR at the same time every day. You can set your watch by it. 10am and 7pm.....like clockwork......and it wasn't the piss down annoying gray on and off drizzle of NYC, but rather a POURING SUN SHOWER for which one takes refuge for an hour and then greets the fresh newly cleansed streets of Guatemala City awaken with the smell of fresh rain, there is nothing more purely cleansing and invigorating for the soul..........and off to the romantic pursuit of che che la fem.......I was in heaven!!!!!!!!!!

The stars SHINE they are gods eyes and each star is unique WE ARE THE STARS. And since all knowledge, and everything that has ever happened is part of the same reservoir of info which is inseparable from and connected to each individual, we know everything there is to know, without being consciously aware of it. All the answers lie, in this ocean into which we can tap and therefore all we really need to do is believe it. In other words, we need to assume its power in order for it to work. Well the more I began to think about this new concept of GOD the more sense it began to make, since I have always rejected the Judeo-Christian idea of God, ever since I was in the single digits and instead of worshiping God the father, I always had a thing for Nature the Mother. I was a pantheist without knowing what a pantheist meant...

No No I mean WHO is the BODY that EATS the FISH and the Chicken and the PIG and eats the FRUIT off the tree and MAKES MONEY AND MATTERIAL THINGS and has LAWS and POLITICS and ISSUES and MORALITY and ART and Suffering and DEATH and LONELYNESS and HORRY and BUEATY and CONEICET and ANGER and LAZYNESS and GLUTOONY and LUST and GREED ....WHO then is he......................

he is a PROUD LAZY GREEDY LUSTFUL JEALOUS ANGRY GLUTTON yes HE is the HUMAN THINKING who doesn't know he is actually a HUMAN ***BEING****....... because of this he loses out. a computer is all on/off the world blinks on/off the computer refreshes itself by blinking on /off the sound you hear is on/off the world is on/off devil/god life/death male/female black/white in/out ....the world is just the blink of gods eye which is you*

44
The Unraveling

This is What Psychosis Looks Like

MY BROTHER JIMMY spent the last five months of his life in Senegal, West Africa. During that span of time, he sent me a slew of emails as his mind gradually splintered, cracked, and finally fell apart. Here are a dozen of the last batch of emails I ever received from him, exactly the way he wrote them (except for the various different colors, fonts, and sizes that he used which, practically speaking, cannot be reproduced here.) I do not believe he would object to my sharing them, not if he thought that perhaps some needed light could be shed on the nature of his illness, or that someone else might be helped by reading them.

"Wow it is so beautiful here I lost my bank card in the taxi and want to rent a beautiful 3 bedroom two bath house across from this beautiful Saly/Portudal Beach it is furnished with HDTV AC everything modern so I need to get this house before it goes off the ?arket. It is only $200 per month!!!!!!!!! U need to go to either a western union or a moneygram ASAP Get one thousand and send it"

"sorry but i am in heaven the love is purely emotional ALSO I WAS IN WITHDRAWAL AND A MAN HEALED ME RIGHT AFTER I TOOK CODIENE LIKE 30 SECONDS HE MUST A KICKED IN THE codiene or some wierd shit this is HEAVEN...NY is hell Bottom line pleasesend the other thousand dollars at the exact same place"

"Would love to hear your thoughts on my trip the beautiful sunset ocean sand roads like biblical toimes muslim chants so spiritual brilliant bursting flaming flowerq of every hue pastel colars goats heards of cattel with giant horns pigs sheep dogs cats lizards roaming..."

"Prices are great bargin taxi ride 40 cents coffee is 50cents per cup restaurant food an omlet costs 40 cents Coke 12 ounces is 50 cents. Aida loves me toooooo much

I think I really am JC and Aida is Mary. Baby Ugo will B jesus i will have nseveral businesses. Guess i was not delusional."

"Imagine having the roof top all to yourself all day long while in the beautiful sun the air the breeze an ocean view of sunset every night a serenety un parrelleled you reach a higher level where you lose fear in your own private parralell universe where you are in control But god sits behind you steering you along but you can lean toward your fancy as you fall into theblack hole of love you fall into the future creating the past moving like a lazer of black light creating your future as you fall and fly like a bird of paradise"

"I MADE IT OUT ALIVE NOW I RULE COME JOIN THE NEVER EVER RVA EVA ENDING GAME CALLED U R IT God has no other choice but to B born out of death The d e v i l created the black hole that bore god...devil created womb of god black hole created by a white needle..."

"Create ad infinitum not the mathamatical infinity it is quantitative a cirle that goes back to where it was born but the spirtiul infin that keepz onnnnn keeeeepppin on on on God izzzzz what happens when a hole is punched in nothingness Adam izzzzz atom Eve is soul 122222222222222 a universe every one goes into a parrallel universe where they didn't die"

"i have not take"en codeien in 33 days i am happy with aida loce i will jave a son a business write a book please vist me you will find paradise here"

"VICKI THIS PLACE HAS FRESH AIR GREAT FOOD FRESH FRUIT VEGATABLES VERY LITTLE RED MEAT OR PORK BUT YES MY GOAL IS TO MAKE A MILLION WITHOUT INVESTING DADS GIFT TO ME"

"vicki u r sick u have chosen hate u idiot scared sick weirdo rot in hell u old spinster bitch"

"THIS IS THE WAY YOU PLAY DARTS..........YOU PUT A HAMMER IN THE PUNGENT HAND AND SMACK THE GIRID OF THE SNOUT BELLIED IA ND MAR CREATURE WHO WHITH PERTURDED EYS SEES WHAT ONLY HE NEEDS O SEE IN ORDER TO SURVIETHE ENERY AND THOUGH WASTED IS SO FASCINATING BECAUSE IT IS ALMOST 90% OF ALL THEIR CREATIVE RESOURSES!"

"thank u –ch i still got a thing for opiates they as zello as thc help as genious T MC KENNA SAID —DISOLCVE boundries and get u out of body ze are putre conscious god s brain is the matter"

45
Soul Searching Across the Pond

AT FIRST I just sat there staring, content to watch the others solemnly rising out of their seats and walking towards the front. But then I thought, oh what the hell, and joined the little procession advancing towards the Anglican priest. Maybe if I took the communion wafer and had a sip of wine from the golden chalice it would fortify me for the big climb to come. Minutes earlier I had been wandering around the magnificent light-filled space under the dome, admiring the statues of Admiral Lord Nelson and the Duke of Wellington, as well as the spectacle of one of the largest pipe organs in the world -- boasting over seven thousand amber-colored pipes -- when I was suddenly startled to hear what sounded like a Eucharist service beginning. Were they about to start a Mass, even though it was early afternoon on a weekday and there must have been at least a hundred tourists prowling through the nave of St. Paul's Cathedral? Intrigued, I had walked over to where the assembled folding chairs were and took a seat.

After receiving communion, I began my ascent to the first of three levels: the circular *Whispering Gallery*, where the peculiarities of construction were such that a whisper into the wall on one side immediately bounced to the opposite side, losing nothing in volume. It would take all of 257 steps up a winding staircase to get there, so I took a deep breath and then began climbing, slowly and steadily. As soon as I got there I needed a rest, so I sat down for a few minutes watching while kids and their parents tested out the acoustic tricks. Then I walked the entire circumference of the gallery twice and sat down again to take in the amazing space, gazing up at the ceiling where vivid frescoes depicting the lives of the saints and prophets adorned the surface, and then peering down below at the striking compass design on the floor whose vectors point towards all corners of the earth. There were two more galleries to go before reaching the top.

Round and round and round I plodded up the narrowest of twisting staircases, trying to ward off vertigo, stopping occasionally just to catch my breath and reorient myself. Finally I reached the passageway that led outside to the *Stone Gallery*, an outdoor balcony that circled the entirety of the dome. The winds were whipping and my open jacket flapped like a flag as I jockeyed my way around the balcony, brushing against other tourists staking out positions and lifting up their smartphones and cameras to capture the stunning views. The blast of air was refreshing and I noticed that most of the morning's clouds had dispersed and the sky was now a sea of pastel blue. But there was still one more gallery to reach, the *Golden Gallery*.

Looking out all around me, I thought perhaps I had come far enough. The city spread out before me in an expansive panorama of buildings and monuments and moving vehicles, human forms darting about in every direction, gray rolling river to one side. It was a 360-degree picture postcard view that alone was worth at least half the price of admission to the historic cathedral. At length I went back inside and looked wistfully at a small door marked: "Way Up," with a bold diagonal arrow pointing the way. I had read in the guidebook that this final stairway was so narrow that only a single person (of normal weight) could manage to squeeze through, that there were over 150 steps to climb up, that it was dark and poorly ventilated, and that, because other tourists would be following behind somewhere, once you entered upon it there was absolutely no turning back. I imagined myself freaking out midway through and having a full-blown panic attack and so decided to pass on it. But as I stood there and observed tourist after tourist enter the forbidding door, including folks who looked to be well over sixty, I couldn't tear myself away. "If *they* could do it," I kept repeating to myself, "then so can I," and resolved to stand there until I could gather up the nerve to join the others, no matter how long it took.

Less than twenty minutes later I stood astride the rails of the *Golden Gallery*, on top of the dome of St. Paul's Cathedral, looking out over London from one of its most famous landmarks. It was my first time in the great city. I took a selfie.

Jean and I are sitting in her cozy low-ceiling living room in a housing complex in South West London, holding mugs of hot tea, facing a wall on which are arrayed family photos in attractive frames, and against which leans a tiny table with a velvet tablecloth on which are perched another group of smaller family pictures. The curtains are drawn and it's early in the evening. Jean has got at least four candles lit and the air has a mild cedar wood scent mingled with eucalyptus and sage. She really appreciates candles, which is a good thing to know the next time I have occasion to bring her a gift. We are, at the moment, talking about my brother.

Jean is, more or less, my sister-in-law. She was my brother's common-law wife. They never came close to actually marrying -- when they met, my brother was still legally married to a young lady from Central America whom he had met on a pleasure trip and married in order to get her to America, borrowing a page from his grandfather's playbook. But Jimmy and Jean did live together in an apartment in Brooklyn for several years and she gave birth to two daughters while there. Unfortunately, I had never gotten to know her very well during those years. I had met her only a handful of times, very briefly, usually when she and Jim happened to stop by my parent's house while I was also visiting.

Jean was originally from British Guyana. One of eleven children, she was smart, ambitious, and determined to succeed. After completing her education, she took a job working with an international organization affiliated with the United Nations. Something to do with recruiting companies to invest in projects in developing countries like her own. A gentleman connected with one of those companies had gotten to know her well, was quite impressed, and offered to sponsor her to come work in America. She found a good job in New York, became a U.S. citizen, lived with the man's family for a while upstate, and eventually took a studio apartment in Brooklyn. She met my brother when he was a postal worker who regularly appeared in the lobby of her building with a heavy sack of mail that took him fifteen minutes to stuff into those pint-sized metal letter boxes. Maybe she thought he was cute or maybe she had a thing for well-built guys in uniforms, but somehow they started dating and were soon a couple.

At first they seemed an odd couple to me. Jean -- mature, businesslike, very responsible -- did not at all seem like Jimmy's "type," nor could I figure out what she saw in him. But I now believe that she was uniquely able to discern something tender and precious within him, to penetrate through layers of bad boy bravado and feigned hipness to detect the core of fear and vulnerability that lay deep inside my brother. It must have both touched her deeply and stimulated her fiercely protective instincts. She probably flattered his vanity by pursuing him, and he must have sensed that she knew and understood who he was, and so allowed himself to be drawn into the emotional safe haven she seemed to be offering. She was the first woman my brother had gone so far as to actually move in with, and for a time it seemed like he might be "settling down" at last, especially after their first child was born.

But when Jimmy's drug abuse and bipolar issues began to spiral out of control and he even wound up getting arrested a few times, Jean began to worry about the effect it would have on her young daughters. Jim would often arrive home disheveled and stoned out of his mind, demanding money to buy drugs or ranting and raving on a manic high. At one point he was on the verge of losing his job at the U.S. Postal Service unless he agreed to enter a drug rehab program, but he resisted and rebuffed all efforts to help. Her patience exhausted at last, Jean decided she could no longer afford to expose her children to such scenes, or expect them to accept such a man as their father. So she ran off to England, where several family members from the former British colony had already settled. After she moved to the UK, I never saw or spoke to her except for the occasional times when she would travel to the States, kids in tow, to visit friends and family. On such rare visits, she would normally call on my parents, who had developed an extraordinary fondness for the polite, well-behaved young girls with their charming British accents.

About a year before Jimmy left for that fateful last trip to West Africa, Jean had traveled to New York and met him for dinner in the city. I remember my brother telling me that the meeting had gone surprisingly well. The two of them had remained friends over the years without any bitterness, and Jimmy had even made several trips to England to see her and the kids. However, in the weeks immediately following the death of our father, which hit him very hard, Jim had attempted to contact her, probably thinking he could use another vacation, an extended period away from home to regather himself and his frayed emotions. But this time Jean was unresponsive, perhaps going through some emotional turmoil of her own. Jimmy complained bitterly for weeks of her lack of response to his emails and phone calls.

Shortly afterwards my brother appeared to be speeding down a steep hill with no brakes. He began hanging out with a coworker -- a fellow cabdriver and ex-con who was dealing weed on the street. Jimmy loaned the guy a lot of money in exchange for a cut of the business, began to smoke or "vape" high potency pot on a daily basis, while at the same time abusing his bipolar meds. And before anyone knew what had happened, he was talking about going to Africa.

When my sister in California -- the only one of the two of us who still had her contact information -- called to inform Jean that Jimmy had died she was shocked and horrified, particularly when the grotesque details of his final months were revealed. Perhaps not knowing what else to do, she reached out to me. It made logical sense. For much of the prior decade I had actually lived with Jimmy, watched him grapple with his demons, witnessed firsthand the cruel vicissitudes of his life, such as his near fatal car accident, his increasing struggle with his manic depression, and the way he had reacted to our father's illness and death. We had grown up together as kids -- we were two years apart -- and had much in common in terms of personality, temperament, and interests. And, at least when he wasn't into hating me, I had been his trusted confidante and helpmate for much of his life. I knew things about him that she didn't. In fact, I probably knew him better than anyone else then living.

Of course, Jean knew Jimmy intimately as well. But over the years she had woven a story about him that she told herself, and perhaps told her daughters -- a story that suited her needs about the man who had fathered her children, and the only man with whom she had enjoyed an enduring relationship that resembled a marriage. There were of necessity mysterious, murky, and ambiguous parts to that story, disturbing parts she perhaps preferred to avert her eyes from or gloss over. But now, in her desperation to understand what had happened, and why this man she had once loved was dead, she needed me to fill in the blanks in the narrative she had so carefully cultivated.

And so she had called me shortly after receiving the awful news. We had somber, lengthy conversations over the phone in which I attempted to provide as much detail as possible about my brother's activities and frame of mind over the weeks leading up to the last time I myself had spoken to him by phone. That was about three weeks before his death. Jean listened in silence, punctuated by little groans and an occasional gasp of disbelief. And then she had insisted that I make plans to come and stay with her in London for a couple of weeks.

I thought about it awhile with some apprehension, but at length decided I would accept her invitation. A couple of months later I was on a London-bound flight. It had been at least ten years since I had last laid eyes on Jean, but when she met me at Heathrow Airport she looked much as I had remembered her. She recognized me as well and flashed a big warm smile. Our visit seemed to be getting off to a good start.

My first day in London was interesting and revealing. Jean took me on a walking tour of her neighborhood, which was known as West Brompton. She showed me the famous hospital whose doctors attended to the royal family, where she had worked for much of the time she had been living in England. Then we hopped on one of those red double-decker buses and I got a brief overview of the downtown area. We disembarked near the West End theater district and walked around awhile.

Back home, as Jean rushed to prepare something for dinner she complained that she hadn't gotten a chance to go to the grocery store in the morning because of some problem with her water tank, and so had to throw together leftovers. The phone rang several times while she cooked. I realized she lived a somewhat hectic life. After dinner we retired into the candlelit sitting room to begin the process of getting acquainted and catching up. It looked like it would be a long process.

The next morning Jean had to wait for a maintenance crew to arrive to check on the water tank, so she armed me with a subway map, pointed the way to the tube station, and told me exactly what line to transfer to in order to get to the British Museum. She thought that might be a good way for me to begin my official tour of London, especially since it was something one could do alone. Ah yes... the fabled British Museum. What could be a better introduction to England's past glories?

I arrived at the entrance to the impressive and stately edifice, as one among hundreds of swarming tourists. I moved slowly and thoughtfully among all those wondrous artifacts -- Egyptian mummies, Ming Dynasty vases, bronze sculptures of Hindu Goddesses, splendid Islamic tiles, African wood carvings, Chinese jade, totem poles, numerous statues of the Pharaohs with some of their non-European noses suspiciously hacked off, laughing Buddhas. A couple of centuries worth of loot and plunder stolen from the peoples whose lands and resources the British systematically ravaged in the course of building the sprawling empire on which, it was said, the sun never set.

Several nights later I was sitting at a round table with a small group of Jean's international friends -- Sarai from Turkey, Leni from Spain, and Dahlia from Algeria. We were greedily dipping into a heaping plate of nachos with melted cheese and guacamole, feasting on mutton with mint sauce from another platter, and washing it all down with tall glasses of *Peroni* beer. A constant hum or drone in the air muffled our conversation but made it seem more intimate at the same time. We were at the *Scarsdale Tavern*, an authentic stereotypical English pub, one that could have come off a Hollywood studio lot with its rich dark wood bar, chalkboard menus, antiquated wall hangings, stained glass, and working stone fireplace. Standing-room-only at the bar and an animated crowd watching a rugby match on a big screen TV completed the picture, assuring me that I was no longer in New York but truly in "merry old England." Getting to experience a "real" British pub had been one of the items on my to-do list, and indeed it was warm and wonderful. And yet somehow, sitting there with Jean's interesting friends, each of whom spoke English with a slightly different accent, I felt as if I didn't belong.

From the day I had arrived in late September we seemed to have been blessed with an unusual stretch of mild, sunny weather -- I had packed my heavy black raincoat in vain -- and for days at a time while Jean was stuck home dealing with the plumbers and repairmen, I did much of the typical touristy stuff on my own. The *Changing of the Guard* at Buckingham Palace, the street performers and magicians working the crowds at Trafalgar Square, cruising the Thames in a flatboat, strolling among exquisitely manicured flower gardens in St. James Park, getting lost in *Harrod's Department Store*, shooting videos of ducks and swans and geese frolicking in Hyde Park, taking in Westminster Abbey and the Houses of Parliament, watching Chinese tourists eagerly prowling through the high-end shops on fashionable Oxford Street, taking a ride sitting on the upper deck of those ubiquitous red buses, right up front against the huge windows, checking out Piccadilly Circus and Covent Garden. What I think impressed me the most was the uncanny, ever present contrast of the sleek and ultramodern with the age-old and moth-eaten. Brash twenty-first century hipness brushing up against stuffy tradition and the dead weight of history. You know, all that pomp and circumstance juxtaposed with scenes of fashionably dressed blokes barfing in the streets outside trendy bars.

Another day and I'm trying something a bit more off the beaten path: the popular flea market on Portobello Road, located in the Notting Hill district of West London. Slowly I make my way among the crowds, past tables and booths overflowing with treasures gathered from attics, garages and dusty old trunks all over England. A plethora of "Stuff:" Cheesy religious paintings with plastic frames, black leather motorcycle jackets, clunky radios from the 1940s, 1960s-era psychedelic posters, Jesus figurines, cookie jars, wooden ducks, crucifixes, woolen blankets and shawls, an old zither. This was once a sleepy winding country path on which cows and hens and sheep planted their hooves in unpaved soil and now it was the site of a frenzied modern-day bazaar. As I pass by the busy stalls where ten and twenty pound notes are quickly changing hands, the road seems to go on forever, meandering gracefully as it slopes downward, then rises again. As far as the eye can see there are still more tables, more goods on display.

But I am not interested in examining anything up close, haggling over prices, or finding a unique tchotchke to take home. Indeed, after dealing with the very unfavorable exchange rate, steep credit card fees and outrageous service charges for changing cash, shopping is the last thing on my mind. Rather I am desperately seeking some place to go to the bathroom. I have now been in London a full week and am a bit worn down, not only from all the pavement pounding I've been doing as a solo tourist while Jean deals with pressing matters at home, but also from something else. I have become aware of tensions rising, and a sense of vague discomfort and slight irritation which I believe to be generated by Jean's manners and attitude towards me.

By nature a frank, candid person, up-front and no-nonsense, and maybe not so big on tact nor overly sensitive to folks with thin skins, Jean just came out and said whatever popped into her mind without much editing or filtering. Which meant that she noticed and commented on my little idiosyncrasies and OCD tendencies. Why did I always seem to leave a trail of shredded bits of tissue wherever I went, why did I pour coffee into my cup right up to the point where it nearly spilled over the lid, or leave splotches of water on the bathroom floor. She informed me that Jimmy had told her a great deal about some of my obsessive tendencies and issues with depression. I wondered what else he had told her about me and how exaggerated or distorted it might have been, especially at those times when he was angry with me.

It seemed it was not enough that I had told her everything I could about my brother, anything I could think of that might make the bizarre way his life derailed and ended in a ditch somehow easier to swallow and digest. Jean wanted to know more about me. Why had I never married? Didn't I get lonely living by myself? Why didn't I work? What had I done with my college education? Did I have a boyfriend? I knew that all of this was entirely without malice or judgment. Jean was not out to interrogate me, embarrass me, or make me feel uncomfortable. She was genuinely curious and interested and just wanted to know me better. She wanted to embrace me as a member of her family, to forge a warm and loving connection with the one person who was closer than anyone else to the man she had sincerely loved and who would always be the father of her children. I tried to understand and to open myself up without fear. But it took a toll on me.

As soon as Jean took care of the broken water tank, she wanted to make up for having left me on my own for the first week of my visit. So she suggested a relaxing weekend spent with her and one of my nieces. On a Saturday we took the train to Wimbledon where the older one lived and enjoyed a leisurely brunch at a local tavern. Kaitlyn, though in her early thirties, looked exactly as I had remembered her when she was about 13 -- the last time I had actually seen her. That had been at a family cookout during one summer when Jean and the kids made an extended visit to the States, to the delight of my mother who had dearly missed her precious granddaughters. Intelligent, polite, free of all pretense, Kaitlyn was a joy to be around.

Later that night my other niece, Theresa, was to join us at a legendary London coffeehouse. The *Troubadour*, on old Brompton Road, was a venerable old relic that dated back to the 1950s. Over the years it had played host to the likes of Paul Simon, Led Zeppelin, Bob Dylan and Jimi Hendrix. The club was located in the Earl's Court district, within easy walking distance from Jean's apartment. We headed over there about 7:00 pm. The ambience of the place immediately sucked you in. The collection of old tarnished coffee pots lined up in the front window, the weird, crooked layout of the interior, the rough-hewn exposed brick, the antique kitchen utensils and musical instruments like mandolins and fiddles dangling from the ceiling, the scratched up wooden floor, all gave the place the air of a *Good Will Thrift Shop*. Homely, ever so slightly musty, and as comfortable as the beat-up slippers you can't bring yourself to throw away.

On this particular night no bands or artists were scheduled to perform, so we just ordered some spinach omelets and beer-battered fish and dug in. Amid the clatter of crockery and silverware I listened carefully to the eager exchange of words and laughter. My younger niece was chatty and vivacious in contrast to her more reserved sister, and she too looked just like I had remembered her. I flashed back in my mind to some happy occasion in the past when the two of them, as young girls, had sat around my mother's dining room table, seducing everyone with their genteel ways and "proper" British accents. And now, so many years and thousands of miles removed, here I was in the midst of this magical reunion.

Yet it was not long before I began to feel vaguely distressed. Listening to these two mature young women talking about their professional jobs, their houses (both had purchased modest homes less than an hour's drive from London), their extensive travels all over the European continent and beyond (Kaitlyn had recently returned from a holiday in Berlin) filled me with amazement and more than a touch of envy. These were the children of my screwed-up brother who now lay in his grave. But they were anything but screwed-up, thanks to the intelligent, careful rearing their mother had provided them. They were my nieces, and they seemed to accept me wholeheartedly and to want to enfold me into their family even though I barely knew them.

This was partly because, no doubt, I was as close as they could ever get to their deceased father, but it was also because they were curious engaged individuals willing to expand their horizons by reaching out to others. That was the way they were raised. And I knew I couldn't hold a candle to them. Not in life accomplishments, not in manners and poise, not in personality. And as the conversation continued and we enjoyed our after-dinner cordials I grew silent and began to recede into the background. When we got home I told Jean I didn't care to watch any late-night TV or sip from a mug of warm milk, as we'd done on most other nights. I went straight to bed.

The next morning the gloom from the night before lingered still. Perhaps it was fitting since this was the day I had planned to go to the *Tower of London*. And it was also the first day since my arrival that the skies were truly gray and misty; the London fog had an iron grip over the city and I knew it would be wise to pack an umbrella. Jean was dealing with a slight cold and would be spending the day indoors. So I walked to the station and boarded the train to Upminster. The stop to get off at was Tower Hill and as I emerged from the underground the massive and imposing landmark was right there. An ancient medieval fortress, the color of soiled sand, stood incongruously in the center of a modern twenty-first century metropolis.

Once I paid my admission and was within its environs, it was as if a time machine had taken me back to the year 1000. And much of it harmonized perfectly with my mood, from the weird wiry gray sculptures of monkeys perched on various surfaces, to the torture chamber in the "Bloody Tower" where were displayed the rack and manacles used to extort confessions from prisoners, to the straight out of Edgar Allan Poe ravens on the Tower Green. I saw the famous "Crown Jewels" up close, examined ancient armaments, swords, and coats of armor, climbed dozens of stairs to get to the top of the castle wall where the sentries used to be stationed, taking in the magnificent views and shooting pictures of the futuristic glass structures just across the river.

Another time we planned a visit to a somewhat hidden-away place the locals called "Little Venice," because it was a picturesque spot where two of London's canals happened to come together. Again, I was impressed with the wide range and diversity of Jean's friends. A willowy blue-eyed blonde who was an art student, a young Afghani nurse, and a much older woman originally from Iran who owned a bridal gown shop. None of us had ever seen Little Venice before and it turned out to be a beautiful day.

But once again I felt lost when it came time to sit around a large table laden with drinks and platters of food. As usual I had little to contribute to the conversation, unless by chance it happened to turn toward some current hot item in the news. But what I could not talk about -- or only barely at best -- was me, my life, my activities, my children, my career, my home, my grandkids, my world travels, my big plans for the future. So mostly I just listened, and ate, and sipped my wine, and wondered how it was that my life seemed all hollowed out, eviscerated of its essential substance, even though I couldn't remember when or where such a gruesome operation had been performed on me.

Back when my brother and my dad were around, everything had seemed different. Even though nothing was different. A handful of years ago, when I was actually living with the two of them, I still would have had little or nothing to say at that table with Jean and her friends. But, under the comforting illusion that I was just living with my dad to help him cope with the unfortunate loss of our mother, I would have convinced myself that as long as all the basics were in place, the rest was trivial and not worth making a fuss about. The odd living situation back then, as awkward and dysfunctional as it was, still provided the manna of life itself, the glue that holds it all together.

There was the protective love, the freedom to say or do anything and have it "understood," the familiar routines and rituals. Living with Dad and Jimmy, stressful as it so often was, had included all of that emotional sustenance. But once that was stripped away, the whole illusion collapsed in on itself like a leaky roof in a bad storm, leaving me raw and exposed. And now my own failure to build the kind of life for myself that could have withstood such losses and weathered such storms stood out in stark relief. It was the signature fact of my life at the present moment.

One evening Jean prepared a special dish from her native Guyana that involved curried chicken, rice, and eggplant (which she called "aubergine"). While she cooked, I attempted to take a shower. It was a frustrating experience, as it had been since I 'd arrived. Jean had to pay for her water usage, which was measured on a meter, just like my electricity usage was at home, and as a result she had installed a handheld attachment to the shower fixture and suggested that I fill the tub a few inches, sit in the shallow water and soap myself up thoroughly, then use the handheld device very sparingly in order to rinse myself off. She said the entire procedure ought not take longer than ten minutes, not counting the time it took to fill the tub bottom with hot water. For someone accustomed to having the shower on full blast for at least a half-hour, sometimes forty minutes, and to washing and conditioning my hair every time I showered, this was a near impossible request. All throughout my visit I had struggled mightily to comply as best I could. But now that only two days remained before I would be boarding my flight back over the Atlantic, I was able to smile in a self-deprecating way at my own ridiculous distress.

Indeed, all things considered, it was near miraculous that I had gotten through the ordeal of this trip as well as I had. Again, I barely knew Jean. And the circumstances which now brought us together -- the untimely, unexpected demise of my brother on the continent of Africa, and the absurd aftermath which led to his remains being left there -- were circumstances guaranteed to generate pain and anguish if dwelled on too heavily. I felt they were best left untouched, frozen in time, forgotten. I would never ever know what really happened, and all I could do was feel a certain sense of relief that my brother was at long last delivered from his suffering. And yet Jean had needed to stir the pot, to know more, to have extended contact and conversation with the one who had known Jimmy best. And so I had come to London. And for the most part it had been a wonderful, surprising treat. After all, London was one of the world's truly great cities, and were it not for knowing I would have a place to stay free of charge, I could have never considered such a trip.

As my visit drew to a close, I suddenly felt a tidal wave of gratitude wash over me. These people had invited me into the bosom of their family and welcomed me as a member. I had lost two essential members of my own family within the space of less than a year. But I had apparently gained several new ones. In two days I would be on a jet plane flying far away from here, with no idea of when, or even if, I might ever see these people again. But at least we were no longer strangers.

Soon after I returned home I had to go to the post office to pick up my mail. Since I knew I would be out of the country for over two weeks, I had arranged to have my mail held. Among the pile of bills, promotional offers and solicitations, there was a letter from the Department of Social Services. After about six years of having been on the waiting list for government-subsidized Section 8 housing, it appeared that I had gotten to the front of the line at last. The news could not have come at a better time.

For several months after my brother's death, I had been struggling to come up with his share of the rent. I had notified Peyton in North Carolina that I might need to consider relocating there again and asked her to keep an eye out for affordable studio or "efficiency" apartments. I had two months' rent on deposit with my current landlady, something she had demanded when my brother and I -- neither one of us having sterling credit -- had originally signed the lease. My plan had been to write the landlady a letter explaining the situation and then relying on the security deposit for my last two months, during which time I would find an apartment in Charlotte, or nearby, with Peyton's help.

But now, happily, I would not need to move down South again. All I needed to do was to find a landlord who would accept my Section 8 voucher, and then move into the apartment of my choice. The voucher would cover any rent exceeding one-third of my monthly income and was a virtual guarantee to the landlord that the bulk of the rent would be paid on time, every month without fail. I breathed a deep sigh of relief.

And so, as I prepared to enter my seventh decade of life on earth, I knew that in spite of everything bad that had happened in my life and everything good that had not happened, it was time now to count my blessings. Over the next several weeks, I went over the hundreds of photos I had taken in London, took a few dozen of the best and created a *Shutterfly* Photobook. I sent it to Jean with my heartfelt thanks for a lovely time in London along with my wish that I will be able to visit again someday.

Before the year ended I located a suitable one-bedroom apartment in a three-family house, less than half a mile from where I used to live with Jimmy. I took a holiday job in *Sears* in order to earn some extra money for moving expenses. By Christmas Day I felt I'd earned the right to just lay in bed, away from the frantic crowds and the frigid cold and just listen to music. No twinkling Christmas tree. No gaily wrapped gifts. No guests, no visitors. Later that afternoon I got myself out of bed, got dressed, and made myself a batch of my old philosophy professor's legendary "Six-Alarm Chili "-- not exactly typical Christmas fare -- and baked a pan of cornbread to go with it. I thought of that famous clever saying: "Today is the first day of the rest of your life." It looked like, from here on, "the rest" would be quite different from what had already slipped into the dustbin of history. Maybe some of it would be good. Fingers crossed.

46
Rocky Mountain High

THE LONG DIMLY lit hallway with its tacky lime-green carpet and dingy wallpaper was starting to seem like a maze that led nowhere, and I kept ending up right back in front of my motel room door. "Oh, come on, man" I thought. "That damn ice machine has got to be *somewhere* on the floor," and so I set out again, in a different direction. Then I see this guy carrying an ice bucket. Great. I'll just follow him. And finally, right there, around a blind corner, was the ice room. The guy looks at me as if to say, yeah, I know, it took me forever to find it too. His face seemed vaguely familiar.

Amid the racket of ice cubes crashing into his bucket, he asked me if I was a new guest at the motel and what I thought of it. I replied that it was strictly a two-star affair, but that the free buffet breakfast and the free hourly shuttle to downtown made it a real bargain for the price. He agreed and, smiling broadly, asked, "And so what brings you to Denver?" I placed my bucket under the ice dispenser. "Oh, I came to visit a friend," I said, noticing the too perfect shape and whiteness of his teeth. I lied. He offered that he had come for the "Great American Beer Fest," a nine-day nonstop celebration of all things pertaining to the golden suds. He asked me how long I was here for, and I told him just a few days. "Well, be sure to check out the 16th Street pedestrian mall and the U.S. Mint." Both were located within easy walking distance of Union Station in downtown Denver, he assured me.

As he spoke I suddenly realized who the guy reminded me of. With his rust red beard, steely blue eyes, and gleaming dentures he looked like a younger version of McNamara, that befogged old man who was constantly walking into my room on the ward at St. Joseph's Medical Center. Oh shit, that was over six months ago and it was the last thing I needed to be reminded of.

After I turned 60 I went into a belated midlife crisis. I had been off all my medications for about two months, thinking/hoping I didn't need them anymore. But depression or anxiety can come out of nowhere, like pigeon droppings when you're walking under the elevated subway tracks. My perspective got increasingly dark and distorted. Then the thought processes started going haywire. Hyper self-consciousness took over. It began the moment I yanked myself out of bed in the morning. Closely tracking every single thought as it bursts into awareness, then instantly thinking: what made me think THAT thought and what other thought SHOULD I be thinking instead? Same with the next thought. Am I really choosing my thoughts or are they random little explosions in my brain synapses? Are they something I am directing or something that is happening to me? Soon it got crazy, out of control. I had even started grinding my teeth because of all the stress. I tried to write down exactly what I was feeling as this was all unfolding. And it went like this:

What a ghastly world -- every news bulletin makes me sick. Everything I hear triggers a terrible thought and that triggers another terrible thought and another in an endless chain. They come fast and furious -- it's like someone is throwing pebbles at me very hard -- every little ping hurts. I just want it to end. STOP!!! I feel raw and exposed. Something essential is missing in me.

There are even more subtle things -- things I can't explain, things so bewilderingly complex and slippery they are impossible to put into words. Like I could be walking through the aisles of Stop n' Shop and all of a sudden the whole question of what it means to exist, to be a living breathing moving animal in a world where untold billions of such lives have come and gone like the flies of a summer -- just lands on my head with surprise and urgency. What does BEING ALIVE RIGHT NOW mean? Shouldn't I be afraid since it all seems so fragile, so tentative?

Then a wave of fear crashes over me. But why aren't all these other people calmly pushing their shopping carts down the aisle afraid? They don't look afraid. Hey you, reaching for that box of Honey Nut Cheerios, aren't you scared? And you, lady, at the fish counter, how can you be so serene and complacent, ordering a half pound of sockeye salmon? My god -- what the hell is wrong with all of you!!!!.

Not surprisingly, I wound up back in the hospital. And this time it was dreadful. Awful food, uncomfortable bed, primitive shower. Inane activities like stringing plastic beads to make necklaces and doing crossword puzzles by the dozen and coloring in coloring books. Doctors with Russian accents. Horrible decaffeinated coffee. The TV in the lounge could get only two channels clearly, but the male patients were always watching basketball anyway. Lights out at ten o'clock. Had to take sleep meds and anti-anxiety meds along with antidepressants. And worst of all was walking into my room only to find McNamara sleeping in my bed!!! The staff had put a huge handwritten sign on the guy's door with the words, in solid blue letters, "JOHN MCNAMARA." But it did no good.

But no. I don't want to think about any of that now. It was more than six months ago. Ancient history.

I came to Colorado for one reason only, and it wasn't for a beer fest. I came for the ganja. New York, for all of its pretensions to being the hippest, most progressive state in the nation is still dragging its heels when it comes to legalizing weed. When my brother was alive, I used to get it from him, or from his friend who was a street dealer. I also had a cousin who used to grow the stuff in his backyard. But now Jimmy is dead, his friend is in prison for attempted murder, and I lost touch with my cousin a couple of years ago after his mom died and he was forced to move out of her house. I knew of nowhere else to get the stuff, had no other contacts. So there was no choice but to travel out of state. And I had never been to Colorado.

Denver seems like a rather cool place. There are all these guys with long beards and ponytails. Women tend to dress very casually, for comfort. Don't see too many high-heeled shoes or tailored suits. Lots of sandals and Doc Martens. There are dogs everywhere, of all shapes, breeds, sizes. So too with wheels other than cars -- skateboards, bicycles, old-fashioned scooters, roller skates, motorized electric scooters, even unicycles. The 1880s and 1890s buildings in the older part of downtown, the whole "Old West" atmosphere greatly appeal to me. I gaze up at the big Rocky

Mountain sky and it looks like a crystal clear blue dome of unfathomable depth and breadth. The patchy white clouds that occasionally drift by look plump, gorgeous, precisely sculpted and palpable -- three-dimensional objects floating in the heavens that you feel you can reach out and grab.

It is unusually hot for late September when I arrive -- in the low nineties with blazing sun. Good thing I didn't bother with a jacket. I've done my research and mapped out at least nine marijuana dispensaries that I plan to visit in the three days I will be here. At my age, and being from out of town, I feel pretty weird when I arrive in front of a pot shop and walk through the door. Similar, I suppose, to the way some young novice might have felt entering a speakeasy for the first time during the Prohibition Era.

It's the same routine at every dispensary. You enter into a small vestibule; there is one person sitting at a reception desk who asks to see your ID. Once you produce a valid up-to-date piece of identification you are escorted through another door, or a heavy curtain is pulled back. Inside is where the action is. Some of the shops are decked out like New Age Zen Buddhist parlors, with potted plants, exotic music playing, oriental rugs, silk curtains, comfy couches to sit on. Others look like cannabis showrooms, brightly lit with all of the merchandise neatly laid out on counters with menus and price lists on the wall and salespeople eager to answer your questions. One dispensary resembled an *Apple* store, with a bank of tables on which sat individual weed samples next to open iPads graphically describing the characteristics of that particular strain. One place even had a gift shop.

The herb itself is displayed in all of its green glory in tall glass jars with labels, presided over by an expert "budtender." Customers are encouraged to come up and examine closely, take a good sniff, etc. There are a dizzying array of names for the various strains -- now in the hundreds -- that pot growers have produced over the last quarter century. Daydreamer, Bubble Gum, Girl Scout Cookies, Sunburn, Strawberry Cough, Granola Funk, Wonder Woman, Witches Weed, Pinky's Advice, Sour Diesel, Juicy Fruit, Death Star, Super Lemon Haze, Blue Dream, Durban Poison, White Rhino, Blue Cheese, Lucky Charms, Trainwreck, Black Tuna, Chocolate Thunder, Orange Sherbet, LA Confidential, Tangerine, Jack's OG, Hog's Breath, and on and on and on. The weed is sold by the ounce or the gram. I've made up my mind to purchase at least a quarter ounce of no less than six different "flavors " over the course of my shopping spree.

After I'm done with the pot shops on the first day, I go and wait in front of the train station for the shuttle bus to take me back to the hotel. When I get there, the elevator takes forever and seems to wobble on the way up to the fourth floor. And once again there is the unmistakable odor of weed. Apparently many a tourist had come to Denver for the same reason I had. Word had gotten out that this particular hotel was "420-friendly." The pungent aroma lingered in the corridor even though I was on a nonsmoking floor. I slip my card key in the slot and open the door to my room. There are brownish stains on the wall next to the bed and one of the lamps is missing a light bulb and the knobby handle I have to use to switch from hot to cold water on the bathroom sink is coming loose and one of the pillowcases has a large tear in it and there are strands of blonde hair in the shower drain and the heavy curtain that I have to pull in order to cover the window at night doesn't go all the way across. But I'm not complaining.

Next morning I get up at 6:00, shower, and go downstairs for the free hot breakfast. Scrambled eggs, bacon, sausages, biscuits, fresh fruit -- Belgian waffles too. They have a pitcher full of batter and a hot open grill on which you pour the liquid and then close the lid. A few minutes later -- a square golden-brown waffle just waiting to be drenched with melted butter and syrup. I loved the free breakfast because it meant I didn't have to plunk down lots of cash on lunch or big meals while I was out on my pot-shopping tours -- which left more cash for weed. And yes, it had to be cash only. Since cannabis is still illegal under Federal law the banks will not do business with the owners of the dispensaries -- so no credit cards allowed.

As I'm walking back to my table with a plate full of eggs and sausage I see the guy from the ice room, the one who reminded me of McNamara, sitting at a corner table with a cup of coffee and a newspaper. I walk over and ask him how he was enjoying the Denver Beer Fest. He says it hasn't officially started yet, but he's been getting a nice preview by sampling from among the dozen or so microbreweries in and around town. With temperatures approaching the mid-nineties, today might be a good day to check out one of those breweries, I think to myself as I head outside to board the shuttle bus to downtown Denver.

Once I am dropped off in front of Union Station I quickly find my way to the famous 16th Street Mall where all auto traffic is banned for a mile. It turns out that three of the pot dispensaries on my list are within easy walking distance, so I head to the nearest one first. There I purchase seven grams of "Green Crack" and a large candy bar containing edible cannabis. The second place I visit, called *Native Roots*, is out of business, apparently for selling to minors or for disregarding one of the other very stringent regulations that must be adhered to in order to maintain a license to deal pot. I decide to leave the third shop for tomorrow, my last day here, and instead head for the *Rock Bottom Brewery* to enjoy some handcrafted beer.

I spend the rest of the day sightseeing and window-shopping and then, feeling hot and fatigued, I find a park bench on the large, well-kept green lawn that graces the impressive state capitol building. Soon the unpleasant thoughts begin cascading -- I wonder what the hell I am doing here anyway. What am I, a "senior citizen," doing traveling halfway across the country all by myself just to buy some weed? It seems absurd, or, at the very least, inappropriate. So what else is new, I tell myself. I think about those dreams I often have, the ones with constantly recurring themes. Like, say, I will be riding on a bus and get off at the wrong stop. I'll wander around, dazed and confused, trying to figure out what to do next. Or I'll be with a group of people on a trip or a tour and somehow I'll get lost, and find out everyone went home without me. Or I'll learn that there's some party to which all are invited, including me, but no one will tell me where it is.

The next morning I got myself up at 5 am. It was my last full day in Denver and I wanted to get as early a start as possible. I showered, dressed, packed up all my stuff, and went down to the lobby to hand in my card key, pay my bill and check out. I had a last hearty breakfast of bacon, eggs, and biscuits, then threw my backpack over my shoulders and headed out to catch the shuttle to downtown Denver. I had two more grass shops to visit. They were both a bit out of the way -- all the way over on Larimer Street. Thankfully, today was not quite as sweltering as yesterday and the day before, so I just started walking briskly. I picked up a few grams of "Kosher Kush" at the first place.

The last shop on my list was called *Ballpark Holistic Dispensary* -- "Ballpark" because it was located near *Coor's Field*, home of the Colorado Rockies baseball team. I walked in, ID in hand, and was escorted to the back. The first thing I noticed was a rack of t-shirts, featuring images of marijuana leaves and the store's logo. Some guy with his back to me was holding up a shirt as if to decide whether it would fit him. Then he turned in my direction. Oops! It was none other than the guy from the motel, young McNamara. I smiled at him and said, "Ah-hah....so I guess beer is not your only vice." He laughed. I asked him his name; it was Jason. He was bright and excited. He told me that for a hundred bucks and change I could take a "Cannabis Tour" where these dudes pick you up in a van and shepherd you to a number of dispensaries where you are encouraged to explore and purchase product. Then it's off to pot-friendly venues where you could freely partake with your fellow weed aficionados.

I asked him if he could recommend any particular strain of weed available in the store. He told me a strain called "Glass Slipper" gave him a soaring high, heightened all his senses, and didn't have a skunky smell. I bought an eighth of an ounce for just under 50 bucks. Before he left, Jason asked me if I would like to accompany him to the first big event of the Denver Beer Fest happening at some popular microbrewery in the heart of downtown. "I'll knock on your hotel door at 6:00. I have a car. No need to bother with the shuttle." I was surprised and felt flattered. Jason was a nice-looking man, and easily at least fifteen years younger than I was. But I told him I had already checked out of the hotel and was, in fact, leaving tonight. "Ah, that's too bad...you don't know what you're missing," he said, smiling with that wide white grin and then waltzing out the door.

After I made my last cannabis purchase it was time to head for Union Station where I would catch my train. Yes, TRAIN. I wanted to bring my stash of weed back home, but if I brought it to the airport I would be under Federal jurisdiction, meaning I would be transporting a Schedule 1 controlled substance and could be charged with a felony were it discovered. I had experienced my share of having my carry-on bags opened and rifled through for no apparent reason, and I couldn't afford to take any chances. So I booked my trip back home on the *Amtrak California Zephyr* line, which originates in San Francisco, stops in Denver, and winds up in Chicago. From Chicago, two other trains would eventually get me to New York's Penn Station. It would take two and a half days, but nobody would be checking my bags.

When I got to the station I threw my heavy backpack onto a bench and headed for the crowded bar. I ordered a pale ale and brought it back to my seat. I took a gulp and then my cell phone rang. It was my upstairs neighbor back home.

"I hate to bring bad news, but I just had to tell you. Remember the book lady, you know, Ruthie the Reader?"

"Sure, I just saw her a few days ago on Gramatan Avenue. She was walking all the way up to Bronxville."

"Well, she got run over, right on the corner of Fleetwood and Grand Street, in front of the *CVS*."

"Oh my God you're kidding...Is she...?"

"She's gone. 87 years old. Gone, just like that."

The "Book Lady" was a fixture in our neighborhood. About 4'11" in height, she had a round, impish face and a crown of short dark gray hair that looked as if she styled it by putting a bowl over her head and cutting off whatever stuck out. She was always outdoors, walking with her specially made walker that allowed her to stop anywhere, set down the walker and sit on its built-in seat. She could sit down wherever she liked and it was her habit to find a bright sunny spot, sit on her walker seat and read a book. When she wasn't walking she was reading. Always reading. You never saw her without an open book on her lap. She would appear in all parts of town -- in front of a store or a restaurant, in a sunny alleyway, on a wooden bench near the *CVS* parking lot, in front of somebody's house, next to a school. Even in the wintertime she seemed to find some little sanctuary, sheltered from the wind, bathed in sunlight. A little old lady just sitting in the sun, quietly reading her book.

Her name was Ruth and we all called her "Ruthie the Reader" (you know, like "Rosie the Riveter.") It was a rare day when I was out walking in the neighborhood that I didn't spot Ruthie somewhere. Once I saw her at the Bronxville Library returning four or five books. I wondered how many she read in a typical week. Because it seemed like that was all she did. You never saw her shopping, or eating, or talking to anyone, or drinking coffee, or staring out into space, or walking a dog, or scratching off squares on a lottery card, or stepping into a car. You only saw her totally absorbed in her book, oblivious to her surroundings, lost in a world of the imagination.

It was almost time to board the Amtrak train. I was not particularly looking forward to the long lumbering train ride. Traveling all night through Nebraska, and all day tomorrow through Iowa, reaching Chicago sometime in the afternoon. A long layover, then the all-night trip to Washington, DC where I'd have to switch trains again. Arriving finally in New York two and a half days after leaving Denver.

I settle into my seat by the window and try to relax. The seat next to me is empty so I put my backpack on it instead of shoving it in the overhead bin. The conductor gets on the horn and announces where the dining car, cafe car, and bathrooms are located. He also tells us about the observatory car. This was a car in the front of the train with huge windows, partial glass ceilings, and very comfortable swivel chairs. "Get a terrific view of the sun rising over Lincoln, Nebraska in just a few hours," he intones.

I listen to conversations going on around me.

"And then I became a Russian translator and worked at the NSA for thirteen years. My daughter did three years in the Peace Corps. She created a program in Thailand to help teenage girls avoid getting pregnant. Now she's an independent contractor."

"My husband and I drove a big rig for years. Hauling a load of hay to one place, picking up a load of timber, hauling it to the next place. We'd take turns driving. We loved it."

"I'm going to visit my daughter-in-law in Springfield. She just had a baby, my first grandchild. I'll pick up a rental in Chicago and drive down. Normally I would never take the train, but I smashed my car on a deer last Tuesday."

After an hour or so the train got dark and the conversations died down. People tried to settle in for the night. I attempted to doze off but couldn't seem to sleep. I tried to imagine what it would have been like had I been able to go to that event with Jason. If he had happened to ask me yesterday, I'm sure I would have said yes. Then I thought about McNamara, whom Jason so uncannily resembled. After finding him in my room for the third time, I had demanded to be given a different room, or moved to a different ward. But they told me not to worry -- McNamara was soon to be discharged; he was going to a nursing home. And so he did. I leaned my head against the window and drifted off to sleep again as the train rattled on into the night.

The observation car was a nice treat in the morning. Getting an up close and personal view of so-called Fly-Over-Country. Cornfields as far as the eye could see, tall silos, bales of hay, grazing horses, humble little churches, decrepit and abandoned buildings which seemed to signify the plight of rural America, those endless *Union Pacific* freight trains -- every car covered in colorful graffiti, the seamy side of Baltimore. I had brought a book to read on the train but when I tried to read I couldn't concentrate. I started thinking about Ruthie the Reader. I could not wrap my head around the fact that I would never see her again around town, sitting in the sunshine, reading her book. A sight as common in my neighborhood as the rail-thin mailman with the long dreadlocks and the bald guy who walks all over with a floral printed tote bag, collecting cans and bottles. I was never to see Ruthie again, not anywhere, not ever. The news was too much to process -- it didn't seem real. Not yet.

I exit the train in D.C. Then I find the track where I will board the express to New York. I climb aboard the more modern *Acela Express* to New York's Penn Station and find a seat. By now I am dead tired and can't stop thinking about Ruthie. How had the accident happened? How could anyone possibly run over a little old lady pushing a walker across the street!!

As soon as I got home, I threw down my bag and my backpack and jumped into the shower. Then I went straight to bed. The next morning I called on my upstairs neighbor to find out more about what happened to Ruthie. She knew someone named Ethel who lived on the block where it happened and who had arrived home a few minutes after the accident. I went to see Ethel to get the details. She told me Ruthie the Reader had been crossing with the light when a pickup truck making a left turn came flying around the corner and smashed into her. What was left of her walker was strewn all over the street as well as a few of her books. An ambulance and the cops were on the scene within minutes, but poor Ruthie was DOA at the hospital.

"I'm sure she never knew what hit her," Ethel said.

Later that afternoon I walked to the corner where it happened to see for myself where Ruthie spent her last moments on this earth. A memorial had already been set up -- there were tall candles at the base of a traffic light pole, bouquets of flowers had been placed there, a stuffed animal teddy bear was tied to the pole, a note from an admirer was scotch-taped above it. And beneath all that, a nice framed picture of Ruthie was mounted on the pole, probably put there by a relative. As I stood there staring in disbelief, at least two people came by to remark what a shame it was that the beloved neighborhood resident had been taken in such an awful way.

The next day I went to a variety store and bought a fuzzy rainbow-colored doll that resembled an owl. For some reason I had always associated owls with reading. Maybe because they have such big eyes. Later that evening I walked over to the memorial for Ruthie the Reader with the doll and some twine and tied the owl to the traffic light pole, just above the teddy bear. I looked once more at the picture of Ruthie, shook my head, and left.

Walking back home I felt lonely and sad. I felt like I was called upon to do something, anything, to alleviate all the needless suffering in the world. But what could I do? Bad things happen and people get hurt. Breakups, divorces, cancer, shooting rampages, shark attacks, wildfires. Little old ladies getting run over by pickup trucks. It was all too much. Maybe a "random act of kindness" was all I could offer. And so when my sister called two days later to ask me if I would consider flying out to LA to babysit her dog, while she and her family go away on vacation next spring, I said no problem.

That night, feeling better knowing I could be useful, I dug out my herb vaporizer and loaded it with some "Glass Slipper." Then I just pulled a random CD from my jazz collection and slid it into my computer. It was "Go" by Dexter Gordon. I took a few tokes of the weed and soon everything got *oh-so-slooowwwwww* and *mellooowwwwww*. The song, "Guess I'll Hang My Tears Out to Dry" never sounded more beautiful.

47
Epilogue

THE QUESTION WITH which I began this memoir now seems so small, so irrelevant. At this moment as I write, life in America seems like something borrowed from the nightmarish plot of a Stephen King novel. The country stands on the brink of a presidential election that, at best will be chaotic, and at worst might lead to bloodshed in the streets. A deadly unknown virus has gone on a rampage through our population, taking the lives of hundreds of thousands of us, and as yet there is no cure, vaccine, or truly effective treatment in sight. Angry protests, demonstrations, riots and destruction have been visited upon some of our major cities, sparked by a seemingly endless spate of police killings of unarmed black people. Massive wildfires rage out west, destroying millions of acres of woodlands and thousands of residential homes in the worst fire season on record. The economy lies in shambles, with millions out of work, families facing eviction, kids forced to stay at home rather than go to school, untold numbers of "Mom and Pop" businesses lovingly built up over decades of hard work, going under in a matter of months. Liquor sales way up, rampant drug abuse on the rise again, sales of firearms at all-time highs.

In the face of all this, the issue of whether I choose to go on living or not is of no significance. Fate may decide. Due to my age, I am considered "high-risk" for Covid-19. But I feel fine physically and don't always wear my mask when I go out. If a vaccine finally becomes available, I probably won't take it. Am I courting disaster? Indeed, I am deeply thankful that I have been as little affected personally by this crisis as I have. No worries as to whether I will be able to come up with tonight's dinner or next month's rent. My current medication seems to be working. So it would seem almost an act of profound ingratitude for me to consider ending my life now, while there is so much heartbreak, suffering and loss happening all around me, and so many people who never expected to but now find themselves in far worse circumstances than I have ever been in. "Social distancing" has pretty much been my way of life, and little has changed in my daily routine other than having to cover my face whenever I enter a bus or a supermarket.

But if the issue of my own self-annihilation has become more or less moot, the issue of mental illness appears more relevant than ever. We now have a man running our country who could arguably be described as a classic sociopath. He has also been called a narcissist, a megalomaniac, a pathological liar, and a person who suffers from delusions of grandeur. He is the most powerful man in the free world, but is seemingly unable to utter a word that a fourth grader might have to look up in a dictionary.

Yet he is so much more than that. He is a first-class entertainer, a con man supreme, a slick dealmaker, and a fiery demagogue who has managed to assemble a devoted cult following for whom he can do no wrong. He is a clever strategist with unfailing instincts who knows how to tweak his opponents and throw them off balance, a quick-change artist who goads his enemies into launching a full-frontal assault and then ducks down just in time so that *they* run smack into the wall instead of him. Then he smiles, and his fans eat it up while his detractors tear their hair out. He is an expert at "flooding the zone," giving his critics so many things to be outraged about at the same time that he creates a three-ring circus where no one knows which act to focus on and everything gets lost in a deluge of white noise. He will say one thing on a Tuesday and reverse himself on Friday and yet has still managed to convince his followers that he is by far the most honest, authentic, and "real" politician they have ever encountered. He is a magician, pulling rabbits out of hats and daring the media to ignore his latest antics -- which, of course, they cannot. So much to love, so much to hate.

Uncanny abilities blended with personality defects, genius laced with poison, extraordinary talent marred by inexplicable blind spots where things like empathy, maturity, and simple decency are supposed to be. The capacity to charm and exasperate at the same time. Mental illness is funny that way.

If anything in the foregoing pages has deeply resonated with you or struck a familiar chord, then my objective will have been achieved. If you feel you learned anything significant from reading this book, please pass it on. And – if even a single one of you was tempted to listen to one of the amazing artists I talked about, and as a result got turned on to the genius of jazz – then this whole endeavor will have been more than worth it.

Made in United States
Troutdale, OR
11/19/2024

25041939R00282